BY THE SKIN OF MY TEETH

BY THE SKIN OF MY TEETH

Flying RAF Spitfires and Mustangs in World War II
and USAF Sabre Jets in the Korean War

Colin Walker Downes

Pen & Sword
AVIATION

First published in Great Britain in 2005
and reprinted in this format in 2020 by
Pen & Sword Aviation
An imprint of
Pen & Sword Books Limited
Yorkshire - Philadelphia

ISBN 9781526781642

Typeset in 10/12 Times New Roman by Concept, Huddersfield, West
Yorkshire

Printed and bound in the UK by CPI Group (UK) Ltd, Croydon, CRO 4YY

Pen & Sword Books Limited incorporates the imprints of Atlas,
Archaeology, Aviation, Discovery, Family History, Fiction, History,
Maritime, Military, Military Classics, Politics, Select, Transport, True
Crime, Air World, Frontline Publishing, Leo Cooper, Remember When,
Seaforth Publishing, The Praetorian Press, Wharncliffe Local History,
Wharncliffe Transport, Wharncliffe True Crime and White Owl.
For a complete list of Pen & Sword titles please contact
PEN & SWORD BOOKS LIMITED
47 Church Street, Barnsley, South Yorkshire S70 2AS, United Kingdom
E-mail: enquiries@pen-and-sword.co.uk
Website: www.pen-and-sword.co.uk

Or
PEN AND SWORD BOOKS
1950 Lawrence Rd, Havertown, PA 19083, USA
E-mail: Uspen-and-sword@casematepublishers.com
Website: www.penandswordbooks.com

Tumult in the Clouds

In memory of

Flight Lieutenant Graham Pearson, DFC, RAFVR
Flight Lieutenant Graham Hulse, RAF
Squadron Leader Douglas Ford, RAF
Squadron Leader Harry Bennett, AFC, RAF

sic itur ad astra

By the Skin of my Teeth is a memoir of flying with the Royal Air Force in war and peace during a career in military and civil aviation covering a half century. The memoir, decorated with *other men's flowers*, consists of personal experiences, reminiscences and impressions, and is written in four parts. 'In Search of Wings' covers the years leading to the graduation of RAF 'Wings'. 'They That Hath Wings Shall Tell the Matter' covers flying propeller driven fighters during and after the Second World War. 'A Few Crowded Hours' covers flying jet-powered fighters before and during the Korean War. 'Pleasant Hours Fly Fast' covers the remainder of Service flying until retirement from the Royal Air Force.

Contents

Prologue

This most excellent canopy, the air, look you,
This brave o'erhanging firmament,
This magical roof fretted with golden fire.

Hamlet

That which hath wings shall tell the matter.

Ecclesiastes

One crowded hour of glorious life
Is worth an age without a name.

Thomas Mordant (1730–1809)

CHAPTER ONE

In Search of Wings

Oh! I have slipped the surly bonds of earth
And danced the skies on laughter-silvered wings;
Sunward I've climbed, and joined the tumbling mirth
Of sun-split clouds – and done a hundred things
You have not dreamed of – wheeled and soared and swung
High in the sunlit silence. Hov'ring there
I've chased the shouting wind along, and flung
My eager craft through footless halls of air.

Up, up the long, delirious, burning blue
I've topped the wind-swept heights with easy grace,
Where never lark, nor even eagle flew –
And, while with silent lifting mind I've trod
The high, untrespassed sanctity of space,
Put out my hand and touched the face of God.

'High Flight' – John Gillespie Magee (1922–41)

LAUGHTER-SILVERED WINGS AND CLOVEN TONGUES

The two world wars produced poetry of high quality and two poets in particular stand out in my memory. In the First World War a Canadian medical officer, John McCrae, wrote 'In Flanders Fields' while serving at a dressing-station during the second Ypres Offensive in 1915. This poem became the most famous of the war and I always associate it with my father, who also fought during the second Ypres battle and was a survivor of the slaughter at the Battle of Loos. Lieutenant Colonel John McCrae, RAMC, died on active service in 1918. In the Second World War an American pilot, John Magee, wrote 'High Flight', a poem that encapsulates all the sensations and joys of flying a high performance aircraft. Born in Shanghai of an American missionary father and an English mother and educated in England, John Magee volunteered from the United States for pilot training with the RCAF in 1940. The following year Flying Officer John Magee, RCAF, joined an RAF Spitfire squadron in England and died in a flying accident. The poem 'High Flight' was among his effects.

From an early age my imagination and day-dreams drifted with *airy navies battling in the central blue* where real aces such as the Red Baron duelled with fictitious ones like Biggles. Both fighter pilots, and the Frog model airplane powered by elastic that I would launch on interception flights against kites flying over Parliament Hill Fields on Hampstead Heath, played a significant part in my aspirations to join the list of Aces. Against my vaulting ambition I had a foe named folly. Wellington said of Waterloo it was a close run thing; so it was for me to slip *the surly bonds of earth* and fly *where never lark, nor even eagle flew.*

To begin at the beginning: airplanes were always somewhere in my life and my first flight occurred in the late 1920s when at the tender age of six I travelled with my parents to the Belgian seaside resort of Blankenberg. We flew in the open four-seat cockpit of a French single-engine biplane flying-boat, taking off at Harwich on the Suffolk coast and landing at Ostend. I do not remember the reason for the trip or my inclusion. Perhaps it was after my nanny had left our household, which was why the weekend jaunt was a near disaster for my mother. My father was busy elsewhere and while walking along the crowded esplanade with my mother I managed to lose her. Luckily I was bilingual so, after the initial flood of fear and panic, I found a sympathetic policeman and a friendly police station from which a near demented mother retrieved me some hours later.

The pilot of the flying boat was a comrade at arms whom my father had met during the First World War while flying with the RAF in France. My father was in his first year of medicine at Edinburgh University when he volunteered for Kitchener's New Volunteer Army in 1914, enlisting in the Cameronians (Scottish Rifles). After participating in the Battle of Loos in 1915, he suffered a severe wound in the chest during the Battle of the Somme in 1916. On recovering from his wound, he decided that living conditions in a tank were preferable to those in the trenches and transferred to the Royal Tank Corps. He fought as a tank commander in the third Ypres battle and in the tank battle of Cambrai in 1917, where he was wounded for a second time. In the preparation for the Battle of Amiens in August 1918, he volunteered for reconnaissance duty with the RAF to coordinate the operations of the tanks of 1st Tank Brigade with the artillery, the RAF and the Canadian Corps. He joined No. 52 Squadron flying RE-8s and it was here that he met the pilot who would be the main influence in developing my interest in aviation. After demobilization in 1919 this avuncular friend of my father continued flying and joined a major petroleum company and flew the company's DH Hornet Moth around the country to air displays and racing car meetings. He owned a diminutive, single seat Comper Swift, powered by a 70 hp Pobjoy engine. He knew Comper while in the RFC during the First World War, and he flew the Swift in air races. I thought this little monoplane the most beautiful of all aircraft and I would day-dream of the day when I might be able to fly one like it. Thanks to this generous benefactor my father and I flew to many air shows and air races around the country, and to the motor races at Brooklands and Donnington.

The war clouds were gathering over Europe in the late 1930s and having been brought up on a diet of First World War reminiscences together with a fund of battle tales, I knew it was only a question of time before I should have to respond to a call to arms. My parents had their own different reasons for deciding I should not go into the Army. My mother being French had spent the First World War in Bordeaux and had relatives in the French Army who had fought in the Franco–Prussian War of 1870–71 and the Great War of 1914–18, and she had no wish to see her son fight in that sort of war. I remember with affection my mother's favourite uncle who saw action during the First World War, and in Indochina and North Africa. Graduating from the Ecole Militaire and the cavalry school at Saumur, he was the epitome of a French cavalry officer from a past generation. He wore a neatly trimmed moustache and dressed immaculately in the Edwardian style, and always with a boutonniere to match the red rosette of the Legion d'Honneur on his lapel. His one regret was never to have led a cavalry charge in any of his wars. He died suddenly in Paris in 1977, the oldest living general in the French army. His ancestor was Eugene Viollet-le-Duc, the architect of the Gothic revival in France and noted for the restoration of medieval buildings and a dictionary of French architecture. On his one hundredth birthday the French Army gave him a birthday party, and with his erect, trim figure and full head of silver hair he looked twenty years younger than his age. His eventual departure at the age of 103 was both unexpected and a little bizarre; and no doubt to his regret. He was too old to die gloriously in battle *pour La Patrie* as he would have wished, but he could at least hope for a warrior's end. However it was not to be; he died while entertaining a lady friend to luncheon at Maxim's. In the enjoyment of the occasion; or in the excitement of the moment; or in anticipation of the afternoon to follow; he choked on a fish bone that even a '37 Chassagne-Montrachet failed to dislodge. His exit had a certain Gascon panache about it; although he came from the adjoining province of the Auverne. Because I lived in

England I did not see this urbane and genial relative often but he left an indelible and illustrative mark in my memory of mores and of living in France during La Belle Époque.

My father, influenced by his experiences during the First World War, decided against the Army, and his short and traumatic experience flying with the Royal Air Force also influenced his decision that I should enter the Royal Navy. The RE-8; also known in cockney rhyming fashion as a 'Harry Tate' after a well-known music hall comedian of the time, was a well tried single engine, twin-seat biplane that was the unglamorous work-horse of the RAF for bombing and reconnaissance. It also had the more sinister name of 'Flaming Wafer' due to its proclivity to crash and burn during landings, particularly when landing in gusty or cross-wind conditions. His contribution to the Battle of Amiens in 1918 ended when his aircraft was shot down over the battlefield on the second day of the battle. His pilot died in the crash landing in no mans land and he suffered severe injuries for a third time. For my father that was the end of a fighting war that included many months in the trenches of the front, two infantry battles, three tank battles, one air battle and many wounds. His injuries kept him in hospital for a year before his medical discharge from the Army in 1920. He met my mother in 1921, they married in 1922 and I was born in London in 1923.

At the outbreak of war in 1939 I was in France staying with friends during a school holiday. I saw the arrival in France of the RAF squadrons of Hawker Hurricane fighters and Fairey Battle light bombers. The majority of these were to remain in France with the loss of more than 900 fighters and light bombers during the German Western Offensive in 1940. Meeting some of the RAF air crew with my French friends they all commented on how young they looked to be flying these planes. Indeed, many of them were not much older than myself, being in their late teens and early twenties. A few years later I met up with some of the survivors from the Hurricane squadrons while flying in Fighter Command. While in France the French radio announced French infantry sallying forth from the Maginot Line to attack the Germans with bayonets fixed and led by the graduates of St Cyr in parade uniforms and plumed shakos. Amid the cries of admiration for the élan of the French troops there was neither mention of casualties nor of the needless slaughter along Marne in 1914–15. Expectations then ran high, fortunately not to be realized, of the French cavalry responding with the graduates of Saumur; with the inevitable same result as that experienced by the Polish cavalry when attacking the German Panzer thrusts into Poland. In endeavouring to return to England in time for the school term, I had some difficulty in getting to Boulogne in time to catch one of the last scheduled ferries back to Folkestone.

On return to school in Dorset my parents decided I should enter the Royal Navy and instructed me to sit for the Dartmouth College direct entry examination. However, I was to circumvent a career in the Royal Navy by failing to pass high enough in the competitive examination for acceptance to Dartmouth. I gave no thought to the RNVR, the 'Wavy Navy', for if I could not join the Royal Navy and put the straight rings on my sleeve I decided to try elsewhere. With my failure to join the Senior Service my parents gave no thought to the Junior Service, and although my mother was not enthusiastic in my interest in the Royal Air Force, never-the-less she always wore a jewelled brooch of RAF wings when I eventually wore a pilot's brevet.

There were some who regarded the RAF with suspicion and considered it not suitable as a career. Inter-Service rivalries between the British Armed Forces were to some extent the result of the British class system. Some years after the Second World War, while a guest of the Royal Yacht Squadron during Cowes Week; my host being my squadron commander on a Royal Auxiliary Air Force squadron, I heard first hand how he, as a prominent yachtsman and MP, became a member of the Royal Yacht Squadron with another well-known yachtsman and MP. Prior to this the RAF members of the squadron, who, if counted on the fingers of one hand would leave fingers to spare, were of very, very senior rank. The names of those proposed for membership were posted with the names of their pro-posers during Cowes Week for vetting by the members before balloting during the week. The dropping of one black ball in the ballot box spelt finis to the expectations of more than one distinguished applicant as the squadron demonstrated the view that *a king can make a knight but not a gentleman*: or a member of The Royal Yacht Squadron. My host and his friend were more successful, despite the reservations of one senior member. This occurred as two senior members in their distinctive squadron dress viewed the posted list prior to the balloting and one was heard to say: 'What's this – Air Commodore Sir Vere Harvey MP, and Group Captain the Hon. Max Aitkin, MP?'

To which the other replied, 'Oh, yes – fine fellows – keen yachtsmen – outstanding war records.'

The first member viewed the list again and said, 'But – Air Commodore and Group Captain – they must be Flying Corps wallahs!'

His companion replied, 'Ha, but it's called the Royal Air Force now.'

His elderly friend was not mollified and continued to complain, 'But, damn it – flying wallahs – good God, we'll be having dirt track riders next!'

From the table of my memory during my adolescence all my summers appear bright and all my winters white. Of course this was not the case but certainly the late summer of 1940 was glorious. While staying with my mother in London during the school holiday I viewed the Battle of Britain being waged at a great height above London. The RAF fighters weaved their white vapour trails through the lace pattern of the *Luftwaffe* bombers and fighters against a backdrop of deep azure. It was very exciting for a schoolboy and I longed to be able to join the gallant Few. Occasionally, among the weaving, diving aircraft, one plane would detach itself with black smoke trailing behind it as it dived or fell to earth. Sometimes a parachute would blossom as if it were a white flower and seem suspended in the air against the blue sky. My mother lived in Hampstead on the north-west side of London. The house was on a hill that overlooked the city and during the night raids on London the fires from the burning docks lit up the sky, and my mother and I would retire to an Anderson air-raid shelter buried in the garden. Wrapped in sleeping bags in our snug cave with her two dogs, who regarded the whole exercise as some game, we listened to the drone of the German bombers overhead and the bangs of the anti-aircraft guns. Shrapnel rained down from the exploding anti-aircraft shells above, and we felt the thud and shake of the detonating bombs. In the morning I would find a few jagged shell fragments in the garden; a compelling argument not to venture outside during the air raids. Living in Hampstead on a hill overlooking London and surrounded by the open parkland and woods of Hampstead Heath and Highgate Woods, we did not expect the village to suffer from the bombing during the Blitz on London; but Hampstead received more than a fair share of the random bombs.

Greater London is a huge collection of urban villages and Hampstead consisted of a largely artistic community with a history of famous musicians, writers, poets, painters and artistes. Consequently, there were no military or industrial targets, but in the adjacent district of Cricklewood to the west, then a largely Irish community, was the Handley Page Aircraft factory producing the Hampden medium bomber and the Halifax heavy bomber. A short distance to the north was the famous RAF air base at Hendon, and so the bombs that fell on Hampstead were in all probability intended for one of these two targets. Although the bombs we received were the result of poor marksmanship on the part of the *Luftwaffe*, there were some who attributed the German's wrath to an evil Nazi plot to blow up Carl Marx resting in Highgate Cemetery; or the affluent Jewish community living in the neighbouring district of Golders Green; or the left-wing intelligentsia of Hampstead Village. Whatever the reason, the result was the unfortunate destruction of two fine old inns on

Hampstead Heath: 'Ye Olde Bull and Bush', the theme of a popular music hall song, and 'Jack Straw's Castle', an eighteenth-century coaching inn on the old toll road out of London to the North; and the site of a gibbet for the hanging of highwaymen preying on travellers to and from London. The name derives from Jack Straw, a common priest who led the peasant uprising in Essex. He became lieutenant to Wat Tyler in the Peasant's Revolt against Richard II in 1381. Jack Straw addressed the assembled peasants on Hampstead Heath from a hay wagon, referred to as Jack Straw's 'Castle'. The original coaching inn was built on this site in 1721, together with horse troughs and a large shallow round stone pond to refresh the horses after their climb up the steep hill from London: and here I would sail model yachts and boats.

Fortunately, despite the debris from the bombs that fell on Hampstead my mother and the house remained unscathed throughout the war. Before marrying my father, my mother was a fashion designer for Coco Chanel in Paris. She had a fashion house at London's 'West End' in Bond Street, and consequently during my school holidays I would meet wives of many well-known personalities. My mother moved in a circle of artistic friends and during my visits from school and later while in the RAF, I met several famous representatives of the arts. Two great opera singers I met after the war remain vividly in my memory: Elizabeth Schwarzkopf who completely overawed me: and the great Italian tenor Beniamino Gigli, who gave me an inscribed silver cigarette case. The violinist, Yehudi Menuhin; the painter, Augustus John and the sculptor, Siegfried Charoux were other established artists I met when visiting my mother in Hampstead. During my adolescent and early maturity years a stay with either of my parents gave me a very different and diverse change of scene. With my mother it was always the arts: with my father it was field sports which included dogs, horses, guns, fly rods, cycling and walking. However, during the half-term break at school it was always my mother who visited me, and she would cause a stir when she arrived in her Singer Le Mans; especially with my housemaster, John Appleby, who was a bachelor. Telling me to bring a friend, we would squeeze into the two-seat open sports car – I do not remember it ever raining at half-term – as my mother roared off at high speed to some hostelry for a lengthy lunch. This was followed by a walk along either the beach or the river before she dropped us off at the school on her way back to London.

The period of the early forties was for me the most influential of my life. It brought the end of my schooling, an abbreviated stay at university, my entry into the Royal Air Force and my participation in the Second World War. My private schooling was considered by some as privileged, although at the time it did not appear so to me. I recall my preparatory boarding school on the Channel coast of Kent, if I recall it at all, as a twentieth-century version of Dotheboys Hall in 'Nicholas Nickelby' by Charles Dickens. My memories of it are of a harsh teaching institution with a brutal and sadistic staff. It was a traumatic experience for an only child brought up in a sheltered existence at home. I remember the inadequately heated class-rooms and common-rooms in winter and the bitterly cold dormitories as I curled into a shivering ball in my bed trying to sleep dressed in socks and flannel pyjamas while wrapped in a woollen dressing-gown. I was awakened, it appeared, almost immediately, while it was still dark, for supervised washing in freezing cold water. This Spartan establishment believed fervently in the benefits of corporal punishment to instil discipline and to develop moral fibre. Even slight peccadilloes and minor infractions in class were subject to the canning of the proffered hand, leaving it inoperative for the rest of the day. More serious misdemeanours were punished at night in the dormitory in front of an attentive audience of classmates. This was in effect a double punishment for the unfortunate culprit as he lay in bed after 'lights-out' trembling in trepidation awaiting the arrival of his beater. The canning was carried out on bare buttocks in the centre of the dormitory, as the recipient clenched his teeth to stifle any cry of pain in front of his room-mates and then attempted to return nonchalantly to his bed; to lie shivering in the dark as he cried himself to sleep. I was a member of the school choir and I recall the discomfort of singing dressed in a thin surplice and Eton collar in the freezing cold chapel with the interminable evensong services. After the service the headmaster, our 'Wackford Squeers', gave his only contribution to the school curriculum when he regaled the assembled school with his derring-do as a staff officer *speeding glum heroes up the line to death* during one of the greatest fiascos of the First World War – Gallipoli. Fortunately, my move from the treble section of the school choir coincided with my departure to my secondary school: a much more benevolent institute of learning where corporal punishment was rare and properly regulated.

The English public boarding school was a good preparation for entry into the armed forces, with uniformed discipline and a system of rewards and punishments. The system was supervised by an appointed student authority responsible to a housemaster for the enforcement of discipline and the administration of judicial punishments. Military discipline was enacted and experienced while serving in the Officer Training Corps (OTC) that provided all aspects of initiation into the British Army. Clayesmore was a boys' boarding school with an Anglican persuasion; located in extensive grounds at Iwerne Minster in the beautiful county of Dorset. The village of Iwerne Minster, as the name implies, was the site of an early monastery alongside running water. It was a small, model English village, created by an enlightened nineteenth-century squire of the manor; with a fine twelfth-century church, and evidence of habitation going back to Roman and Saxon times. Clayesmore School had previously been part of Winchester College before breaking away to become an independent public school. It was at this attractive location that I spent the most impressionable and enjoyable period of my schooling as we attempted to adhere closely to the school motto – *Dieu premier, donc mes freres*. Although in no sense a military academy, Clayesmore made a continuous contribution to the armed services during both world wars. In the Second World War more than half of the school's war casualties resulted from flying service in the RAF.

The teaching staff was recruited from Oxford and Cambridge; prefer-ably with a Blue at cricket, rugby football or athletics. An exception to this was my music master for whom I had great respect, not only for his musical achievements as the school's director of music, but because he served with distinction as a fighter pilot in the RFC during the First World War; surviving 'Bloody April' in 1917. Reggie Sessions produced and directed a fine school orchestra for concerts and theatrical productions. He was also to create a very creditable brass band for the school OTC, with rousing renditions of Sousa for parade inspections despite discon-certing official War Office pronouncements and portents that in the event of hostilities in the neighbourhood the OTC would cease to exist! His organ voluntaries before and after matins and evensong on Sundays did much to make these lengthy services bearable while sitting on the wooden benches. Although my talent as a pianist was a great disappointment to my mother, who played the piano and the guitar, and to my music master, I did learn from him that it was not necessary to be a musician to be musical and to appreciate Mozart. My housemaster, John Appleby, also had an influence on me in passing on some of his love of English literature and poetry; and the art of the printing press. He had a long teaching career at Clayesmore, becoming the school's 'Mr Chips', although, in his case he was known to his boys simply as 'Apples'. The headmaster, Evelyn King, was for us a remote figure that we saw only at school assembly and chapel. However, he was an academic of many parts as well as an astute businessman and a political chameleon. For a while at the start of the war he was an army colonel until he left the army to become a Socialist Member of Parliament. He returned to Clayesmore as headmaster at the war's end, and on losing his socialist seat he became a Conservative Member of Parliament. In his latter years he became an academic once more and a respected author. Of all the teaching staff at Clayesmore the most memorable for me was Carl Verrinder; a truly remarkable man who taught physics, chemistry and many other sciences. I shall always remember his laboratory sessions as both entertaining and exciting. He had an absent minded habit of picking up stray chemical elements littering the benches in his wanderings while supervising experiments. On one occasion, while I was endeavouring to persuade a Bunsen burner to function, I saw our chemistry teacher leap into the air with a shout of pain as he frantically beat at his trouser pocket from which issued smoke and flames. Apparently, in the process of picking up various chemicals and putting them in his pocket, he selected some that when grouped together produced spontaneous combustion. After several attempts to quench the flames with misguided beakers of water directed at his person, we managed to put out the fire; leaving him with charred trousers showing some pink, scorched flesh where his pocket had been. Our wet and embarrassed chemistry teacher limped off to the school sanatorium where the matron removed the remains of his trousers to treat his burns. Carl Verrinder had a very varied life with an inexhaustible supply of energy and his spectrum of interests, for which he had the appropriate talents and expertise, was certainly impressive. As a chemist, apart from an ability to summon up spontaneous combustion, or as a physicist he could have contributed significantly to industry. However, he preferred to devote his time and passion trying to instil his enthusiasm into his students, no matter whether the subject was scientific; the activity sporting; or the art dramatic. As an Oxford Blue he coached the school rugby football, cricket and athletic teams. As an artist and actor he produced and directed the school dramatic society plays, with always one Shakespearean play during the year. And as climber, mountaineer, skier and canoeist he organized and led school trips and expeditions during the school holidays. I was to learn more from him than the rest of the teachers put together, including a more lasting appreciation of Shakespeare than gained in the classroom.

It could be said of Clayesmore that in time of war its main function was the supply of recruits to the armed forces. This included one VC during the First World War. Throughout the Second World War, in addition to a steady supply of volunteers to the three Armed Services, the school provided a contingent from the OTC for the Home Guard platoon of Iwerne village. The Home Guard had developed from the earlier force of local defence volunteers, the LDV, created to protect Britain in the event of invasion. The school's Home Guard platoon formed the major portion of Iwerne Minster's defence of the Realm in providing the resistance to German airborne forces landing in the area; while the remnants of the British Expeditionary Force, recently evacuated from Dunkirk, would tackle the German Panzer force landing on the beaches. Winston Churchill's stirring words on how we should greet a Nazi invasion was

fresh in our minds, *We shall fight on the beaches, we shall fight on the
landing-grounds, we shall fight in the fields, and in the streets; we shall never
surrender.*

I recall the annual return to Clayesmore at the start of the school term
as a major military exercise with hundreds of boys loaded with their
trunks and 'tuck boxes' assembled at Paddington Station. The harassed
school staff deployed everybody and their baggage onto the special train
for Semley, the nearest station on the Great Western Railway for the
school. Here a similar exercise took place to load everybody and everything into a fleet of coaches to the school. Surprisingly, there were no
major problems and no loss of baggage, or boys, in returning to school
that autumn of 1940. After witnessing part of the Battle of Britain over
London during the summer holiday, I continued to be on the fringe of the
air battle as the *Luftwaffe* attacked western targets. On one occasion while
cycling near Blandford Camp I took refuge in a ditch as a German
bomber strafed the countryside. On another occasion an RAF Hurricane
shot down a Bf-110 fighter over the school and it crash-landed on a nearby
hillside. The Hurricane returned flying low over the school before
climbing in a victory roll and I wondered if the pilot was an old boy from
the school. The village alarm sounded and senior members of the cadet
corps rushed to draw rifles and join the local village defenders to apprehend
or battle any survivors of the crash. Led by the solitary representative of
the village constabulary, we advanced in line abreast up the hill with
bayonets fixed to the crashed aircraft. As we nervously approached the
twin-seat Bf-110, which appeared intact apart from a wheels up landing,
we saw the pilot standing by the gunner's machine gun, Luger pistol in
hand, smoking a cigarette. He did not resist and handed his pistol to the
constable. Which was just as well for, although we were issued with blank
cartridges, none of the cadets had any live ammunition. The German's
contempt for this motley band of amateur soldiers was very apparent as
he completely ignored his gunner dying in the rear cockpit. Perhaps our
prisoner considered that his stay in England as a POW would be of short
duration after the German invasion. The injured gunner was taken back
to the school but died in the sanatorium.

The weapons available to the school Officer Training Corps (OTC)
were First World War Lee-Enfield rifles and bayonets, but the Home
Guard members of Iwerne Minster village had to provide their own
weapons such as shotguns, small calibre rifles or First World War
souvenirs. Failing that they had to make do with an army issued pike.
Later, we received the Mills hand grenade that was far more hazardous to
the thrower than any anticipated assailant. A regular army corporal
arrived with two boxes of grenades, together with one box of detonators,

to brief us on the weapon. At least the Army appreciated that for our own safety someone should advise their rustic warriors on the workings, priming and throwing of the grenades. During the briefing and while demonstrating the priming of a grenade, the corporal commented, 'Now then, Gentlemen, these grenades are very dangerous and can be lethal. This detonator can take off your fingers as it is very sensitive to any pressure; which is how it explodes the grenade. Therefore, when inserting the detonator into the grenade like so; both should be treated with the greatest of contempt'! The corporal looked a little askance at the resulting schoolboy laughter. These words of advice were to remain with me thereafter for whenever some danger threatened, or moments of panic arose, the worthy corporal's words would return.

The local Home Guard commander decided the grenades were too dangerous to store in the school armoury and ordered that they be stored in the village Home Guard armoury in a cellar beneath the village pub. The landlord of 'The Talbot Arms' and his regulars decided that tackling General Student's elite paratroops was one thing but drinking their beer while seated above two boxes of live hand grenades was quite something else. They decided to hide the grenades in a safe place and someone had the bright idea to hide the boxes of grenades in the village stream below the bridge close to the pub. That winter a particularly high flood carried them away, not to be seen again for some years. The fate of the detonators is a mystery; but one summer some village children playing in the stream found the hand grenades and started playing catch with them. Fortunately, none of the grenades contained detonators.

Some three years after I left school and returned to England with my 'wings', I attended an abbreviated commando assault course to fill in time before an assignment to flying duties. We carried out firing practice on various weapons that included the throwing of the Mills hand grenade. One nervous participant managed to drop a live grenade after pulling the pin. The rest of us dived for cover behind a rampart but the thrower froze and with only seconds to live, the sergeant instructor, intent on a posthumous VC, was quick and adroit enough to throw the grenade clear before it exploded. I thought back to what mayhem there might have been had we ever practised live grenade throwing in the Home Guard where just carrying a loaded firearm around had been dangerous enough.

During the summer and autumn of 1940 the Iwerne Minster Home Guard kept vigil for the arrival of the German gliders and paratroops. To facilitate this some local artisans built a wooden watchtower some thirty feet high on top of a nearby hill in Cranborne Chase and senior members of the school cadet corps participated in the watches. Few of us were brave enough to venture up the tower for our watch and this prudent sense of self-preservation was confirmed during the first gale of the autumn when the watchtower crashed to the ground; fortunately without any casualties. There was no thought of a replacement watchtower. During the vigils on that hill top in Cranborne Chase, the watches involving the dawn period stand out most vividly in my memory. I sat nervously awaiting the arrival of General Student's Fliegerkorps and as the sunrise appeared so too did a beautiful vista of a verdant and peaceful Dorset. It was hard to realize at such a time that we were at war.

With nothing to do until relieved on watch I listened to the many tales from the local Home Guarders who mostly had rural occupations. One exception was an employee at the pork pie factory in the village. These pies were great favourites in the school where the wartime diet was predictably monotonous. However, after hearing him describe their process of manufacture I could never approach them with the same enthusiasm afterwards, despite the delicious aroma of the hot, tasty and freshly baked pies. At a time when we experimented with the forbidden sins of tobacco and alcohol I found, in common with my friends, that draught cider held more attraction for me than beer. During cycle rides through the local countryside we sampled with awe the locally brewed cider that was of significantly higher alcohol content than the local beer. These cycle rides confirmed an old adage – *Cider is treacherous because it smiles in the face and then cuts the throat.* Listening one night to the cider making process from a fellow Home Guarder employed in the local cider distillery changed my perception. He explained to me that the enzymes in the apple juice required feeding with protein in order to produce the amino acid of the cider. To achieve this they tossed a large hunk of meat and even a carcass into the big distillery vat to produce the required body in the brew. I was surprised to learn what went into this vat and how quickly it disappeared. This may well have accounted for my subsequent and early conversion from the apple to the hop; starting with the sweeter malt stouts before graduating to and appreciating the delights of true English bitter ale. Some years later when stationed in Yorkshire I heard of a tragedy that occurred in the local brewery whose beer, I considered, lacked both taste and strength. It appeared that a brewery worker, maybe overcome by fumes while inspecting the large fermentation tank during the weekend, fell in. Unfortunately, his disappearance was not noted until the start of the working week. In recovering his remains they drained the fermentation tank and hundreds of gallons of beer flowed through the gutters providing a heady effluvium in the town. In rather questionable taste I could not refrain from commenting to friends that apart from the tragedy of the accident, it was also a pity and a waste of the beer as this was the only occasion when this particular brand of beer had contained any body!

Sitting and talking on the hill in Cranborne Chase I also learned quite a lot about farming and horses from one farrier whose personal tragedy was particularly harrowing. According to him he had personally assisted in the home delivery of all his children, treating the process much as he did with his horses. Unfortunately, on the last occasion while his wife was near the end of her pregnancy she developed white leg and he applied horse liniment to the unfortunate woman who died in agony. He expressed surprise at the outcome as it always worked all right with his horses!

The defeat of the *Luftwaffe* by the RAF during September persuaded Hitler to transfer his attentions from the UK to the USSR, and the German 'Blitz' was over by December 1940. By January 1941 it was evident that the threat of invasion was over as the bulk of the *Luftwaffe* flew eastwards. This was just as well for the Home Guard in the rural and sparsely populated county of Dorset, as the elite German airborne forces available for 'Operation Sealion' numbered 8,000 paratroops and glider troops. Battle hardened troops such as these landing around Iwerne Minster would soon mope up any resistance put up by the Home Guard whose only hope was Divine intervention. If General Montgomery, commanding the southern army based at the nearby Blandford Camp, had inspected us in 1940 and witnessed our dilettantish defence of the Realm, he may well have echoed Wellington's words, 'I don't know what effect these men will have on the enemy, but, by God they terrify me!'

By the time the Home Guard disbanded in 1944, when it became obvious there was no further threat of invasion, the school had supplied more than 300 volunteers for an independent platoon for the Home Guard command at Melbury Abbas: a local civil defence contingent, an air observers post on the roof of the school, and the manning of the village fire services. A splendid American Ahrens-Fox fire engine, borrowed from a local museum in the interests of a national crisis, replaced the village fire engine detached to support the fire services overwhelmed by the *Luftwaffe* raids on Bristol. This imposing red fire engine, circa 1920, was the flagship of vintage fire engines. It was the perfect prop for a 'Keystone Cops' type of movie. Indeed, the only call I recollect in response to a village house fire resulted in an enactment of just such a movie, as we endeavoured to unroll and connect 200 feet of heavy hoses, operate the pumping engine and direct the uncooperative jets of water at the fire while contemplating the erection of the fire ladders attached to the sides of the fire engine and the possibility of an opportunity to wield one of the two six pound axes carried aboard the fire engine. It can safely be said that the school more than played its part in the protection of our noble heritage. Fortunately, it was never put to the task of proving this during a German invasion of our cherished land.

They were exciting days during the summer of 1940 with aerial dog-fights, aircraft shot down and boys being machine-gunned from the air. This was much more exciting than the usual aviation side of my schooling that consisted of helping our maths master get airborne in his Slingsby sail-plane from the local hills. After we had hauled the dismantled aircraft up the hill we reassembled it and fitted bungee cords to the release catch on the nose of the Slingsby. Several of us grasped the bungee cords while others held on to the tail. After a headlong rush down the hill to the full stretch of the cords without falling, those holding the tail would let go and the aircraft catapulted into the air. It usually managed to fly about a mile before landing in a nearby meadow. The goal was to pick up lift from up drafts along the hillside or strong thermals beneath the clouds and soar high above the school before landing on one of the playing fields. However, this was not a popular concept in case an ill judged landing put the sail-plane down on a cricket pitch; for there were memories of one 'old boy' flying to the school for the 'Old Boys' annual cricket match and dragging his tail-skid across the number one cricket pitch. These were the days before high performance sail-planes and the Slingsby mostly per-formed as a glider. We never seemed to experience the wind or thermal conditions necessary to achieve much in the way of airborne time or distance. We were always recovering the Slingsby from some field, with an irate farmer armed with his shotgun complaining about the danger to his herd. I always arrived at the glider expecting to find it peppered with number-six shot or the like, although I do not recollect the airplane being damaged in any way. Our maths master, John Simpson, being a pacifist, joined the Friends Ambulance Service, thereby excluding himself from a useful flying contribution to the war effort. The last news I heard of him was driving an ambulance with medical supplies over the Himalayas to China; a far more hazardous occupation. Returning to the school after the war to visit the new chapel I looked at the Clayesmore Roll of Honour. A total of 37 Old Clayesmorians gave their lives during the First World War. In the Second World War, 70 Old Clayesmorians served in the Royal Navy, 130 in the Army and 55 in the Royal Air Force; 43 Old Clayesmorians died in action from 1939–45, and of this total 24 died flying with the RAF.

So the early months of the War passed and in 1941 after four happy years spent at Clayesmore; although I failed to impress their Lordships at the Admiralty; I managed to acquire sufficient academic qualifications to enter university. I left as a school prefect having represented the school in the 1st XI at cricket, the 1st XV at rugby football and the school athletic and boxing teams. I became an undergraduate at Peterhouse, Cambridge, reading engineering, and I joined the University Air Squadron so that I could learn to fly and be accepted by their 'Airships' at the Air Ministry for pilot training in the RAFVR. The University Air Squadron operated de Havilland Tiger Moths provided by the RAF with RAF instructors. The Squadron flew from the grass airfield of Marshall's Flying Training School, outside the city on the Newmarket road. The Tiger Moth was a delight to fly in calm weather but it was very sensitive to rough air and gusty wind conditions. The aircraft was a well-tried training and sports biplane dating from the early thirties and powered by an inline 142 hp Gypsy engine. It had a maximum speed of 108 mph, a service ceiling of 14,000 feet and a range of 300 miles. Light in structure and basic in design it was relatively easy to fly but not easy to fly well. It had characteristics that required full attention and could prove unforgiving to the careless or inattentive pilot. The ailerons, elevators and rudder needed coordination in all manoeuvres, especially during aerobatics when well-executed slow rolls required full and strong application of all three controls. Lockable slats on the leading edge of the upper wing improved low speed handling with a reduced stalling speed. However, the slats required locking during aerobatics and spinning manoeuvres to assist recovery. The RAF Tiger Moths had ventral fillets attached to the upper fuselage at the tail to provide a more effective keel surface area in recovering from a spin. The fuel system in the Tiger Moth was very basic. The fuel was gravity fed from a tank in the upper wing above the front cockpit. When flying the Tiger Moth inverted the engine had no negative G trap in the fuel system and the engine would stop after a few seconds. Restarting the engine in flight required the aircraft to dive sufficiently steeply to turn the propeller and start the engine. Starting the engine on the ground required the propeller to be hand swung with chocks against the wheels as there were no wheel brakes.

Landings were one of the most problematical features of the Tiger Moth as the undercarriage was narrow with no wheel brakes. The aircraft used a tail skid and turning on the ground was achieved by the use of throttle to apply slipstream against the rudder to turn. The closely spaced wheels without brakes for stopping or directional control on the ground often caused the aircraft to swing in cross winds. This resulted in a ground loop with a wing tip striking the ground. Sometimes, in strong winds even the full use of rudder and power was insufficient to stop the swing. It was thus not easy to achieve a true three point landing in which the wheels and tail skid touched the ground together in anything but calm conditions. The easier option was to touch down wheels first holding the aircraft straight with power and rudder, but any attempt to land in this manner elicited abuse from our instructors assigned from the RAF. Drift in cross wind landings is always a problem, even with large and heavy aircraft where the correction technique turns the aircraft towards the wind, crabbing it before skidding it straight at touch-down. In light aircraft such as the Tiger Moth a more effective technique is to lower the wing into the wind and side slip to counter the drift, levelling the wings at touch-down. It is of course possible to combine both techniques. With the narrow width undercarriage I was to find landings in a Tiger required similar techniques to landing a Spitfire, and it was a question of pride when viewed by critical fellow pilots that the landing be a 'three-pointer' with 'wheelers' being greeted with derision.

Flying the Tiger Moth at any time of the year required us to dress as was the custom during the First World War, and flying in the draughty open cockpit with no means of heating could be a very cold affair. We dressed in quilted lined Sidcot flying overalls, virtually unchanged for the previous twenty years. In addition, we wore heavy sheepskin boots and double lined gauntlets. Our instructors flew in much envied and desired leather sheepskin jackets that were not available to us neophytes until we became authentic pilots. Our flying outfit included flying goggles and a leather flying helmet to which we attached flexible rubber tubing to plug into the Gosport speaking tube. This worked very much as a chauffeur's speaking tube and required considerable lung power to convey any information above the sound of the engine and the wind. A personal parachute completed our outfit and periodically we pulled it in front of the packer to reassure ourselves that it would open when required.

The basic theories of flight revolve around the principles devised by a Swiss mathematician and physicist, Jacob Bernoulli, who calculated that as the velocity of a fluid increased there was a resulting decrease in pressure. Hard though it may be for some to accept, air is a fluid, although unlike water it can be compressed, and Bernoulli's theories and the Bernoulli Effect in particular are the explanations of how aircraft fly. For sustained flight an aircraft requires both lift and propulsion, which is achieved by moving the aerofoil or wing swiftly through the air by means of an engine-driven propeller or jet thrust. Lift would not occur on uniformly shaped wings, but by curving the upper surface of the wing convexly, with the lower surface straight or even slightly concave, lift is achieved. This results from the upper and lower air flows over the wing section arriving at the trailing edge at the same time, and as the air flow over the upper surface has farther to travel due to the convex shape than the air flow over the lower surface it travels faster producing a reduction in pressure on the upper surface of the airfoil than the lower surface, thus producing lift to the wing. This is not the end of the design of the wing as, like the birds of the air, aircraft have differing requirements of flight such as lift capability, manoeuvrability, speed, range and endurance. Nature evolved this over aeons of evolution to meet the needs of fast swimming fish and the various requirements of birds. Such factors will govern the design of the aircraft wing to meet the differing operating roles and requirements, and determine whether a thick short wing or a long thin high aspect ratio wing is required.

Following an introduction to Bernoulli's theorems and the revelation that air has similar properties to water, we launched ourselves into the practical application of the effects and further effects of the controls of the Tiger Moth. Stalls, spins and some aerobatics such as loops and slow rolls followed. We then concentrated on circuits and landings, or 'bumps'. The old chestnut that any landing one walked away from was a good landing was often the case when learning to fly with the RFC in the First World War. This was not the view of our instructors from the RAF, who quickly made us aware that flying may be natural for birds, but such was not the case with us. They emphasized that flying was an art and that we take pride in its achievement; to this end the difference between an arrival and a landing was a three-point touchdown. My instructor was a Sergeant Murphy, referred to behind his back as 'Spud'. He had a refreshing Irish sense of humour and, although nothing appeared to faze him, he displayed a strict purist approach to flying. Any sloppy performance or infringement of the principles of flight resulted in a stream of invective shouted down the Gosport tube that was quite a revelation. Transgressions often resulted in violent gyrations ending in inverted flight and the shouted instruction, 'Right then, it's all yours. You have control!' Often in the early phase of instruction, the waving of arms with the control stick in one hand accompanied this instruction. This was quite effective in raising the heart rate until one realized that he carried a spare in the cockpit for just such an impression. Sergeant Murphy had an obsession for precise flying, immaculate landings and a desire to put cocky undergraduates in their place. Any attempt at a wheels first, tail up landing resulted in the full application of power and the shouted instruction to go around and stop leaping over the grass like a demented leprechaun. I got on well with Murphy but then I usually do with the Irish owing to a similar sense of humour and a dash of Irish blood in my mixture. I liked him as an instructor and he was a good pilot. As a result, during my fifth hour of flying and having completed a couple of fairly presentable circuits and landings, on taxiing back for another take-off Murphy got out of the aircraft taking his parachute with him. He fastened his front seat harness, slapped me on the shoulder and shouted, 'Right then; do me a good circuit and landing and bring it back in one piece.' Trying not to appear surprised I waved airily and proceeded to do just that.

One of the apocryphal rules of the air states that although every take-off is optional, every landing is mandatory. It has been said that flying is the second greatest thrill known to man; in which case landing has to be the first! Certainly, the first solo flight has a special thrill matched by few other things in life unrelated to flying. I thought I had done Murphy and myself credit but when I returned to where he was sitting on his parachute he shouted, 'Don't waste my time. Do another and get it right this time'. Whether by luck or intimidation the second effort met with his approval, and I was then in my own estimation an incipient fighter pilot heading for wings and glory.

That evening I telephoned my father to give him the news and he appeared genuinely pleased and I hoped my failure with the Royal Navy was a matter of the past. To celebrate my solo flight I invited Sergeant Murphy to dine at college. Peterhouse, the oldest and one of the smaller colleges, had the enviable reputation of the best dining and, wining in Cambridge. As such, invitations to dine were much desired and being in great demand, very limited and despite the wartime restrictions the college seemed to fare very much as it did before rationing. My gyp – a Cantabrigian valet – who took great care of me in college also served in hall and he made sure my instructor had a memorable dinner. It appeared to me that Sergeant Murphy's attitude towards undergraduates, or maybe just me, softened a little after this and certainly he no longer shouted obscure Irish epithets at me. It was with sadness I learned some years later that Warrant Officer Murphy DFM, lost his life while piloting a Lancaster bomber over Berlin in 1944.

The next five hours of my flying training I spent polishing up my flying on aerobatics, forced landings and instrument flying under a hood. I now started to feel confident that I had command of the Tiger and not vice versa. We also practised engine failures and forced landings, when Murphy would indulge in some very low flying, which was not a good example to set an *ab initio* pilot. However, this impressed me enormously and I looked forward to the day I would skim low level across the countryside. Low flying had an attraction that often proved fatal, and unauthorized low flying was a very serious offence with severe disciplinary consequences. This was necessary to stop the wastage of aircrew and aircraft for more effective use against the Germans. During my last term at school in 1940 the roar of engines overhead disturbed us when a Hampden bomber 'beat-up' the school as it flew very low over the rooftops. In turning around a covert on the school estate to return to the school buildings, the aircraft stalled and crashed into the wood exploding in a ball of fire. We rushed to the crash site but it was impossible to save the crew, and little was recognizable or salvageable of the bomber. It transpired that the two recently graduated and commissioned pilots were on a navigational training exercise with the two pilots exchanging the piloting and navigation. A third member of the crew was an aircraftman air gunner. It was impossible to establish who was at the controls when the bomber crashed, but one of the pilots was an old boy from the school and the assumption was that he was flying the aircraft. Such a waste, but wastage was very much the fate of the Hampden bomber during the early stages of the war. Despite this salutary lesson I, like the rest of my contemporaries, had a sense of infallibility and that such a fate could never happen to us. It was hard to resist the forbidden fruit of low flying despite repeated warnings of the old adage – *There are old pilots and there are bold pilots but there are no old bold pilots.* To us a low level 'beat-up' was a way to impress friends and relatives. While practising forced landings with Murphy, he would select fields that experience told him offered the best prospects for mushroom picking, and we carried a parachute bag with us to collect them. There was one particular wide avenue of tall elm trees that had a great attraction for Murphy as he flew down the avenue between the trees with his wheels a few feet off the ground. I logged all this information in my memory for reference during solo flying, and by the time I had accumulated the grand total of twenty hours I began to feel I was an accomplished aviator.

I had by this time flown the first of my two operational sorties with Bomber Command. The RAF encouraged liaison between the Air Cadet Corps and local fighter and bomber units, and there were many bases around Cambridge. South of the city was Duxford airfield, a famous fighter base that I got to know well when posted there after the war. North of the city was the airfield of Oakington, a bomber base with a wing of Stirlings, the first of the four-engine bombers delivered to the RAF. While visiting the station to inspect the new bomber the squadron commander of No. 7 Squadron offered to take me on an air test to which I readily agreed. Wing Commander Graham had the reputation of a 'hot-shot' pilot having claimed one Bf-109 fighter destroyed over the Dutch coast. The flight plan for my flight changed from an air test to dropping leaflets over Holland and we headed for the Dutch coast at wave top height. This enabled the skipper to indulge in his passion of flying the Stirling as low as possible. Low-level manoeuvrability was probably the best feature of the Stirling, as it was inferior in terms of speed, altitude and bomb load to the later Lancaster and Halifax bombers. I had to stand between the two pilots and the flight was both exhilarating and tiring as our skipper weaved his way over Holland, all the time exhorting his gunners to spot enemy fighters as in shooting down one Bf-109 he had every confidence that he could shoot down another. Apart from some desultory AA fire directed against us we did not meet up with any Bf-109s, and with the

Bf-109 armed with cannon and a considerable advantage in speed and manoeuvrability this was fortunate.

I was not at all sure that I should have been on this mission, but it was certainly a thrilling experience and more enjoyable than the night flight I did in a Halifax bomber in 1944. I did not repeat the experience of a Stirling flight again, nor did I mention it to my parents, but I did fly in a Whitley bomber before joining the RAF. The RAF operated an Operational Training Unit (OTU) with Whitley bombers at Abingdon airfield with a satellite airfield at Stanton Harcourt where my father lived, and he was very hospitable to the aircrew flying from the satellite airfield. The instructors were all on rest from a bomber tour of operations. The squadron commander of the unit was a frequent visitor and my father offered him pheasant and partridge shooting. By way of appreciation, as I was in the Air Cadet Corps with the University Air Squadron, he took me flying a couple of times on a training exercise. The Whitley was a slow gentlemanly type of aircraft and an easy bomber to fly. Early in 1942 the RAF launched the 1,000 bomber raid on Germany with an attack on Cologne; followed by raids on Essen and Bremen. Bomber Command could only produce the magic number of 1,000 bombers by mobilizing the aircraft and crews from the training units. The RAF could not sustain the makeshift effort and it was 1944 before Bomber Command authentically launched 1,000 heavy bombers on raids on Germany. The OTU Whitley aircraft with instructional crews made up a large component of the first 1,000 bomber raid. The comparatively small bomb load of the twin engine Whitley contributed a disproportionately small amount of damage in the raids and the comparatively slower speed and altitude capability of the Whitley resulted in a disproportionately higher rate of casualties from the German anti-aircraft guns and fighters. Among the casualties from Stanton Harcourt during these three raids was our squadron leader friend.

With my accumulated flying experience I was not lacking in confidence in my flying ability, which was more than I could say about girl friends. During my first term at Cambridge I met a lively and attractive girl with a strong interest in horses, sports cars and airplanes. The first interest was a result of her father owning some training stables near Newmarket. Not owning a horse or a sports car, I thought I might impress her with my newly acquired flying skills. The girl responded to my interest by trying to persuade me to do a 'beat-up' of the house. As the stables were close to the Newmarket gallops I had enough sense to disregard such a foolish request. She then suggested that I take her flying but that, of course, was out of the question. However, I did not entirely dismiss the thought from my mind. The opportunity to demonstrate my prowess germinated in my mind when we started cross-country flights. One of our cross-country flights was to visit the Oxford University Air Squadron, a distance of 60 miles to the south-west with a still air flying time of around forty minutes. We would land and refuel the aircraft before flying back to Cambridge. The Oxford squadron would do a reverse exercise by visiting us. I had a friend at the university flying with the squadron and I arranged to visit him. My father had farming friends midway between Oxford and Cambridge and we used to exchange shooting rights with them. I knew the countryside well and while visiting the farm reconnoitred a suitable field in which I proposed to land the Tiger Moth. The plan was to make a pass over the farm, land in the field, give the girl a quick circuit around the house, land back on the field and proceed on to Oxford. The girl had visited these friends with me and although petrol rationing was in effect farmers and horse trainers had a fairly generous allowance. The girl was ostensibly to visit these friends with me but arrive before me, and when I buzzed the farm meet me at the field. There was no air traffic control for us as we had no radio. After authorization of the flight the pilot was responsible for entering the take-off and landing times in the log. The time spent on the ground at Oxford refuelling would make these times flexible without inviting comments.

The day arrived and I checked out and took-off to see my friend in Oxford. It was a nice day and everything proceeded according to my flight plan. I flew over the house waggling my wings and revving the engine. There is a proverb about stolen pleasures being the sweetest, however, as Robby Burns observed, 'The best-laid schemes o' mice an' men gang aft a-gley'. I landed in the field; a large grass meadow used for grazing cattle, and noticed some cows on the far side of the field. I taxied over to the gate by the road and waited with the engine running. Nobody appeared and after a few minutes I started to get anxious. When I saw the cows moving towards me I realized that the sensible thing now was to abandon the caper and take-off for Oxford. It was at this moment that common sense and not the Tiger Moth took-off. In medical terms perhaps it was a question of testosterone flooding the cerebellum; anyway, I switched off the engine. This was not a problem as I anticipated some help from the farm in holding the aircraft while I started the engine, and to move any cows from my take-off path. Still nobody appeared and I set off for the house. I arrived to find that not only had the girl not arrived but my farmer friend and his son were away attending to some emergency. I decided I had wasted too much time and enlisting the help of the farm-hand we returned to the aircraft. As we entered the field I saw with some apprehension the cows gathered around the Tiger Moth, before noticing them contentedly and lovingly licking the wings and fuselage. I rushed towards them shouting and waving my arms; only to stop in horror as I saw strips of fabric hanging from the ailerons, elevator and rudder. Closer inspection revealed holes not only in the control surfaces but also in the lower wing and along the fuselage. With a feeling of acute nausea I realized I could not risk a take-off in that condition. How would I explain my aircraft apparently peppered with light flak damage?

The Tiger Moth's airframe, wings and controls were of wood construction covered with fabric. A varnishing dope tightened and weatherproofed the fabric making it as tight as a drum. It was the smell and taste of this dope that proved irresistible to the cows; similar to a salt-lick in the veldt. The dope also had a slight hallucinogenic effect on the cows. Anyone experiencing the lick of a cow's tongue knows its roughness and abrasiveness which resembled the texture of a number 36 sanding paper or a large bastard file. I was now feeling numb, dumb and emasculated. Recovering from this mentally and physically paralysing attack of the staggers, I began to contemplate the consequences of my stupidity. Grounded by the Squadron and 'gated' by the University – certainly! Dismissed from the Squadron and rusticated from the University – quite likely! Rejected by the RAF and banished to the trenches or the coal mines – a distinct possibility! Recovering from my mental torpor I started to grasp at straws and a plan of action for survival. I walked back to the house leaving the farmhand to guard the remains of the Tiger from further ravaging. The only comment made by the farmhand at this unusual situation was a bemused and descriptive drawn out 'Urrgh'. I instructed him that if questioned he knew nothing and if he said nothing it would be to his advantage. I received the same succinct reply. I returned to the farm and telephoned the squadron, reporting a forced landing in a large field without damage to the aircraft. This was true to the extent that the aircraft was undamaged until the *coup des langues* of the cows; which of course I did not mention. Oh! – *Those cloven tongues like as of fire!* About three hours later a truck arrived with a flying instructor, a fitter and a rigger. I led them to the field where the Tiger Moth appeared even more tattered than when I left it, surrounded by the blissfully contented cows. I prayed my surprise and anguish at this catastrophe appeared genuine, as I sent silent supplications to the Deity. It not being possible to repair the aircraft *in situ* we corralled it and an aircraft transporter retrieved it for recovering at the maintenance unit. To my great surprise and relief the squadron accepted my report. The squadron also accepted my suggestion that an air lock in the fuel line caused the engine to stop; and I had the embarrassment of a commendation for a successful forced landing! I was on tenterhooks for sometime whether the girl's father or my father should get wind of the near disaster. The farmer did not let on that he was an accessory to the fact. This was certainly a salutary lesson and brought home the distinct advantages of all-metal construction for light aircraft. It was probably one of the very few occasions when the tiger succumbed to the cow! The girl explained her absence was due to her parents insisting she accompanied them to a race meeting and being scared to say she was meeting me in case it got out that she hoped to fly with me, she followed them to the races. Under the circumstances it was just bad luck things turned out as they did but I did not intend to push my luck so the matter ended. I suppose she waited until the war ended before getting her first flight. The following year I joined the RAFVR and sailed off to the United States to complete my pilot training. Little did I imagine that the bovine spectre I avoided so fortuitously would follow to thwart my hopes of a pilot's brevet for a second time. From this point the girl's path and mine drifted apart and when I returned I heard she had married into the horse racing fraternity.

Before sailing westwards to complete my training I was inducted into the RAFVR in London. The RAF aircrew induction centre was at St John's Wood, and the Air Ministry commandeered several large luxury apartment blocks near Regent's Park and Lord's cricket ground to accommodate the volunteer aircrew. As aircrew cadets we were discernible by a white flash worn on our forage caps, and leapfrogging the first two basic ranks of Aircraftman 1st and 2nd Class we held the rank of Leading Aircraftman (LAC), indicated by a propeller patch worn on our upper sleeve. Subsequent NCO promotion following the presentation of our 'Wings' would skip the rank of corporal to that of Sergeant Pilot, to be followed one year later to Flight Sergeant Pilot, and ultimately to the exalted and respected top NCO rank of Warrant Officer. I joined other university entrants at the cricket ground for the signing-in and swearing of allegiance to the King Emperor, his heirs and successors. Here we were quickly made aware that Service life was to be very different to that of 'Civvy Street' and the hallowed halls of learning during our Spartan stint in His Majesty's Royal Air Force. We were now subject to King's Regulations and Air Ministry Orders, with sundry directives such as those listed for the enlisting airmen into the RAF. These included such counsel as forbidding gambling for cash; the consumption of food and intoxicating liquor in the barracks; and the commendable prescription to take a bath at least once a week. We were also instructed to be properly dressed at all times while carrying a respirator. We drew uniforms and, to our dismay, full marching kit from the Quartermaster's stores. This was quickly followed by innumerable and interminable inspections and parades while being initiated into the military process of proceeding from A to B and beyond by route marching or double quick time – two things we had hoped to avoid by volunteering to be aircrew. The venerated

grounds of the Marylebone Cricket Club echoed to the bellowed commands of our stentorian drill instructors as they harried us hither and
thither with a litany of commands in preparation for church parades and
station inspections.

Although we viewed it as somewhat irksome at the time, our initiation
process into the military was certainly far less dramatic and arduous
than that experienced by my father when joining the 10th Battalion of
The Cameronians (Scottish Rifles) in January 1915, as part of Kitchener's
Volunteer Army in the popular belief that the war would be over by
Christmas 1915. They landed in France in June with the 9th Battalion and
marched to the Belgian coalfields of Loos on the Flanders Front in time to
join the 9th and 15th Scottish Divisions of General Douglas Haigh's First
Army spearheading the Battle of Loos on 15 September 1915. This was
the start of the Second Ypres Offensive that resulted in gains measured
in yards for a total of 60,000 British casualties against 20,000 German
casualties. The British First Army had only a quarter of the number of
men necessary for the battle, with insufficient and unsuitable heavy
artillery to cut wire and pound the well-prepared German defences. The
attack over open ground, swept by machine-gun fire, while British chlorine
gas was released in the still air conditions, was near-suicidal and 40,000
men fell in the first three hours of the attack. For the Scots the battle was
their blooding and they fought with great determination at great cost
to create a salient in the German lines. German counter-attacks sealed
off the salient and the invested Scottish battalions were cut down as
they attempted to regain the British lines. The subaltern commanding my
father's platoon together with his platoon sergeant, and the company
commander, were killed in the attack but my father escaped unscathed
with survivors of his battalion to regain the British lines two days later.
He received a Mention in Despatches and due to the 70% casualty rate
among the officers in the two Cameronian battalions he was granted an
immediate Field Commission with the 9th Battalion as a Temporary
Acting Second Lieutenant on Probation. The Second Ypres Offensive
resulted in a total of 250,000 allied casualties against German losses of
213,000. The aftermath of the failed offensive saw the battlefields of the
Western Front governed by the machine-gun and barbed wire, and the
start of the Great War of Attrition. Second Lieutenant Bernard Walker
Downes was to remain for some months as a platoon commander in the
pulverised sodden coalfields with the obliterated trenches and torn wire,
the unburied dead and the all-pervading stench, before moving south in
preparation for the Battle of the Somme in 1916.

At university, freed from the constraints of school discipline, one
feature of free expression of dress was a tendency to allow one's hair to

grow longer than had been the case at school. Although encouraged by
the University Air Squadron to keep it at a reasonable and respectful
length – after all it had to fit within the confines of a tight leather flying
helmet and not impede the hearing of instructions shouted down the
Gosport speaking tube – this did not necessarily meet with Service
requirements. At our first parade in uniform with full marching kit the
Senior Warrant Officer, 'God', an 'old hand' from the Guards, walked
slowly behind the ranks of the paraded cadets touching each one in turn
on the shoulder with his swagger cane with the words, 'Get it cut!' When
he arrived behind me I felt the tap and received the same instruction.
I eschewed the free services of the RAF barber, whose ability with
scissors and comb was exceeded by his experience with sheep shears and
the specialty of a razor cut long before it became fashionable. At an
expenditure of a full week's pay I visited the renowned establishment of
Mr Trumper in Jermyn Street to avail myself of his expertise as to how a
gentleman should appear in public. At our next inspection before the
Senior Warrant Officer I was dismayed to hear the repeated words, 'Get it
cut!' echoing along the line. When 'God' arrived behind the cadet standing
in front of me, I heard him sigh and say in a low concerned tone of voice
close to his ear, 'Am I "ertin" you Lad?' To which the startled cadet
stammered, 'Er – er – no – no – Sir.' 'Well I should be,' responded the very
Senior Warrant Officer with a rising intensity of tone in his voice that
finished in a bellow, 'Cos I'm standin on the back of your hair. GET IT
CUT!!'

My billet was in a luxury apartment at the lower end of Avenue Road
close to the entrance to Regent's Park; a very superior residential area.
Before the war the houses along Avenue Road had a local byname of
Millionaires' Avenue. I shared a room that overlooked the park with four
other cadets. When I opened the window I heard gibbons whooping to
one another from the nearby London Zoo.

Before undertaking intelligence and suitability tests we had a very com-
prehensive medical examination, during which I withheld the information
that I suffered from asthma in my childhood and also migraine attacks.
Although these attacks might be as frequent as once a month in my early
teens, by the time I left school they were very infrequent. As I had heard
the medical board was turning down applicants with flat feet I thought it
best to say nothing. In the OTC I had at least learned an old army phrase
– never volunteer anything! The medicos, although quick to reject the
unfortunate 'flatties', were unable to detect my latent asthma and
migraine. I had successfully cleared an anticipated hurdle and the rest was
up to me. It was my ambition and intention to fly Spitfires, failing that,
any single-seat fighter. Fighter and instructional flights were of short

duration and I always had a warning of an impending attack, which, if it happened in the air, would enable me to get back on the ground. My big worry was that if I flew multi-engine aircraft with flights of long duration and if I was the only pilot, I had the responsibility for the safeguard of my crew. I therefore resolved that if I was not successful in obtaining fighters I would come clean regarding my problem. Little did I think that in the Mustang some of my sorties would be in excess of four or five hours. As it transpired, I did not suffer any migraine attacks and it proved to be an adolescent malady.

During the process of the grading tests, medical examinations and drill training a strange interlude occurred. In the middle of the night all the apartments in our block suddenly filled with members of the Metropolitan Police Force supported by our own Service police. Most of the activity was in the apartment next to mine as this massive display of the law paraded through the rooms like an excerpt from *The Pirates of Penzance*. The hiatus abated and the reason for the invasion became apparent with the arrest of a cadet by the name of Cummings. His short stay with us ended with a change of billet to the Bow Street police station where he was charged with murder. It appeared from press reports that the police charged Cummings with the murder of several prostitutes in the West End of London. The press previously reported the murders as the work of a modern Jack the Ripper. The murders were all under similar circumstances in London's West End, whereas the infamous 'Ripper' operated in the Whitechapel area of London's East End. When we tried to associate this violent butchery with the quiet, unassuming aircraftman sipping tea and munching on a NAFFI bun in the canteen, it appeared too incongruous for words.

The senior airman of our particular intake and billet was a regular corporal fitter remustering for aircrew selection. Cummings slept in the same room as the corporal, and the corporal became the star witness in the No. 1 court of the Old Bailey when Cummings appeared to answer the charge of the murder of three prostitutes. An additional charge was the attempted murder of a fourth prostitute. It transpired that Cummings, who kept to himself and was very much a loner, went out on his last hunting sortie in uniform. On entering the room of his intended victim Cummings attempted to strangle the girl. However, she fought back so successfully that Cummings bolted, leaving his service respirator behind. With his name, rank and number clearly marked on the canvas bag of the respirator the police were able to arrest Cummings about four hours later. This was their first positive clue and identification of the modern Jack the Ripper, whom they suspected of at least three other unsolved murders as the modus operandi was similar.

Cummings was convicted of the murder of the three prostitutes and paid the paramount penalty and was hanged. Why this completely unlikely looking young man went on a similar killing orgy to that of 'Jack the Ripper' was not apparent, although suggestions indicated reasons theological rather than sexual. Cummings was, reportedly, an only son dominated by a widowed mother. This reasoning explained the non-consummation of the contracts with the women before their murder. Under the circumstances it appeared strange that he volunteered for aircrew. Some years after the war, I visited the famous museum of the Metropolitan Police College at Hendon when stationed there with No. 601 'County of London' RAuxAF squadron. I saw the famous gas respirator marked with Cumming's name: without this vital clue Cummings may have continued the killings before being detected. Regrettably, this was not to be the only time the RAF received adverse publicity for a multiple murderer. Some years later a pilot with Errol Flynn good looks murdered two women, one in London and the other in the south coast resort of Bournemouth. In this case the motives for the murders were certainly sexual and Neville Heath paid the same penalty as Cummings.

Following the Cummings' arrest, my group moved from our pleasant billet by the park to a slightly less superior apartment in a less affluent area closer to Lord's cricket ground. In this move we were to experience a decline in the quality of our lives as we came under the control of what we referred to as the White City Gang. In the renowned cricket ground and headquarters of English cricket was the headquarters of the aircrew induction centre. The air officer in charge was an Air Commodore Critchley, better known as Brigadier Critchley, CEO of the British Greyhound Racing Syndicate at the White City Stadium. Given a command in the RAF Air Commodore Critchley moved from Shepherd's Bush to St John's Wood bringing some of his staff with him. Some of these he commissioned and the rest he made NCOs, with the sergeants and corporals put in charge of discipline, drill and the daily running of the cadets. The corporals took great delight in the power of authority delegated to them particularly with the university entrants, haring us from dawn to dusk with enough drills, route marching with full pack and equipment, and interminable kit inspections and bed layouts to deter a Guards recruit. The slightest infringements brought abuse with marching or doubling punishments, and we considered them representative of the worst excesses attributed to the dog racing world. The wingless officers, hardly ever seen, kept under cover in the comfortable quarters of the MCC. We accepted this with some grumbling and humour directed at the tormenting NCOs, who being the butt of largely schoolboy jokes reacted with some venom.

For our obvious contempt they were able to exact revenge later to a degree that we could not possibly foresee.

The aptitude and grading tests took place in Abbey Lodge, an apartment block adjoining Regent's Park on Abbey Road. Here the medical examinations took place and our turn came for inoculations. Whereas the previous tests and examinations were in the apartments of the building, the inoculations took place in the basement. These inoculations covered every conceivable disease known to man around the world, and probably many others unknown to man. Never thereafter, despite serving overseas in every theatre, was I to receive so many injections at one time. We paraded *in puris naturalibus* line astern and proceeded down a long corridor past rooms containing the medical staff. Alternately prodded in various tender places and made to cough and bend over, we shuffled along until we arrived at the administration of the needles. Here there were no niceties of new needles as two large hypodermic syringes, more suited to the veterinary profession with the needles blunted by the multiple applications, were thrust into each arm and another two thrust into each breast. The syringes were withdrawn leaving the needles in place while four more syringes were attached with additional inoculations. This was at a time before the problem of drugs and aids but infectious hepatitis was common overseas. At this point some cadets collapsed in a faint. We then dressed and our drill instructors marched us back to our billets in quick time. Dismissed at our billets the orders were to parade in ten minutes in full marching order with an inspection to follow. Such an inspection required boots to be 'spit' and polished, with brass buttons and fittings shining brightly, and the webbing clay piped; somehow we managed to survive.

The following morning we all had varying degrees of fever and sickness. Our arms and chests were so painful it was very difficult to move and the only way we could dress was by dressing one another. After morning roll-call the usual orders followed for marching drill and inspections despite our obvious distress and objections. When the time came for parading some of us were unable to answer the call and some kits were not laid out correctly, and some beds not made. The rest of us reeled around in a comatose state. The corporals went berserk and called the sergeants. They in turn, not getting the response they expected to their orders, called the senior warrant officer. He had an authority amounting to God but even he was unable to work a miracle on the sick cadets. He in turn called a junior officer who sent for the squadron leader in charge. It was very obvious that many of us were sick and in distress, and certainly in no condition to carry out the planned programme. However, the squadron leader disregarded our protests and ordered us back to billets for inspection. By the time the inspection was due some cadets were lying down on their beds and some were in their beds. Others were sitting around unwilling or unable to lay out their kits and during this confusion, among the shouted orders and vague threats the ugly word, 'Mutiny'. Eventually the dog racing gang left us alone while they reported to their master.

The following day our group paraded in some disorder for the morning roll-call and we found ourselves marched to Lord's cricket ground escorted by the instructors, an officer and two RAF policemen. On that famous cricket ground we halted in front of the MCC pavilion and standing on the balcony were the air commodore and his senior officer staff. This was the first and only time during our stay that we saw him or the senior staff. Ordered to attention we listened in astonishment as Air Commodore Critchley informed us that our presence before him was the result of a serious breach of good order and discipline; the consequence of which required the reading of the Riot Act from King's Rules and Regulations. The second in command, a group captain, read the appropriate paragraphs of warning for conduct prejudicial and infractions mutinous. In my feverish state I had the impression of a bad dream and imagined again the strains from *The Pirates of Penzance*, expecting the pompous air commodore to break into song, *I am the very model of a modern air force general*. I am sure none of us comprehended the situation as the whole incident was ridiculous in the extreme and blown out of all proportion, with no attempt to investigate that which should have been obvious to the senior staff. We could only assume the dog track gang had their revenge with a good hatchet job on the recalcitrant cadets; and the hallowed halls of the MCC probably exuded a powerful odour of mendacity. Air Commodore Critchley concluded the parade with remarks concerning the seriousness of our situation and that our fate rested in the hands of the Air Ministry pending an inquiry. As can be imagined this did not go down well with a group of volunteers selected from universities to fly and possibly die for King and Country. We marched back to our billets in an ugly mood and before being dismissed for the day our instructors ordered us to pack our kit for departure to Brighton the following morning.

The word Brighton was familiar to us not only as a famous seaside resort but also as the RAF Disciplinary Centre at Brighton. Known euphemistically as 'Prune's Purgatory' it was a persuasive penitentiary established to curb the excesses of over-enthusiastic and exuberant aircrew. The majority of the 'black sheep' at Brighton were guilty of flying or disciplinary misdemeanours. The modus operandi was a disciplinary course of drill, route marching, cross-country running and a commando type assault course over a period of a month. To house these winged miscreants, the Air Ministry commandeered two of the best hotels on the south coast. The officers occupied The Grand Hotel, and the NCO air-crew The Metropole Hotel. We found ourselves billeted in the Metropole with the staff not sure how to treat us, as we were not only the largest single group sent to Brighton but the only air cadets. The staff probably expected us to be a bunch of rowdy and undisciplined undergraduates, but when it became apparent that we were all unwell from the reaction to a massive dose of inoculations they relaxed and were sympathetic. After a half-hearted attempt to follow the usual routine it became significantly modified. Left very much to our own devices, the commanding officer endeavoured to get the Air Ministry to expedite our embarkation for the completion of our flying training. As a result, our disciplinary course became more of a vacation than a punishment and our stay in Brighton a relief from the St John's Wood Gulag. We never heard the result of any Air Ministry inquiry; and shortly after our departure overseas it was reported that a cadet collapsed and died under similar circumstances. This resulted in some changes in procedures and staff at the aircrew induction centre at St John's Wood.

Ten days after arriving at Brighton we entrained for Manchester and Heaton Park on the north side of the city. Heaton Park was where the Air Ministry located the aircrew destined for the Commonwealth Air Training Schemes in Canada or Kenya. The RAF camp staff lived in the permanent buildings of the park but the transit aircrew had tents, beds and bedding issued for billets. After erecting the tents and settling in we found it necessary to dig irrigation ditches to drain the ponds of water formed by the rain around the tented area. Manchester lived up to its reputation and Jupiter Pluvius was in an ugly mood during our stay. As the tented area reverted to a swamp I decided that being a good camper was hazardous to my health and I moved into the city. I checked into the Midland Hotel commuting to the park for roll-calls and embarkation instructions. After a wet ten days our group proceeded to Liverpool for embarkation on an American convoy sailing for Boston, and from there we joined flying training establishments in the USA. We boarded a pre-war cruise ship, *Thomas H. Barry*, with three other cruise ships converted to troop carriers. The convoy escort consisted of an old battleship, the *Arkansas*, a cruiser and six destroyers.

So we said good-bye and good riddance to an induction process distinguished only by a colleague charged with murder and the only aircrew cadets charged with mutiny. My quest for wings had navigated a bovine confrontation, survived porcine stupidity and demonstrated the advantage of wings over webbed feet. After the war whenever driving down Avenue Road before entering Regent's Park, or on the way to the

West End down Abbey Road past the apartments that housed the aircrew
medical centre, or watching a cricket match at Lord's, or visiting the
London Zoo in Regent's Park, I remembered an anthropoid zoo that
was the RAF aircrew induction centre with names such as Cummings,
Critchley and the White City Gang indelibly imprinted in my mind. I read
Joseph Heller's *Catch-22* many years later and all became clear. Now
when I consider similar examples of military incompetence, abysmal
organization and command, allied to crass stupidity in the best Gilbert
and Sullivan fashion, I remember my induction into the RAF and my stay
in London and Manchester in 1942.

My voyage to the United States was not without incident. Sailing from
Liverpool the battleship *Arkansas* as the slowest ship stationed itself in the
centre of the convoy with two troop transports either side. The cruiser
headed the convoy with the six destroyers stationed three either side of the
troop ships. In this formation we sailed across the Atlantic at a leisurely
cruising speed. Our course took us south in the hope of avoiding the
U-boat packs, and five days out of Liverpool on a fine day with calm seas
I sat on the foredeck taking in the afternoon sun. Suddenly an explosion
appeared aboard the *Manhattan* ahead of us on the starboard station, and
black smoke poured from the ship as it swung out of the formation. The
escorting destroyers circled the convoy dropping depth charges. There
was no sign of U-boats as the convoy slowed and circled the now stopped
and burning *Manhattan*. This continued for an hour as I expected at any
moment the arrival of another torpedo. At sunset the convoy headed west
for Boston with the battleship and the three remaining transports escorted
by four destroyers. The cruiser and two destroyers remained with the
'Manhattan' that now listed visibly. We arrived at Boston without further
incident four days later and the newspapers reported that the *Manhattan*
was under tow. The *Manhattan* arrived at Boston and after repairs
returned to troop carrying for the rest of the war.

I continued by train to Florida to a civil flying school operated by the
Embry Riddle Flying College of Miami. The school operated from an
airfield near Clewiston on the west side of Lake Okeechobee. This large
circular lake measured approximately 30 miles in diameter. South of the
lake stretched the wetlands of the Everglades and to the west and north
the cypress swamp gave way to savannah with cattle ranches and citrus
farms. The airfield was grass without runways measuring just over 1 mile
square and surrounded by a large irrigation ditch. In the centre of the field
the control tower, technical and administrative buildings, together with
the living area formed an island with an access road dividing the field into
the primary and advanced flying landing areas.

The primary area operated Stearman PT-17 aircraft, and the advanced area the North American AT-6, designated 'Harvard' by the RAF. The Stearman PT-17 was a twin-seat biplane larger and more robust than the DH Tiger Moth, with a more powerful Continental radial engine of 220 hp. It had a maximum speed of 124 mph, a service ceiling of 11,000 feet and a range of 500 miles. It was a fine training aircraft and was also popular as a crop dusting aircraft. The PT-17 had a much better performance than the Tiger Moth and had the advantage of wheel brakes and a tail wheel instead of a tail skid. The aircraft was not difficult to fly, but like the Tiger Moth and all good training aircraft it required attention and some muscle to fly well, particularly in aerobatics. The flying instructors were all civil pilots and most of them had long experience in flying instruction; although some had crop dusting experience while others had travelled the country 'barn storming' before the war. My instructor was another expatriate Irishman named O'Neil. He was a large and powerfully built man with black hair and eyes to match the black heart he tried to portray. This Irish-American had a colourful disposition that emerged during instruction. My experience with the idiosyncrasies of Sergeant Murphy stood me in good stead with Mr O'Neil, although he had a more descriptive, demonstrative and violent approach to teaching than the more benign Murphy. This no doubt stemmed from his barn storming days and even minor transgressions of flying techniques produced comments, with appropriate epithets, such as, 'When I say fly at an airspeed of 110 I mean just that; not 109 or 111!': or, 'When I say steer 270 degrees, I do not mean 269 or 271 degrees!' Other transgressions produced more descriptive comments and exhortations to stop flying like a turkey, or worse. Some admonishments often brought a more violent reaction and demonstration of wrath as a sharp rearward jerk on the control column sent the Stearman into a sudden and violent snap roll. Some pupils found this approach to instruction hard to take. When questioned on his hard-nosed attitude to his pupils, O'Neil replied that if his students could not take his haranguing how would they respond to cannon or machine gun fire when up against the *Luftwaffe*? As is often the case, O'Neil's bark was worse than his bite. If one accepted his way of instruction without resentment and was cooperative and eager to learn, he revealed more humane qualities with a bawdy sense of humour. O'Neil was a very experienced pilot with a fund of tall and unlikely tales, and I learned a lot from him apart from flying. He acquainted me with much that was novel to me, including such curious American fraternities as the 'Mile High Club'. According to O'Neil, while endeavouring to qualify for membership of the Club flying a small low wing Piper aircraft he assumed, what in flying parlance instructor's refer to as an 'unusual position', causing the aircraft to go out of control. This caused his companion to panic and become lodged between the control wheel and the seat, sending the plane into a terminal dive. Fortunately for O'Neil he had decided to raise the bar and qualify for the 'Mile and Half High' category that allowed him sufficient height in which to recover. I cannot, of course, vouch for the veracity of what certainly was a most descriptive tale.

I enjoyed flying the Stearman and continued my flying with good assessments. Our American instructors placed greater emphasis on aerobatics than did the RAF instructors, and our ability in this respect was reflected in our overall assessments. A good assessment in aerobatics could significantly improve my chances in requesting an assignment to a fighter squadron after graduation. The PT-17 was a fine aerobatics aircraft but it required strong pressure on the controls for precise aerobatics manoeuvres. This may explain a propensity for snap manoeuvres which required little physical effort being a stalled manoeuvre at speed. Jerking the control stick back smartly sends the aircraft into a rapid roll that is in effect a horizontal spin. Snap or flick rolls look impressive when combined with looping manoeuvres in the horizontal or vertical plane. However, a true slow roll as opposed to a barrel roll or a snap roll requires full and accurate use of all the flying controls with the aircraft flown throughout the entire manoeuvre.

An aviation truism states that the only time one has too much fuel while flying is when the aircraft is on fire; and while performing some solo aerobatics I experienced the first of two incidents during the primary phase of my training. After completing some slow rolls I was halfway through a Cuban eight, a manoeuvre involving two half loops and two half rolls, when black smoke filled the cockpit. Flames enveloped the engine and black oil covered the windscreen. I turned off the fuel cock and side slipped the aircraft to keep the smoke and flames away from the cockpit. My immediate reaction to an engine fire was to leave the aircraft before the fire spread to the fuselage and controls, and in preparation for this I released the safety clip of my seat harness when straight and level. Looking down I saw the uninviting swampland below and I imagined a reception of alligators and water moccasin snakes. The flames from the engine fire no longer enveloped the nose of the PT-17 although there was still black smoke coming from burning oil, and I paused to reassess the situation. The side slipping appeared to extinguish the fire as fuel was no longer entering the engine. Obviously, I could not restart the engine without risking a continuing fire, so I contemplated a forced landing in the swamp. The problem of landing a fixed undercarriage aircraft in water is the very great probability of the aircraft turning over on its back. At this point I remembered a student on the course previous to my own, landing in the swamp at night just short of the airfield and finishing on his back. The upper wing rested on the water and the tail became submerged covering the pilot in the rear cockpit. It appeared he was unable to release himself from his harness and parachute, and by the time the rescue crew reached him he had drowned.

The only other option open to me was a forced landing on the airfield and that required sufficient height to glide to the field. The options and the possible consequences passed through my mind quicker than it takes to read them. Fortunately for me the aerobatics area was not far from the airfield and, as one practised aerobatics at a sufficient safety height to recover from spins, I estimated I could just make it and I stopped the side slip and glided for the field. It was a close call but I scraped over the irrigation ditch bordering the advanced flying area causing an AT-6 to over shoot his landing. The chief flying instructor asked why I did not bale out of a burning aircraft and I answered that I did not care for my chances in the swamp. Inspection of the aircraft revealed that leaks sprayed fuel and oil onto the hot engine. This resulted in a fire and a missing inspection panel in the firewall of the engine bay allowed smoke to enter the cockpit. Closing the fuel cock cut off the supply of fuel to the engine; and side slipping the aircraft extinguished the flames; with the fire damage confined to the engine bay. The initial condemnation for staying with the aircraft changed to commendation for saving the aircraft; and on this occasion the approbation for a successful forced landing was justified. However, a second incident during my primary training nearly obliterated any bonus points accrued by the forced landing.

Navigational flying followed the initial handling phase of the primary syllabus. Florida is relatively flat and in 1942 with the major cities sited along the coast the rural population was sparse. Flying over the wetlands and scrub land held few significant features for identification and our navigation was entirely by dead reckoning (D/R) using map, compass and stopwatch. Therefore, the few roads and railways were important aids to navigation and we resorted to them to reach our identification points (I/Ps). The RAF term for following railways was Bradshaw navigation, taken from the name of a pre-war railway timetable. The small townships always had a distinctive water tower on which was painted the name of the town. Railway stations also had their names displayed on boards easily discernable at low level. Such niceties were not available in Britain with all such forms of identification removed in wartime. This gave ample opportunities to indulge in unauthorized low flying on the excuse of identifying pinpoints. Low flying close to the ground enabled one to appreciate the speed of the aircraft and was an irresistible attraction, with the additional urge to shoot-up targets on the ground; both animate and inanimate. It was on a navigational cross-country exercise I met up with a colleague and we continued low level in formation, taking turns in leading. I took over the lead at one turning point and probably attempted to impress my friend with some very low flying. We did not have radio-telephone communication in our primary training aircraft and I did not notice the departure of my friend until I pulled up to consult my map. I looked astern and saw what I assumed to be my friend's Stearman far astern of me. Wondering why he was lagging behind I throttled back allowing the other aircraft to catch up, and when it did so and flew alongside I saw to my dismay it had two occupants. The instructor in the front seat made gestures to indicate I should follow him back to base and this I did feeling decidedly uneasy. My friend told me later that while following me he saw a Stearman flying above us. The Stearman started to dive down on us and suspecting it to be unfriendly he split formation offering the instructor a choice of targets and the instructor followed me. Instructor Fisher, whom I had flown with a couple of times, was a very different character from Instructor O'Neil, being a very serious and humourless individual. It was just my luck that 'Hawk-Eyes' Fisher spotted us low flying and chased me. O'Neil was unlikely to report a student without a warning in the first instance with an impressive bawling out and possible disciplinary action of his own. However, Fisher had a propensity for strict adherence to the rule book and reported me to the Chief Flying Instructor for unauthorized low flying.

Misfortunes come on wings and depart on foot! A disciplinary board consisting of the Chief Instructor (CI), Chief Flying Instructor (CFI) and Chief Ground Instructor (CGI) met to decide my fate. I listened while Mr Fisher gave evidence that fairly accurately described the circumstances of spotting two PT-17s low flying; however, he was only able to identify me. The CI asked me the name of my companion-in-crime and I answered that we met by chance and I could not identify him or remember the aircraft number. The CI then asked if I was aware of the seriousness of indulging in unauthorized low flying and I could only answer in the affirmative. I also knew that such transgressions usually resulted in termination of the course and a return to Canada for reassignment to other aircrew duties. My turn came to give my version of the incident and I admitted low flying in order to identify my position from a water tower. The CI then asked how low I was flying and I answered about 100 feet. The CI commented that Mr Fisher claimed it was much lower. I replied that from a distance he could not be precise for I was certainly at least 100 feet or more when he formated on my aircraft while I was consulting my map. The CI then asked a question that put a chill to my stomach, 'Well, Mister, tell me; how high is a cow?' Taken aback I muttered something about not understanding the question. The CI continued saying, 'Mr Fisher, who is not only an experienced instructor but also an experienced crop dusting pilot, reports that you had to climb your aircraft to get over a cow!' The CFI and Instructor O'Neil reported on my flying progress with good assessments, as did the CGI on my ground studies. The CI asked me to leave the room while the Disciplinary Board discussed the matter. I returned to the room with just the three chief instructors present. The Chief Instructor commented that normally when faced with a serious breach of flying regulations he had no option but to return the offending cadet to Canada for reassignment. The aim of the school was to produce pilots and a considerable amount of effort and money went into achieving that objective. My instructors spoke well of me and considered me capable of graduating and making a worthwhile flying contribution in the RAF. An act of folly now jeopardized my flying career and was an unnecessary waste with benefit to none but the enemy. However, such breaches of discipline and orders required punishment. As a result the Board allowed me to continue my training and confined me to the base for one month with no weekend passes. It was not difficult to assess the outcome should I reappear before the Disciplinary Board. In thanking the Chief Instructor I felt an enormous sense of relief as I left the room with a smile as permanent as that of the Cheshire cat. I felt sure that O'Neil contributed considerably in the decision not to wash me out and may have put forward the case that I represented only half of the offending breach of discipline. He never discussed the matter again but I am sure he expressed an opinion with my prosecutor. This was the second occasion of fortune favouring fools in my quest for wings, and I averred there should not be a third bovine experience!

During the weekend stand downs I reported as instructed to the aircraft maintenance area for aircraft and hanger cleaning duties. In carrying out the decision of the Board, although I missed out on the local generous hospitality in Clewiston, the rest of my punishment was virtually non existent. The question of race relations and segregation in the southern states of the USA during 1942 was in a very different form than that of today, with certain duties or types of work stipulated for specific workers. Consequently, those in charge of the maintenance area would not allow any other than those so employed to carry out cleaning duties. The engineers made it very clear to me to keep out of the way and not to touch any cleaning equipment. I reported to the chief engineer, a large middle-aged man, with a large paunch, who, when I explained the reason for my presence reacted vehemently, 'Son, this is the engineering and maintenance department, not the goddamn training department. No damn Yankee training chief is going to tell me how I run my goddamn department; and what's more, no white boy is going to do any goddam nigger work. I don't care what you do outside of my department but stay away from my hangers'. I did not need any further problems and I did not wish to be responsible for reviving the civil war, so I did not refer my predicament to a higher authority. I did as instructed and attempted to assume a cloak of invisibility; spending four partially boring weekends mooching around the aircraft, reading and feeding the Coca-Cola dispenser. Any attempt to talk to the black workers produced an embarrassed reaction with a furtive looking around for any repercussions from the supervisors. I limited my approaches to the white engineers and the exercise was not a complete loss or without some educational value. My chats with the engineers taught me not only more about the PT-17 and AT-6, but also much more about matters unrelated to aircraft and flying.

During our leisure moments some students ventured to the coastal areas, to the cities of Palm Beach and Miami on the east coast, or Sarasota and St Petersburg on the west coast. Invitations would arrive at the base for a number of students to visit families in these cities, particularly Palm Beach, where they enjoyed invitations to swimming, tennis and golf, as well as luncheon and dinner parties. The hotels in Palm Beach and Miami offered very generous discounts that made it possible for us to indulge ourselves royally. One aspect of our social life was adjusting to the attraction of the local girls in Florida who matured so much earlier than was our experience back home in Britain. In common with most of my compatriots I found the girls in Florida and Georgia not only physically attractive but fascinating to listen to with their slow and soft Southern accent after the more nasal and rapid accents found in the Northern states. We were to find that in Florida it was not unusual for a girl to be married by the age of sixteen, and even younger. Paradoxically, the age of consent in Florida was eighteen and statutory rape was a felony punishable by harsh imprisonment. For a bunch of virile and aspiring fighter pilots being *strangers in a strange land*, the early blossoming of some of the beguiling girls we came in contact with could be deceptively enticing as well as potentially dangerous. I experienced one such cautionary near involvement that served as a propitious warning while spending a short leave in St Petersburg. This was a pleasant resort on the Gulf of Mexico near Tampa, the principal city on the west coast and the centre of the US five and ten cents cigar industry. At one social function I met a very attractive girl who, to my surprise, reciprocated my evident interest in a very engaging and encouraging way. From her appearance and manner I judged her to be in her early twenties and was surprised when she told me she was about to celebrate her nineteenth birthday. The girl was manifestly concupiscent and my aspirations must have been fairly apparent for a well-intentioned observer suggested that if I intended to further the acquaintance to be warned that I was dealing with jailbait! On questioning him I learned the girl was in fact only seventeen and this information effectively doused any thoughts of a budding relationship. My early return to Clewiston allowed for an amicable withdrawal from a decidedly disconcerting situation; and probably confirmed the impression that the British were somewhat coy and slow on the uptake when it came to the dating game.

The local community in Clewiston went out of their way to offer the most wonderful and generous hospitality, with many families virtually adopting cadets during their stay. For myself, I spent much of my leisure moments locally around Lake Okeechobee where I had some of the best bass fishing and duck shooting available in the States. I was particularly friendly with the engineer in charge of the state water control board in Clewiston who took me on his air boat across the lake and into the Everglades bass fishing and duck shooting. The boat, powered and steered by a radial aircraft engine and propeller, was able to travel at high speed over the shallow and weeded water. In addition to the fishing and duck shooting there were hunting trips into the interior of the cypress swamps and savannah for quail, wild turkey and deer. The wild turkey is a very wary and difficult bird to hunt among the cypress trees and the method used was to appeal to its mating instincts. Taking cover one called up the male turkey by means of a caller that involved scrapping a piece of wood on a piece of slat in an open ended wood box. I found it not too difficult to make a fairly accurate rendition of a mating call and one relied on the intense competitive nature of the wily bird to come near enough for a shot. On one occasion I sat on the ground behind a tree calling to two birds that answered my call. The calls in reply were getting closer when suddenly a panther appeared bellying along the ground and ready to pounce on what he assumed to be a beguiled bird that happened to be me behind the tree. I think we saw one another at the same moment and I do not know which of us was the more startled. For a microsecond we stared at each other and as I raised my shotgun in anticipated defence, the panther leaped into the air and bounded off at speed. This was the only time I saw a live panther in the wild and I regretted that the moment was so fleeting for the rare chance to see this magnificent animal. After recovering from the shock I commented to one of the hunting party who had made disparaging remarks on my ability with the turkey caller that at least my calling was improving as it fooled the panther.

Hunting in the interior there was danger from various species of venomous pit vipers. On scrub lands there were ground and diamondback rattlesnakes that were rarely aggressive unless suddenly surprised. The danger from snakes was far greater in the cypress swamps as here one waded through water inhabited by the copperhead and the water moccasin or cottonmouth, with the water moccasin being the more aggressive. High leather boots encased with wire mesh to deflect a snake strike were used by some hunters, but they were not suitable for rough walking and wading through the swamps. A more comfortable outfit for wading the wetlands was to wear loose fitting trousers with thick socks and canvas boots. The protective theory being the width and looseness of the trousers presented a wide target to a snake strike making it unlikely for the fangs to penetrate the leg. The most poisonous of the snakes in Florida was the small colourful coral snake that did not possess fangs but injected its deadly venom while gripping with its teeth. A coral snake bite was rare which was just as well for the neuro-toxic venom was often lethal. The only worrying moment I had with snakes was while wading up to my waist in Lake Okechobee fishing for bass when a cottonmouth joined me. The snake gets its name from the white interior of its mouth and I saw this clearly as it circled me about twenty feet away with its head raised about a foot out of the water. While considering the best action to take, a second cottonmouth joined the first swimming about ten feet behind it. The second snake also swam with its head about a foot out of the water showing its open white mouth. I assumed the second cottonmouth to be the mate of the first and any action taken against one of the snakes might bring retaliation from the other; and I was unarmed apart from my casting rod. The two snakes continued to circle me about ten feet apart and I felt uneasy as I waited motionlessly to see what their next move might be. Several minutes passed before the snakes lowered their heads and swam away. It was an uncomfortable moment and I wondered at the snakes' interest in me. Was it just curiosity or were they attracted to the bass trailing behind me on a keeper line attached to my waist?

It was during one hunting trip into the interior of the Everglades that the federal agent in charge of Indian affairs took us deep into the restricted area of the Seminole Indian reservation. We left civilization as we knew it far behind as the Seminoles dressed and lived much as they did at the time of the Indian Wars in the late nineteenth century. The Seminole nation came originally from the plains of the Midwest escaping to the South during the Indian wars following the Civil War. Technically, the Seminole nation was still at war with the United States as they refused to sign a peace treaty. I was probably one of the few Europeans to visit the village and I found the Seminoles both curious and friendly. Especially when my turkey caller critic suggested that I would make a suitable suitor for the daughter of the Seminole chief; who appeared quite interested in the idea! According to the federal agent the village elders kept a strict discipline among their people with instances of crime and drunkenness rare. The Seminoles farmed and hunted for deer, and made colourful regalia, curios and handicrafts for sale by the federal agent in the tourist resorts. It was a very interesting and pleasant experience to see these people living as they had for generations, and a relief from the depressing conditions existing for so many of the indigenous people in some of the slum areas of the cities.

The Florida of today with its continuous ribbon development along both coasts is very different from that which existed in 1942 and in the interior where there was swamp and uninhabited areas there is development and population growth everywhere but in the Everglades. The rigid segregation policy that existed then between the white and black population was a situation that was uncomfortable for someone accustomed to living in Britain, where although a class system was prevalent, ethnic prejudices were much less apparent. The invisible Mason-Dixon Line dividing the North and the South was very much in evidence. To the local born whites, or Florida Crackers, the Confederate flag was more popular and more in evidence than the Stars and Stripes; and they kept the memory of the Civil War alive with comments such as, 'I was sixteen before I learned that Damn Yankee was not one word!' One man from whom I endeavoured to get a weather forecast replied, 'Son, here we have a saying that only a fool and a God damned Yankee would forecast the Lord's weather'!

The local town of Clewiston was a neat, well laid out white community with many residents involved in the state water management. On one occasion while I was driving back to Clewiston from Palm Beach along the only road passing through the Everglades to the south of Lake Okeechobee, I saw a body lying on the road. The road was straight, bordered on both sides by wide irrigation ditches. There was no other traffic and when I stopped I saw it was a badly injured black man. The man was unconscious and obviously the victim of a hit and run incident. My companion wanted me to continue saying her father would not like it if we became involved. I had difficulty in persuading her to help me move the injured man into the back seat of the car. There was still no other traffic on the road as I drove to the Clewiston hospital and reported a hit and run casualty to the emergency staff. When the medical attendants saw the casualty was black the hospital refused to admit or treat him, telling me to take him to the medical clinic for blacks. I found the clinic with some difficulty and left him there but by then it was too late to save him. The generous and hospitable friend who lent me his car so that I could take his daughter to Palm Beach upbraided me more for placing his daughter in an embarrassing situation, than for the bloodstains in the car.

I told him that I had difficulty understanding this and I apologized if I had abused his hospitality. Although he was a good and God-fearing man, it was obvious that to him and many like him, the proposition of a white Samaritan, as far as it concerned a black man, did not apply. There was one way of life and one place for whites and another one for blacks. I decided that as a foreign visitor to the United States and staying in the segregated South it was better not to discuss or become involved in controversial matters. Years later during visits to Ireland fishing I also avoided reference to the 'Troubles', for as an outsider such discussions involving implacable views and unshakable historical assumptions can only result in unpleasantness. I tend to take the easy route in such cases and agree with Voltaire – *Il faut cultiver notre jardin*.

Not far to the north of the airfield were cattle ranches with a small settlement and I occasionally joined some friends in visiting the local bar when returning from a hunting trip. There was just a single dirt street with a general store, saloon bar and sheriff's office among the houses lining the street. Outside the saloon bar was a hitching rail for the occasional horse among the pick-up trucks. Inside the bar were lean, tough and weather beaten 'crackers' and cowpokes drinking near proof bourbon chased with beers. Some of the men wore guns and there was much loud talk. Tall tales abounded and no women were present in the bar. Sometimes arguments became heated resulting in a brawl. It was not a propitious place for a tenderfoot to be but the attraction was an authentic Wild West atmosphere and I did not go unless accompanied by friends or local acquaintances. I remember one shooting taking place after an argument, and also another most unusual death in the bar. One local frequenter of the bar supplemented his drinking money by betting he could take any snake bite. When a jar placed on the bar had sufficient dollar bills stuffed in it from a largely drunken crowd, he placed his hand in a glass cage on the bar containing some ground rattlesnakes and allowed one to bite him. The bite of a ground rattlesnake although unpleasant is not as dangerous as its much larger relative, the diamondback rattlesnake. The rattlesnake's haemo-toxic venom infects the blood stream and the resulting sickness depends on the amount of venom injected by the snake's fangs. The man then went home to sleep off the ill effects from the bite before returning to the bar to claim his bet. On this occasion one drunken customer, with possible evil intent, bet that he could not take a coral snake bite. Foolishly the man was drunk enough to insist on taking the bet claiming no snake could kill him, and the bettor produced a small coral snake in a jar. The brilliantly coloured coral snake has to grab its victim with its teeth and from abrasions in the skin the neuro-toxic venom seeps in to attack the nervous system causing paralysis and death from asphyxiation. The man put his hand in the jar allowing the small snake to bite him. He died within an hour of the bite without leaving the bar. I only visited this township a few times but each visit was memorable. On one occasion I reluctantly took a friend's hand at poker when he had to leave the game for a while and to my surprise won the hand. I left the table and the poker player, unable to settle his debt with cash, offered his 0.32 Smith and Wesson revolver in payment. I kept the gun for many years and often wondered about the two notches cut into the butt. On another occasion a man entered the bar calling out, 'There's a nigger hunt on and the sheriff's giving us half an hour start!' At times the twentieth century appeared far away and this last episode sickened me. I decided to stay away and concentrate on my task of qualifying for my wings in preparation for a more dangerous manhunt against a dedicated enemy armed with machine guns and cannon.

Although we had many diversions during the weekend stand downs, for the rest of the week our flying training and ground studies kept us well occupied. We were also quite active in the sporting field and among the sporting personalities to visit us at Clewiston were Bill Tilden to coach us at tennis and Byron Nelson at golf. The United States entered the war in December 1941 following the Japanese attack on Pearl Harbor and the US Army Air Corps had an aircrew induction centre in Miami, taking over several of the top hotels for the purpose. During leave passes in Miami we saw many well-known personalities from the entertainment and sporting worlds. These included the film stars Clark Gable, who became an air gunner; and Jimmy Stewart, who finished the war as a distinguished bomber pilot. As a result of the publicity surrounding such personalities there were plenty of female visitors to distract us from the purpose of our stay in Florida. One I particularly remember was an aspiring starlet named Jinx Falkenbug, visiting her brother in the Air Corps. Whenever such extra curricular activities took us away from our flying, Mr O'Neil's succinct phrase of warning stayed with me as we proceeded off the base, 'Remember son, only birds can drink, fuck and fly'!

One very memorable and entertaining visitor sent to inspire us at Clewiston was Squadron Leader James MacLachan, DSO, DFC; a genuine war hero. MacLachan was famous not only in the RAF, but also with the British public, for continuing to fly fighters on operations while being what the present politically correct people would describe as 'physically challenged'. This he most certainly was; and we called him 'One-armed Mac'! MacLachan flew Fairey Battle light bombers in France before the retreat at Dunkirk; followed by Hurricanes during the Battle of Britain in 1940. In 1941 he was in Malta flying Hurricanes, being successful in claiming eight German and Italian aircraft shot down. It was during a dog-fight with Bf-109s over Malta that he was shot down; parachuting from his aircraft with his left arm shattered by cannon fire. Following the amputation of his arm he quickly set about flying as many aircraft as he could wrangle in order to persuade the Air Ministry that he was fit and competent enough without a left arm to return to flying current fighters on operations. During 1942, after being fitted with an artificial left arm the Air Ministry agreed and he was given command of No. 1 Squadron flying Hurricanes on night interception and intruder operations. No doubt Douglas Bader's legless precedent assisted him in this respect. Following a successful tour on No. 1 Squadron, claiming another five German aircraft destroyed; he spent the last six months of 1942 on a goodwill tour of the United States. MacLachan made a great impression on the Americans during his visit to the US and he managed to persuade the US Army Air Corps to let him fly some current US fighters; and to lend him a P-40 Tomahawk fighter for a tour of the British Flying Training Schools. I met him when he visited us at Clewiston in 1942. He was certainly a colourful character and he put on an impressive display of aerobatics for us in his Tomahawk. He described to me his dramatic combat over Malta chasing a Bf-109 when his Hurricane shuddered with the impact of exploding cannon shells from a Bf-109 he did not see on his tail. He recollected an explosion in the cockpit as a 20 mm cannon shell shattered the instrument panel after passing through his left arm. The cockpit filled with smoke as flames came from the engine and he knew he had to bail out quickly or die. Releasing the control stick he reached up with his right hand and pulled the canopy jettison release cable. The hood lifted from the cockpit as he felt for the seat harness locking pin and pulled it clear. Re-grasping the stick he rolled the Hurricane onto its back, and by dint of part kicking, pulling, pushing and aided by gravity; he fell clear of the aircraft. Tumbling through the air he groped for the parachute ripcord and pulled it, and with a jerk he was floating down towards the Mediterranean some 10,000 feet below.

In commenting on his successful separation from his aircraft, MacLachan thought he was fortunate to the extent that it would have been far more problematical had he lost the use of his right hand! As he descended by parachute a Bf-109 buzzed him without opening fire, and he assumed this to be the German who attacked him. He then viewed the bloody, mangled remains of what had been his left arm and tried to assess his chances of surviving before bleeding to death. By now, due to the physical shock and loss of blood he was feeling light headed, although he felt no pain. Recounting this to me he said, 'You know, it is said that while drowning or being very close to death, your whole life can pass before you in a flash. Well, I can tell you, old chap, that is a load of crap! If I thought of anything at the time it was of the girls I had; with a sense of regret there had not been more!' Fortunately for Mac, he drifted over the island and landed in a field. Immediate first aid applied a tourniquet to staunch the bleeding from the mangled mess that had been his arm and it was found necessary to amputate his left forearm below the elbow. In early 1943 he returned to the UK flying Mustangs on intruder operations; claiming three more German aircraft for a total of sixteen aircraft destroyed. He was shot down over France by ground fire in July 1943 and died of his wounds.

Following the primary phase of our training we moved on to the more exciting advanced training phase with the North American AT-6, to experience at last the thoughts contained in the poem 'High Flight'. We now had an aircraft to fly *where never lark, nor even eagle flew*. The AT-6 was an all-metal monoplane powered by a Pratt and Whitney 600 hp radial engine. It had a maximum speed of 208 mph, with a service ceiling of 24,000 feet and a range of 750 miles. This was a big jump up in performance from the enjoyable Stearman PT-17, being much closer in performance to a current fighter aircraft. There were many new functions and procedures to learn as with the increased performance from the engine came increased complications in instrumentation and aircraft systems. The aircraft controls now included a retractable undercarriage and adjustable wing flaps for landing. The more powerful engine with its variable pitch propeller had a very distinctive noise, especially when in fine pitch. Much stricter attention was required to extract the optimal performance and range from the aircraft. As the AT-6 carried a radio-telephone new operating procedures were required with the additional piloting functions associated with the increased performance of the aircraft. The importance of an accelerated scanning rate to monitor all this new information together with the correct procedures was paramount while flying this advanced training aircraft. Advancing from a primary trainer to an advanced trainer also advanced the scanning rate and attention span to the fine art of paying much more attention for just the slight lapse that could end any aspirations of becoming a pilot. The AT-6 was indeed a fine training aircraft, lacking only the power and speed of an operational fighter. All good training aircraft should have characteristics to curb the careless or inattentive pilot and the AT-6 was no exception; it could bite if abused. The aircraft was not so benign in a stalled condition than was the case with the PT-17, and there were two types of manoeuvres that required more circumspect attention to correct errors that might have more serious consequences. Aerobatics were impressive and exhilarating but required accurate flying with close attention to stalls and spins; and of course, the landing that required particular attention and concentration for the AT-6 had particular problems involving a good landing, as opposed to a tail-up arrival. It was during the circuit and landing phase of our advanced AT-6 training that we needed to exert the most due care and attention; particularly when landing in a cross wind. The AT-6 Harvard shared a common design characteristic with both the Tiger Moth and the Spitfire in possessing a narrow undercarriage. In attempting a three-point landing quick and accurate application of the controls, together with the throttle, was required to prevent any swing developing into a ground loop that could tip the AT-6 ignominiously onto its nose.

We normally flew the AT-6 solo from the front seat, as opposed to the PT-17 that was flown solo from the rear seat. Flying and landing the AT-6 from the rear or instructor's seat was a good initiation for flying any single engine fighter with its long engine cowling and restricted forward vision. As with the primary training phase on the PT-17, instrument flying practice was carried out from the rear seat under a hood. Night flying during the primary and advanced phases was carried out operating from a grass runway formed by goose-necked flares. In addition to night circuits and landings in the AT-6 we carried out night cross country flights using D/R navigation and radio aids, but it was the daylight cross country flights that gave us the greatest enjoyment as these carried us much farther afield. The highest hilltop in Florida reaches a mere 345 feet above sea level and this allowed ample opportunity for low flying. I had some blissful moments flying along silver beaches with my near catastrophe when caught buzzing a cow in my PT-17 a forgotten memory. There was an irresistible urge for the excitement of low flying and speeding close to the ground. Some cross country exercises involved two students with one flying the aircraft from the front seat while the other acted as navigator from the rear seat. This resulted in a very sad occasion for me when two of my friends from Cambridge died in a flying accident. Investigation of the accident attributed the cause to unauthorized low flying. A strange premonition occurred the night before the fatal flight when I visited the room shared by my friends. As I entered their room I saw one of them lying on his bed with a sheet pulled over him. On hearing my voice his head appeared from beneath the sheet and he asked, 'How do I look in a shroud?'

I enjoyed flying the AT-6 very much for it certainly was the best advanced trainer of its day. I experienced no awkward moments during my flying of the advanced phase of our training that passed enjoyably and quickly with only one interruption when a major hurricane struck the east coast. We evacuated all the aircraft from Clewiston north to Georgia, returning two days later when the hurricane moved on to South Carolina. Only slight damage occurred at the base as the hurricane expended most of its force as it passed north along the coast of eastern Florida. After a grand total of around 250 flying hours, the great day arrived early in 1943 for our passing out parade and our course assembled on the parade ground for the presentation of our wings. Watching the parade with a kind of parental interest were all the wonderful and generous people whose traditional Southern hospitality made our stay in Florida so enjoyable and memorable. This was certainly one of the best of times as once more dressed in our RAF blue uniforms with the addition of RAF wings on our chests and the propeller patches on our sleeves replaced with sergeant's stripes, we assembled at the railway station for the journey north to Canada. As we boarded the train many emotional farewells took place with those who for a short time took some unknown foreign students into their homes and hearts.

I had started my journey in search of wings and now as I sat watching the countryside roll by on my return to Canada for embarkation back to England, I felt the satisfaction of achievement together with an innate sense of pride. Despite some mishaps I had succeeded against the odds in my quest to place the coveted replica of eagle's wings on my left breast. In common with my companions I now felt very attached to this symbol of becoming a qualified pilot to the extent that we joked among ourselves of our reluctance to ever take those wings off our chests. We should have been happy to wear them at all times even on our 'civvies' and at night on our pyjamas.

My short year in the United States had been an interesting experience and a great eye opener for me of a very different way of life than my own in England. Despite common antecedents and being *separated by a common language* that in the US was closer to that of Shakespeare than my own; as European stock there was much else that was common but there was much that was new and novel. In general I found Americans to be more direct in their approach; similar in some ways to people from Yorkshire. However, there was always an underlying sense of the aggressive spirit from their pioneer forbears. This was amply demonstrated on the American football field; more so than in the original game of English rugby football. There was also the disconcerting sense of latent animosity still existing between the southern and the northern states stemming from the civil war, and in the south there was the ethnic situation. However, with very few exceptions I was to find sincere friendship with some truly wonderful hospitality and kindness.

One novel experience for me was an introduction to hamburgers and commercial radio, with my initiation to country music that was referred to as 'gopher' music: and purveyors of efficacious snake oil medication as a remedy for all ailments. There were also innumerable gospel preachers and Holy Rollers that conveyed the arrival of Judgement Day. One enterprising preacher always ended his exaltations with the words, 'Send 25¢ and you will receive free of charge a pamphlet entitled, "The Lord is the same on Monday as on Sunday" '. I found this a comforting thought and wondered why none of those lengthy Sunday sermons at school had conveyed the same message!

I considered myself fortunate to have seen much of the eastern seaboard of the US from Florida to Canada, and wondered if I should ever be able to see more of this vast and interesting continent with its diverse peoples after the war. The two-day train journey gave me plenty of time to read and to contemplate my future; and the conundrum – What now? My ambition during the whole of my flying training was to fly fighters and now I hoped and prayed for a posting to a fighter squadron. My flying assessments were high enough for this but in my mind were nagging thoughts that the high casualty rate in Bomber Command during 1942 and 1943 compared with Fighter Command could dictate otherwise. I wondered that should I be successful in flying with a Spitfire squadron, whether my new wings would take me into combat over Europe against the ME-109s and FW-190s of the German Luftwaffe, or eastwards to an unknown Orient to tangle with the Zeros of the Imperial Air Forces of Japan; and thereby hangs a tale.

On Wings of Morning

A sudden roar, a mighty rushing sound,
*   a jolt or two, a smoothly sliding rise,*
a tumbled blur of disappearing ground,
*   and then all sense of motion slowly dies.*
*   Quiet and calm, the earth slips past below,*
*   as underneath a bridge still waters flow.*

My turning wing inclines towards the ground;
*   the ground itself glides up with graceful swing*
and at the plane's far tip twirls round,
*   then drops from sight again beneath the wing*
*   to slip away serenely as before,*
*   a cubist-patterned carpet on the floor.*

Hills gently sink and valleys gently fill,
*   The flattened fields grow ludicrously small;*
slowly they pass beneath and slower still
*   until they hardly seem to move at all.*
*   Then suddenly they disappear from sight,*
*   hidden by fleeting wisps of faded white.*

The wing-tips, faint and dripping, dimly show,
   blurred by the wreaths of mist that intervene.
Weird, half-seen shadows flicker to and fro
   across the pallid fog-bank's blinding screen.
      At last the chocking mists release their hold,
      and all the world is silver, blue, and gold.

The air is clear, more clear than sparkling wine;
   compared with this, wine is a turgid brew.
The far horizon makes a clean-cut line
   between the silver and the depthless blue.
      Out of the snow-white level reared on high
      glittering hills surge up to meet the sky.

Outside the wind screen's shelter gales may race:
   but in the seat a cool and gentle breeze
blows steadily upon my grateful face.
   As I sit motionless and at my ease,
      contented just to loiter in the sun
      and gaze around me till the day is done.

And so I sit, half sleeping, half awake,
   dreaming a happy dream of golden days,
until at last, with a reluctant shake
   I rouse myself, and with a lingering gaze
      at all the splendour of the shining plain
      make ready to come down to earth again.

The engine stops: a pleasant silence reigns –
   silence, not broken, but intensified
by the soft, sleepy wires' insistent strains,
   that rise and fall, as with a sweeping glide
      I slither down the well-oiled sides of space,
      towards a lower, less enchanted place.

The clouds draw nearer, changing as they come.
   Now, like a flash, fog grips me by the throat.
Down goes the nose: at once the wires' low hum
   begins to rise in volume and in note,
      till, as I hurtle from the choking cloud
      it swells into a scream, high-pitched, and loud.

The scattered hues and shades of green and brown
*   fashion themselves into the land I know,*
turning and twisting, as I spiral down
*   towards the landing-ground; till, skimming low,*
*   I glide with slackening speed across the ground,*
*   and come to rest with lightly grating sound.*

Jeffery Day (1896–1918)

Lieutenant Jeffery Day, DSC, Royal Naval Air Service, was shot down and killed on 27 February 1918.

CHAPTER TWO

They That Hath Wings Shall Tell the Matter

I left England early in 1942 and looking out of the porthole of the troop ship as it docked at Liverpool early in 1943, the aspect looked the same as when I left; cold, wet and dismal. After a miserable seven days dash across the Atlantic from Halifax, Nova Scotia, the sunny, warm and comfortable lifestyle of Florida was another world away. The trip across the Atlantic was an unpleasant and uncomfortable one, although no U-boat alerts occurred as far as we knew. Our ship, the *Louis Pasteur*, when it docked at Halifax disembarked 6,000 Italian POWs, and then immediately embarked the waiting British and Canadian aircrew, with some Canadian Army units, without attempting to clean the ship. The Canadians marched on and confronted by the filth and stench left by the Italian POWs in the Augean quarters below deck, about turned and marched off again despite threats of arrest. With stolid British phlegm, or bovine stupidity, we remained onboard. Some efforts followed to redress the problem and the Canadians returned. We sailed unescorted for Liverpool that evening, and to prevent a repetition of the protests we remained battened down for the duration of the voyage under appalling conditions. The Geneva Convention may have applied to the unfortunate POWs but certainly not to British Commonwealth aircrew. A short disembarkation leave at home followed our arrival in Liverpool, before reporting to the aircrew distribution centre at the famous Yorkshire spa town of Harrogate. The town looked shabby after three years of war with its principal hotels requisitioned by the military. To ease the bottleneck resulting from the aircrew output from the Commonwealth Training Plan, the Air Ministry decided that before their assignment the recently qualified aircrew should undertake a modified commando style fitness course. Consequently, before appearing before an assignment board I found myself leaping around the golf course and sand dunes of Whitely Bay, a suburb of Newcastle-upon-Tyne. Returning to Harrogate I restated my preference for Fighter Command and Spitfires. The assignment board stated that the pilot situation in the Command was stable at the time but the Mustang squadrons in Army Cooperation Command needed reinforcing. This sounded ominous but I still had delusions of aerial combat and the prospect of ground support operations did not appeal. The assignment board then dangled the carrot: as my assessments were satisfactory for the purpose if I agreed to take a flying instructor's course, a tour of instructing would give me priority in my preference. This was of course a con but being still naïve in the ways of the military I agreed. My first choice was Spitfires at all costs and I had no wish to discuss the requirements of Bomber Command. If I could have foreseen how my flying instructor's category would dog me years later I might have settled for Army Cooperation Command. In retrospect, some years later after experiencing some of the alternatives it might have suited me very well. The Allison engine Mustang was a nice aircraft to fly low level, although the casualty rate on low level operations was higher than that on high level escort.

My next stop was the Central Flying School of Flying Training Command at the subsidiary flying school near Reading. The grass airfield at Woodley was the home of Miles Aircraft, having merged with Philips and Powis Aircraft. Here I flew my old nemesis, the Tiger Moth, together with the Miles Magister, a two-seat primary monoplane trainer, and the Miles Master, a two-seat advanced monoplane trainer powered by a Rolls-Royce Kestrel in the Mk I, a Bristol Mercury radial in the Mk II and a Pratt & Whitney Wasp radial in the Mk III. The Master was the British equivalent of the Harvard but not as good a training aircraft. It was a robust aircraft of wood construction and although giving the appearance of a two-seat fighter with a high thickness-cord ratio wing, its handling qualities did not match up to that of the North American AT-6 Harvard. The Mark II version of the Master, with the 800 hp Bristol Mercury engine, was the most powerful variant of the aircraft and was used as a Hotspur glider tug for the training of the Airborne Forces pilots. Instructing in the Master was different from any other training aircraft I flew because it had one very unique design feature for the instructor in the rear seat. Forward visibility was poor and in order to be able to see ahead to land the aircraft the instructor in the rear seat had to raise his seat to see over the top of the front seat cockpit canopy. This was achieved by pulling hard on a handle mounted on the front of the Perspex panel over the instructor to pivot the panel upwards and provide a windbreak. This also acted as an airbrake and resulted in considerable airframe buffeting and cockpit turbulence. Accompanied by wind noise and aircraft vibration, the instructor then raised his seat up into the slipstream behind a vibrating Perspex panel to look out of the cockpit and over the top of the pilot in front of him which made for an interesting landing. It was also a decided advantage, as well as a necessity in winter, to wear the *de rigueur* leather sheepskin flying jacket and pants as protection against the elements. Fortunately, I did most of my instructing on the Tiger Moth and the Harvard, with some instructing on the twin engine Airspeed Oxford. However, I did some instructing with the Master II while towing Hotspur gliders at Crouton. This provided some additional unusual moments when, due to the continued use of full power to get the Master and the Hotspur glider airborne and to keep it in the air, the overworked Mercury engine spewed out a coating of black oil over the windscreen making it almost impossible to see ahead. An occasional engine failure necessitated a hurried release from the Hotspur, before being stalled by the towed glider, for a quick forced landing back on the airfield (if one was lucky, as I was when it happened to me!).

The management, design and test flying of all the Miles Aircraft projects at Woodley consisted of a remarkable team of the two Miles brothers, Fred and George, together with Fred's brilliant and ebullient wife, Blossom, as chief designer. This dynamic and innovative team designed and produced while resident at Shoreham, Woodley, Redhill and eventually back at Shoreham again, many interesting concepts and projects primarily of light sporting, passenger and training aircraft in competition with de Havilland. After the war they designed and produced a larger twin engine, civil transport aircraft called the Marathon. The Miles team were certainly unusual in their projects; some being very successful and some not so successful. I recollect one light aircraft design having a novel and unique system for lateral control with the ailerons replaced by stick controlled leading edge wing slats. George Miles often flew the first test flight of a new project but on this occasion their chief test pilot, Tommy Rose, a King's Cup winner and a very extrovert character flew the aircraft. The aircraft took-off heading south and I witnessed its slow and erratically controlled climb to around 200 feet. The aircraft then commenced a slow spasmodic and jerky descent without attempting any turn and disappeared from sight. A search party located the undamaged aircraft in a meadow with no sign of the pilot. Tommy Rose was eventually traced to a nearby pub where he was recovering from an experience he described as trying to walk a wet, greasy pole without a balancing pole in a strong wind!

In 1947 Miles Aircraft ran into financial difficulties and in 1948 the Woodley factory and airfield became part of the Handley Page Aircraft Company which was Britain's oldest aircraft manufacturing company dating back to 1909. Handley Page produced the Hampden and Halifax bombers during the war. In the post-war years Handley Page produced the Victor 'V' bomber, the Hastings military and the Hermes civil transports and high speed research aircraft at its design and production facilities at Cricklewood and Radlett. The company had no experience in designing or producing small, civil aircraft, therefore, on taking over the Miles Aircraft facility at Woodley, Handley Page used the Miles Marathon to enter the medium civil-transport market and the aircraft , now called a Herald, became a fifty-passenger civil airliner and a military transport powered by two RR Dart turbo-props. My own view is that Handley Page, with its experience in the design of bomber and military transport aircraft, would have been more successful with its small eighteen passenger commuter or executive turbo-prop Jetstream had the Miles company been involved in the design and development of the aircraft. Of all the many Miles aircraft projects the most interesting for me was the Miles M-52 reheated jet-powered experimental aircraft intended to break the sound barrier in level flight with a speed of 1,000 mph at a height of 36,000 feet. The authorities at the time, no doubt influenced by the loss of Geoffrey de Havilland while flying the DH-108, favoured an unmanned aircraft to achieve this as it was considered to be too dangerous for the pilots involved. Subsequent test flights with air-launched rocket propelled scale models of the M-52 demonstrated the feasibility of the project by achieving speeds in the region of Mach 1.5. During 1946 a pusillanimous Labour government decided that budget restraints made the undertaking too costly. With this and the danger factor in mind they decided to cancel the piloted M-52 project. Miles had made provision for the safety of the pilot with the unique design of a detachable pressurized cockpit escape capsule for a safe parachute descent. This was later adopted by the USAF for the General Dynamics F-111. As a result of a British-US exchange agreement on high-speed research data (later to be reneged by the US) the Miles design and research data on the M-52 project passed to the Bell Aircraft Company who were researching a rocket propelled aircraft for supersonic flight. In 1947 a rocket propelled Bell X-1 aircraft piloted by Chuck Yeager became the first manned aircraft to fly supersonically in level flight and 'break the sound barrier'. In all probability the success of this flight at the time was due to the Bell Aircraft Company being able to overcome the problem of control stability during transonic flight by the incorporation of an all-moving horizontal stabilizer taken from the design of the M-52. Interestingly, apart from a different means of propulsion, the design of the Bell X-1 closely resembled that of the Miles M-52 supersonic aircraft project with a similar bullet shaped fuselage and conical shaped nose housing the cockpit together with razor sharp straight leading-edge wings. In comparing the appearance of the two aircraft the impression given is that the Miles M-52, propelled by a similar rocket motor to the 6,000 lb static thrust motor installed in the Bell X-1, would have exceeded the speed obtained by the X-1 of 967 mph and achieved its design speed of 1,000 mph. A further spin-off from the design of the all-moving horizontal stabiliser on the M-52 would be seen later with the flying tail plane on the F-86, the succeeding F-100 and all the USAF Century Series of fighters. Influences from both the Miles-52 and the Bell X-1 aircraft are clearly seen in the design of the fuselage and wing of the supersonic Lockheed F-104 Starfighter.

Graduating from the course I started my tour of instructing with a flying school at Theale in the Kennet Valley of Berkshire, which was not far south of my home in Oxfordshire. It was a pleasant spot and the commissioned and non-commissioned flying instructors lived in a requisitioned manor house on a hill overlooking the airfield. This was by far the nicest and most comfortable mess with the best catering I ever experienced in the RAF; added to which was the provision of some excellent fly fishing in the River Kennet. The stables of the estate continued to function as a riding school providing some pleasant hacking. I enjoyed my time at Theale very much and after receiving my flight sergeant's crowns and an 'A' category instructor's rating, I attended a commissioning board and became a pilot officer. In changing from a non-commissioned officer to a commissioned one it was necessary for me to move. I continued my instructing a short distance north at Shellingford in the Vale of White Horse that was even closer to my home at the edge of the Cotswolds. The grass airfield at Shellingford with the wartime huts and the wood and fabric Tiger Moths resembled an RFC flying school of the First World War. As a relatively inexperienced flying instructor and newly commissioned pilot officer, my approach to teaching *ab initio* pilots to fly was more conciliatory than had been my own experience learning to fly with Sergeant Murphy at Cambridge and Mr O'Neil in Florida. It was certainly in marked contrast to the Polish flying instructors training the Polish pilots, who subjected their pupils to much lengthy haranguing and voluble tirades. A memorable example of the differing approach to the technique of teaching occurred when a Polish flying instructor sent his Polish pupil on his first solo flight. There are three simple rules for a smooth landing but unfortunately no one remembers what they are. The student made two unsuccessful attempts to land his aircraft with the engine surging as the pilot opened and closed his throttle while the aircraft bounded across the grass like a mechanical marsupial. This absorbing spectacle, if nothing else, demonstrated the robustness and resilience of the Tiger Moth's undercarriage. At last on his third circuit and multiple attempts at a landing the pilot finally persuaded the Tiger Moth to stay on the ground just short of a hedge on the boundary of the airfield. As he taxied back to his dispersal his irate mentor met him as he parked the aircraft and switched off the engine. With the pilot still seated in the aircraft his instructor proceeded to berate him while all the time belabouring him about the head with his furled flying gauntlets.

I was fortunate to enjoy a comfortable existence during my time at Theale and Shellingford, insulated from the war and with easy access to my home near Oxford. My father assisted this by providing me with a second-hand Morris Minor motorcar and this enabled me to pursue my enthusiasm for game shooting and fly fishing. After the Morris failed to negotiate a sharp bend in the road one night returning to the mess, a Hillman Minx replaced it and there followed a succession of pre-war sports cars in an ascending order of potency. The first was an MG-TC, then a Riley Sprite and finally, just before the war ended, the forerunner of the Jaguar, an SS-100. Fortunately, I did not remain long at Shellingford before starting my progression to Fighter Command by means of an Advanced Flying Unit (AFU) and an Operational Training Unit (OTU), so perhaps the Assignment Board at Harrogate had been right after all. My lasting impressions from the Vale of White Horse were some wonderful walks along the Ridgeway of the Lambourn Downs with its ancient hill forts, and some parachute training at the nearby Army Parachute School at Watchfield. The course culminated in a live parachute jump from a basket suspended from a barrage balloon. This jump was to benefit me a few years later.

The AFU flying Masters and Harvards was at Tern Hill on the English side of Offer's Dyke on the Welsh border and the OTU flying Spitfires was at Eshott on the English side of the Cheviot Hills on the Scottish border. Both were wild border areas and recognized graveyards for aircraft, where the desolate mountains wreathed in mists could reach out and grab erring pilots. By a happy coincidence an old friend from my Cambridge days and the flying school in Florida joined me at Eshott. He told me he had the misfortune to spend the intervening time towing targets at a Royal Navy gunnery school in the Isle of Man, which made me feel better disposed towards the assignment board at Harrogate. The OTU operated Spitfire IIs, and the Spitfire was the most respected and envied fighter of its time, having made its reputation during the Battle of Britain. Popular concepts gave it the credit for defeating the *Luftwaffe* over Britain, but in reality there were nearly twice as many Hurricanes flying in the Battle and they accounted for nearly twice as many German aircraft destroyed. The Spitfire and the Hurricane were both powered by the Rolls Royce Merlin engine but the Spitfire was superior to the Hurricane in speed, climb and dive performance. However, the Hurricane was more manoeuvrable, it was a more stable gun platform and could absorb more battle damage and was more easily repaired than the Spitfire. In an ideal interception profile against the *Luftwaffe*, the Hurricanes would attack the German bombers and the Spitfires their escort fighters. Most of the instructor pilots at Eshott were battle-hardened Canadians on rest from Canadian Spitfire squadrons. The standard of discipline was somewhat more relaxed than was the case in the RAF. They were a wild bunch, causing the officer in charge of the WAAF much apprehension and many sleepless nights; not unlike that of the farmers of old for the raiding reivers across the border. However, they knew how to fly Spitfires in a fashion that brought our respect.

After a short period of familiarization, our RCAF instructors put us through the ringer with intense squadron formation and aerial dogfights. The Spitfire II had a Merlin 45 engine giving 1,175 hp, with a maximum speed of 357 mph, a service ceiling of 37,000 feet and a range of 500 miles. This was a considerable jump in performance to anything else we had flown. The Spitfire II, and its successor the Spitfire V, had a single radiator under the right wing, and one of the major problems associated with it were coolant leaks caused by the Merlin engine overheating. With the undercarriage down, the oleo leg partially obscured and deflected the air-flow through the radiator causing the coolant temperature to rise. When the temperature of the glycol coolant reached boiling point, around 120 °C, the cylinders would expand allowing the surrounding coolant to bleed into the cylinders. The first indication of trouble was a white puff of glycol smoke issuing from the engine exhaust. An attempt to take-off under those conditions would probably result in engine failure on or after take-off. Operating Spitfires in squadron strength exacerbated the problem as the taxiing time was considerably longer. In an attempt to reduce the effect of overheating after landing, some pilots adopted a dangerous pro-cedure when landing by diving the aircraft into the circuit with power off and the radiator flap fully open to lower the radiator temperature. As the Spitfire crossed the start of the runway low level they pulled up in a steep climbing left turn to circuit height while turning through 180 degrees. The approach leg continued through a second 180 degree turn with full flap lowered and the selection of wheels down left to the last minute. The normal procedure was to lower the undercarriage before selecting landing flap, so this technique did not meet with approval for, in the excitement of a squadron landing, some pilots forgot to lower their wheels, despite the sound of a warning horn. One pilot, after an immaculate landing on the runway at Eshott with the landing gear retracted, explained why he disregarded the flying controller's radio warning from the tower by saying he could not hear him for the sound of the horn blowing in his ears! Headquarters decided he was not Spitfire material and better suited to aircraft with fixed undercarriage. To avert similar incidences there was generally a duty controller in a caravan at the end of the runway to fire a red Very flare warning pilots attempting a landing with wheels retracted to overshoot.

The real joy of flying the Spitfire was in its incomparable handling in the air, but first one had to become used to the obstructed view forward by the big twelve-cylinder Merlin engine, which required the aircraft to swing from side to side while taxiing in order to see ahead. Then one became used to the swing to the left on take-off due to the strong propeller torque. Finally, one became accustomed to a tendency to swing on landing due to the narrow width undercarriage, especially in cross winds. After such acclimatization it was not a difficult aircraft to fly, being very responsive to the controls. It was also a very forgiving aircraft both in pitch and yaw, being able to turn tightly while flown to the limit without any unexpected and vicious stall characteristics, unlike many of the Allied and German fighters. It was also a very strong aircraft and stable in high-speed dives. Its main drawback while flying lay with the ailerons due to the fabric covering which resulted in a slower rate of roll than its rivals. The ailerons also became heavy at high speed in a dive. In the air the Spitfire was a delight but on the ground it was another story.

The Spitfire mated the largest possible engine with the smallest possible airframe, leaving little room for even the average size pilot. Larger pilots found that when wearing the traditional fleeced lined leather flying jacket it allowed very little movement in the cockpit. Sitting in the Spitfire the cockpit fitted one as a glove and its design did not incorporate the science of ergonomics. A tall and large pilot had problems even with the seat fully lowered. In the tight fit the sliding cockpit canopy did not provide a good view to the rear and even with a rear-view mirror attached to the windscreen the angle of view to the rear was small, requiring a continuous slight weave while flying to be able to see behind. This was a marked disadvantage considering that the majority of pilots shot down never saw their adversary. The hood opened by releasing a catch and sliding it back and it was extremely difficult to open at high speed; however, there was a cable release to jettison the hood. Although critical of the Spitfire's restricted view, the Bf-109 pilot was worse off in this respect.

The quadrant containing throttle, propeller pitch and fuel mixture controls situated on the left side of the cockpit came readily to hand with the elevator and rudder trim wheels to its rear. A drawback with the Spitfire trim controls was the absence of any aileron trim that resulted in hands-on flying if the aircraft adopted a rolling moment. To correct a wing low attitude the only remedy was for the rigger to dope on a strip of cord along the trailing edge of the opposite aileron. This situation applied to both the Spitfire II and V with fabric covered ailerons. The Spitfire IX and onwards had metal ailerons and the rigger could adjust these by mechanical adjustment, but the Spitfire was still without pilot controlled trim for the ailerons. This feature was particularly irksome for photo-reconnaissance pilots on long high altitude flights. The wheel brakes were air operated by a brake lever on the spade handled grip of the control column through differential use of the rudder. This was a typical feature of British designed fighters up to and into the jet age. The American approach for wheel brakes was by hydraulic control operated by foot pedals on the rudder control bar. Another major inconvenience of the Spitfire was the control of the undercarriage selector lever. The operating lever positioned on the right side of the cockpit made it necessary to transfer control of the aircraft once airborne from the right hand to the left hand to select the wheels. Therefore, it was essential to ensure the throttle friction wheel was tight on take-off otherwise the throttle could vibrate rearwards with loss of power while retracting the wheels. Novice Spitfire pilots were easily discernible from the ground by their switch-back flight during the retraction of the wheels. This arrangement was unique to both the Spitfire and the Hurricane, the difference between the two being the Hurricane's flap control was positioned with the undercarriage selector and the Spitfire's flap control was an on-off selector switch located on the top left side of the instrument panel. The Spitfire's flaps, like the wheel brakes, operated by air pressure with a single position operation, either up or down for landing. The landing flap was very effective with the full down position of 90 degrees, so it was not possible to use them to assist take-off or for turning in combat as was the case with the Mustang. This aircraft used hydraulic pressure to control a variable flap to provide take-off and combat settings as well as a landing position.

The normal maximum manifold boost of the Merlin engine was +12 lb or around 60 in. Certain modifications to the two-speed, two-stage super-charger could increase this to +18 lb. During take-off the torque from the propeller applied a gyroscopic force at 90 degrees and this resulted in a single-engine fighter swinging left or right depending on the direction of rotation of the propeller. The Spitfire accelerated rapidly on take-off and with the tail raised the aircraft required a strong application of opposite rudder to maintain direction. For this reason a take-off power of +6 to +9 lb boost was sufficient until airborne before opening up to full power.

All Merlin Spitfires swung to the left on take-off; but the propeller on the Griffon engine had an opposite rotation, making the Griffon Spitfires swing to the right. I never did find out a logical reason for the two Rolls Royce engines rotating in opposite directions: the last versions of the Griffon Spitfires, the naval Griffon Seafires and the final Spitfire variant, the Spiteful, resolved the torque problem by two contra-rotating propellers.

In the late 1930s the RAF standardized the instrument panel around the blind flying 'Basic Six'. The centre of the panel carried an airspeed indicator in MPH, an artificial horizon, and a rate of climb or vertical speed indicator. Below these three instruments were positioned an altimeter in feet, a directional gyro compass or heading indicator, and a turn and bank or slip indicator. To the left of the flying instruments were gauges indicating oxygen contents, undercarriage lights, brake pressure, trim indicators and the voltmeter. The engine instruments indicating fuel contents and pressure, engine RPM and boost, radiator temperature, oil pressure and temperature were grouped to the right of the flying instruments. The control column had full fore-and-aft movement but was articulated above the pilot's legs for full lateral movement due to the lack of leg room. The two-handed spade-grip incorporated the wheel brakes lever and the armament firing control button with a separate camera gun button. The two-position rudder pedals helped the pilot exert maximum rudder control with the feet in the upper position, and helped to raise his G threshold during high G manoeuvres with the seat lowered.

The Spitfire was not comfortable to fly with its cramped cockpit and lack of creature comforts. Many of its superior performance parameters were a function of simplicity and weight, and the Spitfire's complexity and weight was considerably less than a contemporary US fighter. The US fighters, designed with larger and more comfortable cockpits, had better seats and provided more creature comforts. These fighters had fuller specifications that included full trim controls and good provision for heating and fresh air. In construction, the Spitfire, although strong and robust, was fairly rough and basic when compared with its American or even German counterpart. From a pilot's point of view, although the Spitfire was noisy, draughty, cold, uncomfortable and more tiring to fly on long distance and high altitude flights, it did not possess the complicated electrical and hydraulic systems of the American fighters. It would be some years before the pilot of a British made fighter concerned himself with panels of circuit breakers.

When landing a Spitfire a continuous 180 degrees turn from the downwind leg of the circuit was carried out until touchdown. The steeper the descent and the more continuous the turn meant the quicker the whole squadron could land. The Spitfire was not a difficult aircraft to fly but it was not an easy aircraft to land due to its narrow landing gear. This was especially noticeable when landing in cross winds. Many inexperienced Spitfire pilots preferred to fly onto the runway with power to control any swing that might develop, rather than risk a power off approach with a three-point landing. During gusty and strong cross winds ground loops were a problem that contributed to much damage and even the loss of Spitfires during the training phase. Quite a few alternative postings occurred for the pilots who could not cope with landing a Spitfire under adverse conditions. Squadron strength landings under these conditions with the tight approach to the runway and the short intervals between the aircraft on alternate sides of the runway were always fraught with peril for the inexperienced pilot. Untidy and badly spaced approaches and landings were certain to provoke a public rebuke from the CO or flight commander.

Eshott was a wartime airfield where the accommodation and facilities were very basic. We lived and worked in the ubiquitous Nissen huts. These corrugated-iron sheds were functional but cold, draughty, noisy and cramped; rather like a Spitfire cockpit. We slept several to a hut with one or two small coke-fired stoves that emitted most of the small output of heat up the chimney while filling the hut with noxious coke fumes when-ever the wind blew, which it did frequently and hard in the Border country. The huts were certainly basic and frequent nocturnal bombard-ments of the huts with rocks thrown by merry Canadians returning to their quarters from the mess amply demonstrated their non-insulation. The cold and draughty features of the huts became even more evident when our Canadian instructors returned from celebrating at a local hostelry and fired fusillades from their revolvers at the roofs of the huts. This necessitated the frequent movement of beds to avoid the rain water dripping from the bullet holes and the supply of buckets to catch the rain water. The RAF sensibly only issued a personal sidearm to pilots who were actually participating in operations or stationed overseas.

After several hours spent on intensive squadron formation flying and mock combat it was with some relief I left Eshott for Boulmer on the Northumberland coast near the Scottish border and joined a work-up fighter-bomber squadron of Spitfire Vs. The Spitfire V had the improved Merlin 45 engine giving 1,440 hp, increasing the maximum speed to 374 mph. The aircraft had a variety of armaments carried in four designated type wings. The 'A' type wings carried eight 0.303 in Browning machine-guns with a rate of fire of 1,150 rpm and a muzzle velocity of 2,400 ft/sec. A belt of 300 rounds of ball, armour-piercing, incendiary and tracer ammunition for each gun gave a firing time of 16 seconds. The 'B' type wings carried four 0.303 Browning machine-guns and two 20 mm (0.8 in) Hispano cannon with a rate of fire of 700–800 rpm and a muzzle velocity of 2,820 ft/sec. The 'C' type wings carried four 20 mm Hispano cannon. The early use of the 20 mm cannon using a drum magazine holding 60 rounds, gave a firing time of 5 seconds. Finally, a 'D' type wing contained two 0.5 in Browning machine-guns and two 20 mm Hispano cannon. The 0.5 calibre Browning machine-gun had a rate of fire of 850 rpm and a muzzle velocity of 2,790 ft/sec. Of the types of ammunition used, the ball and armour piercing (AP) were the most effective against aircraft, as on impact the energy of the shell produced red heat igniting any flammable object. Sighting the guns required the use of the GM 2 reflector gun sight, in which a circle of light with a central dot was projected on a glass screen in front of the pilot's line of sight through the windscreen. A broken line running horizontally across the circle with a break in the middle of the line enabled the pilot to adjust the sight to the wingspan of the target aircraft. With the projected display focused at infinity the pilot would then see when he was in firing range. Therefore it was necessary to recognize the target and to know its wingspan. The distance between the sighting dot, or pipper, and the circular ring repre-sented a 50 mph crossing speed to assist assessing the deflection required in a turn while firing the guns against a manoeuvring target. By 1944 the gyro gun sight replaced the GM 2 reflector sight in later models of the Spitfire. The circular ring became a ring of six diamonds, the diameter being adjustable to the wingspan of the target by a twist grip on the throttle. As the pilot tracked the target with the sighting dot the gyroscope moved the display to provide the deflection angle required. Further developments placed a recording camera on top of the sight to record the display when the guns fired enabling the attack to be assessed. As a result of these developments the gun sight became a formidable object over the instrument panel in line with the pilot's face and field of view through the windscreen. This presented a considerable hazard during a crash-landing resulting in many injuries to the face and head; and many pilots who survived a crash-landing retained a lasting memento on their faces. The crash-landing procedure advised placing one arm on the gun sight before impact to prevent or help reduce facial and head injuries.

Further modifications to the Spitfire wing resulted in the clipping of the wing tips for better low-level operation. The reduced wingspan improved the rate of roll with a slight increase in speed from the reduced drag, but poorer manoeuvrability resulted at high altitude. The pilots referred to the low-altitude Spitfire V, introduced to cope with the German high-speed tip and run attacks at low-level, as being 'Clipped, Cropped and Clapped'. 'Clipped' referring to the wings; 'Cropped' to the supercharger impeller reduced to provide 18 lb boost; and 'Clapped' as a result of the reduced engine life. Our Spitfires at Boulmer were Spitfire Vs with the clipped 'B' wing armed with four 0.303 in Browning machine-guns and two 20 mm cannon. The wings had additional hard points for carrying bombs. The dive-bombing phase of our training took place with the air-ground firing on a marshy range some miles up the coast. Dive-bombing involved three attack profiles: attacking from 12,000 feet and releasing the bombs at 8,000 feet; from 8,000 feet and releasing at 4,000 feet; and from 4,000 feet releasing the bombs at 2,000 feet. On one occasion while pulling out of a dive after releasing two bombs at 4,000 feet, the aircraft attempted to pitch-up sufficiently violently to stall the aircraft. A very strong forward pressure on the stick enabled me to ease the aircraft out of the stall into a dive before recovering control at low level without the Spitfire stalling into the ground. It was fortunate for me that I was not on a 4,000 feet to 2,000 feet release dive attack. With the elevator trim wound fully forward and the aircraft vibrating near the stall, I was able to fly back to Boulmer and fly the aircraft on to the runway using the whole length of the strip. It may have been possible to bale out, but the altitude was probably too low and there was a distinct possibility of being hit by the aircraft in the process. The Spitfire's thin wing design with a low thickness cord ratio enabled the aircraft to attain high speeds in a steep dive, as experienced during dive bomb attacks. It was found that the control cables for the ailerons and elevators could stretch under the high G-forces involved. This over-stressing on the control cables allowed the ailerons and elevators to float up, causing a violent pitch-up of the aircraft. The introduction of metal ailerons helped cure the aileron instability. Shortly after my experience we lost a pilot when his Spitfire dived vertically into the dive-bombing range. The assumption was the aircraft experienced complete elevator failure: a wag suggested painting a dotted line along the suspected area of the tailplane, as it was a well-known scientific fact that paper never separates along the perforation line! The aircraft recovery crew dug down thirty feet into the marsh to recover the Merlin engine but there was little airframe wreckage left with which to identify the failure. While attending the military funeral for the pilot I wondered what the coffin contained as it descended into the grave. This enigma would return on future occasions.

The air-ground firing involved both the 0.303 machine-guns and 20 mm cannon. However, for purposes of scoring machine-guns were used as they were more accurate and reliable. The Hispano cannon on the Spitfire V were not reliable due to the drum magazine. If the magazine contained a full load of 60 rounds the spring tension would sometimes jam the feed, and for this reason the armourers often loaded fewer rounds. In the Spitfire IX a belt feed of 120 rounds replaced the drum magazine giving a firing time of 11 seconds. To accommodate the various types of armament the firing button on the stick had a three position pressure switch. Full central pressure on the firing button fired all guns; top pressure on the button fired machine-guns only; and bottom pressure on the button fired the cannon. We carried out air-air firing with both machine-gun and cannon on drogue targets towed several miles out to sea. Again, for scoring and assessment purposes we used machine-guns for scoring the attacks on the drogues with the tips of the rounds painted in various colours for individual identification.

During one armament sortie on the air-air range a newly arrived pilot officer on the squadron reported a complete engine failure. He announced on his radio that he would glide towards the coast hoping to crash-land on the shore. Other members of the flight escorted him while informing sector control at Newcastle-upon-Tyne of the emergency. The sector controller informed the pilot that the RAF Air-Sea Rescue Service had a high-speed rescue launch from Alnmouth, north of Newcastle, in his area. The pilot continued to talk to the controller as WAAF plotters marked his progress on the sector plotting table. His companions offered advice during his glide to the coast, and when the pilot expressed doubts that he could make the coast advised him to prepare to bale out before he got too low and not to attempt to ditch the Spitfire in the sea. Ditching a single-engine fighter, even under the calmest conditions, was likely to result in the aircraft nosing down into the water. The pilot called he could not open his hood and that it would not jettison. The aircraft was now close to the shoreline and the pilot called he was going to ditch. His last call to the controller was to say, 'Thanks'; asking him to tell his mother he loved her. We heard later that while listening to his last radio call the girls plotting his position in the control room burst into tears. The Spitfire landed comfortably on a moderate sea and immediately nosed in and disappeared. Later, the pilot recalled that as he went down he could see the water around the cockpit as the Spitfire settled on a sand bank, less than fifty feet below the surface. He had released the radio and oxygen plugs before impact and as the cockpit carried down with it a large air bubble he could breathe as he disconnected his seat and parachute harness, remembering also to release the Mae West attachment to the dinghy. He then stood up and pressed against the hood releasing it and he shot up to the surface in a big bubble of air. After inflating his Mae West he saw the RAF launch heading for him, having seen the Spitfire go into the sea. He was only in the water a short time before taken aboard the launch with no apparent injuries or ill effects from his submersion. After an overnight stay in hospital he returned to the squadron the next day. The squadron CO decided he should visit sector headquarters at Newcastle as a morale booster to the controllers and WAAF plotting girls. As the pilot officer was not only very young but also tall and good looking, his visit was very successful and the WAAF plotters made a great fuss of him.

A not quite so happy ending resulted from another incident that nearly resulted in serious consequences. While carrying out camera-gun dog fighting the procedure was for each aircraft to take a sighter shot from dead astern of the target aircraft, using a separate camera firing button on the control column. This was necessary in order to align the camera film for calibration. Each aircraft having completed the sighting procedure then established a prescribed separation distance before commencing the dogfight. On this occasion an experienced warrant officer pilot positioned himself astern of his opponent to take his sighter shot. For some reason he thought his camera button was not functioning and decided to use the gun firing button, which normally operated the camera when the guns fired. He assumed the guns were either unloaded or not cocked, and the warrant officer placed the sighting pipper on the tail of the Spitfire fifty yards ahead of him and pressed the firing button. The pilot of the target aircraft reported that when the sighting pilot called in position he saw tracer bullets from the guns pass beneath him as the Spitfire's guns opened up on him. He broke violently away without sustaining any hits and abandoned the exercise. The following morning the squadron commander assembled all the pilots in the squadron briefing room. He recounted the incident in detail in his usual colourful manner ending with the words, '... and the stupid bastard missed him!' He continued his briefing complaining that after all our intense gunnery training and his efforts in driving us hard to ensure that we not only survive against the German fighters but acquit ourselves well against the best of the *Luftwaffe*, here was a pilot who could not hit an aircraft flying straight and level fifty yards in front of him. He did not intend to take a squadron into action that could not shoot down enemy aircraft and was liable to be shot down in the process of trying. He then turned on the unfortunate warrant officer informing him that he was off the squadron immediately as he was no damn good as a fighter pilot. Furthermore, he was going to personally ensure that he would get plenty of experience of knowing what it was like to be shot at as a permanent towing pilot at a gunnery establishment. I never saw the visibly shaken and embarrassed pilot again so I do not know his fate, but it was certainly a salutary lesson to us all and left us wondering what would have been the CO's reaction had the pilot shot down the Spitfire, and whether his punishment would have been less severe!

Our squadron commander, an experienced Canadian fighter pilot, was a very extrovert and unconventional commander. After a few pilots started to do a low level approach with a climbing slow roll over the runway when returning to the airfield, he forbid the practice until we had something to celebrate. He claimed the sole rights to a victory roll as not only the CO but the only one with any German claims. His morning routine after breakfast was to air test his aircraft during which he put on an aerobatics display over the airfield, finishing with a half roll onto his back some fifty feet off the runway and continuing to the end before rolling back and landing. One morning following a mess dining-in night with the usual mess games in which he was always the instigator, he carried out his usual routine. However, on this occasion while flying inverted along the runway he dropped down to maybe less than thirty feet. In recovering to level flight, he did not push the nose up sufficiently before rolling out and his wing tip touched the ground spreading the Spitfire down the runway until it finished in a ball of fire on the airfield boundary. While awaiting the arrival of a new commanding officer I found myself posted south to No. 65 Squadron at Matlaske which I expected to be a Spitfire IX squadron. I enjoyed my stay at Boulmer despite the somewhat Spartan conditions. The squadron, despite its eccentric commander, had a good squadron spirit and was quite independent in its operations. We were firing our guns and dropping bombs every day and I learnt a lot about flying a Spitfire in a fighter-bomber role, and I felt reasonably competent in the role. In fact I now considered myself to be *master of my fate*. During my time off at Boulmer the Croquet River nearby provided some excellent trout fishing, with an occasional salmon for the mess; and the local farmers generously offered us some good rough shooting. The small fishing port of Boulmer was within walking distance from the mess, and produced some excellent lobsters, together with marvellous oak smoked kippers. So it was with a sense of regret I packed my kit into my car and headed south.

During the summer of 1944 the RAF started to build up the numbers of Merlin Mustang squadrons. The Mustang IIIs of 122 Wing, consisting of Nos. 19, 65 and 126 Squadrons that formed the original wing of Merlin Mustangs, withdrew from 2nd TAF (Tactical Air Force) in France back to Fighter Command operating from East Anglia; first at Matlaske and then Andrews Field. Arriving at No. 65 'East India' Squadron I found to my surprise and shock it was a Mustang III squadron. Since joining the RAF my one desire was to fly Spitfires and after a period of two years by dint of good luck I had finally achieved this ambition. I was delighted to be flying the Spitfire, although in the fighter-bomber role, and I was confident with the aircraft and considered myself proficient in low level ground attack. Now without any conversion on type or experience in the role, I found myself on Mustangs. This was typical of the 'P' staff at command headquarters who, for reasons best known only to themselves, juggled the names in a numbers game. My impression of the Mustang, not having flown it, was that it was not so easy or so nice to fly as the Spitfire and inferior in performance. That being the case the prospect of tangling with the Bf-109s and FW-190s now looked more daunting. I was to find I was wrong in this impression in several respects, but it took a little time and some anxious moments. In the end I grew to like the Mustang very much and to appreciate some of its superior qualities.

During the Second World War the results of air combat changed the parameters of fighter design in becoming not just concerned with manoeuvrability and speed, but also the need for increased range and endurance. Air, unlike water, can be compressed and as fighter speeds increased the compressibility of the air affected the control of the aircraft as it approached a critical speed in relation to the speed of sound when the air flow over the wing and control surfaces became disturbed and turbulent air flow around the fuselage resulted in an increased drag factor. Generally, in the conventional wing design of fighters at the time, the thickest part in the cross-section of the wing or main plane occurred somewhere between the leading edge and the centre line of the wing. The design of a laminar flow wing on the Mustang, the first fighter to have such a wing, moved the thickest section of the wing further aft, to produce a non-turbulent air flow in parallel layers over the surface of the wing. This resulted in better control and reduced aerodynamic drag at high speed, giving increased range and endurance. In assessing the Spitfire, the Mustang, the Messerschmitt BF-109 and the Focke-Wulf FW-190, there was no clear overall winner but the Merlin Mustang became generally acknowledged to be the best all-round fighter of the Second World War.

Until the advent of the Mustang the RAF were unable to escort the heavy bombers to their targets, as even with a 90 gallon (Imp.) ventral drop tank on the Spitfire IX its radius of action was around 400 miles. Fighter Command chose to reject the early version of the Mustang powered by the Allison engine and concentrate on improved Spitfire models for the interceptor role. In this respect good high altitude performance was imperative and although the Mustang provided advantages in range and speed its deficiencies at high altitude made it unacceptable. For this reason the RAF's Mustang Is went to Army Cooperation Command where its speed and manoeuvrability were essential in its role of fighter-reconnaissance. By mid 1943 the Mustang squadrons attached to Army Cooperation Command transferred to Fighter Command and after D-day to 2nd Tactical Air Force. The Allison engine Mustang I was faster at low and medium altitude than the Merlin engine Spitfire V but the arrival of the Spitfire IX changed this advantage. The Mustang was heavier by 2,000 lb than the Spitfire and consequently could not climb as quickly. Above 15,000 feet the Mustang's performance deteriorated rapidly due to the lack of supercharging on the Allison engine.

The installation of the Merlin 61 engine with a two-stage, two-speed supercharger in the Mustang III addressed many of the Mustang I deficiencies compared with the Spitfire. The USAAC designation for the aircraft was P-51B, followed after further improvements by the P-51C. The later aircraft arrived for the RAF under the US-UK Lend-Lease arrangement as the Mustang III. However, before going into service with the RAF the Mustang III had the cockpit canopy modified with a bulbous one-piece sliding hood, known as the Malcolm hood after the designer, and this greatly improved pilot visibility. The arrival of the Mustang IV with a full tear-drop canopy improved the pilot visibility even more and was far superior to that of the Spitfire. A second major modification to the Mustang III increased the armament of four 0.5 in Browning machine-guns to six. The two inner guns carried 400 rounds and the two centre and outer guns 270 rounds, for a total of 1,800 rounds. The 0.5 calibre Browning gun had a muzzle velocity of 2,900 ft/sec and was very reliable when geared to 800 rounds per minute. The only problem associated with the gun occurred under high G-turns when a high centrifugal force held back the ammunition belt while firing the guns, causing the breech mechanism to block the feed of the rounds. The Mustang had a reliable K-14 gyro gun sight developed from a British design that enabled proper tracking and deflection shooting. This meant that pilots were more likely to hit the target than miss it with a deflection shot. The USAAC P-51Cs and Ds had a Berger G-suit that was not in the RAF Mustangs. The absence of a G-suit in the RAF continued well into the jet era and it was not until after the Korean War when the Hunter entered service that RAF fighter pilots had this facility in a British built fighter. A third major modification involved the installation of an 85 US gallon (70 Imp.) fuselage fuel tank directly aft of the pilot's seat and below the radio equipment. This affected the aircraft's centre of gravity and therefore its directional stability when full. The effect of this in a tight turn was the aircraft tended to pitch up or tuck into the turn. With the additional fuel tank of 85 US gallon (70 Imp.), two internal wing tanks of 90 US gallon (75 Imp.) each, and two external wing drop tanks of 108 US gallon (90 Imp.) each; the Mustang had a total fuel load of 480 US gallon (400 Imp.). This was sufficient fuel to give the Mustang a round trip of 1,200 miles and an endurance of seven to seven and half hours. The installation of the Merlin 61 engine with a four bladed propeller and a two-stage, two-speed supercharger increased the aircraft weight but resulted in more power and a better performance. The US Packard-built Merlin engine was reliable although not as smooth running as the Allison, and it was hard on plugs that would lead-up at low engine rev settings.

The Mustang cockpit layout was excellent, unlike the Spitfire, with all major levers and switches well placed for operation by the pilot's left hand while the right was free to hold the control stick. The general finish of the aircraft was superior to the Spitfire, rather like comparing an early Jaguar car with a more recent Cadillac. The cockpit, although a close fit, was far more commodious than the Spitfire cockpit. The blind flying instruments followed the RAF's 'Basic Six' panel although they were positioned slightly differently, with the airspeed indicator, the directional heading indicator and the artificial horizon above the altimeter, the turn and slip indicator, and the vertical speed indicator. In similar fashion to the Spitfire, the associated engine gauges were grouped on the right side of the instrument panel. More creature comforts abounded in the Mustang compared with the Spitfire, from the more comfortable seat to the steerable tail wheel controlled by the rudder pedals. This could be disengaged for tight turns by pushing forward on the control column and the differential use of the brakes. There was excellent trim control for all three flying controls, whereas the Spitfire's were not so precise and there was no trim for the ailerons. The heating and fresh air controls were far more effective in the Mustang than in the Spitfire. A folding armrest on the Mustang behind the throttle quadrant rested the left arm on long duration flights. A 'pee' funnel and tube installed below the seat enabled the pilot to relieve himself on long flights. This was a thoughtful feature but proved decidedly problematical in practice. For a pilot to answer a call to nature dressed in full winter flying gear, wearing a Mae West life jacket, strapped tightly into a parachute harness secured to a dinghy pack, while fastened securely in his seat by seat belt and harness presented an almost insurmountable problem. The fact that he was also flying in squadron formation possibly at wave top height, and monitoring his flying controls, flight and engine instruments required the ingenuity and dexterity of Houdini, even with the excellent trim control of the Mustang. There was also the not insignificant distraction of looking out for enemy fighters. Even flying alone over friendly territory at a safe altitude and in ideal weather conditions the satisfactory accomplishment of passing water by the pilot had an additional design hurdle to overcome. The 'pee' funnel was about five inches in length tapering from about three inches in diameter to a flexible rubber tube of half to one inch bore. The pipe travelled along the fuselage and exited behind the radiator by the tail. In theory the airflow passing over the airframe applied suction to draw the contents out into the slipstream. Here was where theory and practice diverted, for to establish the correct exit rate of flow along the pipe required a controlled slow intake rate of

flow into the funnel that under the circumstances was well nigh impossible. I have gone into some detail in this particular provision of pilot
relief in the Mustang as it is not covered or usually discussed during the
aircraft conversion; nor was it to be found in the Pilot's Notes. The first
and only occasion I attempted to utilize this facility I was unaware of the
technique required and after some considerable difficulties, during which I
placed my aircraft and others in dire danger, I experienced an overflow
condition that made the whole process and equipment quite redundant. I
was no better off than the Spitfire pilot on a long high-altitude photo-
reconnaissance flight tentatively peeing down the control column. A
friend of mine flying with the PRU at Benson and plagued with a small or
weak bladder confessed that while flying at 40,000 feet in the freezing cold,
cramped and draughty cockpit of a Spitfire he frequently contrived to pee
neatly down the control column while scanning the sky for enemy fighters.
At the same time rocking the control column to prevent the urine freezing
on the elevator and aileron cables: a good case for photo-recce pilots being
allocated their own personal aircraft! After my unpleasant experience I
made sure to restrict my fluid intake with as many nervous visits to 'the
loo' as possible before take-off. In discussing the problem with other
pilots I found they seldom attempted the facility and, like me, resigned
themselves to the alternative arrangement of British designed fighters.
Probably a combination of nervous energy, profuse sweating and
dehydration during the flight made the use of the equipment superfluous.

The Mustang was an unforgiving aircraft to handle, but once understood and respected it was a superb fighter to fly. The Mustang III
possessed advantages in some performance spheres but was at definite
disadvantages in others, although not falling short on any one aspect
whether flying low-level or above 30,000 feet. Top speed in level flight,
rates of climb and turning circle were generally held to be the most
important factors in fighter performance and in these qualities the Merlin
engine Mustang did not lag. The ability to overhaul an adversary in a dive
or to pull away from him proved an even greater advantage and with its
low-drag airframe and laminar flow wing design the Mustang had few
equals in dive performance and was one of the few propeller fighters to
experience compressibility control problems in a dive. In a vertical dive
from high altitude the Mustang could exceed the critical Mach number of
jet fighters in level flight. The indications of this compressibility problem
were airframe vibration with aileron flutter, followed by a complete loss of
elevator control until denser air and warmer air temperature at lower
altitudes allowed the critical Mach number of the aircraft to rise and the
flying controls to respond. Experiencing this phenomenon in complete

ignorance of flight compressibility for the first time certainly raised the heart rate until control was regained at medium altitudes.

The Mustang was able to hold its own with any interceptor fighter and its crowning advantage was endurance vastly superior to that of the single-seat fighters of its day. In a comparison with its main adversaries the Mustang III was evenly matched against the Bf-109G and FW-190A. The Bf-109G and the FW-190A could out-accelerate and out-climb the Mustang at low altitude, but the Mustang generally had a superior performance over both German fighters. The main advantage of the German fighters lay in the weight of fire of its armament. Against the Bf-109 armed with one 20 mm (0.8 in) cannon and two 13 mm (0.5 in) machine-guns the German advantage over the Mustang was slight; but against the FW-190 armed with four 20 mm cannon and two 13 mm machine-guns, the kill probability against the Mustang if hit was considerable. With the arrival of the long-nosed FW-190D the combat comparison with the Mustang was more evenly matched, although the FW-190D was superior in acceleration, climb and even dive. The long-nosed FW-190D became the finest propeller driven fighter in squadron service with the *Luftwaffe*. In a comparison with the Spitfire IX, the Spitfire proved superior in climb and turning performance to the German Bf-109G and FW-190A, although inferior in rate of roll and dive. The same comparison resulted with the Griffon engine Spitfire XIV against the long-nosed FW-190D. The *Luftwaffe* fighters had an advantage over the RAF fighters in that the Daimler Benz engine in the Bf-109 and the BMW engine in the FW-190 were not only better engineered but had two distinct operational advantages in their design. The fuel injected German engines enabled the German fighters to operate at full power under negative G flight conditions, whereas the fuel flow from the carburettor fed Merlin would stop under negative G conditions. To compensate for this during inverted flight the Merlin had a negative G fuel trap that allowed the engine to operate for six seconds while inverted. A second advantage with the German engines was with the supercharger design that varied the boost automatically with changes of altitude and air pressure to provide continuous maximum power. In early Spitfires the pilot manually controlled the two-stage supercharger, but later Merlin engines switched automatically to the second stage on reaching 18,000 feet. However, the Merlin engines gained more power when using 100 octane aviation fuels while the German engines still operated on 87 octane fuel.

By 1944 the Mustangs were on escort duties with the heavy bombers of the US 8th Air Force attacking V-bomb sites in the Pas de Calais area and with RAF Bomber Command in support of the invasion and advance through France and the Low Countries. After flying the Spitfire I found the Mustang easier to land with its wide undercarriage and to be more comfortable with its roomier cockpit. However, with its greater weight it did not respond to the throttle on take-off as did the Spitfire with the same Merlin engine. With the Spitfire the aircraft accelerated quickly on take-off and as the tail rose the aircraft had a strong tendency to swing left due to the propeller torque, to be corrected by strong opposite rudder. For this reason one never used full throttle on take-off until the aircraft became airborne. Taking-off in the Mustang one allowed the tail wheel to remain on the ground until approaching flying speed so that the steerable tail wheel helped correct the swing. Although I turned down the chance to fly the Allison engine Mustang in order to fly the Spitfire; after I accepted the Merlin engine Mustang for the fine combat fighter it undoubtedly was, I regretted not experiencing the original version of the aircraft. Friends who progressed from the Allison Mustang to the Merlin variant all praised the Allison Mustang as the most pleasant aircraft to fly low level, and considered the Merlin Mustang a distinctly wilder aircraft to fly than its predecessor. The more powerful Merlin engine with its four-blade propeller affected directional stability, particularly in a dive requiring constant trim control. The rasping, crackling, ear-shattering roar of the Merlin and the occasional shudder that it sent through the airframe compared unfavourably with the pilots used to sitting behind the docile and smooth running Allison. Therefore, although the Merlin Mustang was not such a pleasant aircraft to fly its combat potential was unquestionably superior.

When I arrived at the squadron the flight commander asked what experience I had of the Mustang and I replied none, and that my fighter experience was entirely on Spitfires. He responded saying all the available aircraft were on stand-by with full internal fuel and drop tanks. However, one aircraft required an air test to check the drop tanks and he suggested I flew this aircraft. This was a stupid suggestion for someone who had never flown a Mustang, which initially was not the easiest of fighters to fly in a clean configuration. The Mustang loaded with full internal fuel and drop tanks was best described as a flying pig. Not wishing to appear chicken arriving as a new boy on the squadron and being ignorant of the Mustang Mk III, I assumed if I could fly a Spitfire I could fly a Mustang, so I accepted the predicament. Under normal circumstances I should have completed a Mustang conversion course before joining a Mustang squadron, but in the haste to build up the Mustang wings Fighter Command 'P' staff just drafted pilots from within the command. The flight commander gave me a copy of the Pilot's Notes and a senior pilot in the flight showed me over the aircraft. I then sat in the cockpit while he ran over the cockpit layout, engine start up, taxiing, take-off, general flying and landing procedures with the relevant flying and stalling speeds. The first thing I noticed sitting in the Mustang cockpit for the first time was the complication of the circuit breakers situated on a panel on the right side of the cockpit. I asked their function and my 'instructor' replied, 'Well, I have never really figured them out and I just ignore them.' I asked what he did if one circuit breaker popped out and he answered, 'Oh, I just give it a bang and hope for the best.' I asked him if he had done a Mustang conversion and he said he was on Typhoons before joining the squadron. With his guidance I started the engine and my 'instructor' repeated engine settings and limitations with emphasis on the recommended approach and landing speeds while carrying full fuel load and drop tanks. 'Don't forget to increase speed on your approach turn by around ten mph; I don't let it get below 125 mph and if there is a good wind down the runway I add another 5 mph for mother. Keep plenty of power on otherwise you'll fall out of the sky and the Mustang has the nasty habit of flicking onto its back at the stall! Threshold speed should be no lower than 110 mph with power on and if in doubt add 5 mph for someone who cares – Happy landing!'

With this assurance I taxied out, completed my checks, turned onto the runway and started my take-off run. Accustomed to the Spitfire I opened up to about half power and whereas the Spitfire responded to the throttle like a greyhound from the slips, the Mustang responded sluggishly by comparison and I increased the power and pushed forward on the stick to get the tail up to the flying position. The steerable tail wheel initially helped keep the aircraft straight but as the tail raised the aircraft started to swing to the left and increasing more power to get airborne I found that despite using all the strength in my right leg I could not hold the aircraft straight. A transport aircraft uses the terms V1 and V2 to denote take-off commitment speeds, and as in this instance I felt committed not to abandon my take-off and risk a ground loop off the runway with full fuel on board, I continued to pour on the power. The Mustang became airborne in a climbing left turn and at this stage I had insufficient flying speed to straighten my climb away. I am sure that during the next few seconds, although appearing like minutes to me, the viewers in the control tower were laying short odds whether I would clear the high trees bordering the airfield. With a shaking right leg I cleared the trees by a few feet and as I started to build up speed I was able to settle down and trim the aircraft into a climb, waiting for the shakes to subside, the adrenaline flow to return to normal and the sweat to disperse. My reaction at the time to flying a Mustang compared with a Spitfire was not that of riding a wild horse of the American plains but more like riding a hippopotamus compared with a thoroughbred. This was not an auspicious moment to start my vocation as a fighter pilot on the renowned Mustang where due to crass stupidity my first flight on the aircraft was nearly my last ever! I settled down and flew around the area checking out the fuel tanks and burning up the fuel as much as I could. I tried out the undercarriage and flaps, getting a feel at circuit speed and near the stall before calling for a landing. I made a circumspect circuit with a gentle approach turn around 125 mph with a straight approach to the runway. I crossed the threshold at 110 mph to land well into the runway and use up most of the 1,000 yards of tarmac before taxiing to the squadron dispersal. I had by now recovered from my take-off exhibition but was in an angry mood at not being properly briefed on the take-off peculiarities of the Mustang when loaded with over 400 gallons of fuel.

Shortly afterwards I made my first acquaintance with Dr Ernst Mach and the effects of compressibility during high-speed flight. At high altitude in a vertical dive the Mustang, with its low drag ratio from the laminar flow wing design, could run into compressibility problems as the aircraft approached its critical Mach number relating to the speed of sound. The speed of sound at sea level is around 760 mph depending on temperature, and reduces with altitude and temperature until at 35,000 feet the equivalent air speed is less than half that at sea level. The airflow passing over parts of the aircraft will diverge or break away as this airflow approaches the speed of sound. Mach numbers are used to denote the percentage of the speed of sound at a certain altitude, with Mach One representing the speed of sound at that altitude. Every aircraft has a critical Mach number when the airflow over the wing reaches compressibility and shock waves cause the airflow to break away resulting in loss of control. The laminar flow design of the Mustang wing endeavoured to delay this process, and sweeping back the attack angle of the wing on jet aircraft achieves the same purpose. The shock waves created at sonic speed results in increased drag with an ineffective response from the flying controls and even reversibility of the controls; and during the early development of jet aircraft this condition of flight became known as the sound barrier. It was some time before engine design produced sufficient thrust and the use of a swept wing enabled the aircraft to push through the sonic barrier into supersonic flight where the flying controls once more responded normally. The shock wave as the aircraft passed through the sound barrier at Mach One produced a sonic boom that passed along the ground following the flight path of the aircraft. The general effect on a subsonic aircraft as it approached its critical Mach number was a violent vibration and sometimes an uncontrollable pitch up or pitch down of the aircraft, with the controls becoming unresponsive or reversible. As the altitude reduced during the dive the air became denser and warmer, and the critical Mach number for the aircraft rose in ratio. The shock waves then disappeared and the airflow resumed a smooth passage over the contour of the airframe, allowing the pilot to regain control of the aircraft. In the process of attempting to control the aircraft near the critical Mach number a high stress loading was possible that could result in popped rivets, stress fractures and even the break-up of the aircraft. In 1946 Geoffrey de Havilland disappeared into the North Sea during high speed flight testing of the swept wing and tailless DH-108. Although developed from the Vampire, the DH-108 was redesigned so that the twin boomed tail became a single vertical fin and rudder with no horizontal stabilizer and elevator. It was not intended to be a fighter replacement to the Vampire but to be used purely as a research aircraft. Three prototypes were produced and all three crashed, with the second aircraft breaking-up in mid-air. Investigations concluded that during transonic flight an undamped oscillation resulted in a violent pitch up causing the aircraft to shed its wings. Subsequent de Havilland designs reverted back to a reduced sweep to the wing and a conventional tail plane. The aerodynamic phenomenon of sonic flight was not fully appreciated by pilots until the jet fighter arrived on the scene because propeller driven fighters usually experienced too much drag to run into compressibility problems. Some fighters such as the Spitfire and Mustang, which possessed low drag design factors, could approach a speed in a vertical dive from high altitude close to that of a subsonic jet fighter in level flight.

My first acquaintance with compressibility problems occurred during an escort while flying at over 30,000 feet. No one on the squadron thought to mention to me the problems associated with the Mustang when dived vertically from high altitude. The squadron was stacked up in three flights of four aircraft to above 30,000 feet, with my flight providing the top cover. I saw nothing when the squadron commander called the bounce on some aircraft 5,000 feet below us, and my flight peeled over into a vertical dive. I was flying in the number four position and some distance out from my section leader. I followed my leader with a half roll onto my back and pulled through to a vertical dive, a manoeuvre some referred to as a split 'S', and by others as 'a split arse', turn. The airspeed indicator ran rapidly off the clock and the aircraft started to shake with a strong vibration. I looked out at the wings and saw the ailerons fluttering up and down. I pulled back on the stick to pull out of the dive but the elevators failed to respond and I continued vertically downwards. I then attempted to slow down by closing the throttle and moving the propeller to full fine pitch to provide more drag. In order to provide still more drag I attempted to open the radiator flap fully and tried to extend some 10 degrees of flap; but none of these functions had any effect on what appeared to be a vertical terminal dive. As I passed through 25,000 feet there was still no response from the elevators despite pulling as hard as I could. I had by this time lost sight of the other aircraft, and it then struck me that if I continued vertically in this manner there was no possibility of baling out at this speed. Nothing seemed to affect my vertical progress towards terra firma and by now there was an element, if not of terror, certainly of some apprehension of terra firmly within the cockpit. As I passed 20,000 feet the aircraft vibration stopped; the ailerons stopped fluttering; and I felt control coming back to the stick from the elevators. Continuing to pull hard on the stick I pulled out of the dive with my eyeballs somewhere in my flying boots. I was then below 15,000 feet and on reaching 10,000 feet I looked around and found myself alone and somewhat shaken. I started an orbit and seeing nothing I returned somewhat sheepishly to base. It was some time before I fully understood the aerodynamics involved and I had a dressing down from my leader for losing him and not covering his tail during the ensuing mêlée. He was an old hand on the squadron and expressed surprise that no one had thought to brief me on the problem of vertical power dives in a Mustang. I replied that I was used to flying a Spitfire at 300 feet and not a Mustang at 30,000 feet, to which he responded, 'Well, think of it this way: a few moments of practical demonstration are worth a lifetime of theory.'

The missions of No. 122 Wing during the second half of 1944 involved: escorting Bomber Command's strategic day raids on the industrial targets of the Ruhr and V-1 and V-2 launch sites, tactical support of the allied advance through France, Belgium and Holland and attacks on road, rail and water communications and the marshalling areas. Air supremacy ensured low interception by the *Luftwaffe* day fighters already diminished by the split of the fighter force between the Eastern Front and the Western Front where the bulk of the available *Luftwaffe* fighters was engaged in an air battle of attrition with the US 8th Air Force. Bomber Command's heaviest bombs were the 12,000 lb deep penetration bomb and the 12,000 lb 'Block Buster'. The huge 22,000 lb 'Grand Slam' penetration bomb did not become operational until 1945, but I once got a good view of this bomb from the air during the dropping trials. Due to its great size and weight the only aircraft capable of carrying this bomb was the Lancaster bomber. In order to attach the bomb the aircraft was drastically modified by removing the bomb-bay doors, together with the nose and mid-upper gun turrets. I was one of four Mustangs escorting the Lancaster to the bombing range at Martlesham Heath and while up close and slightly below the Lancaster I could appreciate the great size and beautiful proportions of the bomb. Unlike the tin can shaped 'Block Buster' it was conventional in design to achieve the momentum to penetrate deeply into the ground before detonation to fracture the foundations of deep shelters. I was level with the Lancaster when it released the bomb and relieved of ten tons of dead weight the Lancaster leapt some 200–300 feet above me. In my surprise I missed seeing the massive bomb hit the target area below. I remembered the occasion we lost a Spitfire dive bombing and the crash crew recovered the Merlin engine about thirty feet down in the marsh. I wondered how far down the recovery crew would have to dig to retrieve the 'Grand Slam' bomb.

Another task that arose during 1944 involved attacking the V-1 flying bombs launched from coastal sites in Belgium. The V-1, often referred to as the 'buzz bomb' or 'doodlebug', had a pulse-jet engine and carried a 1-ton warhead. It had a short range of around 150 miles and flew between 350–400 mph at below 3,000 feet. To intercept these missiles required the fastest fighters in the RAF and the task fell to the latest Spitfire XIV with a 2,050 hp Rolls Royce Griffon engine and a top speed around 450 mph. The Spitfire XIV, armed with four 20 mm cannon, claimed the majority of the V-1 kills by day with the Mosquito claiming most of the V-1s shot down at night. The AA guns, the new Hawker Tempest and modified Mustang IIIs accounted for most of the rest of the kills claimed, with a few claimed by the first and only Meteor jet squadron just before the end of the war. In order to catch the V-1 flying bomb the Mustang required modification to the Merlin engine to produce its maximum performance at 5,000 feet. The modification to the two-stage, two-speed supercharger increased the manifold boost from the normal 60–80 inches, while using the new 130 octane fuel instead of the usual 100 octane gasoline. This placed a greater strain on the engine producing problems of overheating and the occasional engine failure. Coolant leaks were a common problem and under these operating conditions they increased. An engine change normally occurred every 200 hours and with the increased manifold boost this was reduced by half, as the use of the higher octane fuel caused a reduced engine life through valve burning.

Attacking a V-1 was a hazardous and difficult task. Although it flew straight and level it flew at high speed and presented a small target. Also, because it was constructed from sheet metal it was less vulnerable to cannon and machine-gun fire than a manned aircraft. The hazardous aspect of an attack concerned the 2,000 lb of explosive in the flying bomb, for if the pilot fired at a range closer than 300 yards there was a distinct danger of going down with the V-1 if the warhead exploded. The main danger in flying through the debris of an exploding V-1 was from a rear non-deflection attack. However, if the circumstances permitted and they seldom did, a well-executed high rear quarter attack requiring a deflection shot not only presented a greater target area but offered a better prospect of avoiding any explosion. Such an attack became more feasible when the Meteor entered operational service late in 1944. The average burst of fire during an attack was around three seconds as it was rare for a pilot to hold his aim for longer. The Spitfire with the 20 mm cannon shell had an advantage over the Mustang of impact damage in that a burst of three seconds from four 20 mm cannon produced considerably more weight of metal and explosive than the six 0.5 in Browning machine-guns. However, the six 0.5 in Browning machine-guns were more accurate over longer ranges. Tactics evolved to bring down the V-1 that avoided flying into a possible explosion from the warhead by toppling the gyroscope guiding the bomb. These tactics included the fighter flying in formation on the V-1 and the pilot attempting to get the V-1 to roll by placing one wing over that of the V-1 thereby removing the lift from that wing and causing the V-1 to roll; or under the wing to strike physically the flying bomb's wing tip upwards with the fighter's wing tip. The V-1 had wings skinned in rolled steel, whereas the fighter's wing tips were of far weaker light alloy so that actual contact with the V-1 wing was hazardous and several attempts at this manoeuvre resulted in a damaged wing tip or aileron. Consequently, not many pilots adopted this method of downing the V-1, but among those claiming successes with the wing tipping manoeuvre were the gallant and tenacious Polish pilots on the RAF Polish Mustang squadrons. As it was necessary to tip the V-1 wing through 90 degrees in order to trip the gyroscope, there was a likely chance of damaging a wing tip or an aileron in the process. Several Polish pilots landed with a damaged wing after an attack on a buzz bomb in this manner, and on one such attempt the pilot was killed when his Mustang crashed after a jammed aileron caused his aircraft to roll uncontrollably.

By the later part of 1944 the V-1s with their short range operated from mobile launch sites on the Belgian coast. To intercept the V-1s Fighter Command carried out standing patrols called Diver Patrols over the English Channel and to the north of the Dover Strait. Pairs of fighters patrolled at 10,000 feet awaiting instructions from sector control for a vector to intercept the buzz bomb. The fighters then went into a slight dive to gain maximum speed at full throttle and maximum revs to intercept the V-1 that was usually heading for the London area. Around London was a defensive zone for the guns of AA Command, and barrage balloons flew over sensitive areas such as Buckingham Palace, Westminster and the Port of London. While in the dive there was some apprehension whether the engine would give up the chase while gaining slowly on the V-1 at over 450 mph. The tendency was to open fire out of range for fear of flying into the debris should the warhead explode. Firing at 400 yards or more at such a small target from a bucking fighter meant the shells or bullets were sprayed around the V-1. To ensure a hit on the V-1 the pilot needed to be patient to the extent of waiting until he was within the 300 yards range and it was difficult to keep the gun sight pipper on such a small target for more than three seconds; requiring short bursts of fire. As far as the Mustang was concerned the six Browning guns gave a total of 80 rounds per second for 20 seconds before the four outer guns fired out leaving an additional ten seconds of firing for the two inner guns. Thirty seconds is a long time to be firing at a target yet the V-1 often, and maddeningly, continued its burping way undisturbed with no apparent ill effects. Most pilots did not consider it was a fair exchange to sacrifice their fighter for one V-1, although I am sure there were some on the ground that would offer another view.

The Mustang squadrons of No. 122 Wing had served either with 2nd Tactical Air Force in France or with Desert Air Force in Italy, and as such were completely independent squadrons with their own technical, administrative, medical and motor transport services. In addition, each squadron had a small single engine two-seat Auster monoplane, similar to the Piper Cub, for communication duties. The aircraft was intended for use as an airborne taxi, although it spent much of its flying hours on recreational jaunts. The aircraft used 80 octane gasolines suitable for motor vehicles, and for some this was an attractive means to supplement the recreation gasoline allowance. The 80 octane fuels did not contain the colouration to identify the higher 100 octane aviation fuels used by the Mustangs. The colouration enabled detection by the Special Investigation Branch (SIB) units investigating the pilfering of aviation fuel. A more relaxed and informal approach to discipline and the dress code existed on the wing as was the normal case within Fighter Command. Crumpled and stained dress caps in the best operational and Pilot Officer Prune fashion abounded. Pilot Officer Prune was a cartoon character used in the RAF flying training publication, 'Tee Emm', to denote anything that resulted in a careless and stupid approach to flying. One issue contained the poem that summed up ten typical examples of Pilot Officer Prune's approach to flying.

Ten Little Fighter Boys

Ten little Fighter Boys, taking off in line,
   One was in coarse pitch, and then there were nine.
Nine little Fighter Boys, climbing 'through the gate',
   One's petrol wasn't on, and then there were eight.
Eight little Fighter Boys, 'scrambling' up to Heaven,
   One 'weaver' didn't, and then there were seven.
Seven little Fighter Boys, up to all the tricks,
   One had a 'hangover', and then there were six.

Six little Fighter Boys, milling over Hythe,
  One's pressure wasn't up, and then there were five.
Five little Fighter Boys, over France's shore,
  One flew reciprocal, and then there were four.
Four little Fighter Boys, joining in the spree,
  One's sight wasn't on, and then there were three.
Three little Fighter Boys, high up in the blue,
  One's rubber pipe was loose, and then there were two.
Two little Fighter Boys, 'homing' out of sun,
  Flew straight and level, and then there was one.
One little Fighter Boy, happy to be home,
  Beat up dispersal and then there were none.
Ten little Spitfires, nothing have achieved,
  A.O.C. at Group is very, very peeved –
'Fifty thousand Smackers thrown down the drains,
'Cause ten silly buggers didn't use their brains!'

In addition to the crumpled dress caps, the squadron pilots also affected a style of dress that left the top button of their uniform tunics undone to denote fighter pilots. Colourful scarves would replace the official black neck ties, and suede or desert boots often replaced the standard black shoes. This informality often produced rebukes and orders to leave the mess when confronted by the base commander, always referred to as the 'Station Master', or one of his senior officers. As far as the squadron pilots were concerned the only important function of the base headquarters, apart from the provision of food and billets, was the issue of the operational recreation gasoline allowance. The gasoline was essential for scouring the countryside for suitable hostelries, or for visits to London on stand-downs. The person responsible for issuing the gasoline coupons was the base assistant adjutant. This WAAF officer may not have been the most attractive of the WAAF serving on the base, who were usually to be found in the motor vehicle section, but she was without doubt the most popular of the WAAF with No. 122 wing. The squadrons competed in ensuring that the Assistant Station Adjutant did not lack in invitations to dine out or for a trip to London during her tour of duty with the wing, with an anticipated expectation of an extra coupon or two to their recreational allowance.

The RAF Mustang III was fully camouflaged but early in 1945 No. 65 Squadron received the first P-51D or Mustang IV. These aircraft were unpainted with a bright polished metal finish. They also had a redesigned tear-drop canopy that resulted in a reduction of the dorsal fuselage to incorporate the sliding hood, and this created some directional instability.

A dorsal strake or fillet attached to the fin empennage increased the keel surface and corrected the directional instability. The P-51D incorporated further external wing weapons attachment points, although we were not to use them. Similarly, the P-51D incorporated a tail warning radar device that sounded a warning bell in the cockpit when aircraft came within a 12 degree cone. The RAF disconnected the tail warning as unsuitable for our type of operations. The tail warning radar was no doubt welcomed by the photo-reconnaissance pilots. As a result of these modifications the Mustang IV weighed around 500 lb more than the Mustang III. In theory this gave the Mustang III a slightly better performance than the Mustang IV although this was not discernible. A clean Mustang IV with the Packard Merlin 68 engine of 1,790 hp had a top speed of 440 mph in level flight and with full fuel loads of 400 gallons (Imp.) in the inboard and outboard tanks a range of 2,000 miles. I personally preferred the Mustang IV finding the changes to my advantage, mainly with the better opening canopy and the better all-round visibility.

During the final year of the war from 1944–45 a little known campaign, described by a participant as *A sort of separate war*, waged along the western seaboard of Norway and over the narrow straits of the Skagerrak, between the southern tip of Norway and the northern coast of Denmark. The German occupation of Norway offered a ready base for naval operations against Allied shipping in the North Atlantic. Beaufighter and Mosquito fighter-bombers of Coastal Command operating from the east coast of Scotland harassed the shipping of supplies from Germany to Norway and the iron ore from Norway to Germany. To counter the RAF activity the *Luftwaffe* maintained two fighter *gruppen* of 50–100 Bf-109s and FW-190s along the Norwegian coastline. Battle-weary but experienced *Luftwaffe* fighter squadrons and pilots were withdrawn from the air battle of attrition against the escorted raids of the 8th USAF on Germany, where the *Luftwaffe* was losing two or three pilots a day, for a rest in Norway. Many famous *Luftwaffe staffels* of Bf-109Gs, such as the famous 'Ace of Spades' *staffel* and their aces, rested on the airfields along the coast and the Lista Peninsula in particular on the southern tip of Norway. The prospects were some easy pickings from the Beaufighters and Mosquitoes attacking shipping and coastal targets in the fjords along the coast, and along the Skagarrak between Norway and Denmark. With the arrival of the Merlin Mustang it was possible to provide a fighter escort of equal performance to the *Luftwaffe* fighter squadrons intercepting the rocket and cannon firing Beaufighters and Mosquitoes.

The first long-range escort by Mustang IIIs was in May 1944 and thereafter the shipping strikes were rarely without the benefit of Mustang protection. The airfield selected for the Mustangs was Peterhead, the most easterly airfield in Scotland from which the nearest point in Norway was over 300 miles away. Peterhead was a small fishing port 30 miles north of Aberdeen on Kirkton Head. Most of the shipping strikes were within a 500 miles radius of action from Peterhead involving a flight of four to five hours or more over water with half of it flown at very low level. Although the US Mustangs were regularly flying escort missions of up to 1,200 miles round trips lasting seven hours, there was a significant difference in these missions. The American Mustangs escorted the American heavy bombers of 8th Air Force at an altitude of 20,000–30,000 feet, whereas the North Sea strike missions to the Norwegian coast flew just above wave top height at 50–100 feet to stay below the radar warning horizon and to avoid alerting the *Luftwaffe* fighters.

The element of surprise in attacking shipping and coastal targets was vital. The flight across the North Sea was a hazardous affair during the long summer days, and was doubly so during the short winter ones. The Mustang pilot's life depended on the smooth running of the single Merlin engine, for if it quit there was insufficient time or height in which to bale out of the aircraft. To bale out of a Mustang was a difficult procedure, requiring the aircraft to be flying relatively slowly and on an even keel. Under ideal conditions and the canopy successfully jettisoned, the pilot released his many and various attachments to the aircraft and attempted to stand on the seat and dive towards a wing tip. The only other possibility of baling out without hitting the tail of the aircraft was to drop out inverted with as much negative G as possible. The chances of successfully ditching a Mustang could be assessed as nil and I know of none who succeeded. Even with the calmest sea, and the North Sea was seldom calm especially during winter, the engine radiator located behind the pilot acted as a scoop and ensured the aircraft nosed in when it touched the water. A theory postulated but never demonstrated, suggested that if the Mustang touched the water first with a wing tip the immediate drag at the wing tip would skid the Mustang around on top of the water like a skipping stone.

The North Sea, named the German Sea before the First World War, evolved from an ancient inland sea and is a shallow and notoriously rough and unreceptive sea even during the summer months. It is also a cold sea and with normal flying clothing and a Mae West life jacket a pilot's expectation of survival in the sea was a question of minutes. During the winter and spring months our doctors calculated a swimming pilot succumbing to hypothermia within four to five minutes. Such was the prospect for the sailors on the Murmansk convoys if torpedoed. If a pilot baled out and got into his one-man K-type dinghy successfully, with any sea running the dinghy would capsize and climbing back into the dinghy would soon exhaust even the strongest swimmer. We practised this under ideal conditions in the swimming pool and it was not easy dressed in flying clothing. But allowing that everything occurred according to the book with the pilot secure beneath a spray cover, the prospect of rescue miles from land was doubtful. The RAF high-speed rescue launches operated close to the coast from Fraserburgh. The only chance of survival and rescue many miles into the North Sea lay with the airborne lifeboat carried by a converted version of the Wellington bomber called the Warwick.

The Coastal Command strike wings were based on the North Aberdeenshire coast of the Moray Firth. The Beaufighter Mk Xs, powered by two Bristol Hercules radial engines of 1,770 hp, operated from Dallachy; and the de Havilland Mosquito Mk VIs, powered by two Rolls Royce Merlin engines of 1,460 hp, operated from Banff. Both the Beaufighter and the Mosquito aircraft carried a crew of two. The Beaufighter Mk X had a maximum speed of 300 mph and a range of 1,500 miles. The armament consisted of four 20 mm cannon in the nose, six 0.303 inch machine-guns mounted in the wings, with one defensive dorsal mounted machine-gun operated by the navigator. The aircraft could carry one 500 lb bomb under each wing and some were modified to carry one 2,000 lb torpedo under the fuselage. The Beaufighters carrying torpedoes were renamed 'Torbeaus'. The Mosquito Mk VI, a fighter-bomber version of the multi role aircraft, had a maximum speed of 400 mph and a range of 1,500 miles. The armament was normally four 20 mm cannon and four 0.303 inch machine-guns in the nose. The Mosquito could carry a bomb load of 2,000 lb in the bomb bay. One interesting variant of the Mosquito Mk VI was the Tsetse Mk XVIII with a 57 mm Molins gun mounted in the nose in place of the cannon and machine-gun armament. This gun was the equivalent of a six pounder naval gun with an automatic feed mechanism to give a rate of fire of forty rounds per minute. The Molins gun had considerable recoil when fired and the crew could feel and count the rounds as the gun fired. Flames from the muzzle blast enveloped the nose, and fumes from the burnt charges entered the cockpit. The vibrations from the gun caused dust and dirt to float around the cockpit and the instrument panel would bounce on its anti-shock mounts, making it difficult to read the instruments. The feed mechanism for the shells occasionally jammed; but the Molins gun was a very effective weapon when used against the anti-aircraft batteries, ship superstructures such as the bridge or the conning towers of U-Boats caught cruising on the surface. A Molins gun attack was usually made while in a 20 degree dive from a height of around 2,000 feet, and opening fire in short bursts from 1,000 yards range.

Both the Beaufighters and the Mosquitoes carried four 3 inch free-flight rocket projectiles (RP), with 25 lb solid heads, mounted on rails under each wing. The 3-inch rail mounted rocket projectile had a large circular error of probability (CEP) and this gave a wide spread when fired in salvo; and they were usually fired in ripple. Efforts were made to harmonize the alignment of the rails to be in line with the anticipated attack angle of the aircraft. The 25 lb solid head replaced the 60 lb high explosive head on the shipping strikes as it was not only more accurate but also more effective in penetrating a ship's hull both above and below the water line. The RP attacks were usually initiated from a height of 2,000 feet in a 45 degree dive angle. Cannon fire commenced at a height of 1,000 feet, with the rockets fired at a height of 500 feet.

The shipping strikes on the convoys along the Norwegian coast and on ships sheltering in the deep fjords protected by high mountain cliffs were hazardous and stressful for the strike crews, with many factors opposing the strike aircraft. The first imponderable factor was of course the vagaries of the Scottish, North Sea and Norwegian weather. This could cover every facet from poor visibility due to mist and fog; rain squalls and continuous heavy rain; to snow storms from gales sweeping across the North Sea; and usually there was a low, thick cloud base. Many of us flying across the North Sea to Norway during the winter months were conversant with an old proverb – *A Scottish mist will wet an Englishman to the skin.* And many of us after two hours of formation flying at low level above a cold, angry and unforgiving sea before meeting the opposition could empathise with Robert Browning's words – *To feel the fog in my throat: The mist in my face.* Waiting to greet the strike aircraft when they arrived in Norwegian waters was heavy and accurate anti-aircraft fire from either the shore or ship anti-aircraft batteries, with guns ranging from multiple 20 mm and 40 mm cannon up to the deadly 88 mm AA gun. The efficient German *Kriegsmarine* manned the ships and there were also heavily armed flak ships. Another daunting weapon thrown up at the attacking aircraft were rockets that on reaching their apogee released a parachute with a steel wire deployed from the descending rocket head to which was attached an aerial mine. This presented a slowly descending protective curtain of wire and explosive to entangle the propellers and wings of the attacking Beaufighters and Mosquitoes. Finally, Bf-109 and FW-190 fighters from Luftwaffe staffels based along the coast waited to intercept the incoming strike aircraft and their escorts. The strike force could be as many as forty aircraft with a squadron of twelve escorting Mustangs, therefore, if the strike force was intercepted the Luftwaffe fighters usually had a numerical advantage over the escorting Mustangs. The German fighters would also have a morale advantage in fighting over their own territory, and they had a combat advantage of height with an operational advantage of being able to out-accelerate and out-climb the

Mustang at low altitude. However, adverse weather conditions often dictated whether the fighter interceptions were successful. The strike aircraft suffered considerable battle damage from the anti-aircraft fire, with the loss of many aircraft and their crews. As the task of the escorting Mustangs was to protect the strike force from intercepting fighters, they were usually above and out of range of the defending guns. For all the surviving aircraft there was the long return flight back to Scotland with a possibility of ditching in a rough sea when the only chance of survival came either from the German air-sea rescue service, or the presence of patrolling Warwick aircraft equipped with the airborne lifeboat and Lindholme dinghies.

In January 1945 No. 65 Squadron relieved the Polish Mustangs of No. 315 Squadron at Peterhead. Squadron Leader Ian Strachan led the squadron on the 400 miles flight from Andrews Field in Suffolk to Peterhead giving an indication of the average distance for a strike mission to Norway at low level. No. 19 Squadron, commanded by Squadron Leader Peter Hearn, DFC, arrived at Peterhead later in the month to form a Mustang wing under the command of Wing Commander Peter Wickham, DFC. This gave the Mosquito and Beaufighter strike wings at Banff and Dallachy some added protection from the *Luftwaffe*. Interestingly, No. 19 Squadron while at Peterhead had two pilots who became post-war sporting personalities: Flight Lieutenant Alan Sheriff played cricket for England and Flight Lieutenant Bob Weighill captained the England rugby XV. Squadron Leader Strachan was shot down at the end of January and Squadron Leader Ian Stewart took over command of 65 Squadron only to be shot down in March. Squadron Leader John Foster then became the commanding officer of No. 65 Squadron. Johnnie Foster was an experienced pilot and at the age of twenty-three he was not much older than me, and younger than his two flight commanders. However, he had maturity and a sense of leadership far beyond his years. I served under several squadron commanders and certainly Johnnie Foster rated number two in my experience.

Often it was a dull, grey overcast day at Peterhead as the Merlin engines started up and thirteen Mustangs taxied to the runway for take-off. Whereas a wing commander commanded a bomber squadron, a squadron leader commanded a fighter squadron. The squadron's unit strength was sixteen aircraft, operating twelve in the air in three flights of four aircraft with one reserve aircraft. The pilot strength could vary between twenty and thirty commissioned and non-commissioned pilots, divided into 'A' and 'B' flights, each commanded by a flight lieutenant. In the air the wing leader, or a squadron commander or a flight commander, led the leading flight. The flight commanders scheduled pilots from their flights so that senior pilots led flights or sections, leaving the junior pilots as the wingmen; the responsibility of the wingmen being to protect the tails of the section leaders. To quote an old adage – *A full belly neither fights nor flies well*. Despite eating a full breakfast the stomach would feel empty when lining up at the end of the runway for the engine and take-off checks. The chill of a Scottish mist seemed to enter the heated cockpit and penetrate the body as each pilot hoped nothing occurred to make the Mustang abort the flight; with a suspicion of 'lack of moral fibre' (LMF). As all aircrew were volunteers, cases of LMF were rare. If everything was satisfactory the twelve Mustangs and the reserve aircraft took-off and the squadron formed up at 1,000 feet in loose squadron formation of three flights and headed for the rendezvous with the strike force of Mosquitoes or Beaufighters over Fraserburgh near Kinnaird Head.

A frequent target was the shipping in Alesund Fjord, between Bergen and Trondheim, some 500 miles from Peterhead and the extreme range of the Mustangs. The squadron would settle down at low level on one side of the strike force and ease down to a height of 50 feet above the waves. The rotation of the fuel tanks was the first airborne check to ensure that all the tanks fed correctly. If one aircraft experienced some fuel flow problem the reserve Mustang took its place before returning to Peterhead. Flying close to the wave tops often resulted in sea spray breaking over the aircraft and a salt layer built up on the windscreen, causing the formation to increase height. The Mosquito leader of the strike force took care of the navigation while maintaining strict radio silence. The Mustangs only concerned themselves in maintaining visible contact, while often flying through low scud and driving rain. While flying low level over the sea through the line squalls in open squadron formation there could be a momentary flood of fear as the loosely formating aircraft disappeared from sight, resulting in an instant decision to either concentrate on course, height and airspeed and hope to emerge in contact with the others without a collision, or to pull-up and lose contact with the formation with a possible return to base and scathing condemnation. Obviously, the first course was the selected choice and momentarily even nonbelievers placed their destiny with The Deity.

The low level portion of the mission to Norway lasted about two hours and it was possible to succumb to a sense of monotony to dull anticipation of things to come, although flying formation at wave top height entailed full concentration. As a safeguard against errors in concentration most pilots trimmed their aircraft in a slight nose up attitude to avoid flying into the sea, which required a constant forward pressure on the stick. The Mustangs cruised to the target area with the fuel mixture control leaned off, the propeller pitch coarsened and a medium to high manifold boost in order to achieve maximum range and endurance. Instead of cruising revs at around 2,100 rpm, the revs were reduced to 1,800 rpm at around 30 inches of manifold boost. However, with the reduced rpm and lean fuel mixture the notorious Merlin plugs soon began to carbon or lead up. Flying low level to Norway made each participating Mustang pilot an instant expert in detecting the slightest change of engine note, with an instant response before the Merlin engine began to splutter. As a precaution against this problem every fifteen minutes the engine revs were increased to 2,100 rpm, together with an increase in boost for up to one minute, to burn off the lead or carbon deposit on the plugs before resuming the cruise settings. While carrying out these engine checks the flow and balance in the fuel tanks was checked before once again settling down and hoping no seagull found its way into the radiator or the carburettor and supercharger intake in the nose. The Mustangs took-off on the fuselage tank and, after fuel flow checking all tanks, flew the outward leg of the mission on the drop tanks. With a total of 480 US gallons the aircraft did not handle well until lightened considerably of fuel. The stability of the Mustang was not at its best with a full load of fuel, and the aircraft did not respond to its full combat potential until the fuselage tank became half full and the aircraft cleared its drop tanks. The overload tanks were dropped as the strike force approached the target area or on sighting enemy aircraft and they then flew on the fuselage tank before switching to the wing tanks. Tangling with Bf-109s and FW-190s with the drop tanks on was like entering the boxing ring with one hand tied behind the back. In dropping the external tanks it was necessary for the aircraft to be flying straight and level and the tanks released with some positive 'G' to ensure a clean release. There was a danger otherwise of a tank curling around the wing tip and damaging an aileron.

Often approaching the Norwegian coast there was overcast, and, if the overcast lifted the mountains of Norway became visible, and under any other circumstances were beautiful to behold. The strike aircraft pulled up to around 2,000–3,000 feet for their rocket attacks on the shipping ahead and the Mustangs moved up to combat power as they released the drop tanks and climbed to below the main cloud base or 5,000 feet. Any interception by the *Luftwaffe* usually resulted in a confused mêlée with the radio jammed with calls and instructions. It was the wingmen's job to protect their section leader's tail and sometimes they could be faced with the decision to do so or break away to attack another aircraft. If successful they could by this means leave the ranks of permanent wingmen. Rank, seniority and combat experience dictated the selection of the flight and section leaders in the squadron, and those other than flight or section leaders had few opportunities to fire their guns and prove themselves

My first flight at the tender age of six with my parents in 1929. The flight was from Harwich to Ostend in a Type FBA17H22 French Navy flying boat, powered by a Hispano-Suiza engine of 180 hp. The aspiring aviatrix is my mother.

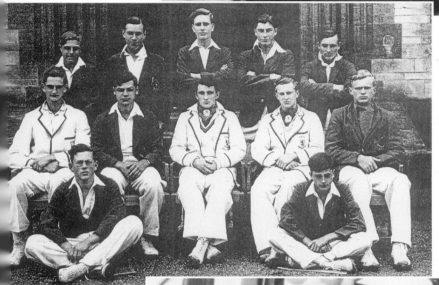

Clayesmore 1st XI. Spin bowler CWD is extreme right in the back row.

At Clewiston, Florida in 1942.

CWD flying the North American AT-6A, designated 'Harvard' by the RAF, at 5 BFTS, Clewiston, Florida in 1942.

Right: A Stearman PT-17 primary trainer at No. 5 BFTS, Florida, 1942.

CWD with the AT6A after a flight in 1942.

Central Flying School

Tiger Moth

Miles Magister

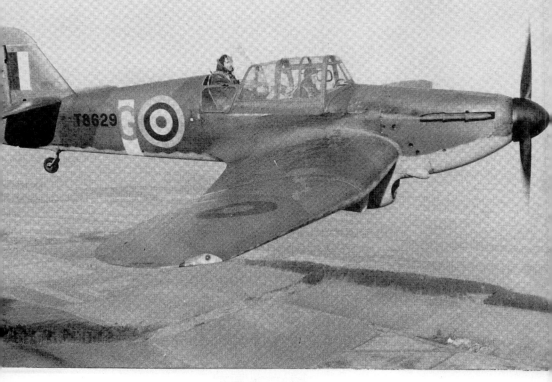

Miles Master Mk. I

Some of the aircraft types flown during my instructor's course at Woodley during 1943.

SUMMARY of FLYING and ASSESSMENTS FOR ~~YEAR~~ COMMENCING ~~1st~~ 7th OCT. *1943.

[* For Officer, insert "JUNE"; For Airman Pilot, insert "AUGUST."]

	S.E. AIRCRAFT		M.E. AIRCRAFT		TOTAL for ~~year~~ PERIOD.	GRAND TOTAL All Service Flying
	Day	Night	Day	Night		
DUAL	3.10	1.00			4.10	174.25
PILOT	400.00	17.20			417.20	579.15
~~PASSENGER~~	—	—	—	—	—	753.40

ASSESSMENT of ABILITY

(To be assessed as :—Exceptional, Above the Average, Average)

(i) AS A DH 82 † PILOT .... *Above Average*

(ii) AS PILOT-~~NAVIGATOR/NAVIGATOR~~ INSTRUCTOR .... *Above Average*

(iii) IN BOMBING .... N/A

(iv) IN AIR GUNNERY .... N/A

(v) IN S.B.A. .... N/A

† Insert :—"F.", "L.B.", "G.R.", "F.B.", "Instructor", etc.

ANY POINTS IN FLYING OR AIRMANSHIP WHICH SHOULD BE WATCHED

Nil.

Date 17th July 1944. Signature ...... C. R. Walwin, S/L.

/or. Officer Commanding 26 E.F.T.S.

FORM OF FLYING INSTRUCTOR'S CERTIFICATE FOR INCLUSION IN THE FLYING BOOK

178290 F/L C.B.W. DOWNES

Part I Category	Date	Signature of C.O., C.I., or Officer i/c Training.	Rank (Not below W/Cdr), appointment, and name of Unit.	For A.2 and A... only, No. of A.M.O. in whi... award was pro... gated.
A2.	7/9/44	J. R. A. Cube...	W/CDR. C.O. OXFORD UNIVERSITY AIR SQUADRON	N 165/45

Part II. This Instructor is competent to fly for instructional purposes th... undermentioned types of aircraft, on which his knowledge and pro... ficiency have been tested by a qualified instructor not below A.2 category.

Aircraft Type	Training role	Signature of C.O., C.I., or Officer i/c Training.	Rank (Not below W/Cdr), appointment, and name of Unit.	Date
OXFORD D.H.82 MASTER MAGISTER HARVARD		J. R. A. Cube...	W/CDR. C.O. OXFORD UNIVERSITY AIR SQUADRON	1/7/47

My flying instructor rating.

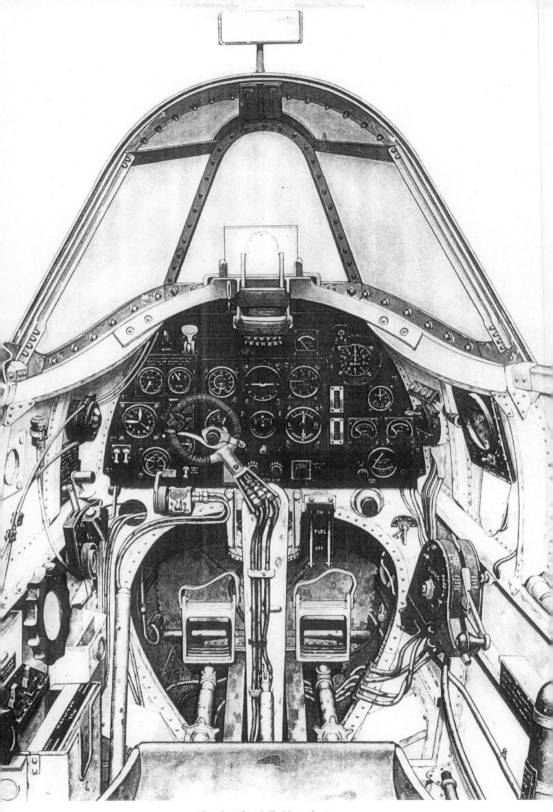

The Spitfire Mk V cockpit.

P-51 MUSTANG

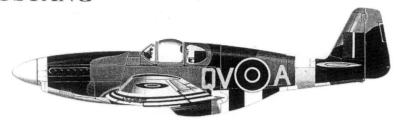

6. Control column and cockpit detail.
7. Cockpit controls:
1 cockpit floodlight
2 gunsight
3 cockpit floodlight
4 cockpit floodlight
5 throttle
6 compass
7 clock
8 suction gauge
9 manifold pressure gauge
10 remote control
11 altimeter
12 directional gyro
13 flight indicator
14 RPM counter
15 oxygen flow blinker indicator
16 mixture lever
17 propeller control
18 carburetor mixture control
19 undercarriage position indicator
20 air speed indicator
21 turn and bank indicator
22 rate of climb indicator
23 coolant temperature gauge
24 oil temperature and fuel and oil gauges
25 oxygen economizer
26 cockpit cover jettison hand
27 cockpit floodlight switch
28 control column
29 gun and bomb switches
30 parking brake
31 instructions for parking brake
32 engine primer
33 oxygen pressure gauge
34 oxygen system warning ligh
35 bomb lever
36 undercarriage selector
37 booster pump switches
38 supercharger control
39 warning light for supercharger
40 starter
41 oil dilution switch
42 ignition switch
43 compass light switch
44 gunsight lamp switch
45 cockpit floodlight switch
46 fuel cock and tank selector
47 hydraulic pressure gauge
48 fairing door emergency control

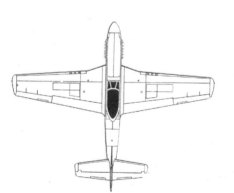

The North American P-51C Mustang.

1D Mustang

Dimensions
Length: 32ft 3in (9.84m)
Height: 13ft 8in (4.17m)
Wing span: 37ft 0½in (11.30m)
Gross wing area: 233sq ft (21.65m²)

Weights
Empty: 7,635lb (3,466kg)
Normal take-off: 10,100lb (4,585kg)
Maximum loaded: 12,100lb (5,493kg)

Power
1 × Packard V-1650–7 (licence-built Rolls-Royce Merlin 61 series) 12-cylinder liquid-cooled Vee piston engine rated at 1,490bhp at take-off, and 1,720bhp at War Emergency setting

Performance
Maximum speed: 437mph (703km/h) at 25,000ft (7,625m)
Initial rate of climb: 3,475ft/min (1,060m/min)
Service ceiling: 41,900ft (12,780m)
Combat range: 950 miles (1,526km)
Operational range: 1,650 miles (2,655km) with two drop tanks

The P-52D Mustang.

A de Havilland Hornet long-range escort fighter.

The Oxford University Air Squadron at summer camp in Shoreham in 1947. I am seated 5th from the right holding a Border Terrier.

No. 41 Squadron Meteor VIIIs, Biggin Hill, 1951.

A de Havilland Vampire Mk 5 with No. 601 Royal Auxiliary Squadron, North Weald, in 1949. (Reproduced from the book *'Til We Meet Again* by John McQuarrie, 1991, published by McGraw-Hill, Ottawa.)

Meteor VIIIs of No. 41 Squadron in 1951.

No. 41 Squadron in front of my personal Meteor VIII 'D' at Biggin Hill in 1951. I am 5th from the left.

CWD with his flying Dachshund at Biggin Hill in 1951.

No. 41 Squadron at readiness at Biggin Hill in 1951.

No. 41 Squadron formation team with the photographer Russell Adams at Biggin Hill in 1952. CWD
is on the extreme right.

My Flying Assessment, 41 Squadron, Biggin Hill, 1952.

H44774 Wt.8943-P.103 20,000(2) 5/51 Gp.840 F. & C. Ltd., London   41 SQUADRON   **R.A.F. FORM 414 A**

SUMMARY of FLYING and ASSESSMENTS FOR ~~YEAR COMMENCING 1st~~ FROM :- APR. *1952

[*For Officer, insert "FEBRUARY"; For Airman Pilot, insert "AUGUST."] — JAN. 1953

	S.E. AIRCRAFT		M.E. AIRCRAFT		TOTAL for ~~year~~ SQUADRON	GRAND TOTAL All Service Flying
	Day	Night	Day	Night		
DUAL	—	—	—	—	—	225 : 05
PILOT	3 : 25	—	372 : 45	8 : 50	385 : 00	1993 : 20
PASSENGER	—	—	—	—	385 : 00	2218 : 25

ASSESSMENT of ABILITY   (To be assessed as :—Exceptional, Above the Average, Average, Below Average)

(i) AS A ~~FIGHTER~~ DAY †PILOT ..... Above the average

(ii) AS PILOT-NAVIGATOR/~~NAVIGATOR~~ ..... Above the average

(iii) IN BOMBING ..... N/A

(iv) IN AIR GUNNERY ..... Above the average

(v) IN INSTRUMENT FLYING ..... Green Ticket Holder.

† Insert :—"F.", "L.B", "G.R.", "F.B.", "Instructor", etc.

ANY POINTS IN FLYING OR AIRMANSHIP WHICH SHOULD BE WATCHED

An exceptionally able leader.

Date ..... 5 JAN 53   Signature .....   SQN. LDR.

Officer Commanding ..... NO 41 (F) SQUADRON

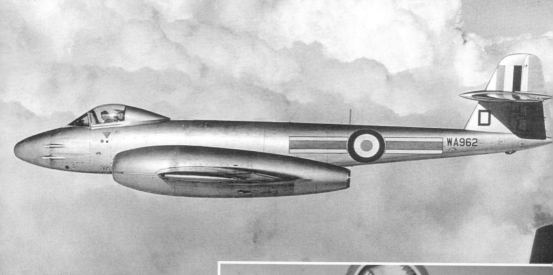

CWD flying Meteor VIII 'D' for Downes.

I am standing 3rd from the left with 'Charlie' Flight, 335th FIS, USAF, at K-14 Kimpo, Korea in 1953.

A North American F-86 Sabre cockpit, Nellis AFB, USAF, 1953.

'Charlie' Flight, 335th FIS, heading for 'Mig Alley' in 1953.

The Yalu River, 'Mig Alley', North Korea, 1953.

'Charlie' Flight returning from 'Mig Alley' in 1953.

'Charlie' Flight over Seoul and K-16, Korea, 1953.

An USAF Aeronautical Chart showing the west coast of North Korea from the Yalu River on the Manchurian border to the Han River and Seoul in South Korea – Scale 1:1,000,000.

Flight into Manchuria and a visit to the Chinese air base at Feng-Cheng, June, 1953

unless separated during a dogfight. Some followed a 'Lone Wolf' philosophy to acquire 'ace' status, but most recognised the need for flight discipline in being a team player. With a long return to the safety of base it was necessary to be watchful of the Mustang's fuel state and the 'bingo' call indicated only sufficient fuel for a safe return to Peterhead. Often due to low cloud and poor visibility there were no interceptions by the *Luftwaffe*. The return to base was made in loose formation at medium altitude if visual flying permitted, otherwise it was a single or formation return on instruments, arriving back at Peterhead low on fuel. The effect of the mission after four or more hours of concentrated attention and effort left most pilots feeling weary almost to the point of exhaustion. The high concentration required flying formation at low level in borderline weather conditions for several hundred miles across an inhospitable sea; the steady flow of adrenaline in some active combat against an opponent with the odds weighed heavily in his favour, followed by the long return to base in bad weather while low on fuel left most pilots physically and mentally drained. This condition would be remedied in the bar and followed by a deep and forgetful sleep afterwards.

The Mosquito strike wing at Banff and the Beaufighter strike wing at Dallachy kept the two Mustang squadrons at Peterhead active. The Mustang pilots had the compensation that the strike pilots had by far the tougher assignment in attacking ships against intensive anti-aircraft fire, despite the fact that the Mustangs were outnumbered by the German fighters. For most of the Mustang pilots it was the psychological factor of flying low level on one engine for long periods over the North Sea in winter that was the hardest part to take. Faith is of course a great help in the face of adversity, anxiety and stress; and we had this in spades with the Packard Merlin. One particular discomfort experienced in the Mustang that was hard to take on a daily basis was sitting on the dinghy seat pack for several hours. The packing of the K-type dinghy left an uneven and lumpy surface to the seat that created pressure points. We tried to ease this by shifting position on the seat but after several hours it did not make much difference as the backside became bruised and numb. Towards the end of the war a water cushion arrived on the squadron which when strapped on the dinghy pack made the seat more comfortable as well as providing drinking water if adrift in a dinghy. However, with the cushion filled with water the parachute and dinghy pack became heavy to carry. It also became as hard as a wooden seat and very cold; neither condition conducive to easing the occupational affliction of sedentary pilots. The most popular solution to achieve a comfortable seat with a precaution against subzero temperatures was to place just enough scotch and water with a little air in the cushion to float just clear of the dinghy pack.

Looking across at fellow pilots on the long outward leg of the mission it was interesting to see what some pilots carried on the cockpit combing between the windscreen and instrument panel. Apart from a map there might be a sandwich; or an orange, apple or banana from the aircrew special rations. While pealing a banana or eating an apple presented no problems after removing one's oxygen mask, I never worked out how to peal an orange satisfactorily while flying at wave top height. Other items visible included the aircrew chocolate ration, and once I saw a pilot smoking a cigarette with the canopy partially open, presumably with the oxygen turned off to prevent an explosion. There was one young pilot officer who always carried a book on the combing. It was not a bible and if asked why he always commented there was not much to do on the way across the North Sea to Norway. Although I spent some of my formative years sailing the Solent and the English Channel I could never come to terms with the North Sea. Flying over the North Sea was never for me – *the blue above and the blue below*. The North Sea for me was always a dark, dangerous and angry sea with the wind blowing the tops off the waves, and the sky above an overcast grey. There were many times when I would feel *fog in my throat*; even on the return to Scotland there was still what Joyce described so aptly in 'Ulysses' – *The snotgreen sea. The scrotumtightening sea!* For if the aircraft experienced problems the chances of survival, even when baling out successfully, were very remote.

One outstanding, extrovert personality on the squadron was Flight Lieutenant Graham Pearson; an experienced and aggressive fighter pilot with a reputation of being a bit wild and unusual, even among a bunch of fighter pilots. He was two years older than me and we became firm friends. He acted as my mentor, while leading me astray on and off the squadron. One mission in particular was typical of his press-on approach to life. While returning to Peterhead from Norway a Mosquito pilot who had been hit while attacking the shipping called to report that his remaining engine was about to fail and he would have to ditch the aircraft. By sheer luck Graham Pearson picked up the Mosquito below and gave it top cover as it started to loss height. Sector control had a fix on the aircraft and reported a Warwick with an airborne lifeboat heading towards them. The Warwick intercepted them when the Mosquito was about 100 miles out from Scotland and shortly afterwards the Mosquito called that he would ditch. The Mosquito made a perfect touch-down on the water and after jettisoning the escape hatch, the pilot and his navigator climbed into a circular J-type dinghy. The Mosquito remained floating on the water for a while, probably due to the wooden construction and near empty fuel tanks. The Warwick flew overhead and dropped smoke flares to establish wind speed and direction. The Warwick carried a lifeboat of twenty feet in length with large flotation chambers fore and aft. The lifeboat carried sails, oars and two small outboard engines, together with survival gear, rations, an emergency radio and signalling gear. The Warwick flew into wind over the dinghy at 1,000 feet to drop the lifeboat so that it would land on the sea upwind of the dinghy. Three large parachutes lowered the lifeboat down to the sea with an automatic release to disengage the parachutes as the lifeboat touched the water. The lifeboat hit the water and two rockets in the bow fired two drogue sea anchors to reduce drift, as a rocket on each side amidships fired a lifeline for the dinghy crew to pull themselves to the lifeboat. Unfortunately, the Warwick pilot did not release the lifeboat sufficiently far upwind of the dinghy and it landed in the water to one side and level with the dinghy. Only two of the parachutes released and the remaining chute filled with air acted as a spinnaker sailing the lifeboat away downwind. The Mosquito crew tried paddling to catch it but the wind was too strong and the lifeboat drifted away from them.

Graham Pearson called to say he would try to deflate the chute by firing at it. He made a firing pass at the chute before calling he was out of ammunition. The chute continued to fill with air and draw the lifeboat farther away from the Mosquito crew in the dinghy. 'GP' then called that he would attempt to deflate the chute by hitting it with his wing tip. As the Mustang skimmed the waves and dipped one wing it flicked the top of a wave. There was a good chance that it would cartwheel into the sea if not from hitting a wave then in becoming hooked up on the parachute. Fortunately he missed the chute and I think this must have shaken even his flamboyant approach to life as he did not make a second run. He was by this time low on fuel and although still early afternoon the light was fading and he informed sector control he was returning to base, leaving the Warwick orbiting the unfortunate Mosquito crew to drop a larger Lindeholme dinghy to them. The Warwick remained until dark and dropped float flares before returning to base. An extensive search the following day produced no trace of either the dinghy or the crew of the Mosquito.

Graham Pearson had another unusual and interesting trip to Norway just before the war ended. Over the Skagerrak on the way to Kristiansand in low scud and poor visibility that made contact with the Mosquitoes difficult, the strike force was attacked by FW-190s. The last heard from GP was that he was involved with some F-190s and while attacking one of them he called that he was hit. Nothing more was heard or seen and he was posted as Missing in Action. About two weeks later he walked into the squadron pilots' crew room wearing a smart Swedish air force flying jacket he exchanged for his tattered fleece-lined leather jacket and flying boots. He told us that while firing at an FW-190 and assuming his wingman was behind him, found to his dismay that the aircraft behind him was the wingman of the FW-190 he was following. He received some damage from an explosive 20 mm cannon shell near the radiator, and anticipating some coolant problems he dived to sea level and out-ran the FW-190 before pulling up into cloud. He had a plan in his mind that should such a thing happen to make for a Swedish air force base near the Norwegian border, and his engine held out long enough for a crash landing in Sweden. Although the Swedes impounded the Mustang and interred him they treated him very well while confining him to the base. However, as he presented a problem due to Swedish neutrality they decided to relieve themselves of the problem by putting him aboard a civil BOAC Mosquito flying the secret missions to Sweden to carry steel ball bearings back to the UK. He squeezed himself into the Mosquito cockpit between the pilot and navigator and after an uncomfortable flight arrived back in England. He told me that had he known the war would end so quickly he would have remained in Sweden until after VE Day to find out if it was true what was said about Swedish girls!

The European war ended on 8 May 1945, and the Mosquitoes and Beaufighters of the strike wings operating from late 1944 experienced far greater losses than the escorting Mustangs, with more than 100 aircrew lost mostly from surface anti-aircraft fire while attacking shipping and coastal targets. The Mustang losses from anti-aircraft fire were nearly non-existent with only one possible loss in this manner. The experienced and battle-hardened *Luftwaffe* fighter squadrons on rest in Norway from the air fighting over Germany also experienced losses, together with aircraft from the operational training bases along the Norwegian coast. Consequently, the calibre of the German pilots attacking the strike force could range from recognized 'aces' to inexperienced tyros.

Between January and May 1945, No. 65 Squadron was consistently more successful in its claims against the *Luftwaffe* than No. 19 Squadron, with 14 German aircraft claimed destroyed in combat over Norway and eight probably destroyed; for the loss of four pilots. No. 19 Squadron claimed five German aircraft destroyed for the loss of six of its pilots. The *Luftwaffe* claimed many successes against the RAF over Norway but, as with the RAF claims, post war analysis showed them both to be exaggerated. One of the losses on 65 Squadron that occurred in February 1945 had an interesting sequel. During a dog-fight with Bf-109s while escorting Mosquitoes on a shipping strike in Alesund Fjord, Warrant Officer Caesar was reported shot down with his Mustang crashing into the sea. Apparently a *Luftwaffe* ace from the 'Ace of Spades' staffel fired at him setting the Mustang on fire. The German pilot made enquiries after the war with the RAF regarding the strike operations over Norway and their losses on that date, and after receiving the name of his adversary gave his version of the combat. He said that during a dogfight with several Mustangs and while in a tight turn he put a burst of fire into one of them setting the aircraft on fire. Following the Mustang in a diving turn he waited to see it crash into the sea, when to his surprise the Mustang suddenly decelerated by lowering some flap and he overshot the Mustang. The Mustang pilot raised his flaps and closing behind the Bf-109 opened fire from short range setting the aircraft on fire. The German pilot had just enough height to bale out of his burning aircraft and was picked up by a German gun-boat, who saw the burning Mustang crash into the sea. Warrant Officer Caesar was by this time either too badly injured or too low to bale out, or both. The German pilot stated in his report that the Mustang pilot was the bravest pilot he fought against over France, Germany, Russia and Norway, and he wanted his squadron and his family to know how he died. A similar act of gallantry brought the only fighter VC of the war when Flight Lieutenant Nicholson stayed in his burning Hurricane to shoot down a Bf-109 during the Battle of Britain, before baling out with severe burns. A similar recommendation for the award of the Victoria Cross to Warrant Officer Caesar did not receive official approval due to lack of confirmation. The next highest award for a non-commissioned officer is the Conspicuous Gallantry Medal and presumably the lack of confirmation also precluded the award of this rare decoration, thereby rendering Warrant Officer Caesar ineligible for any recognition of his gallantry.

Shortly after VE Day Wing Commander Peter Wickham, DFC, received the DSO; and led the Mustang wing to rejoin No. 122 Wing at Bentwaters in Suffolk. Squadron Leader Johnny Foster received a well-deserved DFC for his leadership of 65 Squadron, as did Squadron Leader Peter Hearne commanding 19 Squadron. Flight Lieutenant Graham Pearson received a DFC in recognition of his claims against the *Luftwaffe* of four aircraft destroyed, and he continued to lead me astray during our leisure moments in London with some memorable parties at his mews cottage near Regent's Park.

The pink granite town of Peterhead is still an important fishing port as it clusters around the busy harbour that is now a satellite of Aberdeen in support of the North Sea oil industry. Gone are the women and girls from the wharf gutting and preparing the fish with blue fish frozen fingers for the night train to London. Gone too are the vast amounts of herring from the Dogger Bank: a daily fish auction when the boats dock now distributes the catch throughout the European Economic Union. The dignified granite city of Aberdeen is the UK Dallas of the North and the centre for North Sea oil prospecting; and the North Sea still takes a toll on those who dare to transgress it. The airfield at Peterhead has like other wartime airfields reverted back to farmland and only an isolated and forlorn looking control tower remains with some old Nissen huts to remind one of the snarling, crackling sound of perhaps two dozen Merlins lining up for a trip to Norway. There were good moments when Jupiter Pluvious would relent and allow one to see the beautiful countryside of Aberdeenshire, with its abundance of famous waters in the pursuit of salmon and sea trout. Just a short distance north of the airfield the Ugie produced a few early salmon, sea trout and river trout, and in Loch Strathbeg were rare Loch Leven trout. In later years I fished more famous waters in the area at more expense and less success.

It would be remiss of me at this stage of my memoir to leave Aberdeenshire without mention of a most remarkable woman: Lady Mac Robert of Dounside, and her heroic, magnificent and generous gestures to the Royal Air Force in memory of her husband, Sir Alexander, and her three sons, Alisdair, Roderick and Iain. All three sons were to die while flying: Alisdair in a pre-war flying accident, Roderick flying a Hurricane fighter and Iain flying a Wellington bomber over Germany. There being no heir to the barony Lady Mac Robert's response was to donate a Sterling bomber to Bomber Command bearing the family crest and the words 'Mac Robert's Reply'. This unequalled gesture was followed by the donation of four Hurricane fighters to Fighter Command; three of them honouring her sons. At the time of purchase in 1941 a four-engine Sterling bomber cost £25,000 and a Hurricane fighter £5,000. Lady Mac Robert's final magnificent gesture to the Royal Air Force was to donate her home, Dounside House near Aberdeen, as a holiday and retirement home for RAF officers under the Mac Robert Trust; and build a nursing home for the RAF Benevolent Fund named Alestrean House in memory of her three sons. A truly wonderful lady!

By May 1945 the RAF Mustang squadrons, including the Polish wing, were all in East Anglia. The sixteen Mustang squadrons in the UK numbered 300 aircraft; a formidable force, although small when compared with the US 8th Air Force's 1,600 Mustangs in Europe. The Mustang wing at Bentwaters consisting of Nos. 19, 64, 65, 118, 126 and 234 Squadrons formed a super wing under the command of Wing Commander Michael Donnet, DFC, formally of the Belgian Air Force, as part of Tiger Force for the invasion of Japan. We were to be the escort fighters for the new RAF Lincoln bombers entering service in 1945. The Lincolns, developed from the Lancaster bomber, the most famous of the bombers of Bomber Command, would be the RAF's principal bomber force for the final assault on Japan. At the time of VE Day Tiger Force was to support the invasion of Singapore before the assault on Japan, but Singapore fell without invasion and after the Americans captured Okinawa it became the main base for the invasion of mainland Japan. The Air Ministry intended replacing the Mustang with a smaller single-seat development of the Mosquito named the Hornet, which had the same wooden construction as the Mosquito. The wood construction of the Hornet gave it a light weight for its two Merlin 130/131 engines of 2,030 hp, and with the contra-rotating propellers it had no swing on take-off. A top speed over 450 mph, a range over 2,000 miles and an armament of four 20 mm cannon plus 2,000 lb disposable stores, made it a formidable escort fighter and was faster than the current propeller fighters. The Hornet had a slight edge in speed and range over the Mustang. The safety advantage of two engines for the long sea crossing of 400 miles to Kyushu, the nearest island in Japan, appealed to us and we eagerly awaited their arrival. However, the Hornet production was delayed until after VJ Day on 15 August when Tiger Force disbanded. Prior to this we carried out training exercises with the new Lincoln bombers in preparation for escorting them to the Land of the Rising Sun. The Lincoln was larger and more heavily armed than the Lancaster bomber, and it carried an even heavier bomb load. We also carried out camera-gun combat in preparation for the anticipated combat with the Japanese Zero fighter while escorting the Lincoln bombers to Japan. The Japanese Zero with its lower wing loading was more manoeuvrable with a faster initial acceleration and rate of climb over the Mustang and the Hornet; making it essential to maintain our speed and dive advantage over the Zeros.

> *Gin a body meet a body*
> *Flyin' through the air,*
> *Gin a body hit a body,*
> *Will it fly? And where?*

On 14 June 1945 four of us were returning to Bentwaters after a camera-gun dog-fight exercise some miles off the coast. We were descending in a line astern tail-chase with me bringing up the rear, when at around 10,000 feet some US P-51 Mustangs bounced us. Such encounters had become almost a daily activity with the concentration of US and RAF squadrons in East Anglia, including the enthusiastic participation of the Polish Mustang squadrons. As we broke hard into our attackers, I glanced up to see a silver Mustang coming down on me in a steep diving turn – *I looked and behold a pale horse: and his name that sat on him was Death.* This was certainly a Revelation as I pulled left as hard as I could. In a fleeting second I knew the US Mustang would hit me, and there was nothing I could do to change the situation. A violent bang and shudder occurred as the US Mustang's right wing sliced into the fuselage behind me. The force of the impact sheared off part of its wing and the US aircraft rolled over and dived steeply into the sea. No parachute appeared but I was not looking for one because I had my own problems as my aircraft half rolled into a steep dive. I assumed the tail or at least the flying controls severed and I pulled the canopy jettison lever before releasing the seat harness and attempting to bale out of the aircraft. The canopy curled around as it released and the front corner of the metal frame struck me behind the left ear, as my head was not lowered sufficiently due to the negative G while inverted. The blow was very violent and I must have momentarily lost consciousness for my next impression was the aircraft was no longer inverted but in a near vertical dive. Instinctively I pulled back on the stick as it was not possible to bale out with the slipstream pushing me back into the seat. To my surprise the aircraft responded and came out of its dive. I could hear nothing on the radio or make any call as the radio which was behind my seat had sustained damage in the collision. The turbulence within the cockpit without the canopy was considerable and disconcerting. My head ached from the blow from the canopy as I felt a warm flow of blood running down my neck and chest. With the Mustang vibrating strongly it was difficult to control the aircraft, and I could only maintain lateral and directional control by flying the aircraft cross-controlled with strong right rudder and left aileron. I turned towards the coast and prepared to get up on the seat any moment and dive for the wing tip hoping the aircraft did not roll over me as I did so. I then wondered if perhaps it was better to let the aircraft roll and then push forward on the stick to give enough negative G to clear the tail. I felt around to check the dinghy connection to my Mae West and I disconnected the oxygen and radio plugs as these connections could throttle me or break my neck. I surprised myself that after an involuntary call to The Almighty in my momentary flush of panic I carried out these actions quite calmly, confirming Dr Johnson's view that one's imminent demise can *concentrate the mind wonderfully.*

The engine was running smoothly and, although the radiator appeared to be operating, the engine temperature had started to rise. I was now down to 3,000 feet and unable to climb as with full power I could not control the aircraft. I looked around but could see no one and felt annoyed at my abandonment by my colleagues (who were looking for two Mustangs in the sea). Fortunately, the weather was clear but over the sea a thick haze caused poor visibility making it difficult to see anything. I had a glimpse of the coastline ahead and decided to bale out when over land. The engine temperature had by now risen considerably and it continued to rise as I waited for the signs of a coolant leak due to the over-heating. My immediate concern was whether I had sufficient altitude to bale out successfully when I crossed the coast. I reached the coast at Aldeburgh with Bentwaters 10 miles to the south-west. It had become quite a strain flying the aircraft cross-controlled with my head aching from the blow by the canopy, and I felt blood from the wound in my neck continuing to run down inside my shirt.

The engine temperature was now dangerously high and I knew it was decision time to either get out or make an attempt to land the aircraft before the engine failed. I had no means of contacting either the control tower at Bentwaters or aircraft in the circuit, and a landing would be a one shot chance with no possibility of an overshoot and a go-around. The runway at Bentwaters was much shorter than an emergency landing strip at Woodbridge, a further 5 miles to the south-west, and I decided my chances of putting the aircraft on the ground safely would be better if I could reach Woodbridge. The airfield was built during the war, together with one in Kent and another in Yorkshire, for bombers returning with battle damage in bad weather as all three emergency strips were equipped with FIDO, a runway fog dispersal system. There was no circuit aircraft to worry about at Woodbridge and I had a clear descending straight-in approach to the 3,000 yards of runway. I decide to try landing the aircraft with the landing gear down, and still with sufficient height to bale out I lowered the undercarriage. The aircraft responded without loss of control as long as I maintained a speed of 150 mph. White puffs of glycol coolant started to appear from the Merlin's exhaust and I knew I did not have much time left on the engine before it seized. I flew the Mustang onto the runway without flaps and the tail up, closing the throttle on the runway, cutting the fuel and switching off the ignition. The Mustang continued straight along the runway until the tail wheel touched down when there was a vibration as the tail wheel tyre burst.

I got out of the aircraft to see the radiator twisted out of line with a great gash in the fuselage aft of the cockpit. The empennage appeared to be a few degrees out of the vertical and this may have accounted for the tail wheel tyre bursting. Looking at the Mustang it was hard to imagine how the engine kept running and how the flying controls still operated. The impact from the collision occurred at probably the only place along the fuselage that was strong enough to absorb the blow while still allowing air to flow through the radiator. It was clear that the US Mustang's right wing had passed very close to my right wing; and had the impact been anywhere else, fore or aft, my Mustang must have suffered fatal structural damage and gone in with the American aircraft. Several jeeps, two crash trucks and an ambulance arrived and some incredulous observers viewed my Mustang. A physical reaction set in and I felt shaky with blood from my wound now below the waist. The ambulance crew put a first aid dressing on my head before taking me to Ipswich hospital where they stitched up the gash to my head and neck. I arrived back at Bentwaters still wearing my bloodstained shirt with my head swathed in a large bandage looking like a turban. Waiting to greet me were our new wing leader, Wing Commander Max Sutherland, DFC, together with the squadron commander, flight commander, and Graham Pearson, my flight leader, who could not resist his penchant for The Bard by commenting – '*What bloody man is that!*'

Shortly afterwards two USAF majors arrived for a preliminary inquiry into the accident. The squadron commander and my flight commander gave statements, together with my flight leader; and I explained the cause of the accident involving the loss of the American pilot and his aircraft. The two Americans were singly unimpressed with my explanation being quick to emphasize that the leader of the flight of US Mustangs was a very experienced fighter pilot and one of the top aces of the 363rd Fighter Squadron and the 357th Fighter Group at Leiston. He was also on his last flight with the squadron before returning to the US for a promotional tour of the States. I assumed from this that he was the pilot who collided with me and hence my angry response to say it depended how one spelt 'ace'! The essence of the two USAF majors interrogation was to imply that culpability for the accident lay with me as a junior, and by implication, an inexperienced squadron pilot. Max Sutherland led me away saying there was bound to be some flak from the Americans and it would be better if I went to ground until required for the official court of inquiry. In my turbaned state and throes of an unremitting headache, I was reluctant to go home and confront my parents. Graham Pearson with typical generosity solved the problem for me by suggesting I hole-up in his mews cottage in London. As I gratefully accepted the keys he said, 'Now's your chance to show off at the usual watering holes looking like a genuine war hero'!

The next day the air and sea search continued for the missing US pilot. No wreckage or body was found and in all probability both aircraft and pilot lay some twenty fathoms down on the seabed of the North Sea, and I was fortunate not to be resting nearby in my Mustang. The Americans returned to question me further but Sutherland informed them I was on sick leave. A formal Court of Inquiry later exonerated me of any blame for the accident. It was not until some years later I learned that the pilot who hit me was a Lieutenant George F. Barrett; an inexperienced pilot who had recently joined the squadron. He was still on his initial training with the squadron and not listed as operational. This made it clear that the blame for the accident rested with the flight leader. The RAF Official Records Office briefly summed up the incident succinctly by stating:

'Mustang KM316 of 65 Squadron hit by USAF aircraft 14 miles ENE of Orfordness on 14 June 1945. Aircraft not repaired and Scratched off Command'. During the last six months of the war I managed to thwart the grim reaper but the USAF nearly succeeded where the *Luftwaffe* had failed. Flying Spitfire Vs in a ground support role I yearned for Spitfire IXs in a fighter interception role and was initially disappointed to be flying Mustangs on long range escort. However, on that unforgettable day in June 1945 I was thankful to be flying in a Mustang and be able to fully appreciate the quality of construction of the P-51 Mustang by the North American Aviation Company, when over the North Sea I beheld *A Pale Horse*.

It was during our preparation for Tiger Force that the first post-war general election took place and the nation showed its gratitude for Churchill's leadership by defeating him at the polls. It seemed to many of us a mistake that he was not given a mandate to settle the problems of post-war Europe and to settle with the Japanese in the Far East. The first major Allied conference of post-war Europe took place at Potsdam near Berlin during July 1945 without the presence of Churchill or Roosevelt, who died in April. Although the war with Japan was still in progress most of the conference business at Potsdam concerned the reconstruction of Europe. Many people in Britain and the Socialists in particular, regarded Joseph Stalin (responsible for more deaths among his citizens than Hitler killed in the concentration camps) as 'Dear Old Uncle Joe'. The British cabinet appeared prepared during renditions of 'The Internationale' or 'The Red Flag'; to give in to his demands. One outcome of this was that forty Rolls Royce Nene jet engines sent to the USSR enabled the Mig-15 fighter to appear in the skies over Korea before the US F-86 Sabre Jet. The Mustang wing at Bentwaters flew to Tangmere on the south coast to escort the Allied participants to the Potsdam Conference. I was delayed by an engine problem and taking-off late in the afternoon flew through a thunderstorm en route to Tangmere and experienced a severe electrical storm with violent discharges of lightning. Recalling advice from those who experienced large tropical storms in the Far East, I lowered my seat and placed a map over my head as I turned up the cockpit lights and concentrated on my primary flying instruments. The soundness of this advice became apparent when after experiencing several intense lightning flashes the aircraft received a lightning strike with a big bang and a great flash of blinding light. Had my eyes not been shielded I must surely have become momentarily blinded and the aircraft uncontrolled. As a result of the strike the compass went haywire and despite replacing the compass and degaussing the aircraft before swinging the new compass, the compass was always erratic and unreliable on that particular aircraft. This experience was to stand me in good stead when I experienced flying in tropical storms. I experienced another lightning strike some years later in a Meteor jet as the lightning entered the aircraft at one wing tip and exited at the other wing tip, and again we could never completely degauss the aircraft and get a compass to function accurately. My third lightning strike occurred while flying a Canberra at 50,000 feet through the top of the inter-tropical front lying across Malaysia.

From Tangmere we escorted the new Prime Minister, Clement Atlee, and his cabinet to Berlin and the wing landed at Debelsdorf, an ex-*Luftwaffe* ME-262 base east of Lubeck. Here we stayed during the period of the conference before escorting the UK participants back to England. During the conference we flew wing strength formations over Berlin and along the Unter-den-Linden in a show of strength for the benefit of the Soviets. Our stay at Debelsdorf was certainly an eye opener on how the other half operated and lived compared with us and it appeared the only thing in our favour was victory. The German fighter squadrons were an elite force in the *Luftwaffe* and the jet pilots of the ME-262 squadrons were the *crème de la crème* of the fighter force. It amazed us to see the luxurious appointments of the base; in particular the officers' mess. This had the appearance of a luxury country hotel with a hunting lodge interior. In addition to a very comfortably furnished lounge was an attractive dining room with tables set for four. This was unlike an RAF mess with its large communal dining tables. To ensure an exceptional degree of comfort and privacy the mess provided individually furnished bedrooms and bathrooms; and to take care of these rooms and to serve the meals in the dining-room were tall, long-legged and good-looking blonde Valkyries. This was certainly quite unlike any RAF mess! At first the mess staffs were nervous and anticipated a fate worse than death from their conquerors, but they became relaxed with the occupation of largely Anglo-Saxon troops, rather than ravishing Slavs and Tartars. We had strict orders regarding fraternization on pain of court-martial. Obviously the girls were hand picked as part of the benefits provided for the ME-262 pilots in anticipation of maintaining a high morale with a sense of Valhalla; and for the propagation of *der meister rasse*! It was a bit of a strain for healthy young pilots used to making the subject of girls a topic in the mess when 'shop' talk was taboo. In no time the girls became congenial in the knowledge that the Allied military authority would protect their honour. Some more handsome members of the wing even received glances indicating little resistance should the victors take advantage of the spoils of war. It was perhaps as well our stay at Debelsdorf was of short duration as it would have spoiled us for a return to our more Spartan world in the RAF.

The crowning jewel of this *Luftwaffe* home-from-home was below the building in the cellar that acted as an air raid shelter. In a large room, lavishly decorated in the style of a Bavarian Hofbrauhaus, was a panelled bar with recreational facilities and decorated with antler heads, crests and trophies. The wine and beer cellars ensured a steady libation of entertainment while under bombardment. With all these delights we were in grave jeopardy of forgetting any problems associated with fraternization and courts martial. During our stay we were unable to leave the base due to the presence of German Werewolves. These guerrilla fighters ambushed individuals and during our stay killed a British army dispatch rider. Field Marshal Montgomery's personal staff officer returning to Twenty-First Army Group headquarters suffered the same fate. Under the circumstances we had no desire to explore off the base. After a pleasantly unexpected and very educational diversion to Debelsdorf, with a contrasting view of life style in the *Luftwaffe*, we returned to our bare and draughty Nissen huts at Bentwaters to reflect on a different military philosophy, and a grudging envy for an elite German approach to service morale.

Following VJ Day the Air Ministry called for volunteers for the occupational force in Japan, I decided against this opportunity to see The Land of the Rising Sun as there appeared to be much more interesting prospects in Europe. There are pundits and moralists who state with 20/20 hindsight that the use of the atomic bomb against Japan was unnecessary and that the Japanese were ready to surrender. I think that anyone who took part in the Battle of Okinawa would readily dispute this assessment. The amphibious assault on the island chosen in preference to Formosa (Taiwan) or the Philippines as the final springboard for the invasion of Japan claimed the most casualties of any Allied campaign against Japanese forces in the Pacific War. The scale of the assault was comparable with the Allied landing in Normandy, consisting of over 1,300 ships landing over 150,000 veteran troops on a small island defended by over 120,000 fanatical Japanese troops with the heaviest concentration of Japanese artillery of the war. The Americans lost over 700 aircraft and the Japanese lost over 1,000 kamikaze aircraft in attacks on the Allied fleet resulting in the sinking of thirty-eight ships. Total American casualties were around 50,000 killed and wounded against 110,000 Japanese troops killed. This was a taste of the resistance that could be expected in an assault on the Japanese homeland. The planning for the final assault against Japan, 'Operation Olympic', anticipated an attack on Kyushu, the southernmost of the Japanese home islands, during the autumn of 1945 using a force of 770,000 men with anticipated casualties around 270,000. Estimates of Allied casualty figures ranged from a low of 100,000 to a high of 500,000. The invasion of the Japanese home islands was to be a far greater enterprise than the Normandy landings. The 400 miles of open sea from the start line on Okinawa to the rocky coastline of southern Kyushu made it a far more hazardous operation and vulnerable to attacks from a still formidable force of more than 1,000 kamikaze aircraft, with an anticipated fanatical defence by the Japanese of their homeland. After the consolidation of Kyushu, the island would become a huge invasion base for massive air attacks on the main island of Honshu, to be followed by invasion in the spring of 1946.

The initial strategic bombing attacks on Japan inflicted little damage to the home islands apart from the attacks on the major cities. The series of fire bomb raids on Tokyo inflicted more casualties than the two atomic bombs on Hiroshima and Nagasaki combined. By June 1945 the six major industrial cities of Tokyo, Osaka, Nagoya, Kobe, Kawasaki and Yokohama were devastated with over 250,000 people killed. It is true that elements of the Japanese cabinet wanted to negotiate peace terms but the Potsdam Proclamation broadcast to Japan in July demanded unconditional surrender, and the militarists retained a veto over cabinet decisions. The Allied demand of unconditional surrender strengthened Japanese determination to fight to the end. President Truman commented that he hoped there was a possibility of preventing a similar Okinawa situation from one end of Japan to the other. It was this consideration that decided him to authorize the use of 'a new weapon of unusually destructive force' during August 1945 to end the war. President Truman knew that possession of a nuclear attack capability guaranteed that the Allies could not lose the war and further, could now end it quickly. However, it was necessary to demonstrate this in order to save Allied lives. He had an additional incentive to end the war quickly by August as the Soviets announced plans to invade Manchuria, Korea and Japan early in August and threatened to over-run the northern island of Hokkaido: he was alarmed at the prospect of Soviet penetration in Asia. An atomic bomb dropped over Hiroshima on 6 August, followed by another over Nagasaki on 9 August added another 3 per cent to the existing devastation of the Japanese cities. The Japanese war cabinet faced with Armageddon recommended to the Emperor that he accept the terms of surrender, and the war ended the following day. As one of those waiting to play a part in the final assault on Japan I had no qualms about the Americans bringing an early conclusion to the war with the use of the atomic bomb. Those who condemn the use of the atomic bomb to end five years of war against a cruel, remorseless and fanatical enemy in order to save the needless slaughter of American and Allied lives, do so without consideration of Cicero's *O Tempora! O Mores*! I think it safe to conclude that had the Germans or the Japanese possessed nuclear weapons, they would not have hesitated in using them against military and civilian targets. If Truman had decided against the use of the two atomic bombs against civilian targets in order to preserve US casualties, the war would have continued into 1946. The US strategic bomber offensive, with the use of conventional bombs, would have intensified with even greater devastation of Japanese cities and loss of life. The objection to the use of the atomic bomb was the horrific and immense number of indiscriminate casualties to the civilian population. Continued and increasingly massive B-29 bomber raids against the Japanese home islands would have reduced all the major cities to rubble. In addition to this massive US strike capability, the US had available large numbers of an improved version of the German V-1 flying bomb: the Republic JB-2 'Loon'. Also, by 1946 the US had developed the German V-2 rocket into the A-4 missile. In addition to these new weapons of destruction were chemical and biological weapons available to both sides that posed the question whether the Japanese would in desperation resort to their use. A final consideration for an immediate end to the war by the use of atomic weapons was the declared intention of the Japanese to summarily execute all Allied POWs held by the Japanese in the event of an Allied invasion of Japan.

The use of the atomic bomb not only saved the Allied forces from experiencing extensive casualties in an invasion of Japan, but also countless Japanese civilian lives making the casualties of Hiroshima and Nagasaki fade into insignificance in comparison. The moral question is: did the end justify the means? The alternative suggests that it did, for had the atomic bomb not been used against Japan the war would have continued for two or more years with estimated Japanese casualties exceeding five million. The Soviets would have occupied the northern Japanese island of Hokkaido and probably tried to extend their occupation further. Without the US nuclear deterrent, the enormous land, sea and air forces of the Soviet Union would have overwhelmed the western European countries, turning them into satellites of the USSR. President Truman's decision to use the atomic bomb on Japan to end the war quickly, horrific though the consequences were, was his *least abhorrent option*, not only for the Allies but also for the Japanese.

After VJ Day in August, Tiger Force disbanded and we moved to Fairwood Common in South Wales for an armament practice camp before joining Nos. 19 and 64 Squadrons, first at Hethel and then Horsham St Faith near Norwich, to await the arrival of the Hornets. At this time Fighter Command practised for the victory fly-past over London and Buckingham Palace led by Group Captain Douglas Bader, the famous legless 'ace'. After Bader returned to the RAF from being a POW he received promotion to Group Captain and was made responsible for leading the victory fly-past. I never served under him but frequently saw him sitting on the bar of the mess holding court. He had many admirers and like many strong personalities he was open to criticism. Certainly Bader was a controversial figure as a result of his 'Big Wing' theories on how to fight the Battle of Britain. AVM Leigh-Mallory, the AOC 12 Group, gave Bader, then a mere squadron leader, full command of the five squadrons comprising the Duxford wing. Bader's theory was that the *Luftwaffe* should be attacked in wing strength and that he alone should control this large and unwieldy formation of aircraft in the air against the massed German bombers and fighters, without control from the sector commander. Pilots who flew in the Duxford wing said that taking-off and forming up this number of aircraft at combat altitude could take thirty minutes or more, half the endurance time of the fighters. I knew one pilot, who flew as wingman to Bader, who commented on his lack of consideration for those following him. I knew another who was a POW in the same prison camp with Bader who, despite the loss of his legs, insisted on his inclusion in all the escape plans despite the rules of the escape committee that only those actually planning an escape knew the plans. Fortunately, Bader's involvement was vetoed by the senior British officer in the camp. There were many who criticized his insularity and intolerance, but he was undoubtedly a war hero and one could not but admire his personal courage and intense determination. Both during the war and after, his example and inspiration gave encouragement to the disabled and for his services to the disabled, both military and civilian, he received a well-deserved knighthood by the Queen. While practising for the fly-past the erroneousness and egotism involved in the 'Big Wing' concept became readily apparent as the distance covered and time involved in forming up the squadrons and wings before flying up the Thames to London made Bader's 'Big Wing' theory ridiculous. The airborne control of several squadrons during an air battle becomes too inflexible and with the first 'Tally-Ho' call from Bader leading the charge, the whole Duxford wing became a confused free for all. Wing Commander Paddy Barthropp, DFC, AFC, who flew in the Battle of Britain and was a personal friend of Bader, commented that the Duxford 'Big Wing' concept as defined by Douglas Bader, was a complete mystery to him and many others because to assemble three or, in Bader's case, five squadrons in the air into a controllable wing directed against the *Luftwaffe* bombers and fighters took far too long with the *Luftwaffe* bases some 20 miles or so across the Channel. The 'Big Wing' controversy continued after the war, but the outcome was the Duxford Wing attacked the German bombers after they had dropped their bombs on their targets.

   I viewed the Battle of Britain from the ground as a school boy, so any views I have come from knowing many of those who took part in the battle and who knew the major personalities concerned. With the usual 20/20 hindsight one can blame ACM Sir Hugh Dowding, CinC Fighter Command, for allowing the 'Big Wing' controversy to blow-up to such an extent that the personal rivalry between the Group commanders seriously jeopardized the cooperation between 11 and 12 Groups in intercepting the *Luftwaffe* attacks on south-east England during a critical stage of the battle. It would appear that Dowding had the power, if not to sack Leigh-Mallory, at least to place the Duxford base within the 11 Group area or transfer some of the Duxford wing squadrons to 11 Group. This Group, commanded by AVM Park, was the vital Group for the defence of London and the south-east, and Park, the chief architect of Dowding's plan for the Battle of Britain, was Fighter Command's most able air commander. It is the opinion of many that such a move would have resulted in a more effective use of the Duxford squadrons. Following the victory over the *Luftwaffe*, while a grateful nation celebrated, the Air Ministry retired Dowding and relegated Park to Training Command. Air Marshal Keith Park's value as an air commander was later recognized when he became AOC Malta and responsible for its successful defence in 1942. He went on to become CinC RAF Middle East and then commanded the Allied Air Forces in the Burma Campaign against the Japanese. Air Marshal Sholto Douglas, Assistant Chief of Air Staff, who had chaired the infamous 'Big Wing' debate, succeeded Dowding as CinC Fighter Command and Leigh-Mallory took over command of 11 Group. This was a typical example of politics in high command and when the Air Ministry under the command of Air Chief Marshal Sir Cyril Newall, Chief of the Air Staff, published an official history of the Battle of Britain, Air Chief Marshal Sir Hugh Dowding's name as CinC Fighter Command did not appear. This is comparable to the Admiralty publishing an official history of the Battle of Trafalgar and not mentioning Nelson; or the War Office writing of the Battle of Waterloo and omitting mention of Wellington; or indeed, a history of Britain during the Second World War without mentioning Churchill. Prime Minister Winston Churchill in his speech on the outcome of the Battle of Britain, a battle of greater significance in Britain's survival than either Trafalgar or Waterloo, said, 'Never in the field of human conflict was so much owed by so many to so few.' He was surprised and shocked at the Air Council's treatment of the man who, in the opinion of most people, was largely responsible for saving Britain in 1940. Churchill in a minute to the Secretary of State for Air, Sir Archibald Sinclair, rebuked him for being associated with such maliciousness, although it should also be noted that Churchill did nothing to intercede on Dowding's behalf. ACM Dowding was the mastermind for the air defence of Britain, and the leader and inspiration of the 'Few'. The omission of Lord Dowding from the official history was indeed shameful. In war a successful commander-in-chief is often judged by the attrition advantage over the enemy. As the victors, official RAF aircraft losses during 1940 amounted to half those experienced by the *Luftwaffe*. ACM Sir Hugh Dowding can be assessed not only a successful but also an effective commander-in-chief.

The same cannot be said of Sholto Douglas as CinC Fighter Command during 1941 and 1942 when he and Leigh-Mallory, then AOC No. 11 Group, initiated a policy of mass offensive fighter sweeps called Rhubarbs over Northern France. The intent was to draw the *Luftwaffe* fighters up into combat, and when this failed to achieve the objective the fighter wings escorted formations of bombers, renamed Circuses, to induce the *Luftwaffe* to fight. This resulted in a World War One type of an air battle of attrition in favour of the *Luftwaffe*. The rationale for an aggressive fighter policy over occupied Europe regardless of casualties was an attempt to maintain a moral ascendancy over the *Luftwaffe* following its defeat in the Battle of Britain. This aggressive policy found favour with the Air Council and also with Churchill who sought to demonstrate Britain's determination to take the war against the Germans into Europe. Churchill wished to appease Soviet pressure for a second front and impress on them Britain's intention to invade Fortress Europe. This was ultimately demonstrated by the fiasco and failure of the Dieppe Raid in 1942. The RAF's offensive sweeps in 1941 and into 1942 turned the victory and the attrition advantage over the *Luftwaffe* in 1940 into an extensive and expensive defeat, with heavy aircraft losses and the aircrews either killed or taken prisoners of war. In a defensive air battle, as in the Battle of Britain, there is always a possibility to recover the aircrew shot down to continue to fight. The fighters and the bombers involved in these sweeps would have been better and more successfully employed in other areas of operations. The offensive fighter sweeps over Western Europe proved costly to the RAF, and were only superficially effective as a slight deterrent to the Germans in reinforcing their Eastern Front.

When Leigh-Mallory became CinC Fighter Command after Douglas he conducted a war game to vindicate the 'Big Wing' theory. The exercise was a fiasco and showed vital fighter airfields to be bombed before the 'Big Wings' were even airborne. As an interesting footnote to the 'Big Wing' controversy, on 15 September 1940, the day the Duxford wing claimed its highest total of German aircraft destroyed, post-war studies indicated they were more than the total losses of all German aircraft flying against the UK on that day. Indicative of this is the fact that from 8 August to

11 September 1940 during the height of the Battle of Britain, the RAF claimed 1,631 German aircraft destroyed with 584 probably destroyed, and of this total of 2,215 aircraft only 316 enemy aircraft wrecks were counted. When confronted with these figures Bader suggested the discrepancy could be found in the English Channel. The total official British figures for claims of *Luftwaffe* aircraft destroyed by the RAF and AA Command during the accepted period of the Battle of Britain were 2,698. Post-war official German quartermaster figures admitted losses due to all causes during this period as 1,733. Leigh-Mallory's shortcoming as a commander-in-chief was further exposed when as CinC Allied Expeditionary Air Forces following the Normandy landings in 1944 his assessment for the support of ground forces and his poor appreciation of bomber operations upset the respective Allied bomber chiefs and army commanders to the detriment of the land battle. ACM Sir Trafford Leigh-Mallory died in an air crash in 1944 en route to taking up his appointment as Air CinC Southeast Asia, and his replacement was his old nemesis, Sir Keith Park.

Group Captain Douglas Bader, DSO, DFC, was without doubt the most famous RAF fighter pilot of the Second World War, despite the loss of both legs in a flying accident before the war. This was in part due to an admiration for his example of willpower and sheer determination in persuading the Air Ministry to let him fly fighter aircraft again when war broke out in 1939. To me, Bader demonstrated an insatiable desire to emulate the Italian Air Marshal Balbo, after whom large formations of aircraft were named, in controlling *airy navies grappling in the central blue*, and as such was an ideal choice to lead the Victory fly-past over London. The fly-past appeared very impressive when viewed from the ground but in the air it was hard, sweaty and tedious work as the many squadrons and wings passed overhead in close formation. Bader may have had his critics but he was respected by fellow countrymen and foes alike. This was exemplified when the *Luftwaffe* permitted an RAF aircraft to drop a new pair of artificial legs onto an airfield in France after Bader was shot down in 1941. Although Bader was the best known of the disabled RAF pilots during the war, he was not alone as several other pilots used the Bader precedent in persuading the Air Ministry to let them continue to fly disabled.

I knew four other pilots in Fighter Command who flew fighters without the use of one or two legs and they continued to fly jet fighter aircraft after the war, thereby avoiding the very significant problem of controlling propeller torque. Hughie Edwards and Tommy Burn each flew with one leg, and Roy Morant and Colin Hodgkinson each lost the lower part of both legs. All these pilots shared similar characteristics in being strong personalities with great determination in developing powerful upper body strength as a compensation for their disability. They were also consummate exponents in the art of gamesmanship to even the odds against them. Bader was a keen golfer and played a good game despite his two artificial legs, and overawed those playing with him by insisting on walking the course and rejecting any form of assistance. Edwards and Burn were both keen squash players and would demoralize those playing against them with a very aggressive approach to the game. Their specialty was to go crashing to the floor while attempting, for a disabled player, an impossible return of the ball. This had a daunting effect on any opponent showing sympathy for or a deference to their disability. Morant became the CO of a Vampire jet fighter squadron and led the squadron formation aerobatics team. Hodgkinson had an interesting escape following a forced landing in a Spitfire when the engine crushed his two artificial legs below the amputations, trapping him in the cockpit of the burning aircraft. He was able to undo his harness and crawl out of the wreckage unhurt to fly again.

Squadron Leader James MacLachlan, DSO, DFC, was another example of an indomitable spirit after the loss of his left arm while in combat with Bf-109s over Malta in 1941. A short list of unforgettable characters I met while flying in the RAF would certainly include James MacLachlan, together with Graham Pearson, for their approach to operations that in the Royal Navy would be described as the 'Nelson Touch'. Douglas Bader would also figure on this list for his unquenchable determination and personal courage. My list would also include my boss on 41 Squadron, Dusty Miller, for his exceptional leadership; and it would probably conclude with an American, Lonnie Moore, while in Korea; for his dedicated combative attitude with exceptional piloting ability.

Although we still waited re-equipping with the DH Hornet, the Mustangs returned to US control under the Lend-Lease Agreement. The total production of the North American P-51 Mustang was approximately 15,000 aircraft built either in Los Angeles, California, or in Dallas, Texas. As a temporary measure we became a Spitfire IX squadron, equipped from a squadron converting to the Spitfire XIV. With the advent of the Spitfire IX some of the drawbacks associated with previous models were remedied with the addition of a second radiator under the left wing, which removed the engine overheating problems associated with lengthy taxiing. A Merlin 61 engine with a four bladed propeller replaced the three bladed propeller and increased the power to 1,650 hp, the top speed to 408 mph, the rate of climb to 4,800 ft/min, and the service ceiling to 43,000 feet. Although the Merlin Spitfire IX was nicer to fly than the more powerful Griffon engine Spitfire XIV, whose propeller revolved in the opposite direction to a Merlin Spitfire, it could not compare with the Spitfire XIV in climb performance and its maximum speed of around 450 mph. The Spitfire V was the most numerous of the variants, but from a pilot's viewpoint the Spitfire IX was the ultimate and by far the nicest Spitfire to fly ever built. No other Spitfire could compare with it in terms of manoeuvrability and the sheer joy of flying. In returning to the Spitfire I now found myself criticizing the aircraft in comparison with the Mustang. After a while at Horsham St Faith we moved north to a pre-war bomber base at Linton-on-Ouse in Yorkshire. The Hornets started to arrive together with a couple of Mosquitoes for the twin-engine conversion. The Hornets were fast and at their best at low level. However, there were many problems and my impression was that despite the confidence and safety aspects of having two engines in the Hornet, the Mustang would have served us better on Tiger Force had we escorted the bombers to Japan. When the Hornets eventually arrived in the Far East they experienced problems with engine over-heating, together with airframe problems associated with the wood and glue construction under the tropical conditions. Had the war continued into 1946, the continued development of the P-51D would have resulted in a much lighter P-51F or Mustang V with a more powerful US built Packard Merlin 100 of 2,218 hp, a modified leading edge to the wing, a modified landing gear, and a longer cockpit canopy resulted in a slightly different appearance to the aircraft. The P-51F or Mustang V had a design speed of close to 500 mph, with a greatly improved rate of climb, and a range of 1,200 miles. It would certainly run rings around any other propeller aircraft at the time, although still inferior to the jet fighters starting to emerge. Further developments of the Mustang resulted in the Twin Mustang P-82 with a range of 4,000 miles that saw service as a ground attack and night fighter during the Korean War.

It was about this time I thought it might be fun to do the Air-Sea Rescue course at Calshot in the Solent. This was an old flying-boat base in a unique situation overlooking Southampton Water. It became famous as the base for the pre-war RAF High Speed Flight during the Schneider Trophy races. It was at that time a base for the Air-Sea Rescue Service operating in the English Channel, with a squadron of pre-war Supermarine Walrus amphibians and its wartime replacement, the Sea Otter. The Walrus was an amphibian biplane powered by a pusher 775 hp Bristol Pegasus engine, with a speed of 135 mph and a range of 600 miles. The Sea Otter differed from the Walrus with a conventional propeller powered by a Bristol Mercury engine of 800 hp. Each aircraft carried a crew of three or four and both handled like a big, heavy Tiger Moth. There was also a squadron of high-speed RAF Thorneycraft rescue launches. We travelled from the mess to the hangers and slipway by a small gauge railway that ran the mile long length of the Calshot Spit.

We started with lectures by an unfortunate flight lieutenant we called 'Captain Cuttle', whose task it was to acquaint a bunch of airlubbers with matters nautical. There is of course an affinity between water and air, but this was not apparent as aircrew from Bomber, Fighter and Coastal commands struggled with rules of the sea, ship's rigging, and the various types of rope and knots. Our task was first to learn how to survive in a fragile emergency dinghy on an angry and unforgiving sea, and then to handle and sail the airborne lifeboat. The Airborne Lifeboat Mk 1A owed much of its wartime design and development to Uffa Fox, the celebrated designer of many planing dinghies and, later in 1947, the famous International Flying Fifteen planing keelboat. The lifeboat had a length of 23½ ft, a beam of 5½ ft, a draught of 1 ft, and a weight of 1,600 lb. The construction was of mahogany frames with a mahogany chine hull. On contact with the water the three parachutes attached amidships released, as two rockets in the bow fired two drogue sea anchors, and two rockets amidships fired lifelines. The lifeboat was equipped with a small Bermuda type foresail and mainsail with a drop rudder and centreboard. In addition to the survival gear, rations, signalling flares and rockets, the lifeboat carried oars and two small 4 hp Britannia outboard motors giving the lifeboat a theoretical range of 100 miles. It also carried an emergency radio, and as our floatation waistcoats were named after a famous film star because of its generous chest measurement so too the emergency radio, which was shaped to be held between the knees and cranked by hand to provide the electrical power, was also referred to in the feminine gender. The airborne lifeboat with its large floatation chambers fore and aft, small centreboard and small Bermuda sloop rig, experienced considerable leeway in the slightest breeze and handled like a Thames barge under jury rig. As I had some sailing experience I had an advantage over some of my other airborne colleagues who found its handling and the terminology involved a new experience. After a series of lectures, Captain Cuttle had his just revenge when he had us dumped into dinghies set adrift in the Solent. The airborne lifeboats had a frustrating inability to sail upwind as we tried to progress against wind and tide in broad reaches. However, they did provide a considerably better survivability factor than the aircraft dinghies. In the days before immersion suits it was cold and very wet work and we were grateful not to be in the Merchant Navy sailing the Atlantic convoys. The only consolation resulting from battling the elements in the Solent was the regular issue of the Royal Navy rum ration. The Bomber Command aircraft dinghies carried rum among the emergency rations, but in Fighter Command we had to make do with some nourishing Horlicks Malted Milk tablets.

The pilots on the course had an opportunity to fly and I had several flights with the Walrus and the Sea Otter. The latter was a bit more powerful but the Walrus handled better. As a result I had a great deal of respect for the air-sea rescue pilots. We taxied from the hanger to the slipway and slid down into the water and as the nose of the aircraft plunged into the waves I saw green water through the windscreen and water poured in through gaps in the cockpit canopy. We were usually quite wet by the time we got airborne. We opened the throttle and ploughed through the waves while rocking the elevators back and forth to unstick the hull and get the aircraft onto the step to get airborne. Once airborne the aircraft was cold and draughty and the noise made conversation difficult. The slow wallowing and noisy Sea Otter was in very marked contrast to my sleek, fast, comfortable, manoeuvrable and beautiful Mustang. However, the Walrus and Sea Otter provided a valiant and invaluable service to the aircrew of Bomber, Fighter and Coastal commands, saving many lives in the process. Getting the aircraft back to the slipway was quite an experience as when the aircraft touched down on anything but a flat calm sea the impact of the waves against the riveted hull made it feel and sound as if the hull keel had parted company, and once again we had a salt water shower. We taxied to the slipway, lowered the wheels and were hauled up the slipway as water drained out of the hull. In contrast to getting wet on our nautical exercises, our flying duties did not entitle us to the rum ration. My first attempt at a take-off was interesting as due to the distraction of the salt water shower I just opened up the power and no matter how I tried to get the aircraft up on the step we just seemed to dig deeper into the waves. After ploughing down the Solent for a while I asked my instructor, 'Are we ever going to get this sea-pig airborne?' He replied, 'Not until we raise the wheels!' This performance no doubt confirmed his view of fighter pilots. One of my instructors won a well-deserved DFC in a Walrus by landing to pick up a bomber crew within range of the German guns on the French coast. Despite the rough seas, the crew managed to get the bomber crew aboard but with the rough sea and extra weight the pilot could not take-off and he taxied back towards the English coast being fired at from the shore and chased by a German E-boat, until it was driven off by some RAF fighters. The bomber crew were eventually off-loaded into an RAF rescue launch and the Walrus was able to take-off and return to Calshot. Our course finale and graduation was the live drop of an airborne lifeboat by a Warwick aircraft that we sailed back to Calshot. It was a thoroughly interesting and enjoyable course for most of us, especially me, and we gratefully acknowledged our appreciation and thanks to the long suffering Captain Cuttle and his crew. The experience certainly stood me in good stead later on when I was involved in some ocean sailing races. An additional good aspect of the course was the provision of some ex-*Luftwaffe* sailing boats as war reparations for leisure sailing. These were later presented to the RAF Yacht Club in the Hamble River, where I sailed them again after joining the club.

Yorkshire is one of my favourite counties and Linton-on-Ouse was a comfortable pre-war base conveniently sited between York Minster and Harrogate; so I enjoyed my stay in Yorkshire. The living conditions and the flying were good as we converted onto the Hornet without any problems. I enjoyed flying the aircraft and the Mosquito was also nice to fly but not to the same extent as the Hornet with its greater power-to-weight ratio. The de Havilland Mosquito was one of the fastest and most versatile aircraft of the Second World War, and it was used in a variety of roles as an all-weather fighter, an attack fighter-bomber, a tactical bomber, a pathfinder bomber, a conversion trainer, and for photographic reconnaissance. My experience of the aircraft was limited to the trainer version in flying the Mk III, manufactured in Britain, and the Mk XXIV, manufactured in Canada. The various marks of Mosquito handled quite differently depending on their respective roles, and this also applied to the country of manufacture. The Canadian built aircraft were heavier both in structure and in their handling characteristics. The Mosquito cockpit was cramped for the crew of two, resulting in considerable problems when endeavouring to bale out of the aircraft through the entry hatch under G conditions, or evacuating the aircraft through the canopy hatch after ditching. The pilot's field of view over the nose was good, although restricted to the side by the Merlin engines and to the rear where the high speed of the Mosquito offered some protection. One particularly irksome design feature in the cockpit was the location of the fuel cocks behind the seat. The Mosquito with its Merlin engines inherited some overheating problems from the early marks of the Spitfire while stationary or taxiing. During take-off there was a marked swing to the left and the aircraft had a high critical safety airspeed of 200 mph before climbing away in order to maintain directional control in the event of a single engine failure on take-off. The small rudder area and low slung engines produced some loss of directional control with heavy rudder loads when manoeuvring at low airspeeds. The aileron control could vary from light to heavy depending on the version and mark of Mosquito. Although aerobatics were possible these were normally limited to rolls, but precise slow rolls were not easy as the aircraft tended to lose airspeed and fall out of the manoeuvre when inverted. Consequently, it was more usual to barrel-roll the Mosquito to maintain height and airspeed. Stalling was straight forward but spinning was avoided due to the lack of rudder effect at low airspeeds. Generally the Mosquito handled well with few flying problems, although flying with one engine caused heavy rudder loads, especially when manoeuvring at low airspeeds; and engine failures while flying the Mosquito were not uncommon. It was particularly important when carrying out a single engine approach and landing that the airspeed did not fall below 160 mph when below 1,000 feet until committed to the landing. It was impossible to overshoot the Mosquito on one engine without sufficient height to build up to safety airspeed in excess of 160 mph, and ignoring this crucial factor resulted in many fatalities with these handling characteristics of the aircraft. Although the Mosquito was considered to be a 'pilot's airplane', with its diverse demands it could be unforgiving but, pilots liked it and it was a very remarkable aircraft.

There were less problems flying the Hornet Mk. 1, it being a scaled down version of the Mosquito with a greater power to weight ratio and a lower wing loading. The layout of the cockpit of the Hornet was an improvement on the Mosquito from a pilot's viewpoint, although still in typical British fashion it was compact to the extent of being a snug fit. It had excellent all-round visibility apart from some downward restriction of view from the large under slung Merlin engines. The Hornet handled very well from take-off to landing. The contra-rotating Merlin engines ensured that there was no engine torque induced swing on take-off. The rate of climb was excellent and the single engine performance was very good presenting few problems, apart from care required during asymmetric low speed handling due to the small rudder design inherited from the Mosquito. Stalling the aircraft was straightforward, although the small rudder area restricted spinning on the aircraft. The provision of a dorsal fin extension with modification to improve the elevator control arrived on the Hornet Mk. 3. Aerobatics were a delight and one pilot on the wing added a signature manoeuvre to his demonstration aerobatics display with a high speed low level pass with both engines stopped and the propellers feathered. He then pulled the aircraft up into a climbing roll before restarting one engine, unfeathering the propeller and finishing his display with a single engine approach and landing. This manoeuvre certainly drew attention and exhibited an implicit faith in the de Havilland Hornet's reliability in restarting an engine in flight. Operationally, if taken out of its main low level strike role the Hornet's handling performance deteriorated with altitude and it was not suited to a high altitude escort and air combat role.

I was by now a flight lieutenant and no longer flew the wingman positions but led sections and occasional flights. Nearby we had some rough shooting available, and not far to the west lay James Herriot country and the delightful Yorkshire Dales where the upper reaches of the Wharfe and the Skirfare passed through an area of magical beauty as the rivers flowed through limestone valleys cut by glaciers. On cloudless days of summer it was a naturalist's nirvana as the wild brown trout tested the dry fly angler to the utmost, but in winter it was quite another matter. So it was with some surprise and annoyance that one day in 1946 my flying instructor's 'A' category rating caught up with me as my card popped out of some dusty file in an Air Ministry 'P' Staff office for a flying instructor at Oxford University Air Squadron. I had cursed this diversion in my flying career, for, although I had achieved my ambition to get on fighters, it had retarded any hopes I might have had of being a distinguished fighter pilot by arriving on a fighter squadron near the end of the war. Added to this was the fact that the war ended before I had acquired any seniority of rank. I protested the posting but to no avail and I left the inspiring moors and dales of Yorkshire for the dreaming spires of Oxford. I now had the rare experience of flying with both Cambridge and Oxford University Air Squadrons. To misquote Shaw *A nice sort of place Oxford, for people that like that sort of place. They teach you to be a gentleman there. At Cambridge they teach you to be an engineer or such like!*

For the next two years I was away from fighters and although I missed the flying there were compensations as I readjusted to flying the Tiger Moth again, with some additional flying on Harvards and twin-engine Oxfords during the summer camp. Although annoyed at being taken off fighters, I enjoyed my time at Oxford as many members of the squadron were experienced RAF pilots from the war. I met up with an old friend from my Spitfire days studying forestry who while I joined a Mustang squadron he joined a Spitfire IX squadron. On his first operational mission on the squadron flying wingman on a large fighter sweep over France they were intercepted by a large formation of ME-109Gs and in the confusion of the dog fight, while trying to look in all directions at once and at the same time follow his leader, he failed to see an ME-109 heading straight at him. The German pilot was also a new hand and presumably looking everywhere but ahead of his aircraft and the result was a head-on collision. He did not know much about the collision recalling only a big bang and the jarring impact. The next thing he recalled was dangling from his parachute with a broken arm and leg. He landed in a field and passed out to wake up in a *Luftwaffe* hospital. He noticed another injured German pilot in the bed next to him who turned out to be the ME-109 pilot he had collided with, and whose experience and injuries were similar. They became quite good ward mates and he said the Germans treated him well while he was in the *Luftwaffe* hospital. The two tyro fighter pilots used to take walks on their crutches together and have races along the hospital ward. When the Germans decided he could walk without his crutches they transferred him to Dulag Luft for interrogation, and from there he moved to Stulag Luft III before being transferred to a POW camp in Poland. In the prison camp anyone volunteering for camp fatigues was castigated by his fellow prisoners as a collaborator. He found that the German guards called for prisoners to collect their laundry and take it to a nearby concentration camp for women who would do the washing. The Germans issued bars of soap for the washing and he made sure that he obtained a double ration. Soap being a very desirable commodity in the camp his extra supply made him popular with the Polish inmates. In addition, being young and reasonably good looking, he found himself in demand and thus able to be selective. Taking advantage of the situation he negotiated favours in return for his extra bars of soap, as well as ensuring a good service for his own laundry. Some of his fellow POWs could not figure out why he often had a smile on his face when returning to the camp. His explanation to the escape committee for his apparent collabora- tion was that he was planning to use his exit pass out of the camp as a means to escape. The committee accepted his explanation but before having to report back on the extent of his plans the Russian advance threatened the camp and the Germans marched the prisoners-of-war westwards into Germany until the advancing British troops rescued them.

The Oxford University Air Squadron had its headquarters in town with gardens backing on to the Isis, a tributary of the Thames. It was a pleasant spot and popular with the undergraduates as the mess served excellent food at very reasonable prices. Initially, we operated our aircraft from a grass airfield at Shillingford, where I had instructed during the war. Shortly after my arrival the squadron aircraft moved to Abingdon, a wartime bomber base that in 1946 became a Transport Command base operating C-47 Dakota aircraft. We flew our Tiger Moths from the grass areas of the airfield operating from one of the pre-war hangers. Scattered around the airfield in dispersal sites were many abandoned aircraft from the war including several bomber versions of the Mosquito. These aircraft remained unattended for about two years until some mechanics arrived to service the engines and the aircraft were refuelled. As the Mosquitoes became serviceable they were flown to Palestine by mercenary pilots attached to the fledgling Israeli air force. Not surprisingly some did not make it to Palestine and among those that did not complete the journey was 'Buzz' or 'Screwball' Beurling, one of the top scoring Allied fighter pilots against the Axis air forces, and Canada's highest scoring ace of the Second World War. I met Beurling briefly when he was a gunnery instructor at the Central Gunnery School, but he was not an endearing character being unpopular with both the RAF and the RCAF. He was very much a 'rebel without cause' but he was a naturally talented fighter pilot with an instinctive ability at deflection shooting, although he did not have the inclination or patience to impart this skill to others. When the RCAF demobilized him after the war he was unable to adjust to civil life and after a period of 'living rough' offered his flying services to the Israelis in 1948. He died on a ferry flight from England to Palestine when his aircraft crashed after take-off following a transit stop at Rome International Airport.

During the university summer break all members of the air squadron attended a mandatory two-week camp at an airfield near the coast, and I have amusing memories of both the camps I attended. Apart from taking all our Tiger Moths to camp the RAF provided a Harvard trainer and a twin engine Airspeed Oxford for advanced training during the camp. In my first year at Oxford the camp was at Shoreham-on-Sea in Sussex near the seaside resort of Brighton. Shoreham airport was a small civil grass airfield and was home to the Miles Aircraft Company and the South Coast Flying Club. During our stay the airport organized a weekend air show and flying display. I was asked to demonstrate the Tiger Moth, and an undergraduate pupil asked to fly with me during the display. As he was a member of the squadron indemnification was not required! After take-off I made a low pass with a steep turn around the spectators, before pulling up for a couple of slow rolls across the airfield. Climbing up to demonstrate a loop, I continued into a second loop, rolling out on top of the loop to put the aircraft into a spin. I delayed my recovery as long as I dared in order to make a steep dive and low pass alongside the crowd to finish the show. My rear seat passenger had remained silent during the whole display and as I prepared for a tight, side-slipping, short landing close to spectators I laughingly called out to him, 'How did you enjoy that? I bet 50 per cent of the people down there thought we would have an accident!' A faint voice filtered through to me from the speaking tube, '50 per cent of the people up here have!'

The second summer camp was at RAF Chivenor, an RAF flying training airfield on the North Devon coast at the mouth of the River Taw, near Barnstable. On our last weekend at the camp, three ex-RAF undergraduate friends and I decided to play golf at Westward Ho, a famous links course on the south side of the Taw estuary. The weather was sunny and warm as we set off in two cars for the 40 miles drive via the towns of Barnstable and Bideford. After the golf game that my partner and I won, despite protests of cheating, we returned to Bideford for the dinner to be paid for by the losers. Bideford is an interesting small town at the junction of the Torridge and Taw rivers with a long history as a naval shipyard. We had a convivial evening and on leaving the pub at closing time, someone suggested skinny-dipping from the beach in Bideford Bay. Not for a moment did I suspect any skulduggery but while the two of us were swimming we noticed that the other two had left the beach, and arriving back at the car naked and wet we discovered they had departed taking our clothes and shoes with them. My car at the time was a rare 1937 Auburn roadster that was a potent automobile even ten years after its manufacture. It had a big straight eight cylinders Lycoming engine giving immense low-end torque that resulted in acceleration over a quarter mile that was bettered at the time only by the 1938 supercharged Cord. Regrettably, this performance was not matched by the Bendix cable operated brakes that had to be finely adjusted otherwise the Auburn could become lethal in the wet. This may be the reason for my father's generosity in providing the more suitable alternative of a new MG. The Auburn had an interesting gear shift, similar to that on the French Delage and Delahaye: the Cotal electric 'H' box that could be switched off when not in use. In the event of an electrical failure there was provision for a standby manual gear shift that was inserted into the floor. This feature was to prove a significant factor in subsequent events to follow. Although the weather was fine we had a cold, draughty and uncomfortable 40 miles drive back to Chivenor. There was little traffic on the road but in passing through Bideford and Barnstable I had occasionally to stop at traffic lights and I feared that some diligent upholder of the law would see us 'au naturel' and charge us with indecent exposure in public. I had visions of a friendly bobby leaning over the car to say, "ello, 'ello, wot 'ave we 'ere – a couple of Lord Godivas?!' Fortunately, the only surprised reaction occurred from the service police on guard duty when we passed through the camp gate. By the time we arrived at the mess we were certainly dry but cold and shivering with goose bumps forming on goose flesh. I found my belongings in my room and while soaking in a hot bath I contemplated my revenge.

This was to occur unintentionally on the instigator of the prank shortly after our return to Oxford. Our tormentor returned by air and I returned via London in order to visit a girl friend. I arrived in Oxford the following day to be greeted by my friend in a very agitated state to tell me that he and his wife had been awakened at five o'clock in the morning by the local police, accompanied by two detectives from the London CID, to inquire as to his whereabouts and activity over the past twenty-four hours. Although his wife was able to provide an acceptable alibi for him, he wondered but said nothing regarding any possible involvement on my part as the police did not offer any explanation when producing his service hat for identification. I had borrowed the hat after losing my own while at Chivenor. The hat was found in a stolen car used in a major robbery, and as it had his name marked clearly inside (shades of the Cumming's affair(!)) he was implicated in the police investigation. I assumed the thieves were foiled in an attempt to steal my car for a fast getaway by the unusual gear shift arrangement and looked elsewhere. They probably took the hat to distract and divert the police after the robbery. I was impressed at the speed by which the police traced my friend through the Air Ministry to his digs in Oxford. I gave a statement to the police explaining the presence of the hat that satisfied them and they returned the hat to its rightful owner. I then sent a suitable and contrite floral apology to the wife for the shock and embarrassment she experienced. There were no further repercussions from the authorities and this seemingly casual incident brought home to both of us the wisdom of the advice Polonius gave Laertes in *Hamlet, Neither a borrower nor lender be: for loan oft loses both itself and friend: and borrowing dulls the edge of husbandry.* Shortly after this episode my father gave me my first new car, an MG-TD, a less lethal vehicle than the Auburn.

During my stay at Oxford I flew some trips to Vienna in the Dakota as supernumerary pilot and it was an interesting experience. This was my first visit to Vienna and I hoped to see something of this fine city, but as it was divided into four zones occupied by British, American, French and Russian troops this became difficult. Fortunately, the British occupied the most interesting part of the city, with officers accommodated in the Sacher Hotel near the Opera House. The Allied troops used military script as payment in authorized places and it could not be used in the Austrian economy. The Austrian schilling became devalued with people carrying bundles of the old currency into the banks and coming out with just hand-fuls in exchange. We solved the problem of entertaining ourselves, and at the same time supporting the local economy, by carrying a parachute bag filled with coffee or cocoa that fetched a good price on the black market. This was of course illegal but we could only use the Austrian schillings in Vienna and they could not be exchanged for any other currency. We therefore took just enough to cover our expenses when visiting the restaurants and night clubs that were prohibitively expensive. This was the only way in which we could get out of the Officers' Club and entertain ourselves during the couple of days we spent in Vienna. We did not really consider these transactions black market (as with penicillin in the film *The Third Man*) and we considered the transactions were more that of a faintly grey market. We attempted to delude ourselves that we were doing the deprived Austrians a favour, but, as the saying goes, there is no way to be half pregnant! Unfortunately, in the process of enjoying ourselves I picked up a souvenir that I could have done without during one of my Dakota trips to Vienna. I have never been airsick in my life and shortly after a trip to Vienna I started to feel quite ill while flying. I fought this off for a couple of days until one morning while shaving I saw a gaunt yellow face I did not recognize looking back at me with matching yellow eyes from the mirror. My suspicions of jaundice, or to be specifically more medically correct, infectious hepatitis became apparent when on relieving myself I saw what appeared to be Guinness. The doctor shipped me off to the RAF hospital at Wroughton where I spent a couple of weeks before being released with strict instructions to consume no alcohol for at least six months. It was interesting that the majority of the injuries in the RAF hospital were not from flying accidents but from motor cycle accidents, mess games and rugby football. One squadron leader in the psychiatric ward appeared perfectly normal to me, despite completing three tours of bomber operations including one on pathfinders. His problem arose while instructing at a bomber OTU when he became obsessed at losing sight of the airfield and would not leave the circuit. I should have thought that a rest from flying in some ground job would solve his maladjustment. However, after several days of hourly sessions with the hospital's psychiatric staff, they diagnosed his mental ailment as stemming from being locked in a cupboard for some hours when he was a child. It seemed to me that some of the psychiatric staff could have benefited from the odd trip with Bomber Command to the Ruhr or Berlin.

During my time on the squadron I had one flying accident that occurred while landing in a Tiger Moth. However, I was not injured and the only injury to my companion was to his pride. The CO of the squadron was Wing Commander John Embling, DSO, a pre-war graduate of the university and a very experienced bomber pilot during the war. I liked Embling but he did not do much flying during his command and one day he suggested we carry out some simulated instrument flying in preparation for an instrument rating check. He acted as safety pilot from the front seat while I carried out instrument flying under a hood covering the rear cockpit. We returned to Abingdon to change seats and I found I could not release the hood so that I was unable to see what transpired. Embling attempted to land as close to our dispersal as possible and to do so had to pass over our hanger. He certainly succeeded beyond his expectations making the closest touch down to our dispersal ever achieved on the squadron. He made a very tight power off descending turn at low speed but neglected to take into account the strong wind blowing at the time. The aircraft hit a wind shear over the hanger and we dropped like a stone from about fifty feet. We just missed landing on the hanger roof as we ploughed into the grass beside the perimeter track. The impact was very severe and fortunately there was no fire. When I extracted myself from the wreckage I saw the propeller and wheels were sheared off and the upper wings had folded down from the middle leaving the fuel tank hanging precariously over Embling's head and held on by just one bolt from one of the wing struts. Embling remained motionless like Damocles in a state of shock and as I clambered over to him I noticed fuel from the tank dripping down on top of him. A single spark would probably have consumed both of us in flames. I asked him if he was alright and that he must get out of the cockpit quickly as there was a danger of fire but he made no reply. I called to members of the squadron who, not having far to run, had arrived on the scene before the crash crew and we got him away from the wreckage As it turned out Embling was only bruised and shaken but the accident was very embarrassing for him and I felt very sorry for him. As I was blind for the whole manoeuvre there was little I could contribute to the accident report as clearly the cause was pilot error and the less said the better other than to emphasize the strength of the wind. Embling was a very experienced pilot but at the time of the accident he was not in current flying practice on light aircraft, especially under windy conditions. He left us shortly after the accident and I heard later that he was killed while on a Meteor jet conversion course. He was a victim of the deadly 'phantom diver' peculiarity of the Meteor when during an approach to land if the pilot selected his wheels down with the air brakes out the aircraft rolled on its back with insufficient height in which to recover. Embling's replacement was a Wing Commander Christopher Foxley-Norris, DSO, also a pre-war graduate of the university and a Battle of Britain fighter pilot. He commanded one of the Mosquito squadrons on the Banff strike wing while 65 Squadron was escorting them to Norway. He went on to become an Air Chief Marshal and I met him again in Singapore after I retired from the RAF when he commanded the Far East Air Force.

Apart from my touch of Blue Danube hepatitis, I enjoyed my two years at Oxford and in 1948 in response to a request to return to a fighter squadron the Air Ministry posted me to No. 601 'County of London' RAuxAF Squadron at Hendon, in the north-west London area. The 'P' Staff no doubt felt they had met me halfway in that I could serve a double purpose in having a flying instructor's rating. An auxiliary squadron had three regular RAF officers on the squadron establishment with two General Duties officers and one engineer officer, with the appropriate staff all reporting to an auxiliary commanding officer. The squadron pilots and most of the engineering and administrative staff came from the auxiliary air force. My duties were to act as temporary squadron CO during the week then handing over to the auxiliary commanding officer at weekends. I took over from an ex-Battle of Britain pilot, Flight Lieutenant 'Chips' Carpenter, DFC. The squadron flew the Spitfire XVI, which was similar to the Spitfire IX but with a Packard Merlin 266 engine giving 1,705 hp. The aircraft had the clipped wing for low-level operation with a 75 gallon (Imp.) fuel tank installed behind the pilot. The Spitfire XVI with a full fuselage tank was unstable and unpleasant to fly, especially during mock dog fights. The Spitfire and the Mustang when flown with a full fuselage tank responded in a similar manner by tucking into a turn and for this reason for normal flying we never flew with more than 30 gallons in the rear fuselage tank. A bubble canopy replaced the sliding canopy giving much improved visibility. The aircraft armament was two 20 mm cannon and two 0.5 in Browning machine-gun. Hendon was a famous pre-war fighter base but during the war due to its small size within a built-up urban area it became an air communications base. We shared it with No. 604 'County of Middlesex' RAuxAF Squadron and a communications squadron operating Avro Ansons. The runway was a short 800 yards with a high railway embankment at one end and two pre-war hangers at the other. The airfield, being surrounded by housing, was not suitable for the operation of modern fighter aircraft. At other RAuxAF airfields, such as Biggin Hill to the South, there were longer unobstructed runways suitable for operating Griffon engine Spitfire XXIIs. The Spitfire XXII was a development from the Spitfire XXI and fitted with a bubble canopy. It became the mainstay of the Royal Auxiliary Air Force until re-equipped with Vampire or Meteor jet fighters. The Spitfire XXI was an inferior development of the Spitfire XIV: the best and fastest of all the Griffon Spitfires. However, we only had the more pleasant to fly Merlin Spitfire XVI, and before allowing a new pilot to take-off and land the Spitfire at Hendon, I would give him some circuits flying from the back seat of a Harvard. The new pilot would then fly the Harvard to Fighter Command's communication airfield at Bovingdon, to the north of London, with me following in the Spitfire. The new pilot would fly some circuits in the Spitfire landing on a measured length of the runway similar to that of Hendon. If the landings were satisfactory he would fly the Spitfire back for his first landing at Hendon. A few pilots over-shot the short runway without serious consequences to the surrounding housing; but on one occasion an Anson from the communications squadron had an engine fail on take-off and it crashed into a shopping area in Edgeware killing the crew of two and three civilians.

By this time the development of the Spitfire from the Mark I to the Mark XXIV saw the engine power and fuel capacity doubled, and the weight of the aircraft increased by 60 per cent. The Spitfire became 25 per cent faster and it could fly 35 per cent higher, climbing nearly twice as fast. To achieve these figures there were many changes to the airframe and engine. The use of the bigger Griffon engine brought about many changes of propeller ending with either a five-blade or a six-blade contra-rotating propeller. The direction of rotation also changed so that the Griffon engine Spitfires swung to the right on take-off. The nose section was strengthened to accommodate the larger, heavier and more powerful Griffon engine. The tail section required substantial enlargement for the more powerful engine and larger propeller, with further strengthening to the fuselage. The addition of more amour plating and the metal covered flying controls added further weight. These changes, together with a wider track and taller undercarriage to allow for a larger propeller, resulted in very different aircraft with inferior handling compared with the Merlin Spitfires. The differences in the Merlin Spitfires and the Griffon Spitfires were such that the last marks of the aircraft should have been renamed. This did not occur until the final version of the Spitfire emerged with a redesigned laminar-flow wing and was renamed the Spiteful, but by this time the jet fighter rendered both the Spitfire and the Spiteful obsolescent. The Spiteful, although being capable of nearly 500 mph, had a handling that was markedly inferior to the Griffon Spitfires and it did not enter squadron service.

The Auxiliaries were the weekend air force, as most had civil jobs during the week. They spent their weekends flying with one midweek night at the town headquarters and a mandatory two weeks at summer camp. No. 601 'County of London' Squadron was probably the most dilettante of the auxiliary squadrons with the reputation of being 'The Millionaires Squadron'. The pilots were not millionaires but certainly from the life-style of some and the expensive cars parked outside the mess one might get that impression. The squadron had some unique idiosyncrasies such as scarlet silk linings to the uniform tunics, always worn with the top button undone, and scarlet socks. It also numbered some well known and even famous personalities in its membership. The first post-war commanding officer of the squadron was a pre-war member: Group Captain the Hon. Max Aitkin, DSO, DFC, son of Lord Beaverbrook and an MP. He had a distinguished war record as a Hurricane pilot during the Battle of Britain, and commanded the Mosquito strike wing at Banff during my time at Peterhead. The 'A' flight commander was Group Captain Hugh 'Cocky' Dundas, DSO, DFC, a Battle of Britain Spitfire pilot and the youngest to reach his rank at the age of twenty-three while with Desert Air Force in Italy. The 'B' flight commander was Wing Commander Paul Richey, DFC, a Hurricane pilot in France and author of 'Fighter Pilot'. Another senior pilot was Wing Commander Gordon Hughes, DSO, DFC, a photo-reconnaissance pilot. A distinguished barrister acted as the squadron adjutant and a well-known Harley Street specialist as the squadron doctor. The majority of the squadron pilots had war-time experience up to the rank of squadron leader, and it was not an easy task to maintain some sense of order, discipline and purpose with a bunch of opinionated civilians bent on making the squadron a superior private flying club for visiting friends around the country. An attempt to conduct some serious ground studies at the midweek gathering and dining-in night at town headquarters usually resulted in energetic mess games following the dinner. There was slight resentment by some regulars against the auxiliaries but usually this only resulted in some banter, and there existed a sort of university 'Town and Gown' atmosphere between the two groups. The main reason why the auxiliaries devoted all their free time to the squadron was a love of flying and nostalgia for the RAF without the service restrictions. For some the time required for the squadron became too much either from family or business pressures, and one of these was Max Aitken who left the squadron and gave up his parliamentary seat to take over the running of the Beaverbrook Press. The command of the squadron passed to 'Cocky' Dundas during a summer camp spent at Tangmere on the Sussex coast. It was here that he had flown with Douglas Bader before it became the Central Fighter Establishment; although the CFE eventually moved north to West Raynham in Norfolk.

During the year spent at Hendon, I had one interesting diversion while competing in the Daily Express Air Races at what is now Birmingham Airport. For the auxiliary trophy each squadron entered two aircraft and as the competing aircraft varied from Vampire jets to various Merlin and Griffon Spitfires, it was a handicapped race. This put Paul Richey and me, representing 601 Squadron with our Spitfire XVIs, ahead of the field at the start. I think for a brief period of the race around the pylons the commentator announced I was in the lead but, before I reached the finish line, two Vampire jets and a couple of Griffon Spitfires relegated me to fifth place.

My only incident on the squadron occurred while air testing a Spitfire when I had to carry out a forced landing. After completing the air test with everything appearing satisfactory I decided to do some aerobatics, and while pulling out of a loop the propeller started to speed up causing the engine to vibrate. Realizing that the propeller blades were about to part company with the aircraft I shut down the engine before it failed, and looked for somewhere to land the aircraft. Fortunately, the weather was fine with only some scattered cumulus cloud. I recognized the town of Banbury below and remembered a large disused grass airfield at Croughton to the south where I had flown Master tugs and Hotspur gliders. With this useful local knowledge I had little difficulty in landing the Spitfire on the field without damage to the aircraft. The fault in the propeller was the loss of oil from the constant-speed unit, allowing the propeller to over-speed. The squadron maintenance crew replaced the propeller unit and I flew the Spitfire back to Hendon.

During my time with the squadron we lost two Spitfires with one fatality, which occurred during the first summer camp at Tangmere, and regrettably this could have been avoided had I been present at the briefing. The squadron operated a training flight, in addition to the two operational flights, to train new pilots on the Harvard and Spitfire before being cleared for operational flying. With many experienced ex-wartime pilots on the squadron the senior members liked to relive the memories of the war flying in full squadron formation, referred to as a 'Balbo'. Unfortunately, on this occasion I was flying with a pilot on a training flight and in my absence the CO with the senior flight commander decided to mount a full squadron formation of twelve aircraft and one of the training pilots was detailed to make up the formation. This pilot had little experience on the squadron but elected to fly in the formation. Manoeuvring a squadron or wing formation in open or battle formation is carried out by cross-over turns. In turning a squadron of three flights through 90 degrees while in open battle formation, as the inside flight cannot slow down to turn inside the leading flight, it passes under the leader before turning sharply into line abreast formation on the opposite side of the leader. Similarly, as the outside flight cannot speed up on the outside of the turn, it crosses over the leading flight to take up a line abreast position on the opposite side of the leading flight. The two outside flights therefore reverse positions on the leader and in the process the sections of each flight similarly change positions requiring a degree of flight manoeuvring and throttle control. Unfortunately, the pilot concerned due to his inexperience collided with one of the Spitfires, lost control, crashed and was killed. The other pilot managed to bale out of his aircraft and he survived.

By the end of 1948 it became obvious that Hendon, which had operated the Hawker Fury before the war, was unsuitable for current fighter aircraft and both squadrons moved to North Weald, a famous pre-war and Battle of Britain fighter airfield near Epping Forest on the North-East side of London. Within a short period we started to convert to the de Havilland Vampire powered by a single DH Goblin jet engine of 3,350 lb static thrust. The Vampire had a maximum speed of 550 mph (Mach 0.78), a climb of 4,800 ft/sec and a range with external fuel of 600 miles at sea level and 1,200 miles at 30,000 feet. The armament was four 20 mm Hispano cannon, and fighter-bomber variants carried a 2,000 lb external ordnance load. This performance was a considerable jump to that of our Spitfires and the absence of any torque gave an initial impression of the aircraft flying ahead of the pilot on take-off compared with the

Spitfire. The small twin boomed jet was a delight to fly, being the jet equivalent of the Spitfire IX. The Vampire was easy to fly with no vices and from the pure enjoyment of flying I cannot think of any other aircraft quite like it; which accounted for its early popularity with other air forces in Europe and elsewhere. When the RAF started to produce squadron individual and formation aerobatics displays, the Vampire was the natural and favoured aircraft for the flying displays, and was able to keep the presentation within the circuit of the airfield and within sight of the spectators on the ground. The main drawback of the aircraft was that it did not have the operational performance of the Gloster Meteor that out-climbed it and was faster. The Meteor was more of a handful and more difficult to fly with the two engines and the associated asymmetric problems, and it killed more pilots in training. After our departure from Hendon the airfield became a housing estate, with the RAF Museum emerging from the remains of the two Auxiliary Air Force hangers. The distinctive Tudor style officers' mess became a hall of residence for the University of Middlesex.

I spent an enjoyable, if at times contentious, attachment with the auxiliaries and before the end of my tour I left the fun and frolic of the 'County of London' squadron for a staff appointment at No. 11 Group headquarters as the personal staff officer, or aide-de-camp, to the Air Officer Commanding, Air Vice-Marshal Stanley Vincent, DFC. This was to be the first of my two staff appointments during my RAF career, and although reluctant to give up a flying appointment, I was glad to remain in the premier fighter group of the RAF. Stanley Vincent was the only RAF pilot to shoot down a German aircraft in both World Wars; and he was generous in the time given to me to keep in current flying practice on operational aircraft. Shortly after my appointment as his ADC, Air Marshal Sir Basil Embry, DSO, DFC, who had a distinguished war record as a bomber pilot, became Commander-in-Chief Fighter Command and Stanley Vincent retired. Conversely, Air Marshal Sir Harry Broadhurst, DSO, DFC, Commander-in-Chief RAF Germany and 2nd TAF, had a distinguished war record as a fighter pilot before taking over command of Bomber Command. Both men had strong and powerful personalities; and both men made significant changes in their commands as both became operationally more effective at the height of the Cold War. Both Embry and Broadhurst were very protective of their reputations and both liked to have a say in and give endorsement to the various appointments in their commands, and they would take many of their appointees with them to new commands. Basil Embry was considered by many to be a prospective Chief of the Air Staff, and on one occasion when this was suggested to him he replied that as a practicing Roman Catholic this was not possible. In

his opinion there would never be a Catholic or Jewish head of any of the
Armed Services, and as far as I know this has been the case. Basil Embry
retired from the RAF to become a sheep farmer in Western Australia, and
I met him again when flying in the State Governor's HS 125 executive jet.
He appeared to me to have mellowed a lot, as I found him good company.
Harry Broadhurst was to model Bomber Command along similar lines to
the Strategic Air Command of the USAF commanded by General Curtis
Le May. Broadhurst became the only RAF air marshal to eject from an
aircraft when returning from an overseas trip in a Vulcan bomber as the
co-pilot. The aircraft crashed while attempting to land in thick fog at
London Heathrow; the nearest airport to Bomber Command Headquarters. The two pilots of the Vulcan ejected successfully but the
remainder of the crew, not being equipped with ejection seats, were killed
when the aircraft crashed.

When Stanley Vincent retired I continued as ADC to his successor,
AVM Thomas Pike, DFC, a decorated night fighter 'ace' during the war.
Pike had a particular attachment for North Weald, for when posted there
as a junior pilot officer from the RAF College at Cranwell during the late
twenties to fly the RAF's first all metal fighter, the Armstrong Whitworth
Siskin, he met and married the daughter of the local rector. Pike
subsequently made his home near North Weald. He recalled how shortly
after his arrival the squadron met with disaster when half the aircraft were
damaged or destroyed by fire. North Weald was the first airfield designed
as a modern fighter base and after the construction of a large hanger, a
concrete apron in front of the hanger provided parking space for the
squadron aircraft. To prevent the spillage of fuels fouling the concrete the
aircraft parked over metal grills that drained the leaks into pipes
connected to the domestic rainwater drainage system. The rainwater
drained into a ditch running alongside the roadway passing the airfield.
One weekend during stand-down of the squadron someone tossed a
lighted cigarette butt into the ditch and ignited the fuel floating on the
water. The fire spread rapidly up the pipes erupting out of the drainage
grills under the parked aircraft. Those Siskins parked over the drainage
grills, although of metal construction, caught fire and suffered considerable damage. This resulted in a rework of the drainage system and luckily
for the engineer responsible, there were no 'correction' camps in Britain.

AVM Tom Pike, who was AVM Broadhurst's Senior Air Staff Officer
in Desert Air Force, would later be knighted as CinC Fighter Command,
and eventually become Marshal of the RAF as Chief of the Air Staff. Pike
liked to fly the aircraft in his command and when visiting one of his fighter
wings would fly to the base in the appropriate aircraft. We would drive
from London to our communication squadron at Bovingdon and from

there take either two Vampires or two Meteors to the air base in question. During bad weather or when visiting a non-flying unit such as sector headquarters or radar stations, Pike flew his personal Anson while I acted as navigator. I travelled extensively with him within Fighter Command and 2nd TAF in Germany, keeping in touch with the latest aircraft developments. In the course of my duties I met many top military commanders, as well as senior members of the Government and some visiting foreign dignitaries, making me appreciate that *no man is a hero to his valet*. These various VIPs always appeared to us lowly underlings as larger than life figures and even supermen, but when viewed up close and in normal contact one gained a different opinion as they were fallible like the rest of us.

The job involved long hours and although not over-possessive of my time, I did not get much opportunity to pursue leisure interests. Pike was a keen pilot and was generous in the time he allowed me to visit squadrons in the group to fly the Vampires and Meteors, and to maintain my instrument rating status. On one occasion I flew down to Tangmere to fly the new Meteor VIII on 43 Squadron when it became the first squadron to re-equip from the Meteor IV to the Meteor VIII. I was flying above 40,000 feet when there was a bang and the bullet-proof windscreen started to disintegrate and only the several laminations of glass held with vinyl stopped it hitting me in the face. I expected it to break completely any moment as I reduced height and landed as soon as possible. Inspection of the windscreen attributed the cause to a combination of windscreen construction, outside air temperature, windscreen heating and cabin pressurization. The failure was the only one recorded for the Meteor in the Command and the OC Flying at Tangmere expressed the view that this was to be expected if inexperienced staff officers flew the new squadron aircraft. I did not like this particular wing commander who did most of his commanding of the wing from the ground and I decided he should not get away with this unjustified slander. I mentioned the incident to Pike when I reported my impressions of the new Meteor and casually let slip the wing commander's comment. He must have mentioned this to the SASO, Ruper Lee, who apparently delivered a monumental rocket to the wing commander. By a coincidence the CO of 43 Squadron at the time was my wing leader from my Mustang days at Bentwaters, Max Sutherland, who when he saw me getting out of his damaged aircraft said jokingly 'I might have known it!'

Pike was Director of Operational Requirements at the Air Ministry before taking over 11 Group and as such involved in the Hunter day and Javelin all-weather fighters to replace the Meteors in 1954. The English Electric Canberra jet bomber was another aircraft he had an interest in before it entered service with Bomber Command. The Air Council went to view the Canberra at the Warton factory and evaluate the aircraft. Pike accompanied them and suggested to Rollie Beamont, the chief test pilot, that I should fly with him on the demonstration flight. I sat in the navigator's seat behind the pilot where the view of the outside world was a glimpse of the sky forward through the pilot's canopy. During the flight I saw as much of the ground as I did of the sky as 'Bee' hurled the Canberra around through an almost continuous series of rolls and loops. For a bomber this was very impressive to me as the passenger, and the watching Air Council were suitably impressed by 'Bee's demonstration. He went on to impress the world attending the Farnborough Air Show, and I was able to appreciate fully his demonstration skills in flying the Canberra from ground level while handling a gin and tonic! I had a great respect for 'Bee' personally and as a pilot, but he had to be one of the fiercest handling pilots I ever flew with. This gave me quite the wrong impression of the aircraft for later, when I was at the Central Fighter Establishment, I flew the Canberra on overseas visits and I found it to be an easy and well-mannered aircraft to fly. It was a delightful aircraft for long range commuting when as far as the handling was concerned it resembled a jet propelled Anson. I considered Squadron Leader Roger Topp, AFC, to be the best demonstration pilot on the Canberra, and this also applied to his leadership of the RAF's Hunter formation aerobatic team when his commanded No. 111 Squadron.

There were two problem areas with the early model Canberra: one concerned with baling out of the aircraft and the other with its electrical systems. Initially the aircraft had no ejection seat and the crew endeavoured to bale out through the entry door. Later, when fitted with the ejection seat, the pilot fired the seat through the canopy and the navigator through an escape hatch. Several injuries resulted until explosive bolts fitted around the canopy and the hatch released both before the ejection guns fired. This resulted in a successful ejection if the crew were in their seats, however, if the navigator was out of his seat in the bomb aiming position in the nose, any G force made it impossible for him to return to his seat. On a visit to the Martin Baker factory to see James Martin, the managing director and chief designer, I found him on the floor of the corridor in front of his office attached to a strong bungee cord stretched down the corridor. On a word from him he was released and the bungee catapulted him along the corridor. On seeing my surprise at the MD of Martin Baker Aircraft flying along the corridor he got up and said he was trying to solve the problem of the navigator in a Canberra returning to his seat in a high G situation. James Martin was a remarkable man with an extra-ordinary inventive mind in designing aircraft, ejection seats and many other aeronautical inventions that included equipment such as an airborne balloon-cable cutter attached to an aircraft wing. He inspired great loyalty among his employees and he persuaded one brave engineer named Benny Lynch to do the first live ejection demonstrations from the open rear cockpit of a modified Meteor III aircraft. Lynch carried out many live ejection demonstrations to the extent that it was said that his joints creaked as he walked. The day I met him this problem was eased with a little sherry in the mess to lubricate his joints before the demonstration ejection.

The other problem with the early Canberra concerned the electric trim control. Nearly everything in the Canberra, apart from the primary flying controls, operated electrically and some Canberra aircraft crashed owing to a runaway on the elevator trim. A good friend of mine at The Central Fighter Establishment (CFE) had the problem while low flying and the elevator trim ran forward which caused him to fly into the ground. By the time I flew the aircraft this problem no longer existed and I grew to like the Canberra a lot; especially the luxury of a navigator aboard to see one returned home safely. The aircraft was not as fast as the Meteor but it could climb to 50,000 feet which was useful in allowing a pilot to climb above the weather, except perhaps in the tropics where the tropical storms can reach up to this altitude.

After a year as Pike's ADC I thought it time to get back to regular flying and I suggested to the AOC that while appreciating the opportunity and experience, I thought a year was sufficient as his Personal Assistant and suggested that someone else now to gain the experience. I asked to return to a squadron and he agreed, asking me where I should like to go. I replied that I should like to command a flight on 41 Squadron when it moved to Biggin Hill. I had established through 'P' staff that 41 Squadron was in the process of converting from Hornets to Meteor IVs at Church Fenton in 12 Group, and moving to Biggin Hill to join 600 and 615 Auxiliary Squadrons, also converting to Meteor IVs. Although my time as ADC was a staff appointment I managed to get in quite a lot of flying time on jets and the Anson, and consequently I was in current flying practice with no need for a conversion course. There are times when it is a definite advantage to have the right contact in the right place and at the right time; now for once these factors all coincided for me. To my great relief Pike suggested in the right quarters that they try to accommodate my wishes, and when 41 Squadron arrived at Biggin Hill I became the 'A' Flight commander.

In retrospect, when considering the 1939–45 war, I was very fortunate in finally achieving my ambition to fly fighters and doubly so in that the war, in so far as it effected me, proved very benevolent in contrast to many of my contemporaries. My tour of flying instruction in Flying Training Command, following my Wings graduation, kept me out of combat for eighteen months and during that time I did at least have an experience of what it was like to fly in Bomber Command. The flying instructors in Flying Training Command had the opportunity to fly one operational mission with a bomber squadron and early in 1944 when asked if I should like to fly an operational mission, as a newly commissioned pilot officer I did not have the nerve to decline with thanks. The procedure for these initiation flights was usually to fly on a diversionary raid that was mounted in the hope of diverting some of the attention of the German night fighter force from the primary target. However, the German air defence system from 1944 onwards was such that it assessed the RAF raids very accurately, allowing the main night fighter force to be concentrated on the main targets, leaving the AA guns to cope with the diversions. The Lancaster had a limited and cramped crew space and the supernumerary observers generally flew with the Halifax squadrons. The Handley Page Halifax although slightly inferior to the Avro Lancaster in terms of performance and bomb load, was slightly roomier inside and had the comforting reputation of being a rugged and dependable aircraft able to withstand battle damage. It was on such raids that the war correspondents generally flew when reporting on Bomber Command's operations; Ernest Hemingway flew a similar sortie to mine in a Halifax bomber, as well as on a B-25 Mitchell medium bomber raid. I flew in a Halifax of No. 77 Squadron of 6 Group out of Elvington in Yorkshire with a Canadian crew captained by Flight Lieutenant Thompson, DFC, RCAF: Canada was second only to the RAF in supplying air crews to Bomber Command. We flew on a diversionary raid on Emden while the main bomber force headed for Essen in the Ruhr. We were fortunate that we met little opposition with the German fighters which were either preoccupied with the main force or thwarted by the adverse weather.

We flew the whole mission through overcast and I saw little of the ground during the flight and experienced little evidence of AA fire, other than the occasional glow in the cloud and a bump of the aircraft as a shell exploded nearby. We flew the 350 miles to the target in cloud at 18,000 feet by means of D/R navigation with guidance from Oboe, which placed us accurately over the target area. The Oboe system was an improved version of the radio beam guidance of the Gee system. The Germans managed to jam the Gee system but not Oboe where radar stations on the UK coast enabled the aircraft to fly a grid to the target. It was a very effective aid to navigation but unfortunately did not have the range to extend its grid guidance to targets as far as Berlin. Over the target we bombed blind by the use of the H2S radar that gave a radar picture of the ground. As our target was the docks it stood out clearly on the radar screen for the bomb aimer to drop the bombs accurately. We had no attacks from night fighters, and being above or in cloud we avoided the cones of the searchlights bracketing us that would require a violent corkscrew evasion manoeuvre. On the debriefing after landing the crew summed up the mission as a 'milk run', but I could see the strain on the crew during the six hours of the flight. I could imagine the strain of a tour of thirty missions flying during a 'hunter's moon' over the Rhur, or on the long flight to Berlin while running the deadly gauntlet of a greatly improved and highly efficient air defence system. Each bomber raid was a roll of the dice and synonymous with the infantry 'going over the top'; its outcome dependent upon weather, enemy dispositions, sheer chance and a lot of other factors that could not be controlled. It was a game that if played long enough one could only lose and it is a wonder that some aircrew in Bomber Command survived as many as three tours, when it was calculated that only one third of them survived a first tour of thirty missions, and only a quarter survived two front line tours in Bomber Command.

Requiem for a Rear Gunner

My brief sweet life is over: my eyes no longer see.
No summer walks – No Christmas Trees – No pretty girls for me.
I've got the chop: I've had it: my nightly ops are done:
Yet in another hundred years, I'll still be twenty-one.

R. W. Gillbert

By 1944 Bomber Command's aircraft loss rate on raids over Germany averaged around 5 per cent, and occasionally rose to nearly 10 per cent. The Nuremberg raid in March 1944 resulted in the worst loss rate on a single raid when 96 aircraft failed to return out of a force of nearly 800 aircraft, a loss rate of 13 per cent. In Bomber Command alone some 56,000 air crew died out of a total RAF loss of 70,000 air crew killed in all war theatres during the Second World War. These losses exceeded those sustained by the much larger USAAF with 52,000 air crew dead. However, it was the USAAF who suffered the most disastrous losses in proportion to their gains during the daylight raids on the ball-bearing factory at Schweinfurt and the oil fields at Ploesti in Romania. The two raids on the Schweinfurt factory in 1943 suffered losses of over 15 per cent and such unsustainable losses resulted in the suspension of further raids until the bombers were provided with fighter escort to and from the target area. Whatever damage occurred to the Schweinfurt factory it had little effect on the availability of ball-bearings to the German war machine. Similarly, the raids on the Ploesti oilfields resulted in the loss of 350 aircraft with little oil loss to the Germans until the oilfields were occupied by the Red Army in 1944.

The advent of a British socialist Government in 1945 fuelled criticism of RAF Bomber Command and in particular the Commander-in-Chief, Air Chief Marshal Sir Arthur Harris. This criticism resulted from studies on the effectiveness of the RAF policy of night area bombing, as against the USAF policy of day precision bombing. What the critics chose to ignore is that up to 1944, precision targets could not be identified at night, and the lightly armed RAF bombers could not survive over Germany in daylight without prohibitive losses. Over and above these factors was a more unpredictable but crucially important factor – the European weather. It was not until 1945 that navigational aids became available such as an improved Oboe system, GH and H2S that enabled Bomber Command to find and attack targets regardless of weather. ACM Harris was not the originator of the area bombing policy, although he did fervently believe in it. The critics conveniently forget that Britain was fighting a total war against Germany and Japan requiring unconditional surrender by both enemies. Bearing this in mind, there was no other way to carry the war to Germany, and the British people, who had suffered extensive bombing of their major cities, desperately wished to hit-back at the Nazis. Much of the venom against Harris focuses on the bombing of Dresden. However, this target was not the choice of Harris or the RAF, but one of several cities in eastern Germany on the target list from Eisenhower and the Chiefs of Staff to give support to the Russian front. The Soviets specifically requested the destruction of Dresden as a focal point for communications in the transfer of troops and supplies between the German western and eastern fronts. The Allied air forces, after receiving political approval, bombed Dresden to destruction with the RAF by night and the USAF by day. Incendiary bombs are the most effective conventional weapons for the mass destruction of a city and the incendiary bombs used in the raids against Dresden produced a fire storm that destroyed the city with a loss of life estimated at around 50,000 dead. It was the ultimate terror raid and a grim reality of total war. The German refugees from East Germany that poured into Dresden with the advance of the Soviet forces and terrified by reports of rape and pillage by the Soviet troops, fled out of the city to block the roads thus achieving the Soviet objective in disrupting German communications and reinforcements to the Eastern Front. The devastation of Dresden did not materially influence the outcome of the war as the war was effectively won at that stage, but for the German people it was a portent of what might occur to other German cities by prolonging the war. The Dresden raids on 13–15 February 1945, followed requests from the Soviets to also bomb the cities of Berlin, Chemnitz and Leipzig to prevent German reinforcements to the Eastern Front. On 3 February 1945 the USAF launched 'Operation Thunderclap' against Berlin. One thousand B-17 bombers of the US 8th Air Force bombed Berlin to destruction with an estimated loss of life of between 20,000–30,000 German civilians. The higher casualty figures for the Dresden raid was due to the intensive firestorm that developed in a city crowded with refugees escaping from the Soviet advance. In the post-war analysis and criticism of allied strategic bombing offensives, it is the Dresden raid that is remembered and the one that specifically fuelled the outcry at the destruction by the RAF of a historically important city crammed with refugees when the war was virtually won. The destruction of the other cities is conveniently forgotten as the vigorous criticism of RAF Bomber Command and its Commander-in-Chief continues. The moral and political outcry at the devastation of Dresden was the result of the efficiency of its destruction, although the participation of the USAF is muted in the attacks against Harris. It is now known that Germany was well advanced in the production of a nuclear bomb and if the Nazis had been the first to use the atomic bomb or fitted nuclear warheads in the V-2 rockets aimed at British cities, would the reaction to the destruction of a historic German city have been the same?

> *To murder thousands takes a specious name,*
> *War's glorious art, and gives immortal fame.*
> Edward Young (1683–1765)

Controversy always encourages a 'What if?' analysis by historians and as far as the Dresden raid and RAF Bomber Command controversy is concerned, 'What if the war had ended in 1944?' It is suggested by some military historians that with complete allied air supremacy the Allies lost a great opportunity to end the war in 1944 by 'Blitzkrieg' strategy. Despite the wish of the commanders of the Allied army groups to thrust eastwards from Belgium into Germany in the summer of 1944, the Supreme Commander, General Eisenhower, decided on a 'broad front' strategy for an advance along a linear front. The result of this allowed the Germans to regroup for a counter-offensive through the Ardennes with considerable losses in Allied lives, the murder of prisoners of war, an increased death toll in the Nazi concentration camps, and the Soviets reaching Berlin first. Had Montgomery's 21st Army Group in the north and Bradley's 12th Army Group in the south been allowed to make independent thrusts for Berlin, they had every prospect of succeeding in advancing the surrender of the German forces. With the surrender of German forces in 1944, the

Dresden raid would not have taken place; and along with many other assumptions resulting from such a scenario, is the likelihood that post-war Europe would have been different.

If history requires someone to be responsible for the incineration of 50,000 civilians and the unnecessary destruction of the historical city of Dresden, it should not be the commander-in-chief of RAF Bomber Command. Air Chief Marshal Sir Arthur Harris did not target Dresden and he did not politically authorize the raid or its destruction. As the C-in-C of Bomber Command he ensured that his bomber crews carried out the raid effectively as directed by the Chiefs of Staff in conjunction with the USAF. More deserving of censure is General Eisenhower who supported the Soviet request to bomb Dresden to destruction and who when given the opportunity to end the war in 1944 allowed it to continue until May 1945.

Bomber Command and its long-time Commander-in-Chief, ACM Sir Arthur Harris, were not treated well by the British nation following the end of the war in Europe, despite public appreciation and gratitude. The refusal by both the coalition government of Churchill and the new socialist government of Atlee publicly to acknowledge the debt owed to Bomber Command by the awarding of a campaign medal, or even a clasp to the Defence medal, to the air and ground crews was a disgrace to the many thousands of volunteers from the British Commonwealth that came from afar to fight in the air war of attrition against Germany. It was also a national shame to the memory of over 55,000 aircrew of Bomber Command who did not return home from the raids into Europe. Was the British Eighth Army more deserving of recognition by a clasp to the Africa Star medal than the contribution and sacrifices of Bomber Command in winning the war? The answer is obviously not, but elements within the government in Britain thought differently. A total of 40 per cent of Bomber Command crews came from beyond the shores of the British Isles: of this total Canada provided a majority of 60 per cent. Australia, New Zealand and South Africa, together with Czechs, Frenchmen, Norwegians and Poles provided the remainder. Even the Soviets acknowledged a debt to Bomber Command and its commander-in-chief, Sir Arthur Harris. It is strange that Churchill, of all people, who was so effusive in praise of Fighter Command with his *Finest Hour* speech, made no similar reference to Bomber Command. In his victory speech to the nation he first spoke of the events of the war and the achievements of all the Services, before speaking of the liberation of France and the land battle into Germany, but he made no mention of the part played by Bomber Command in making it all possible, while saving innumerable Allied lives following the D-Day landings. There is no doubt that had the

Dresden raid not taken place both RAF Bomber Command and its Commander-in-Chief would have been judged differently by the post-war generation. My night with Bomber Command gave me a great respect for the bomber crews that flew night after night in all weathers over Germany. To those of us in Fighter Command there was an excitement and pleasure in flying a high performance fighter aircraft and it appeared to us, quite wrongly, that the bomber pilot had little opportunity to feel this joy as he concentrated on the job in hand with the survival of his aircraft and crew. The greater responsibility towards one another among the bomber crews led to a greater sense of esprit de corps than was apparent among fighter pilots, with the fighter aces being by definition individualists. Bearing in mind the task of the bomber pilot, I was grateful in my selection to fighters. The government that denied the aircrew of Bomber Command due recognition by a campaign medal or clasp was the same mean-spirited and niggardly government; subsequently endorsed by succeeding governments and the bureaucracy; that withheld the payment of the supplemental flying pay entitlement of RAF aircrew incarcerated as POWs for the period of their captivity.

Although the chances of survival were far better in Fighter Command than in Bomber Command, there was always the spectre that tomorrow might be the day; but if a pilot failed to appear in the mess the system did not allow for this to prey upon the mind. The mess bar and rowdy mess games provided a suitable wake process and a safety valve that precluded public mourning so that any grieving was private. Consequently, there were times when pilots suffering from hangovers were not at their sharpest when this may have mattered the most. Of course, the possibility of injury was always present with the hope that any quietus be swift and merciful; the great dread being a 'flamer' and surviving badly burnt. We had one such pilot, Flight Lieutenant Ron Hibbert, who rejoined the squadron shortly after VE Day. He had flown Spitfires on 65 Squadron when based at Hornchurch during 1941. Hornchurch was a grass airfield on the north-east side of London and was a prominent fighter base during the Battle of Britain. The Spitfire wing was involved in the mass daylight offensive sweeps over France and Belgium escorting bombers sent to draw the Luftwaffe fighter force up into combat. In order to extend the range and endurance of the Spitfire V some squadrons were operating with a 90 gallon 'slipper' drop tank carried beneath the fuselage. As his Spitfire was on the take-off run and was about to become airborne, the engine exploded in flames and a crash landing into some buildings on the airfield boundary was imminent. Hibbert quickly assessed that his chances of survival were improved if he baled out onto the grass as the entire internal fuel contents of the Spitfire was situated between him and the big, heavy

Merlin engine. Releasing himself from the seat and parachute harnesses, he lowered the side entry flap of the cockpit and dived headfirst towards the wing. Unfortunately for him the 90 gallon drop tank also parted company with the aircraft, caught fire and Hibbert fell headfirst into the fireball. A crash crew extracted him from the flames and although only his arm was broken, his face and hands were severely burnt. His flying helmet, goggles and oxygen mask provided little protection from the intense heat and his face was virtually gone. Fortunately for him, as it turned out, the medical officer arriving shortly after the ambulance was conversant with the latest developments on burn treatments and stopped the medics from applying any first aid treatment such as Tannafax jelly. They wrapped the pilot up to keep the air off the burn area and after administering morphine sent him in the ambulance across London to the Queen Victoria Hospital at East Grinstead on the south side of London, where the RAF's Special Burns Unit was based under the direction of a New Zealand surgeon, Archibald McIndoe. It was McIndoe and his team who pioneered the remarkable developments in treating severe burn injuries and the skin grafting techniques to repair the appalling disfigurements. The problem with most burn injuries was due to the initial first aid treatment with salves, sulphur powder or tannic acid jelly to soothe the burn area and prevent infection. Unfortunately, this had the effect of creating shrinkage and the resultant scarring made any skin grafting difficult and often impossible, with a resulting disfigurement. McIndoe's procedure was to keep the burn area untreated and unhealed with constant saline jet washing, leaving the flesh open and raw until the area was ready for the skin graft from suitable areas of the body. This was a long and painful process but it prevented the burnt tissue from scarring.

I became friendly with Hibbert while we were based at Hethel and he told me something of his ordeal. Initially it was thought that he had lost his sight when his eyelids suffered from the burning that removed most of his eyebrows, together with parts of his nose, lips and ears. He said the worst of the ordeal came when he was shaved between the continuous saline washings to prepare the bare skinless flesh for the skin grafts. The skin graft was achieved by creating a tube of flesh and skin taken from his inner thighs and attached to the upper torso, and from there the tissue was moved to the face for the grafts. This process was very painful lasting many months and involved many operations. His eyesight was saved and eventually became fully restored. McIndoe created new eyebrows, lips and ears. Before starting on his nose McIndoe asked what shape he would like and he chose to go classic Grecian. The complete process took two years by which time he had a presentable face with no disfigurement from the burns. His hands remained scarred as they were not receptive to skin grafts, but fortunately he only experienced a slight impairment in their use. His wife, who went through a rough period until she was able to see him, expected the worst and was very relieved at the result even with his changed appearance, commenting that she thought he looked more handsome. McIndoe created The Guinea Pig Club for the exclusive membership of his patients and he held an annual reunion to which most of his patients attended, and he particularly liked to have Hibbert present as he regarded him as one of his prize achievements. Although initially the pilots of Fighter Command provided a majority of the members of the Club, after the Battle of Britain it was the aircrew of Bomber Command that contributed a considerably larger membership to the Guinea Pig Club.

The Special Burns Unit at East Grinstead became world famous for the reconstruction of appalling burn injuries. Naturally enough, many of the patients became remorseful and reclusive during treatment; and the hospital staff worked just as hard to repair them psychologically as physically. The Guinea Pigs were encouraged to go out to theatres, restaurants and pubs, and McIndoe was always able to find attractive volunteers to accompany them, thus preparing his patients for a return to an acceptable life. For his great service to the armed forces and civilians, Archibald McIndoe received a very well deserved knighthood. It is largely due to his contribution in pioneering the new techniques of skin grafts that many badly burnt air crew were able to return to society. As for Hibbert he had a completely reconstructed face that did not show the terrible burns he suffered. In appearance, if his face was studied up close, the skin texture of the grafts showed only a slight appearance similar to that of orange peel, and only when he became excited or inebriated did the demarcation line between the surviving skin and the skin grafts become apparent, as the grafted skin from his body could not flush. It said a great deal for his courage, resolve and determination that he persuaded the Air Ministry to let him fly again and to return to his old squadron to fly not only the Spitfire again but also the Mustang, and our new aircraft, the Hornet.

Chance is a strange factor while flying as one starts hopefully with a full bag of luck and an empty bag of experience. The trick while flying is to fill the latter before emptying the former! I was certainly successful in this respect in avoiding any major injuries while flying Spitfires and Mustangs. During the last ten years I had successfully survived a few incidents that could be assessed as close calls, but nothing compared to a highly respected New Zealander I knew with a very distinguished war record. Air Commodore Al Deere had claimed twenty-two German aircraft destroyed during his four operational tours on fighters. In achieving this with the award of the DSO and DFC, he records in his autobiography *Nine Lives* that he also set an individual record for the number of RAF aircraft he lost in the process, either in combat or flying accidents, having survived eight bale outs or crash landings with various injuries. The cat is said to possess nine lives and New Zealanders are often addressed in the RAF as 'Kiwi', and this particular Kiwi certainly emulated a cat by surviving to a ninth healthy life before his retirement. Some cat! – Some Kiwi!!

In looking back on my time spent on Spitfires and Mustangs, it had really come too late in the war for me to achieve any of the aspirations I dreamed of years before. My contribution to the operational outcome of the war was, at very best, insignificant, and in trying to evaluate my flying career to date I came to the conclusion that although I considered myself a reasonably good pilot with some of the 'right stuff', it was not of *such stuff as dreams are made on*. I lacked some of the ingredients for a successful fighter pilot; namely chance, purpose, insularity and consequence. In retrospect had I the ability to *call back yesterday, bid time return*, I may have reconsidered photographic reconnaissance. That being said I had a good run on the two best Allied fighters of the war: the Spitfire and the Mustang. With a few notable exceptions I enjoyed the experience, and survived it intact: the best of all aspirations! I may have experienced one or two anxious or even sphincteral moments before returning to the comparative comfort of base, but it was certainly a doddle compared to a tour on Bomber Command. My career as a fighter pilot on propeller driven fighters ended with my staff appointment to No. 11 Group, Fighter Command. My career as a jet fighter pilot commenced with my arrival on No. 41 Squadron at Biggin Hill in the spring of 1951, to fly *cloud-encircled Meteors of the air* into *the high, untresspassed sanctity of space*.

CHAPTER THREE

A Few Crowded Hours

The best private flying club in the world was the modest appellation conferred on RAF Biggin Hill by some of the Royal Auxiliary Air Force pilots during the 1950s. Formed in 1917 Biggin Hill had many attractions and was arguably the most famous fighter station in the RAF, having the best record of any in Fighter Command with over 1,000 enemy aircraft claimed shot down. During the Battle of Britain, when it was home to some of the RAF's most famous fighter squadrons and their pilots, it was a constant target of the *Luftwaffe*. Situated on top of an escarpment of the North Downs above Westerham in Surrey, the birthplace of General Wolfe and the home of Winston Churchill, Biggin Hill is a convenient 20 miles from Piccadilly Circus. By 1951 the airfield had one main north-south runway with the pre-war hangers destroyed by the *Luftwaffe* replaced by modern structures. However, the pre-war red-brick Officers' Mess was undamaged and not only provided a comfortable home but was unique in the RAF with its terraced gardens, swimming pool and situation perched on the edge of the escarpment overlooking the green Weald of Surrey.

It was to this pleasant environment that No. 41 Squadron moved from Church Fenton in Yorkshire; converting from the de Havilland Hornet long-range strike and escort fighter to the Gloster Meteor IV interceptor jet fighter. No. 41 Squadron also joined the two RAuxAF squadrons converting from the Spitfire XXII to the Meteor IV who called Biggin Hill home. No. 600 'City of London' Squadron, commanded by Squadron Leader David Proudlove, RAuxAF, was a little less flamboyant than its sister squadron, No. 601 'County of London' Squadron based at North Weald. The honorary air commodore of No. 600 Squadron was HM Queen Elizabeth, The Queen Mother. No. 615 'County of Surrey' Squadron commanded by Squadron Leader Neville Duke, DSO, DFC,

RAuxAF, had as its honorary air commodore, the Prime Minister, Sir Winston Churchill. No. 41 Squadron, formed during the First World War as a scout squadron flying SE5 fighters based at St Omer in France took as its squadron crest the Croix de Lorraine from the city arms. During the Second World War the squadron operated various marks of Spitfires until it converted to the DH Hornet in 1947. By 1951 the UK based Hornet squadrons re-equipped with the Meteor, leaving the Hornet in service only overseas in Malaysia and Hong Kong.

Three notable fighter pilots held commands at Biggin Hill during my stay on 41 Squadron. In 1951 Wing Commander Arthur Donaldson, DSO, DFC, commanded the station. He was one of three well-known brothers in the RAF who were fighter pilots and who were all awarded the DSO. He was followed in 1952 by Wing Commander 'PB' Pitt-Brown, DFC. The OC Flying was Squadron Leader Ray Hesselyn, DFC, DFM, a New Zealander who became a noted ace while flying from Malta in 1942. The first commanding officer of No. 41 Squadron at Biggin Hill was Squadron Leader John 'Dusty' Miller, DFC, AFC. Miller won his DFC the hard way flying Beaufighters on anti-shipping strikes. He proved to be an outstanding squadron commander dedicated to making No. 41 Squadron the best operational squadron in Fighter Command. At a time when there was considerable competition within the command to produce the best formation aerobatics team and the best individual aerobatics pilot, Miller did not allow this distraction to deter from the operational role of the squadron. I rated him as the best squadron commander I served under, and it was largely due to his enthusiasm and drive that during his leadership the squadron achieved the best gunnery and aircraft serviceability record in Fighter Command. The squadron had a good mix of experienced and inexperienced pilots: in addition to them coming from all parts of the British Isles the squadron included an Australian, a Canadian and a New Zealander; with an American Marine Corps pilot on exchange with the RAF. I was indeed very fortunate to have command of a flight on a squadron not only technically and operationally proficient, but also possessing the best squadron spirit I ever experienced during my flying career.

The Gloster Meteor was the first British jet to enter service in 1944 and was one of the few fighters capable of catching the V-1 flying bomb in level flight at low altitude. The first Meteor Mk 1 was equipped with Rolls Royce Welland engines producing 1,700 pounds static thrust (lb.s.t); and the first squadron was RAuxAF Squadron No. 616, who became not only the first but also the only Allied jet fighter squadron during the Second World War. The second squadron was another RAuxAF Squadron, No. 504, just before VE Day with the Meteor Mk III equipped with Rolls

Royce Derwent engines producing 2,000 lb.s.t. The Meteor and the German Messerschmitt ME-262, that entered service before the Meteor, were the two most impressive fighters of the Second World War. The Meteor, although successful against the V-1 flying bomb, was never involved in air combat and one can only speculate at the outcome of such an engagement with the ME-262. The German ME-262 although equipped with slightly less powerful jet engines, was faster than the Meteor due to its swept-back wing design. The Meteor with a conventional straight wing design and more powerful engines had a better rate of climb; although the ME-262 could incorporate rocket motors to boost the aircraft's climb performance. In dog-fighting manoeuvres, as both aircraft suffered from turbine failures, engine and throttle handling required great care; and re-lighting an engine in flight was more problematical with the ME-262 than it was with the Meteor III. The Meteor had the advantage of air brakes to decelerate the aircraft in the air, which the ME-262 did not possess. The German fighter was slow to decelerate and would have benefited from the use of an air brake, especially in combat and during circuits and landings.

The German ME-262 may have differed considerably from the British Meteor in aerodynamic design with the innovation of a swept wing, but both aircraft experienced problems with their engines. The ME-262's Jumo axial-flow engine was an advance in design over the Rolls Royce Derwent centrifugal engine, but was of less power. The centrifugal engine had more aerodynamic drag but it handled better and was more reliable with longer engine life. The Derwent engines gave the Meteor better initial acceleration and were also less susceptible to ingestion damage. The big advantage of the ME-262 over the Meteor operationally was in its armament. Whereas the Meteor carried an armament of four 20 mm cannon the ME-262, designed as a bomber destroyer, carried a much heavier armament with four 30 mm cannon and it could also carry batteries of free flight rockets. Four 20 mm cannon continued as the armament of all day and night interceptor Meteors. Neither the early Meteors nor the ME-262 were equipped with an ejection seat; this was to follow later with the Meteor Mk VIII.

I never saw the ME-262 in flight but I did see some on the ground at Debelsdorf in 1945. Seen up close the shark-like German fighter looked sleek, elegant, menacing and very fast, even while resting on the ground and made the Meteor look almost pedestrian by comparison. Fortunately for the Allies and the US 8th Air Force in particular, the ME-262 spent a lot of its operational life on the ground plagued by engine problems and the many opposing concepts for its operational role. It is easy to imagine that if the *Luftwaffe* had been able to operate the interceptor version of the ME-262 fighter in sufficient numbers against the US 8th Air Force during 1944, the daylight raids on Germany could not have been sustained despite the large force of escorting US P-51 Mustangs. Fortunately, German political distractions with the operational use of the ME-262, especially Hitler's obsession with the bomber version, enabled the US attrition rate to stay within acceptable limits. Allied test pilots who flew the ME-262 reported that the swept wing delayed the onset of compressibility allowing the aircraft to attain a higher limiting Mach number than the Meteor more quickly. This was particularly significant in a dive until the ME-262 experienced a loss of flying control. The compressibility effects on the Meteor Mk IV were less dramatic. As the aircraft approached the limiting Mach number the flying controls became heavy and airframe buffeting occurred. To be followed by a strong pitch-up with a wing drop; accompanied by noises of protest from the engines. The airframe drag on the Meteor was such that a reduction in engine power would quickly return the aircraft to normal flight control. The initial problems with the directional control and stability of the Meteor Mk IV would eventually lead to a complete redesign of the tail in the Meteor Mk VIII.

As the Meteor Mk III and Mk IV were not equipped with an ejection seat the bale-out procedure was very problematical and the only procedure that offered a fair prospect of success was to reduce speed to below 200 knots and drop out inverted with some negative G to clear the high set tailplane. The CO of 245 Squadron, Squadron Leader Bird-Wilson, DSO, DFC, experienced a unique method of baling out of a Meteor III when during an aerobatics display he pulled out of a high speed dive at low level and found himself flying upwards in his seat as his aircraft disassembled itself around him. Fortunately, he reached sufficient altitude to release himself from the seat and pull his ripcord for a safe landing. Inspection of the wreckage established that the D-doors covering the main landing wheels had sagged open under the high G force to an extent that the slipstream ripped them off the under surface of the mainplane, leading to a break-up of the airframe. This problem, together with others, was addressed when the Meteor IV entered service in 1946. The Meteor IV had an increase in engine power with RR Derwent 5 engines producing 3,500 lb.s.t. A reduced wing span not only increased the airspeed at low altitude, but also improved the rate of roll. It was with this aircraft the RAF High Speed Flight established a world speed record in excess of 600 knots.

The advent of jets into the RAF brought about a change of calibration of airspeed from mph to the nautical knots, together with a Mach number indicator to represent the percentage of the speed of sound at that altitude. Range became measured in nautical miles instead of statute miles with 1 nautical mile equal to 1.15 statute miles. The next development of the Meteor was a two-seat trainer version that made the conversion of pilots from propeller driven aircraft to jets at the OTUs much easier and with fewer accidents. Both the Vampire and the Meteor were eventually produced in a trainer version. The Meteor VII retained the basic airframe of the Meteor IV with the same tail design and a lengthened nose section to incorporate the two-seat tandem cockpit. It was lighter in weight than the Meteor IV with a better rate of climb, and as such was preferred by some pilots for aerobatics displays. The side-by-side seating arrangement in the Vampire trainer, although preferred by some instructors, resulted in more weight with reduced performance and visibility.

The most significant improvements in the Meteor came with the arrival of the Meteor Mk VIII, which became the definitive model of the Meteor with a redesigned tail to overcome control difficulties at high Mach numbers. A lengthened nose section compensated for the increased weight and additional fuel tankage. It retained the short-span wings that improved the rate of roll and the handling became greatly improved at high speeds. The aircraft with up rated Derwent 8 engines of 3,600 lb static thrust had a service ceiling of 44,000 feet, a rate of climb of 7,000 ft/min and a range of 700 nautical miles. Whereas the Meteor IV had difficulty reaching a speed close to Mach 0.8 with heavy controls and wing drop, the Meteor VIII could be persuaded to reach Mach 0.82 before shaking and snaking with a heavy nose-up stick force. The air brakes were very effective with a rapid deceleration, and when first experienced it felt like running into a giant sponge. The general control with the new tail was a great improvement on the Meteor IV. The aircraft incorporated an improved air conditioning system that reduced windscreen and canopy misting and icing. A big improvement from the pilot's peace of mind in the Meteor MK VIII was the installation of a Martin-Baker ejection seat, aided by an improved cockpit canopy. It was the first RAF aircraft to be so equipped and by these means the Meteor VIII, although not a 'pilot's' airplane in the sense of the Vampire, became a comfortable aircraft to fly with well-balanced flying controls and effective trim controls up to a height of 30,000–35,000 feet. Above this height as the speed built above Mach 0.78 the controls became progressively heavier, and in particular the ailerons, with reduced trim control, had the tendency to drop a wing. However, even in a dive from high altitude the drag factor of the airframe design was such that the compressibility effect of loss of control approaching sonic speed was not too apparent and a reduction of engine power was sufficient to stabilize the aircraft.

To pilots accustomed to the noise of propeller driven fighters, the relatively quiet and vibration free flight of a jet fighter was not only impressive, but the take-off and climb performance of the Meteor when first experienced was breath-taking. A major drawback was the voracious thirst of the centrifugal turbojets that limited the flight duration to less than one hour and this quickly led to the addition of an external ventral slipper tank of 105 (Imp.) gallons added to an internal fuel capacity of 330 (Imp.) gallons. Although simple to operate the turbojets required close attention during start-up while feeding the high pressure fuel supply to the engine so as not to flood the turbine, known as a wet-start, and not to exceed the maximum jet pipe temperature of around 500 °C. Slow adjustment of the throttle controlled jet pipe resonance which could cause turbine blade failure which, if it occurred at high RPM, could result in a catastrophic engine fire. The simplification of the engine controls reduced the workload of the pilot considerably with the absence of fuel mixture and propeller pitch controls, and the absence of a propeller eliminated the torque-induced swing on take-off.

As a counter to this simplification was the fact that events occurred more quickly in jets than with propeller driven aircraft, requiring an accelerated rate of scan to monitor both engine and flight instrumentation. An additional welcomed factor was the tricycle undercarriage allowing unrestricted forward view over the nose, and which also allowed the full application of the brakes on landing without the risk of the tail rising with a nose-over. The ability to apply maximum braking created a problem of aquaplaning on wet runways and the danger of sliding out of control when the main wheels locked-up. This was corrected by squeezing the brake until detecting lock-up, releasing and squeezing again. This problem was solved by one of the brake modifications that followed with the arrival of the Meteor VIII into service with the installation of the French designed Dunlop Maxaret braking system that allowed the brakes to release automatically when the wheels locked-up. Anti-skid brakes became standard on all military aircraft and civil airliners long before the device appeared on motor-cars as the adaptive braking system or ABS. The use of an anti-skid device on the brakes greatly increased the pressure that could be applied to the brakes without manipulation by the pilot thus greatly reducing the landing distance on wet runways. It also allowed an effective braking technique at high runway speed when the elevator could still apply a tail moment down force on the main wheels to enable the tyres to bite into the water on the runway.

One of the problems associated with turbine engines was the fracture or loss of a turbine blade that could chew up the turbine resulting in an engine fire and failure. A minor 'panic' encountered in the early jets was a flame-out of the engine caused by a compressor stall which in turn was caused by harsh use of the throttles, particularly during dog-fights at high altitude. Unlike the DH Goblin engine in the Vampire that possessed no re-light facility, thereby leaving the pilot with a choice between either a forced-landing or baling-out of the aircraft, the RR Derwent could be re-started in flight. The procedure for a re-start was to glide the aircraft to below 15,000 feet at a speed not in excess of 160 knots to prevent the wind milling turbine speeding up, then careful use of the high pressure fuel control and throttle usually resulted in a re-light of the engine. Single-engine flying was straightforward provided the speed was not reduced to below 160 knots until committed to the landing, and provided the selection of the wheels and flaps were not made with the air brake out. This produced a phenomenon known as 'phantom diver' where the Meteor rolled out of control with insufficient altitude in which to recover, and several Meteor pilots met their deaths by this error. The final turn for the landing was carried out at 140 knots and full flap selected. A half throttle engine setting of not less than 7,000 rpm was maintained to the touch-down point at around 100 knots. In this manner, should an overshoot be required, the engine rpm could be rapidly increased without a compressor stall, bearing in mind that most of the thrust from the engine did not occur until the throttle was opened above 90 per cent of the rpm range. It was, therefore, advisable not to attempt a power-off approach as the turbine could not respond quickly enough to prevent the aircraft stalling if the airspeed became too low.

The Meteor VIII could be considered the definitive Meteor in regard to flying and performance and it became the RAF's principal interceptor equipping fifty-nine RAF squadrons. Various additional versions of the Meteor such as the two-seat all-weather Mk XII and Mk XIV were produced. The interceptor Meteor VIII followed the progression of most RAF interceptor fighters, in eventually converting to the ground attack role, as was the case during the Korean War with Australia's No. 77 RAAF Squadron. The Meteor IX was basically a Meteor VIII fitted with cameras in a fighter reconnaissance role. The Meteor under a licensed manufacture by Avions Fairey in Belgium and Fokker in the Netherlands provided the aircraft for their respective air forces. In addition to Australia, the Meteor also saw service in the Argentine, Brazil, Chile and Equador. The RAF's principal fighter became somewhat of an archaic aircraft during the period of the transonic fighters in the early fifties with such interceptor fighters as the North American F-86 Sabre, the Russian Mig-15 and the French Dassault Mystere, until replaced by the Hawker Hunter in 1954.

Aerobatics in the Meteor were exhilarating after flying propeller aircraft owing to the power available to cover a large area of sky without the need to regain speed and height in a sequence of manoeuvres. Stalling the aircraft was quite straightforward but deliberate spinning was avoided. Conventional aerobatics presented no specific problems, and with the great thrust available it was possible to do outside loops or 'bunts'. Unless one had the arms of a gorilla, to get the necessary forward push on the stick for this manoeuvre I found it necessary to push as hard as possible on the stick with the right arm while pulling with the left arm holding the instrument panel. This particular manoeuvre became a popular inclusion for an aerobatics display but I did not particularly enjoy it for the negative G force required was considerable. With ones eyeballs out on organ stops, all the accumulated dust, dirt and rubbish down in the cockpit and fuselage, including an occasional dropped tool, floated around the canopy like goldfish in a bowl. It did at least recover the odd spanner dropped by a careless rigger but I suppose it was the novelty of a manoeuvre that is now a standard item by modern light aerobatics aircraft with their high power to weight ratio and increased airframe stressing. During one Farnborough Air Show Jan Jurakowski, Gloster's Polish chief test pilot, who later became Avro Canada's chief test pilot for the ill-fated Arrow supersonic interceptor, demonstrated his famous cartwheel manoeuvre on the Meteor VIII. Several of us tried to emulate Jura without success. We assumed we could fly the Meteor through the cartwheel when approaching the stall in a vertical climb by applying full power to the outboard engine while closing the inboard engine to idle. Several pilots, including myself, in attempting the manoeuvre finished up in a spin and as a result Fighter Command banned the manoeuvre. What we failed to realize, or appreciate, was that Jura's Meteor VIII was not to the same configuration as the Meteor VIIIs in Fighter Command. The manoeuvre could only be performed with the external stores attached at the wing tips that Jurakowski was demonstrating for the first time. The added weight of the rocket projectiles mounted on the wing tips provided the necessary momentum for a flywheel effect as the Meteor pivoted around its axis to complete the cartwheel. Jan Jurakowski as an exceptional test and demonstration pilot, as well as a brilliant engineer, had calculated this in demonstrating his unique manoeuvre in the Meteor: but then Jura was special; as a test pilot, as an engineer, and as a person.

The Martin Baker ejection seat underwent many design changes and modifications before it became the efficient means of survival that it is today. In the process it saved many lives on many types of aircraft with air forces around the world. Initially when it first arrived on the Meteor VIII it was a relatively straightforward design where on firing the seat a single charge propelled the seat up a rail and out of the cockpit, thereafter it was up to the pilot to release himself from the seat and to pull the parachute ripcord. Among the many things that could go wrong was not sitting up straight in the seat resulting in spine injuries. Then there was the question of jettisoning the cockpit canopy before ejection, otherwise the seat fired through the hood, inflicting head and face injuries, and crash helmets for RAF pilots did not appear until several years later. Another form of injury was caused by not retracting the legs and feet resulting in serious injuries to both. When the seat was clear of the aircraft it would tumble, disorienting the pilot attempting to release himself from the seat and achieve sufficient separation from the seat before opening his parachute. Lastly, there was the danger of anoxia at high altitude that required a free fall from the rarefied air and sub-zero temperatures to a safe height for a parachute descent.

James Martin attempted to take care of the correct cockpit posture before ejection by making the pilot pull a blind over his face to fire the seat, thus keeping his back and head in line and to bring the arms into the body to avoid flailing, as well as offering some protection to the face and head. The only drawback occurred during very high positive G forces when the pilot had difficulty raising his arms sufficiently to pull the blind. The US ejection seat fired from the seat pan provided an advantage under high G conditions and later versions incorporated restraining strap modifications to ensure the correct body alignment on ejection. However, back and leg injuries still occurred because the single charge of explosive in the ejection gun was very violent. This was resolved by making the initial charge softer and as the seat moved up the rail a stronger second charge sent the seat clear of the aircraft and the tailplane. Leg and foot injuries were reduced by incorporating thigh shields to the seat and leg straps to pull the legs against the seat as it started to rise. Injuries sustained while shattering the canopy on the way out were reduced by incorporating miniature detonating cords along the canopy that exploded the hood into small pieces as the seat started to move. To enable a stabilized and safe free fall before the automatic disengagement from the seat and the automatic opening of the parachute, the seat incorporated a rocket to deploy a drogue that stabilized the seat into the correct attitude for the release of the pilot, with an automatic barometric release mechanism to allow the seat to fall free to 15,000 feet before releasing the pilot and automatically opening the parachute. Finally to prevent anoxia, a small emergency oxygen bottle carried with the dinghy pack operated a supply of oxygen into the pilot's face mask until he reached a lower safe altitude. These modifications took several years to materialize and incorporate, by which time higher aircraft performance made it necessary for the pilot and navigator to be able to eject at zero airspeed and zero altitude. This was achieved by incorporating rocket propulsion in the place of an ejection gun to take the seated pilot or navigator to a sufficient height for his safe release from the seat and the safe deployment of the parachute.

An early modification to the Meteor VIII ejection seat resulted in my first incident on the squadron. The modification was the provision of an emergency oxygen bottle for safe ejection at high altitude. The bottle was placed in front of the dinghy pack in the seat pan. This resulted in no known problems until one day during a Fighter Command exercise the squadron scrambled to intercept a mock raid by aircraft from RAF squadrons based in Germany. The squadron aircraft were parked on a concrete servicing area in front of the squadron dispersal and to expedite our take-off, instead of our normal take-off towards the south against the prevailing wind, which entailed a lengthy amount of taxiing around the airfield perimeter track, we taxied rapidly across the rough grass of the airfield to the south end of the runway. I was leading the flight of four aircraft and, turning onto the runway, opened up to full power. About halfway along the runway I attempted to rotate the aircraft to lift off the runway but I found I could not move the stick far enough back to raise the nose. My first impression was that the elevator control was jammed, but on reaching down I found the emergency oxygen bottle jammed between the seat and the control stick. With the weight of the dinghy and parachute pack plus myself strapped tightly into the seat, I could not move the oxygen bottle. As I struggled with it my R/T connection to my helmet disconnected and when I called on my R/T to announce my intention to abort my take-off my wingman did not hear the call and, despite my hand signals to indicate cutting engines, he still attempted to stay with me as I closed both throttles and the high and low pressure fuel cocks shutting down both engines. To my surprise I saw my wingman Dougal Dallison, a New Zealander, still with me but he quickly overtook me before we reached the end of the runway. I was then behind him as we left the runway at speed and crossing a wide grass strip headed for the boundary fence and hedge. I pulled in behind him and followed him through the gap he cut through the fence and hedge. We continued into a wheat field and I stopped about one third into the field, but my faithful wingman continued until he stopped just short of a wood. Both my engines had stopped with the turbines just windmilling and so my engines injected nothing while travelling across the field and there was no damage to my aircraft. However, my number two sustained some damage going through the boundary fence and hedge, and as his engines were still running they ingested quite a lot of wheat together with one partridge. The fortunate aspect of the incident was the fact that in taking-off towards the north, instead of towards the south as was normal practice, we were able to take advantage of the only overshoot area available off the runway. Our normal direction of take-off allowed no overshoot area before crossing the main Bromley to Westerham road and crashing into houses bordering the road in Biggin Hill village with probable fatal results. Further incidents resulting from rough taxiing across the grass were prevented by the building of concrete readiness platforms at the ends of the runway for the aircraft on readiness, with a telephone connection to sector control to enable the aircraft to respond rapidly to the order to scramble. Ironically, both aircraft sustained some damage as the salvage crews endeavoured to get the aircraft back on the airfield. As far as I can recall, my previous windscreen incident on a Meteor VIII and the emergency oxygen bottle incident were the only such incidents recorded in Fighter Command and must constitute the only pioneer contribution on my part for safety modifications to the Meteor. The modification to the seat pan placed a lip on the front of the seat to prevent any possibility of the bottle vibrating out of its housing during rough taxiing.

Shortly after this incident Sir Winston Churchill became the British Prime Minister for the second time and the two auxiliary squadrons arranged for their respective honorary air commodores to visit Biggin Hill to inspect their squadrons on the same day. Coincidental to this, Fighter Command had a defence exercise that gave the Queen Mother and the Prime Minister the opportunity to see the Biggin Hill wing in action. The auxiliaries entertained their honorary air commodores to a luncheon in the mess before an inspection of the squadrons to be followed by a fly-past. No. 41 Squadron was not involved in the function and during the proceedings waited at readiness on the north operational readiness plat-form (ORP) of the runway. The Queen Mother and the Prime Minister inspected their respective squadrons and the two squadrons took-off for the fly-past. Shortly after their departure from the airfield we received scramble instructions and the twelve Meteors lined up in pairs for the interception of a raid coming from the European mainland. I was leading the squadron and a Canadian pilot, Flight Lieutenant MacDonald, was my number three, leading the second pair in my flight. The usual procedure for a flight or squadron stream take-off was for the pairs of Meteors to take off at ten seconds intervals, with the odd numbered pairs in the sections pulling high on take-off and the following even numbered pairs staying low to avoid turbulent slipstream and to pick up speed to facilitate a quick formation join up. All the Meteors had a full fuel load of 330 gallons internal fuel and a ventral overload tank of 105 gallons. MacDonald either attempted to lift off too soon with the full load or selected wheels up too soon on becoming airborne as he encountered my slipstream. Whatever the reason, the Meteor sank back onto the runway and slid along the remainder of the runway before crashing through the perimeter fence, crossing the main road and crashing into a house. The impact demolished the house, and the Meteor, with over 400 gallons of fuel on board, exploded in a massive fireball that enveloped the house. MacDonald and two elderly residents of the house died instantly. I was unaware of the disaster until informed over the R/T before continuing with the squadron on our interception. Fortunately, MacDonald's wingman and the aircraft following were not involved in the accident and on completion of the exercise we diverted to Manston in Kent before returning to Biggin Hill. This was our first fatality and major accident, and most unfortunately it was witnessed by our distinguished guests. However, before they left the airfield they were to witness a double tragedy.

The proverb that *misfortunes never come singly* became a reality when, as the two auxiliary squadrons approached Biggin Hill for their fly-past and were informed of the disaster on the airfield, they turned over the airfield to divert to another airfield and a Meteor IV of No. 600 Squadron, now led by Squadron Leader Jack Meadows, DFC, AFC, RAuxAF, whose pilot was paying more attention to what had happened on the ground than to his formation flying, collided with his section leader. The other pilot managed to bale out of his aircraft and landed on the airfield close by the impact of the two Meteors. Considering the height and time available to him to accomplish this without an ejection seat it was some achievement. The offending pilot was not so fortunate and died in the wreckage of his aircraft. One error compounded by another resulted in the loss of four lives, three aircraft and the destruction of a house. It was certainly a day to remember by all concerned and it was very fortunate that the death role on the ground was not considerably greater. It was particularly sad for us as MacDonald, an experienced and excellent pilot, was a good friend and a popular member of the squadron. I had the unpleasant task as adjustment officer of being responsible for attending to his personal effects for his next of kin, while the CO wrote the usual letters of condolence. The task of an adjustment officer is an unpleasant one and often leads to some embarrassing situations; and once again the squadron assembled to pay their respects to an empty box as it descended into the ground to the echo of the shots fired by the honour escort.

I do not recall The Queen Mother visiting Biggin Hill again during my time there, but Winston Churchill did visit unofficially on a couple of occasions. The Prime Minister liked to talk to the pilots on the squadrons and as a battalion commander in the Royal Scots Fusiliers while out of office during the First World War in 1916 he was proud of his military associations. His sense of sartorial individualism saw him frequently dressed in his Air Commodore's uniform with RAF wings and campaign ribbons from the Boer War and the First World War. I had seen him on several occasions without speaking to him but on one occasion I did speak to him while in the mess at Biggin Hill when he was en route to his home at Westerham. There happened to be a cocktail party in the mess at the time and the great man's appearance created a stir as usual. I recall him asking me to find him a comfortable chair in a quiet corner of the mess so he could talk with some of the squadron pilots while smoking the inevitable cigar accompanied by a glass of cognac. He asked that we try to keep the ladies from speaking to him as he was too tired to keep getting up to greet them. Churchill had not been well and showed his approaching eighty years. Despite rumours to the contrary, although he appeared frail at the time his mind remained as sharp as ever. Bearing in mind that he continued as Prime Minister until 1955 and then lived in retirement for a further ten years, the reports of his decline were probably exaggerated. At the risk of echoing a popular comic song consisting of only two lines – *Lloyd George knew my father – My father knew Lloyd George* – sung over and over again to the tune of 'Onward Christian Soldiers,' I mentioned to the Prime Minister, while he was questioning me on the Meteor, that he had known my father during the First World War. At first he showed polite interest as obviously my name meant nothing to him until I said my father was his ADC while he was with the 9th (Scottish) Division of First Army on the Western Front in January 1916. To my surprise he said, 'Ha yes, a tall young Scot with a passion for firearms.' Churchill had resigned from the Asquith government in 1915 and returned to the Army after a period of eighteen years. It was expected that he would be given command of a brigade in First Army with the 9th (Scottish) Division. My father was serving with the 9th Battalion of The Cameronians (Scottish Rifles) having received a field commission during the Second Ypres Offensive at the Battle of Loos in September 1915. He was assigned to Churchill's personal staff as his ADC while escorting him around the 9th (Scottish) Division and First Army. Political infighting resulting from Churchill's resignation from the Asquith government quashed the command of a brigade but he was given command of the 6th Battalion of the Royal Scots Fusiliers, and my father returned to his regiment. However, Churchill did not remain long at the front with the Royal Scots before leaving to join the government of Lloyd George in 1916, becoming Minister of Munitions in 1917. Therefore, he was not with the 9th (Scottish) Division when it moved from the pulverized sodden land of Flanders south to the open rolling chalk-downs of the Somme in June 1916 to join Fourth Army in preparation for the Somme Offensive in July 1916. Churchill asked after my father and I told him he had survived the severe wounds he received during the Battle of the Somme in 1916, the Battle of Cambrai in 1917 and the Battle of Amiens in 1918. Churchill expressed interest and concern, saying he was glad to hear that my father had not only survived the war but was still alive and able to live an active life. While standing with a group at the entrance to the mess as the Prime Minister took his leave, I was surprised when he moved over to me to say, 'Thank you. I enjoyed our talk. You should be proud of your father, he was a brave man. Please pass on my regards to him.' My father, who always spoke well of Churchill, was both surprised and pleased that the Prime Minister remembered him.

In the era of the propeller driven aircraft, despite constant warnings, people still managed to walk into whirling propeller blades with fatal or horrendous injuries. So it was with jet propulsion engines when people passed too close to the engine intakes, but unlike propeller aircraft steel grills could be placed in the intakes of the jet engines to prevent ingestion. It was standard procedure for these guards to be placed in the engine intake whenever ground running the engine, and although the grill mesh was not small enough to prevent small objects being ingested into the engine, it would prevent a human body from being sucked into the engine intake. One day while standing outside the squadron dispersal during a Meteor ground run, I saw an airman walk across the front of the aircraft and in an instant disappear as if in a magic show, followed by a loud bang as the impeller turbine disintegrated. Running over to the aircraft as the fitter shut down the engines, we found no protective grills over the engine intakes and no sign of the airman, apart from one black shoe lying on the ground. Looking inside the engine intake some ragged remains of clothing and body parts were seen and yet again I attended another farewell and customary consignment of a largely empty box into the ground. Even with the engine intake guards in place, if a human body was drawn against the grill at high engine power the suction applied at the intake by the jet engine was such that the lungs would collapse and the victim suffocate before the engine could be shutdown; but at least the body would remain intact for burial.

One of the joys of flying a jet propelled fighter after flying a propeller driven fighter was the greater power and speed aligned to a greater smoothness and simplicity of controls with relative quietness. Gone was the rasping, clattering noise of the twelve cylinders combined with the propeller noise as the propeller heaved the aircraft into the air with the blade tips approaching the speed of sound, before the aircraft settled down to a lengthy climb to altitude. Instead, the surge of the jet thrust projected the aircraft rapidly into the air and the rate of climb to altitude was initially quite breathtaking. With the pilot insulated within the pressurized cockpit, the whine of the jet engine penetrating the flying helmet was muted and soon ignored, and the flight was smooth and seemingly effortless. Accustomed to the vagaries of the piston engine and propeller pitch noises accompanied by the occasional airframe shake, flying a jet was a completely new environmental experience. Gone too were the complications of engine boost, propeller revolutions and fuel mixture control with carburettor heat control, to be replaced by a simple use of throttle to control the turbine revolutions and jet pipe temperature. The monitoring of the engine instruments was similarly simplified from several dials to basically a group of four: the engine revolutions and the jet pipe temperature, grouped with the fuel pressure and oil temperature gauges, while keeping a watchful note of the fuel contents. The sensation was that of riding a projectile into space and in a few short minutes one was through the overcast to the troposphere, when after a climb of around 6 vertical miles the tropopause was reached on the edge of the stratosphere. With a little imagination, as the blue of the sky deepened and the perception of the curvature of the earth emerged, one felt one was on the edge of space itself. However, to achieve this would require a few hundred miles more altitude; through the stratosphere, ionosphere, mesosphere and finally the exosphere, a distance of around 650 miles. At the tropopause, and above the weather, the view below was either a bright white carpet, or more rarely in Europe a patchwork quilt of greens and browns edged by the blue-green of the sea. Flying in the tropopause, at the edge of the effect of weather, as the aircraft turned one could view one's progress through space marked by the condensation trails of the jet engine as it traced a broad white chalk line across the sky against a deep azure board. At such times, if flying alone with the radio silent, there was an incredible feeling of not being part of this world, especially if above cloud, and regardless of one's religious beliefs the effect was one of wonder, empathizing with John Magee in a perception of being able to *touch the face of God*. With the sight of another aircraft the spell and any illusions were broken and one contemplated a return to earth, often dependent upon the guidance from the ground via radio, radio compass or radar control. If flying on instruments the descent through the darkening clouds would reveal the real dark, dreary, wet and forbidding world below; but for a few short magical moments one had soared with angels. The great joy of flying a jet fighter was that no matter how life appeared to mere earth bound mortals, one could *slip the surly bonds of earth* and enter another world of bright sunlight and sun drenched clouds.

One of the great flying experiences of which I never tired was the awesome manoeuvrability of flight in a jet fighter. The power of the jet engine and the ease with which it could perform aerobatics covering great areas of sky, enabled one to soar over towering cumulus cloud mountains and around the soft rounded cotton wool tops, before plunging down deep running canyons and through narrow winding ravines, without the danger of impact if the judgment was not fine enough. Here one could effortlessly traverse the great white crags *as hills peeped over hills, and Alps on Alps arose,* with vaulting zooms and darting dives interspersed with loops and rolls. It had been difficult, if not impossible, remotely to experience this effortless flight in any propeller driven fighter and it was always a source of great pleasure for me until recalled to the operational role of being a fighter pilot. Since most of our flying was conducted in some form of formation flying, the opportunity for personal indulgence such as this usually resulted while on an air test or a cross-country exercise or on simulated camera gun combat when the right conditions prevailed.

When flying at night one was usually alone on a cross-country flight, or practising circuits and landings. Flying at high altitude above cloud would bring a sense of awe and wonder at the magnificence of the night sky, seen with a brilliance and clarity never experienced on the ground. Often the feeling of remoteness would be replaced by a sense of extreme loneliness. The ground, if seen at all, was only discerned by shades of darkness and a town or a city identified only by strings of fairy lights strung along the streets, no matter the hour of the night. On occasions, especially when flying over the overcast, a sense of remoteness and loneliness could be almost overpowering; until the spell was broken as one was connected to another aircraft or reconnected to earth by a voice on the radio telephone. These were all magical moments never remotely contemplated, or even dreamed of, while flying propeller fighters. They are still treasured memories in the twilight of my non-flying days.

During a Fighter Command exercise against the Vampire wing at North Weald, while leading my flight over East Anglia I witnessed a mid-air collision between two Vampires at 30,000 feet. The impact was that of an explosive shell and from the fire-ball pieces of wreckage fluttered down with no sign of a white parachute emerging. We reduced height looking for signs of survivors and on reaching 20,000 feet I heard a call from my squadron commander, 'Dusty' Miller, that he had a fire warning light on his port engine. This was followed by a call reporting an explosion. On checking over his aircraft I could see that flames coming from the engine jet pipe were getting bigger and assumed a disintegrating impeller turbine had ruptured the fuel line. I called for him to eject as the fire in the port engine was now intense and threatening the aileron control. An ejection appeared to be his only option before losing control of the air-craft. Miller turned onto an easterly heading with a hope that the aircraft would fly itself seawards. He closed down the live engine, reduced speed to around 150 knots, trimmed the aircraft, and remembered to lower his seat and head as he jettisoned the canopy. Then drawing his feet back towards the seat, he reached up and pulled the blind over his face, firing the ejection gun. He recalled a violent thump and loud bang as the charge propelled the seat up the guide rails taking him clear of the Meteor. This was before modification of the ejection seat would provide a double charge ejection gun to help reduce the very jarring shove in the backside as the single ejection gun fired. This was also before further modification to the seat provided a rocket propelled drogue to stabilize the seat. As it was the seat began to tumble and with the blind off his face he could see the sky and earth reversing positions. An automatic barometric release unit had yet to be incorporated in the seat, but he knew he was at a safe altitude to release the seat and open his parachute. Feeling for the seat harness release he turned it and when the sky appeared above him, punched the release and kicked away from the seat. He then remembered to wait for a separation from the seat before pulling the parachute ripcord. This was necessary because before the fully automatic sequence of events that would result in suspension from the parachute when clear of the seat, there were instances when the pilot was not so fortunate and the ejection seat became entangled with the parachute. Eventually the whole process became fully automatic because the pilot could be unconscious from the moment of firing the ejection seat to the time he arrived safely on the ground: but in the early days of the 1950s one had to work for the banana. Miller was around 10,000 feet when his chute opened and swinging gently he could see below a reassuring green patchwork quilt of open countryside.

'Dusty' Miller recounted that his descent was very quiet and peaceful as he contemplated whether he could control the chute to avoid hitting any obstacles such as high tension wires, houses or trees. All those easy instructions during pilot training on how to control one's descent could now be demonstrated as he tried to assess the wind speed and direction. Fortunately for him, the weather was fine, the wind speed moderate and he was over farmland. For a short while he was almost enjoying the seemingly gentle descent but as the earth started to approach rapidly he saw he was heading for some farm buildings. Fortunately, before he could consider any guidance to his descent he passed them by and arrived on mother earth just inside a meadow of grazing cows. He landed in an untidy heap and while struggling to release his parachute, the wind dragged him into a hedgerow. He had barely disengaged himself from the parachute harness when some farm labourers arrived on the scene followed by the inquisitive cows. On feeling himself all over he found his limbs all in place and, when asked, was able to pronounce himself in fine fettle. His flying helmet, goggles and gloves had protected him from any scratches from the hedgerow, and he was able, as a devout Catholic, to make an appropriate number of 'Hail Mary's' in thankful salutation to whatever providence had prevailed to provide such benevolent conditions for his first, and he hoped, last parachute descent. Equally fortunate was the fact that his Meteor crashed in open country without causing any civilian casualties. He was taken to the nearest RAF station at Wattisham and after a cursory inspection by the station doctor, declined his offer to send him to the RAF hospital at Ely. A service car drove him back to Biggin Hill where his anxious family, and squadron, awaited his arrival.

Not all my time at Biggin Hill was duty bound as I enjoyed more leisure time than was the case when I was flying with the auxiliary air force or during my tour as an ADC. It was after my arrival on 41 Squadron that I decided to divest myself of my half share in a four-seat Percival Proctor single-engine monoplane used by the RAF as a light communication aircraft during the war. The RAF had little use for these aircraft after the war and many were sold off as surplus war equipment. During the last year of the war I had a friend who was a flight commander on a communication squadron that flew me to Paris shortly after the liberation. After VJ Day I decided to obtain my civil flying licences. My friend was now commanding an RAF communication squadron at what is now Gatwick International Airport and I accompanied him to one of the war surplus sales, and on a sudden whim we decided to buy a Proctor that was in good condition with low flying hours. We purchased it very cheaply and were able to enlist 'volunteers' on the squadron to help service the aircraft; so the upkeep when shared between us was no more expensive than running my sports car. The other incentive was the fact that my friend lived in Jersey and we anticipated that the aircraft would enable us to visit the Channel Islands and France at weekends. The grand prix motor circuit had started up again and we flew to many of the motor races. The process of private civil flying in the immediate post-war years was fairly relaxed and being service pilots enabled us to get away with a lot that would not be possible in later years. My friend used to fly regularly to Jersey to visit his girl friend and I was certainly not utilizing my share of the Proctor, although financially this did not amount to much and I was by then a member of 'the most expensive private flying club in the world', No. 601 RAuxAF Squadron! My friend nearly wrecked the Proctor, fortunately without any personal injuries and I decided to sell him my share of the aircraft. We had a lot of fun with the Proctor on some of our jaunts together with a few exciting moments, but I had started to renew my interest in sailing and I could not indulge in both pastimes. As a result of one close call, and as my father thought I should get into less trouble sailing than joyriding around Europe in the Proctor, he generously helped me in the acquisition of a 28 foot Bermuda rigged sloop that I kept moored at the RAF Yacht Club in the Hamble River. Whenever time permitted I spent my time sailing the Solent area and along the west coast, with an occasional trip to France. I got to know the area well and crewed on several larger yachts in the Channel races and during Cowes Week when I joined the Royal London Yacht Club.

Some of my most enjoyable sailing during my tour at Biggin Hill was with a friend who was flying with the auxiliaries. We crewed for his younger sister in her International Dragon Class yacht and competed in several of the races at the Royal Beaumaris Yacht Club in North Wales, where my friend lived. He was the only son of an extensive estate along the shores of the Menai Straight, and as the only member of his family to break with tradition and blot the family escutcheon by joining one of the services other than the Army, he liked to have some RAF support when visiting the family. My initial visit had perceptions of 'Brideshead Revisited' as the family residence was an impressive stately home. The baronet, the epitome of his class during a different era, had a resemblance to the actor C. Aubrey Smith in one of his military roles. At my first meeting with him I felt very much as I did in the presence of my head-master at school. However, he proved to be very approachable, and with a mutual interest in guns, shooting and fishing, as well as being well versed in battle tales by my father, I established a good rapport with him. The general had served with distinction in the infantry during and after the First World War and I encouraged him to talk of his experiences in The Great War, much to the feigned chagrin of the family having listened to them many times before. I recounted some of my father's exploits while serving with the Scottish Rifles at the Battle of Loos and the Battle of the Somme. He was particularly interested to hear how my father as a very junior subaltern platoon commander endeavoured to deceive the Germans that he had a Lewis machine-gun in his section of the line when they were in very short supply. He mounted a dozen rifles on each of two wooden frames placed on top of the parapet of the trench with the triggers tripped to fire the rifles in quick succession. The firing of the rifles sounded as two quick bursts of fire from a machine-gun and he hoped by this to persuade the Germans to do their probing raids elsewhere. The distance between the opposing front line trenches in the coalfields around Loos was often less than 200 yards and at night both sides carried out patrols and the repair of the barbed-wire in no-man's-land. In order to deter this activity on his company front he modified a Stokes 3 inch trench mortar into a cannon to fire grapeshot. The cannon, primed with two mortar charges and filled with various scraps of metal – bullets, shot, shrapnel and nails – was placed on top of the parapet of a forward sap and lined up on the barbed-wire in no-man's-land. Sandbags placed on top, at the sides and the rear of the mortar protected the gunner. On a dark night with no moon, when wiring parties and reconnaissance patrols were anticipated, my father took up position behind his cannon, while a brave volunteer crawled out through the barbed-wire pulling a length of wire behind him. Out in the barbed-wire he went to ground in a shell-hole and taking up the slack on the wire with signalling tugs to my father holding the other end, he waited for the Germans to come within range of the cannon's lethal charge. The signal came to hand and my father fired the cannon. The resultant bang sounded to those on 'stand-to' in the trench as if a mortar bomb had exploded in the sap as the mortar disintegrated with the barrel becoming a serrated funnel – *As cannons overcharged with double cracks.* My father regained consciousness on the far side of the trench with nothing more than a broken shoulder and punctured ear drums. Cries from the barbed-wire indicated that at least some pieces of metal had found human targets and the cries brought rifle fire to bear under the light of Very flares. The brave scout out in no-man's-land, although considerably shaken, survived the hail of fire and returned to his front line intact before dawn. My father was taken to hospital and given 'Blighty' leave and the experiment was not repeated.

One of the many problems confronting the troops in the front line trenches came from snipers, and these skilled sharpshooters using special Mauser rifles with telescopic sights caused many casualties to any of the troops exposing themselves above the trenches. The snipers, adept and ingenious in concealment, and changing their hides frequently, proved to be difficult to locate and harder to kill with the standard .303 Lee Enfield rifle. My father, while on leave in London following his discharge from hospital and visiting some of the famous London gunsmiths, came across a second-hand Jeffrey big-game double-barrelled rifle. There not being much demand at the time for such a rifle, my father was able to buy it very cheaply. The rifle chambered for the 0.600 nitro-express cartridge was intended to bring down a charging elephant, rhinoceros or buffalo at short range and had a considerable bullet drop at longer ranges. Nevertheless, the close proximity of the opposing front-line trenches made the rifle, when fitted with a telescopic sight, a feasible counter to the sniper threat operating from a hide. One sergeant in his company had been a gillie in the Highlands before joining the army and was expert in detecting a sniper's hide. After setting up a decoy, my father firing from a forward sap would place several of the big and heavy slugs into or around the detected or suspected hide. Although he made no claim of kills with the rifle, it proved an effective deterrent with a subsequent uplift in company morale, and he became in demand within the battalion to take care of snipers.

My Welsh friend's sister was an attractive and athletic girl who handled her Dragon very competently, and I had an immediate, restrained and unrequited crush on her. I looked forward to my visits to Wales when I would borrow a Meteor jet from the squadron and fly to RAF Valley in Anglesey to be met by my friend's sister. This privilege was traditional in the RAF during stand-downs, and regarded by the RAF as useful flying practice. The Army was not so accommodating in the loan of their tanks or the Royal Navy with their ships on such occasions. Although our presence was required for dinner and breakfast, my friend preferred that we stayed on the small island belonging to the estate in the Menai Straight, where a fishing lodge overlooked fish traps to catch salmon heading for Welsh rivers. I have very pleasant memories of this island retreat where, after some evening fishing, we sat on the terrace or in front of a log fire in the lodge for lengthy nightcaps before retiring, to be lulled to sleep if not by alcohol by the sound of water flowing over the fish weir. Arising early we would fish again before joining the family for breakfast. The general would brief us on sailing tactics and boat handling for the race before we sailed the Dragon across the Straight to Beaumaris. Our skipper was a demanding sailing master but we never managed to win a race for her. Following the race the general, who always followed the race from the clubhouse balcony through a telescope, would hold a post-mortem examination on our tactics, handling and mistakes. Our skipper obviously inured to this procedure would take it patiently and stoically, but afterwards would vent her displeasure on her crew. I imagined the general holding similar debriefings in his command following military manoeuvres. These idyllic days of summer in Wales were regrettably short and few in number but the memory would return frequently over the years, especially when abroad. Sadly, after I departed the UK for the US and then Korea, my friend was killed in a motorcar accident. The grim reaper was to deprive me of my two best friends in the RAF during my absence from the UK.

An activity over the English Channel that occupied us at Biggin Hill was air firing exercises. This was carried out initially on drogue targets towed over the sea a few miles off the coast. Flat banner targets replaced the drogue targets that gave a better sighting target and were easier to score with the cannon shell tips marked with different colours. This routine training was followed once a year by a detachment to the Fighter Command armament practice camp at Acklington on the Northumberland coast, that was close to the wartime Spitfire OTU I attended at Eschott. We stayed at Acklington for two weeks of concentrated air–air firing exercises. An amusing episode with revealing social mores occurred on one particular armament practice detachment when the squadron CO was ill and I was acting CO. We had an excellent two weeks firing on banner targets with the innovation of some towed glider targets. It was not possible to score the hits on these targets in the same manner as the banner targets as the hits were not clearly defined and one shell might indicate more than one hole. An audio wire recorder in the glider registered the sound of the hits and gave a good indication of the extent of the hits made. The main advantage of the glider target was that it resembled an aircraft and made the pilot range his sight while tracking the target.

There were no incidents during our stay and at the end of our detachment we decided to give the squadron ground crew a party at a local pub in Acklington village, paid for out of the 'pilots' fund', which normally took care of expenses for amenities in the pilots' crew room. The process of this fund was very democratic with the subscriptions determined by needs and rank. On leaving the pub at closing time, most of the squadron moved next door to the village hall for the monthly village dance, for which there was an extension of the drinking licence. On entering the hall we saw a few men gathered around the bar and a few couples dancing to a local band. However, seated all around the dance floor against the wall were dozens of hopeful women and girls in the proverbial wallflower situation. To enliven the proceedings, I offered to donate a bottle of scotch to the winner of a mandatory pilots' dancing contest to be judged by the two flight commanders and myself. The winner would be the pilot dancing with the most unprepossessing partner. As a result, that particular monthly dance was probably the most successful dance in the village hall since the departure of the Americans in 1945. The outcome of our socializing occurred the following morning when the squadron adjutant informed me that I had a rare 'orderly room' for hearing one of the squadron airmen charged by the RAF police of being improperly dressed after curfew and for conduct prejudicial to the good order and discipline of the Service. A service policeman gave evidence that the airman charged was caught creeping into camp in the early hours dressed only in his shirt and socks. The airman explained that after the dance at the village hall one of the women invited him back to her home. Acklington was a small mining village situated over a coal field that extended far out under the North Sea. The airman's 'date' was married to a miner working on the night shift but unfortunately he returned home unexpectedly due to a mishap at the mine. In the general panic of escaping out of the window the airman either could not find his clothes and shoes thrown out in the dark after him, or else he abandoned them as he legged it back to camp, The airman was clearly guilty as charged, but in mitigation I considered that the squadron bore some responsibility for the offence in placing him at the scene of the crime. That being the case there was the squadron's reputation to consider and in such matters the course of justice must be seen to be done. There was also the question of safeguarding the physical well being of the airman concerned. I found the airman guilty with a warning as to his future conduct and confinement to camp for the duration of our stay; and the cost of the items missing from his service kit during the offence to be deducted from his pay. However, the airman's punishment was not onerous as he was put on the advance party returning to Biggin Hill the following day. We flew out of Acklington two days later and the pilots' fund reimbursed him for the missing items of service kit. Our two weeks of intensive flying and gunnery resulted in the squadron achieving the highest air firing scores in Fighter Command. It was interesting to see the coast of Northumberland again, although much had changed in the years since I fulfilled my ambition to fly Spitfires and experienced at Eschott the thrill and joy of flying the aircraft. Our torment-ing Canadians had returned home, to the regret of many of the local girls, taking some of them home as wives. The airfield had returned to nature and only a few abandoned, riddled and leaking Nissan huts were left as a remembrance of things past. On the Boulmer airfield further up the coast there were no snarling Spitfires, only a few dispersed Bloodhound guided missile sites patiently waiting to sniff out any attacking Soviet 'Badger' bombers should they come from the East.

A London Particular. During my last year at Biggin Hill in 1952 *the yellow fog that rubs its back upon the windowpanes* of London was a killer fog and a notable catastrophe that brought disruption and death despite frequent warnings to the government in the past for the need of a Clean Air Act. The worst of these fogs occurred during the autumn and early winter months. It was estimated that by the end of the year as many as 12,000 people had died from respiratory complaints, mostly among the elderly. It appeared that the low lying areas of London along the Thames Valley created natural fogs, and when this occurred with a low level temperature inversion and no wind to disperse the fog, it mixed with the dense London smoke pollution from coal burning boilers and domestic fires to form a thick blanket of dense yellow smog like some monstrous catarrh. The dense smog stayed at ground level enveloping everything and making movement in the city almost impossible. Biggin Hill, sited on the escarpment of the South Downs a few hundred feet above sea level, escaped most of the effects of the smog and we were still able to fly. Flying over the yellow sea that covered London presented an incredible sight with the belching smoke stacks sticking out above the thick yellow blanket of smog. As the smoke emissions curled back down towards the ground, the smog blanket grew denser day by day until the weather factor changed with a wind to disperse the smog. Through this blanket covering the city I could still see church steeples poking out into a clear blue sky. The worst of these fogs lasted for as much as a week, before the inversion lifted and the wind dispersed the smog. I experienced the effects and difficulties of travelling in London when caught out in the city. The choking yellow smog reduced visibility to a few yards and just crossing a street was both a difficult and dangerous navigation exercise. Driving a car was well nigh impossible and the effect of the smog was plain to see as shirt collars and cuffs became quickly blackened by the soot. Thick, filthy yellow-black mucus blocked the nose and throat making it difficult to breathe; and in clearing the nose the filth was clearly evident in the handkerchief.

As an occasional sufferer of asthma I was very glad to be out of the smog area at Biggin Hill that remained mostly in the clear with only occasional patches of mist or fog. Similarly, my mother living at Hampstead above the smog level remained in the clear though unable to travel. Those that travelled by the London Underground system were no better off as the smog penetrated into some tunnels and stations, and the passengers on reaching ground level became as immobile as the rest. After the killer smog of late 1952 and early 1953, the government finally passed the Clean Air Act that at last brought an end to the 'Pea Soup' fogs of London and made even *a foggy day in London Town* a rarity and an exception to a previous frequent occurrence. There is no better description of a *London Particular* than that written nearly 100 years earlier by Charles Dickens in 'Our Mutual Friend' – *Animate London, with smarting eyes and irritated lungs, was blinking, wheezing, and choking. Divided in purpose between being visible and invisible, and so being wholly neither. Even in the surrounding country it was a foggy day, but there the fog was grey, whereas in London it was at about the boundary line, dark yellow, and a little within it brown, and then browner, and then browner, until at the heart of the City it was rusty-black.*

One of the most significant events during my time on 41 Squadron was my selection to attend The Day Fighter Leader School (DFLS) at the Central Fighter Establishment at West Raynham in Norfolk during 1952. The CinC Fighter Command, Air Marshal Sir Basil Embry, directed that all squadron commanders and flight commanders must complete this course before being confirmed in their appointments. The course involved the most intensive and rigorous fighter flying in the RAF, and was the forerunner of the USAF and USN 'Top Gun' schools in the USA formed after the Korean War. The flying on the course was conducted in simulated wartime conditions with little or no flying restrictions, and even under weather conditions that would normally ground the day fighter squadrons. The high standard of flying required made it necessary for the students to have more than just a little experience of jet fighters before attending the course, which some 'old hands' found to their cost.

The low level ground attack sorties had no height restrictions and were normally carried out at around 50 feet in altitude at a speed of 360 knots on the Meteors, and later at 420 knots on the Hunters. This equated to a ground distance covered in still air of 6 or 7 nm per minute to facilitate accurate D/R navigation at low level. The normal height restriction in the RAF for low flying was 250 feet and infringements below this height were subject to disciplinary action, but such a restriction was not feasible under mock combat conditions. The relaxation of the normal low level flying restrictions resulted in a high rate of bird strikes. *The air bites shrewdly – it is a nipping and an eager air.* I happened to be one of those to collect a bird strike while flying at zero feet and 360 knots, around 420 mph or 670 kph. The gull splattered the whole windscreen of the Meteor and the effect was as if hit by a large raspberry jam puff. The effect of suddenly flying blind at zero feet altitude can be quite disconcerting, especially while looking for landmarks. Fortunately it was no more serious than that as the bullet proof windscreen was tested to withstand the impact of a five-pound chicken fired from a pneumatic cannon at a speed of 500 mph. The many laminations of armoured glass sandwiched with vinyl did their job and although the result was messy it did not prove dangerous: with the number of turkey farms in the area I was glad the turkeys did not fly.

A bird strike on the windscreen was preferable to one in the engine intake that could cause a turbine failure. The squadron experienced some of these and I was glad to be flying Meteors with twin Derwent engines. The large compressor blades in the centrifugal RR Derwent engine in the Meteor, and the DH Goblin engine in the Vampire, did quite a good job of mincing the birds without throwing a compressor blade. When the axial flow compressors in the Rolls Royce Avon and Armstrong Siddeley Sapphire arrived with the Hunter and when one of the many small blades running the length of the compressor became dislodged, it churned through the many stages of the compressor as it passed through the engine, causing at least an engine fire if not a catastrophic turbine failure.

The only other worrisome incident I experienced on the course occurred shortly after one take-off when on selecting the cabin pressurization I became enveloped in a white cloud of kerosene mist, which temporarily blinded me shortly after becoming airborne. My wingman reported that I had a cockpit fire but when I turned off the pressurization and motored open the canopy hood the kerosene mist cleared from the cockpit. My oxygen mask protected me from inhaling any fumes and although my eyes were watering and smarting my goggles had kept the kerosene out of my eyes. I flew around for a while to clear the fumes and burn off some fuel and landed without incident. The engineering staff tried to maintain that it was impossible for the fuel to get into the pressurization system but somehow during refuelling the kerosene had entered the airframe and cockpit of the aircraft and the cockpit pressurization had produced a dense white cloud of kerosene mist. I never heard of a similar case but then the pilot may not have returned to report the incident. At that time the RAF and the USAF had different policies regarding the turbine fuel used by jet aircraft. The RAF preferred to use aviation kerosene called Avtur, whereas the USAF used aviation gasoline called Avgas. The Avtur fuel, although more expensive to produce, was a safer fuel and with its higher temperature of combustion offered less of a fire hazard than the high-octane gasoline fuel.

In 1952 the directing staff on DFLS consisted of experienced wartime senior pilots, some with wartime 'ace' status. During my time on the course the CO was Wing Commander Prosser Hanks, DSO, DFC, an ex-Battle of Britain 'ace'. The senior instructor was Squadron Leader Billy Drake, DSO, DFC, another Battle of Britain pilot, who made a reputation in Desert Air Force as a high scoring fighter ace with 24 German and Italian aircraft claimed destroyed. Billy Drake, a descendent of Francis, was a well-known personality in Fighter Command, and I got to know him well during the fifties. His aggressive character as a fighter pilot carried over into the mess as the enthusiastic instigator of mess games following a dining-in night such as 'Mess rugby', 'High cockalorum', and 'Are you there Moriarty?' These mess games, together with motor cycle accidents, accounted for the majority of orthopaedic cases in the RAF hospitals at Halton, Ely and Wroughton! As an accomplished skier with strong legs, Billy Drake's speciality was leg wrestling and with his opponent's reflexes dulled by alcohol, he was seldom bettered at the game. The DFLS course was a wonderful experience and was without question the most intensive and enjoyable flying I had experienced to date. By a function of chance and good luck all my flights went well, especially in leading missions and I graduated with a rare 'Exceptional' leadership assessment. I am sure it was this assessment, together with my squadron assessments in flying and gunnery of 'Above Average', that was instrumental in my selection at Fighter Command to fly with the USAF fighter squadrons during the last year of the Korean War. In the same way as my flying instructor's category followed me around, so too did the DFLS assessment follow me two years later for selection to the directing staff of DFLS and the Fighter Combat Wing that replaced it.

So it was that when Fighter Command called for volunteers to go to Korea towards the end of 1952, my name was put forward by Biggin Hill and in January 1953 I joined a squadron leader and ten other flight lieutenants from the Fighter Command day fighter squadrons on a BOAC Stratocruiser bound for New York on the way to Nellis Air Force Base,

Las Vegas, Nevada. Only the squadron leader, Max Higson, and I had wartime flying experience as the remainder of the pilots were post-war entrants into the RAF. I was then in my thirtieth year and I recalled the time eleven years previously, when I had sailed to the USA in search of my wings, that three of the cadets in our intake were in their mid to late twenties and married, two having volunteered for pilot training from the police force and one remustering from ground crew. The rest of us regarded them as very elderly, certainly too ancient to be aircrew. Perhaps our more junior companions regarded Max and me in the same light as being too old for active jet operations, but I was to find a few pilots older than us on the 4th Fighter Interceptor Wing (FIW) at K-14, Kimpo, in the 'Land of the Morning Calm'.

The history of Fighter Command pilots flying with the USAF during the Korean War originated from Air Marshal Sir Basil Embry, CinC Fighter Command, wanting to send a Meteor squadron to Korea, but was unable to do so. The Royal Australian Air Force was represented in the United Nations forces in Korea by No. 77 Squadron flying P-51 Mustangs. The Australians decided to convert the squadron to Meteors and the Meteor VIIIs arrived from the UK with RAF instructors to assist in the conversion. Subsequently, the RAF provided about 40 per cent of the commissioned pilots on the squadron. Initially, a handful of experienced pilots from the Central Fighter Establishment went to Korea as observers and one, Wing Commander John Baldwin, DSO, DFC, a distinguished wartime Typhoon ground attack pilot, was lost in action. Although a very experienced pilot, Baldwin had limited jet-flying experience when he arrived in Korea. The Commander-in-Chief Fighter Command was anxious that Fighter Command should have jet combat experienced fighter pilots on his squadrons at a time when the 'Cold War' was at its most intense phase. He arranged with the Chief of Staff of the US Air Force that the RAF could send qualified fighter pilots on detachment to the USAF to fly with the USAF fighter squadrons in Korea. In order to ensure that these pilots were suitably prepared to join the US squadrons they would have to attend the same tactical weapons training as the US pilots before joining USAF squadrons in Korea. Training on air-air combat, air-air gunnery, and air-to-ground firing with rocket and bomb attacks was carried out at The USAF Tactical Weapons School at Nellis AFB in the Nevada desert, using F-80 'Shooting Star' and F-86 'Sabre Jet' aircraft. In order to maximize the number of combat experienced pilots in Fighter Command, it would have been more beneficial for the RAF to have a similar arrangement to that agreed by the USAF with the RCAF, in sending fighter pilots to Korea with an abbreviated tour of fifty missions. The USAF would not agree to this and insisted on a full tour of

100 missions for the RAF pilots. Understandably, when the USAF was fully geared up to produce as many jet combat experienced pilots as possible, it was reluctant to support the additional time required for a double intact of RAF pilots at Nellis. Under the new arrangement four more Fighter Command pilots arrived in Korea in 1952, joining the two F-86 Fighter Interceptor Wings. When they returned at the end of 1952 it was decided to send a further twelve pilots from Fighter Command and I was included in that number. The armistice at the end of July 1953 ended any more detachments from the RAF to the USAF in Korea and the RAF and the RCAF had provided twenty fighter pilots from each air force to the USAF fighter squadrons during the Korean War.

Before leaving for the US we were equipped with a vast amount of arctic clothing and flying kit, including the new RAF G-suit. As it turned out this large bag of luggage was largely excess and redundant ballast as I preferred, apart from a useful arctic parka, to use the USAF equipment. We embarked on a BOAC Stratocruiser for New York and after the usual round of sightseeing flew on to Washington, DC. In the US capital we had briefings at the British Embassy with some further sightseeing before flying on to Las Vegas via Chicago and Denver, Colorado.

Nellis Air Force Base lies a few miles out of Las Vegas in the Nevada Desert. We were a little surprised to find that jet pilots were segregated to the extent of having their own Bachelor Officer Quarters and a mess dining hall for 'Jet pilots only'. Although the tactical weapons course was divided into two phases, the first on the F-80 and the second on the F-86, as experienced jet fighter pilots we were exempted from the first phase apart from some day and night navigational exercises and instrument flying without a cloud in sight during the whole of our stay. The Lockheed F-80 Shooting Star was a good handling aircraft with an equivalent performance to that of the Meteor VIII. Powered by an Allison J-33 turbojet engine of 5,000 lb.s.t, it had a maximum speed of Mach 0.8; and a rate of climb close to 7,000 ft./min. Wing tip overload tanks gave the F-80 a very useful range of 1,300 nautical miles. The two-seat trainer version of the F-80, the T-33, was the nicest weekend aircraft I ever flew and I envy those who have the means to buy a civil registered version as a personal aircraft.

Moving on to No. 97 Squadron for the F-86 phase of our course we joined, as far as the RAF was concerned, a still quite select group of pilots to experience the envelope of transonic flight and break through the popular misconception of the 'sound barrier'. With but a nodding acquaintance of Dr Mach and compressibility problems during my Mustang flying, any near approach to this invisible 'barrier' in the Meteor was accompanied by much buffeting with strange airframe convulsions and noises of protest from the engines. This was to be the real thing at last and after a familiarization flight I carried out my first 'Mach run' and delivered the expected sonic boom at the base as evidence of joining the then fairly exclusive club of those exceeding the speed of sound.

The single engine F-86 Sabre is one of the great fighter aircraft in the history of aviation, and a very different fighter to the twin engine Meteor I had flown during the past two years. As I climbed into the F-86 cockpit for the first time I felt very much as I had done all those years ago when leaving my Spitfire and climbing into the Mustang cockpit for the first time. The F-86 cockpit was more cluttered and complicated than the Meteor or any other aircraft I had flown up to that time. There were different concepts in an American designed fighter than an RAF one, such as controls, systems and instrumentation, with some innovations that were new to me. The biggest and most important difference in concept and design being in the hydraulic system that controlled the flight controls, air brakes, flaps, wheel brakes and the operation of the undercarriage. In support of this system was an auxiliary emergency system enabling the aircraft still to fly and be controllable even with the engine flamed-out, as long as the turbine was able to windmill and supply sufficient limited hydraulic power, with electrical backup supplied by the emergency battery. The cockpit although not spacious was nevertheless comfortable, with excellent all-round visibility through the bubble canopy. Reassuringly, it had an ejection seat and this differed in design from the RAF Martin Baker ejection seat. Whereas the British ejection seat was fired by pulling a blind over the face, the US ejection seat was fired by pulling handles at the side of the seat. I personally favoured the British design as I considered it offered better chances of escaping injury on ejection. The US ejection seat, however, had the advantage of being able to be fired while experiencing extreme negative G conditions, when it may have been difficult if not impossible to reach up and fire the Martin Baker seat. The F-86 had a very efficient pressurized and air conditioned cockpit that was the best I had experienced up until that time. The pressurization control had two settings; one for normal high altitude flying when the 11 psi pressure produced a cockpit altitude of around 10,000 feet, and the other being a combat setting of 5.5 psi that reduced the effect of sudden decompression in the event of failure, allowing the pressure demand oxygen system to automatically supply increased flow under pressure into the face mask. The pilot was protected from battle damage by two armoured panels fitted fore and aft of the cockpit, in addition to the heated armoured glass windscreen panel. Demisting and de-icing of the windscreen and cockpit canopy was very effectively cleared by high-pressure hot air blasts from nozzles around the windscreen and canopy, controlled by a trombone type slide lever on the left side of the canopy.

A prominent feature in front of the pilot and above the main instrument panel was the radar ranging and tracking gun-sight. The throttle, air brakes, flaps and undercarriage controls were conveniently placed for the pilot's left hand. The flight and navigational instruments followed a conventional layout, with the associated engine instruments to the right of the flight instruments. Below the main instrument panel in front of the pilot was a panel for the control of armament and ordnance. The radio panels were along the right side of the cockpit. Among the innovations in instrumentation was a tachometer calibrated in percentage power instead of precise rpm. This was a better and more logical interpretation of the power from the turbine, rather than a read out of the very high rpm involved, bearing in mind that 90 per cent of the available engine thrust occurs in the last 10 per cent of the rpm range. Another innovation was the provision of a G-suit. Although the Americans had used G-suits towards the end of the Second World War, the RAF did not equip their fighters with this combat convenience until the arrival of the Hunter into service in 1954. The F-86 used nose-wheel steering for taxiing by depressing a button on front of the control stick. This was an improvement on the RAF system of taxiing by differential braking. Also situated on top of the stick, and conveniently placed for the pilot's right thumb, was a 'coolie hat' shaped button for the aircraft's pitch and roll trim, replacing the manually controlled trim wheels on the left side of the cockpit. Yet another innovation was the use of an integrated flying and crash helmet to protect the pilot, with a moveable sun visor. The flying crash helmet was not adopted by the RAF for general pilot's use until 1954. In Korea we removed the sun visor in preference to regular detachable flying goggles, as the visor tended to restrict or obscure vision while in combat.

Unlike the Meteor, that used a battery trolley accumulator for starting the engine, the F-86 in typical US fashion used a Houchin, Ford V-8 engine powered, 24 volt starter generator, producing 1,000 amps for start-up power. Selection of the low and high pressure fuel cocks required careful advance of the throttle to prevent the jet pipe temperature exceeding a maximum of 600 degrees Centigrade until the engine ran up to idling rpm. In flying the F-86 with its single axial flow turbine engine, the initial acceleration on take-off was slower than the Meteor with its twin centrifugal turbine engines, but after a nose-up take-off run of 10–15 degrees with an unstick airspeed of 115 knots, the rate of climb built up until it was faster than that of the Meteor. The F-86Es at Nellis had recently replaced the F-86As and were a big improvement on the original aircraft. Although the E model was similar in appearance to the A model it had the important difference of featuring an 'all-flying' tail, that greatly improved the control and handling of the aircraft at sonic speeds. The introduction of duplicated hydraulic powered flying controls on the F-86A with irreversible control surfaces successfully helped to counter the undesirable side effects of compressibility but the elevator, as in previous fighter designs, controlled the longitudinal attitude in flight with some instability at sonic speeds. The 'all-flying' tailplane moved the horizontal stabilizer in conjunction with the irreversible elevator and the result was greatly improved control as the aircraft went sonic in a dive and then transonic coming out of the dive to subsonic flight. The design of the hydraulic system on the F-86 was far more complex than hitherto had been the case of current fighters; and it is not surprising that the designer of the hydraulic system with its emergency back-up system was rumoured to have suffered a mental breakdown as a result. It would be some years before the UK designed fighters started to catch up in the design of hydraulic control systems. The F-86E was powered by one General Electric J47-GE-13 turbojet engine producing 5,200 lb.s.t. The maximum speed at sea level was 590 knots or Mach 0.9, and 520 knots or Mach 0.88 at 30,000 feet. The aircraft had a rate of climb of 7,250 ft/min and a service ceiling of 47,000 feet. An internal fuel capacity of 437 US gallons gave it a combat radius of 280 nautical miles. The armament consisted of six 0.5 inch M-3 machine-guns with 267 rounds per gun and a firing time of 15 seconds at 1,100 rounds per minute.

The speed of sound at sea level is around 760 mph at a standard temperature of 59 °F. The higher the temperatures at sea level the higher the speed of sound to around 790 mph at 105 °F. The speed of sound reduces with an increase in altitude and a reduction in temperature, until at 35,000 feet the equivalent air speed is less than half that at sea level. To achieve a speed of Mach One in the F-86, the speed of sound at that altitude, it was necessary to dive the F-86 steeply from above 35,000 feet, and with its swept wing design the aircraft passed quickly through Mach 0.96 into the compressibility area of transonic flight. A slight pitch-up and vibration occurred as the F-86 passed through this envelope before going sonic and the control returned to normal. A maximum speed of around Mach 1.01 was reached but as the altitude decreased and the critical Mach number increased the aircraft returned to subsonic speed. The compressibility or shock waves forming on the aircraft as the airflow became supersonic and broke away, set up abrupt changes of air pressure that created the sonic boom or bang, much in the same way that pressure changes from a whip lash produces a crack and a lightning bolt a clap of thunder. The sonic boom created by the aircraft will follow the aircraft's flight path along the ground, and it was customary for pilots to aim this at some specific target area. As a result the base at Nellis and the town of Las Vegas were subjected to many such booms during the day until complaints from hospitals and irate owners of broken windows resulted in the issue of orders directing all pilots to aim their sonic booms at the open desert area.

Flying the F-86 was, of course, the fastest I had flown in level or vertical flight at the time and the F-86 was for me the ultimate fighter and it continued to be for some time afterwards. The aircraft was a stable and controllable platform in both air-air and air-ground gunnery. During the course we carried out air-air combat with camera guns and realistic missions against targets involving guns, rockets, napalm and bombs. The desert provided unlimited space for the appropriate tactical weapons ranges and in the process I spread a lot of ordnance around the desert to the north of Las Vegas. I became accustomed to the use of the radio compass by which all USAF pilots navigated and it certainly made navigation over the featureless desert much easier. This was a navigation aid absent from the RAF fighters until the introduction of DME, measuring the distance and vector to a base beacon. During my navigation exercises I added two more unauthorized firsts to my flying compendium. The first was in registering a minus altitude by flying an F-86 at 100 feet over Death Valley that lay 200 feet below sea level. This would stand as the lowest point of my low flying until I landed with a Herald alongside the Dead Sea in Israel at 1,200 feet below sea level. The other was a truly awe inspiring experience when I flew down part of the Grand Canyon on the Nevada–Colorado border above Lake Mead with the canyon walls towering hundreds of feet above, hemming in my F-86 as I flew at 300 knots 100 feet above the river.

It was a relief to drive into Las Vegas of an evening to sample some of the many attractions of that truly unique oasis in the desert. Despite the fact that we were on the flight line by 5.00 am, the temptations were too great as the hotel casinos offered many allurements of food, drink and entertainment at surprisingly low prices. The hotels also provided top class shows with world renowned artistes, and the legs of the equally renowned show girls had to be the best, and longest, in the entertainment business. For some of us there was the temptation of the gaming tables but with our rates of pay we were fairly immune to any dreams of avarice. Similarly, any thoughts regarding those long-stemmed and unadorned American beauties quickly evaporated when it became evident that mink coats and sports convertibles did not figure in our conversations. However, it was all a new experience of entertainment on the large scale and a very enjoyable experience as many of us appeared bleary eyed on the flight line the following morning. The words of advice from Mr O'Neal, my voluble Irish-American instructor of my Clewiston flight days, when faced with the hedonistic temptations of Miami would echo back to me during our stay at Las Vegas; perhaps they helped, but the selection of full emergency oxygen when boarding my aircraft prior to our first flight of the day probably helped more.

One young 2nd lieutenant on an adjacent F-80 course to us was very attracted to the bright neon of Las Vegas and surprisingly did not have his wings singed. His passion was the dice game of craps at which he was either very knowledgeable or extremely lucky, and probably both. In a short period of time he successfully parlayed a modest stake into some $6,000, a not inconsequential sum in 1953. This was just enough for him to realize his dream of owning a red Cadillac convertible. He turned up at the flight line with his pride and joy and parked it next to the squadron offices, to show the car off to his envious fellow students. This was strictly contrary to base regulations as no private cars were allowed on the operational area of the base let alone the flight line. An F-80 after completing a weapons sortie taxied into the squadron dispersal with one of its 3-inch rockets still on the rocket rail under the wing, and as the aircraft swung into the parking bay the rocket released and firing up headed for the squadron building about three feet off the ground. The rocket had a solid practice head with no explosives but in other respects it was a standard rocket and on entering the building it passed through the main administrative office with several clerks present, collecting one typewriter in the process, before passing through the building and exiting where the lieutenant had parked his car. The rocket hit the Cadillac head-on and passed through the V-8 engine block, the front and back seats and came to rest halfway through the spare wheel in the trunk of the car. Miraculously nobody was hurt but the Cadillac was a write-off having been drilled from end to end. The unfortunate lieutenant was unable to claim on his insurance as the car was parked illegally in a prohibited area. The loss of the car may have saved the lieutenant from a reprimand, although I do not imagine this was much consolation to him under the circumstances. Although very young he showed a true gambler's philosophy when I commiserated with him on his loss. With a certain *savoir faire* he shrugged his shoulders and said 'Yeah, well as they say you win some and you lose some. I'll make it back and those SOBs can eat their hearts out watching me cruise 'The Strip' in my next one'!

Las Vegas

In Nevada did a gleeful Satan
Some Neon Pleasure Domes decree;
And Silver like a mighty torrent ran
Through coffers too numerous to scan,
Onto that vast and waterless sea:
From the many casinos built on sand
That makes up this exotic wonderland.

After a thoroughly enjoyable stay in Nevada we headed for Los Angeles to visit the North American Aircraft factory at Longbeach, home of the P-51 Mustang in the forties and the F-86 Sabre in the fifties. We also visited the Douglas Aircraft factory and both were a revelation after visiting British aircraft factories. I understood how the P-51 Mustang was so superior in build quality compared with the Spitfire, together with the American ability to produce such vast quantities of well-built aircraft. While at the North American plant I saw the prototype of the F-100 Super Sabre; a third generation jet fighter developed from the F-86 Sabre and the first production aircraft of the 100 Series of fighters to fly supersonic in level flight. A short leave followed in the Los Angeles area and invitations came from the entertainment world of Hollywood where the British colony of actors headed by Deborah Carr and her husband Tony Barclay, an ex-Battle of Britain pilot, took an interest in us. I visited some of the film studios, one of which was endeavouring to make a film with Marilyn Monroe before she was replaced by Kim Novak. The Australian actor Peter Finch took me to a very weird party given by Vivien Leigh at David Niven's house, with many British expatriates present including Joan Fontaine. Such generous hospitality was both entertaining and enjoyable if a little revealing at times, and part of any long standing illusion of Hollywood was shattered in the process. Particularly while having a drink with David Niven, who perhaps revealed more than he should have of his early days in Hollywood.

Three very enjoyable lunches and a round of golf provided lasting memories of my stay in Hollywood and San Francisco. When visiting the film studios in Hollywood I met an attractive girl who was the personal assistant to Cary Grant, and she introduced me to the film star. Whether it was because I was a compatriot or off to the war in Korea I do not know, but Cary Grant was extremely friendly and hospitable. I found him very pleasant and entertaining; in fact exactly as he appeared in his films. He invited me to lunch with him and his secretary at his favourite steak restaurant. It was a small and unpretentious restaurant that claimed to serve the best steaks in the world, a claim readily confirmed by Cary Grant as a regular customer. The restaurateur obtained his beef exclusively from a free-range ranch in Kansas. The meat travelled from the abattoir to the restaurant by truck, keeping it chilled but not frozen; it was then hung at a constant temperature to age and tenderise naturally before serving. The result was certainly the best steak that I had eaten. Cary Grant was an excellent host, entertaining us with many amusing and revealing anecdotes. I was so impressed by my meal that I was determined to repeat it before I left Hollywood, as I anticipated it would be some time before I was likely to have the opportunity of a good steak before returning to

Europe. I invited Cary Grant's secretary to lunch with me and at first she demurred. I then pitched the 'off to war' routine and she agreed warning me that the restaurant was very expensive. However, I assessed the opportunity merited any liquidity problems that might result. I was not disappointed and we had another superb meal accompanied by a very acceptable Californian cabernet. This was just as well in helping to anaesthetise the shock of the reckoning. My companion had not exaggerated, but then, perfection does not come cheap; and as it turned out this was one of my better investments.

Before leaving Hollywood I decided to try out the famous Brown Derby restaurant. I was with Tom Sawyer, one of the pilots in our group and we were in uniform waiting in line for a table when the maitre d' approached me to ask if we would like to join Miss Dinah Shore at her table for lunch. Miss Shore happened to be one of my favourite singers at the time and I readily agreed. She was lunching with her agent and there was probably an ulterior motive for the invitation as a photographer joined us shortly afterwards to take photographs. Despite this, we had a most enjoyable meal as Dinah Shore was not only very attractive but very pleasant and genuine company as we talked about the war in Europe when she entertained the troops. At the time Miss Shore had a TV programme sponsored by Chevrolet and she jokingly prevailed on us only to drive a Chevrolet while in the States. As it happened I did rent a Chevrolet convertible while in San Francisco, where we moved for processing to Japan and Korea from Camp Stoneman. I rented a small studio apartment on Nob Hill and thoroughly enjoyed a short but busy time exploring the Bay area. On one occasion I drove down the coast to Carmel to play golf with three of the RAF pilots: Max Higson, Tom Sawyer and John Chick at the famous Pebble Beach course. Fortunately, while investigating a teeing-off time and the cost of a round, a charming lady approached me inviting us to be her guests. This was another example of the wonderful and generous hospitality extended to us while we were in California. I remember I lost at least one ball to the Pacific, so the golf may not have been that good but the location was and it was certainly a memorable day. We topped off the trip on the way back by calling in on Steinbeck's Cannery Row in Monterey. All in all it was a busy and hectic month before my departure to Japan. I deliberately delayed my note of thanks to our charming and generous benefactor in Pebble Beach until I arrived at Kimpo, as I felt sure she would appreciate it more coming from the war in Korea than from San Francisco. I also had a short but enjoyable stay in Sausilito, an artists' colony across San Francisco Bay, but this was of a more personal nature – *Just one of those things*. With all this going on it was with many regrets I boarded a Douglas DC-4 for Honolulu, promising myself that one day I would return to San Francisco. However, it would be many years before I could do so and when I did, it just did not seem to be the same; or perhaps it was I that was not the same.

The flight to Honolulu took twelve hours and my first impression of the famous Waikiki Beach was a disappointment as I expected it to be, like everything else in the United States, so much bigger. It certainly looked very different in 1953 than it does today with no high rise buildings and only a few beach houses with just three hotels on the beach, one white, one brown and one pink. Another twelve-hour flight brought us to Wake Island for a refuelling stop before the final twelve-hour flight to Tokyo. Our stay in Tokyo at the Daichi Hotel, near the Imperial Palace and the previous headquarters of General Douglas MacArthur, was unmemorable apart from an introduction to Tokyo nightlife and the Japanese style of entertaining in days before it became prohibitively expensive. After a short stay in Tokyo our orders came to proceed to Korea, with six of us to join the 4th Fighter Group at K-14 Kimpo and the other six to join the 51st Fighter Group at K-13 Suwon. All the airfields in Korea, as is the military custom, were designated and called by a K number, with the two fighter interceptor groups based near Seoul at Kimpo and Suwon. We left the main transport air base of Tachikawa near Tokyo aboard a Douglas C-47 Dakota. This twin-engine transport was the tried, trusted and reliable workhorse of the Second World War as troop carrier, freighter and glider tug. As a troop carrier it would carry thirty troops on benches lining the sides of the cabin, and in civilian trim as the DC-3 the aircraft carried twenty-eight passenger seats. As we sat on the benches facing one another I reflected on an Indian Air Force Flight Lieutenant friend flying Dakotas during the period of the partition of India in 1947. As a result of the massacres taking place between the Hindus and Moslems there was a general state of panic as Hindus in the new state of Pakistan tried to get back into India, and the Moslems in India tried to get into Pakistan. My friend told me that his squadron had the task of flying back and forth across the border with their aircraft packed with refugees. No luggage was allowed on board and the cabin was stripped bare with the unfortunate refugees packed like sardines in a tin but without a key. The overloaded Dakota staggered into the air with just enough fuel for a round trip of 200 miles. Unofficially, there were no air fares involved but much gold and jewellery changed hands in establishing priorities, and no doubt the impecunious had to make do with shank's pony. My friend told me that his record for the number of refugees packed into his Dakota was 118, and looking at ourselves half filling the aircraft this seemed not only inconceivable but physically impossible. I wondered if this was an activity noteworthy enough for entry into the Guinness Book of Records, as it seemed a more significant achievement than the number of students packed into a telephone booth or a mini motor car, not that the FAA or CAA would sanction such an undertaking. Following the Indian transmigration my friend retired from the air force and moved to Nepal where he joined Royal Nepal Airline as senior pilot. He later became the personal pilot to the King and commander of the Royal Flight with the rank of full colonel. We were to meet again in the seventies when I was involved in the sale of HS-748 aircraft to the airline and the Royal Flight. The aircraft ordered for the Royal Flight had to fulfil a military role and consequently the cargo door was modified for the dropping of supplies and paratroops. Following the delivery of the aircraft to Nepal, my friend was demonstrating to the King and his cabinet the dropping of paratroops using the current Dakota aircraft and I was scheduled to accompany him on the drop. At the last moment he asked if I minded stepping down so that his son could fly with him in the co-pilot's seat. I watched the paratroops drop without incident into a valley and the Dakota returned to make a low pass down the valley. My friend did not see some high tension cables strung across the valley until the last moment. He banked the Dakota and pulled up in an effort to avoid them but a wing tip hit the cable, cart wheeling the aircraft into the ground with the loss of my friend, his son and two dispatchers.

Very little was seen during the flight to Korea until scattered clouds allowed a glimpse of a bare and inhospitable land of craggy, treeless mountains in varying shades of brown, capped by sugar icing. Approaching the K-14 airfield on the south side of the Han River a few miles west of Seoul, the aircraft passed over a wide estuary with many dark brown islets breaking the light brown coloured water of the estuary. The airfield came into view surrounded by the flat brown paddy fields. We landed on the single macadam airstrip surrounded on both sides by the aircraft revetment areas for the multitude of aircraft operating out of K-14. The 4th Fighter Interceptor Wing with its F-86 aircraft operated from the north side of the airfield with the 67th Tactical Reconnaissance Wing (TRW) operating F-80 and A-26 aircraft, together with the Meteor VIIIs of 77 RAAF Squadron, on the south side of the east-west runway. This was 'The Chosen – Land of the Morning Calm', and it would be my home for the next nine months. Kimpo airfield was an ex-Japanese fighter base during the Second World War and was set in the midst of what was then entirely a rural and farming landscape. To the east low hills merged into the mountain range south of Seoul, and 3 miles to the north of the airfield the Han River ran north-west from Seoul before joining the Imjin River, which formed the western extremity of the front line. The two rivers formed an estuary 2 miles wide with extensive mud flats on an ever widening outflow into the Yellow Sea some 20 miles to the west. Millions of geese and duck could be seen on the mud flats during the day before they flew onto the paddy fields in the evening. The rice paddy fields surrounding the airfield stretched 10 miles to the west and south to the port of Inchon. *Odours, when sweet violets sicken, live within the sense they quicken.*

The weather in Korea is seasonal with a long, cold winter during which the mountains are covered with snow, followed by a short almost pleasant spring and then the long hot, humid and unpleasant monsoon of summer; to be followed by a short colourful respite of autumn before reverting back to a cold bare winter. Depending on the season the surrounding paddy at Kimpo changed from white to brown to green to brown and back to white. The winter months on the whole were the preferable period of the year for us as although the temperature dropped to well below zero, the flying weather was at its best with high pressure systems bringing many days of clear blue skies. Another redeeming factor was the relief from the excessive sweating while operating under the hot and humid monsoon conditions that brought a shortage of water and led to uncomfortable and persistent skin ailments. The major redeeming factor of winter was perhaps the welcome freezing of the rice paddy and the consequent relief from the ever pervading effluvium of the night soil fertilizing the paddy fields. The arrival of spring turned the paddy overnight into a carpet of bright green for a short while before the harvest returned the paddy to brown again to match the shades of brown of the hills, river, mud flats and sea – it was on the whole a very brown landscape.

Spring in Korea

Modestly it comes: hesitant to show
A nakedness expectant of reprimand.
Winter's mantle falls as departing snow
Reveals the brown and forbidding land.
A vernal breeze blows across the Chosen,
Now loath to show a resplendent array,
While still so bare, desolate and frozen;
Ravished by numbing winds from Cathay.
Suddenly; overnight, like a curtain rising,
The paddy is green and life is opportune.
For a short magical moment it is Spring;
Prior to the long discontent of Monsoon.
Then: brief respite with a golden autumn;
Until grim winter completes the continuum.

North of the airfield and parallel with the Han River ran a ridge on which surveillance radar searched for enemy aircraft that only came at night. The radar also provided some limited tactical air control of not much significance. Between the ridge and the air base of K-14 was the small rural village of Kimpo supporting the farming community. In the familiar pattern of US military bases overseas the village had developed into a shanty town of shacks and was a rats' nest of brothels, bars and outlets for the black market trade. Despite official efforts to place this out of bounds to service personnel it seemed to thrive from the presence of the base. One particularly unpleasant incident involved an American sergeant who, finding a Korean rifling his kit in his tent on the base, drew his 0.45 automatic and shot him dead. It appeared the sergeant was in the habit of frequenting one of the establishments in Kimpo City and the jungle telegraph conveyed details of the incident to the occupants. While awaiting an enquiry into the shooting the sergeant returned for a final tryst: as he was leaving he was set upon and emasculated. He managed to reach the base gate holding the severed parts before collapsing. The incident was given wide coverage on the base to act as a deterrent.

Anyone flying into Kimpo International Airport today will find very little to identify the K-14 airfield of 1953. Today the concrete runway is double the length of the old macadam air strip and on the north side a large aircraft parking area has replaced the revetted area. A modern control tower, terminal buildings, maintenance hangers and car parks confront the disembarking passenger where once stood a small wooden control tower, and the 4th FIW Quonset huts. The only visible signs of what had been a Japanese fighter base were the huts on a slight rise on the north-east perimeter that in 1953 housed the officers' club and quarters. The south side of the east-west runway, the area that accommodated the 67th TRW and 77 RAAF Squadron, became a ROK air transport base and it looked much the same as it did in 1953 when I delivered an HS-748 Executive VIP aircraft to the Presidential Flight in the early seventies. A thriving industrial town has replaced the shanty village of Kimpo. A straight multilane double highway has replaced a meandering dirt road, known to some at K-14 as the Shakuhachi Pass, as it followed the Han River upstream through agricultural farmland to Seoul. The shakuhachi is a Japanese bamboo flute; traditionally an ancient spiritual instrument used by Japanese monks in the thirteenth century to 'Blow Zen'. Visitors to Seoul pass rapidly through an industrial sprawl to Yongdunpo, once an independent rural township on the south side of the river, and now an industrial suburb of the metropolis of Seoul. There is no longer evidence of the fighting that took place as the battle zone passed twice through the area, taking heavy US casualties. Some evidence of the destroyed bridges during the war remains, but many new bridges now span the wide expanse of the Han River leading to what once resembled a pre-war Japanese city and is now a huge modern high-rise city with a surging economy. The ancient defensive wall still rings the city on the north side, before the bare rugged mountains merge with those of a hostile north.

The Korean peninsula has a mountain range running north-south covering the eastern half of the country, with the mountains fanning out east-west in the northern part of North Korea to heights approaching 10,000 feet. A fertile alluvial coastal strip runs down the whole length of the west side of the Korean peninsula providing one fifth of the land suitable for arable cultivation that is mostly rice production. At the time of the Korean War the bulk of the rice production lay within South Korea with the main mining and industrial resources with hydro-electric power being in North Korea. The principal areas of population and industry in North Korea are contained within the western coastal strip, together with the principal lines of rail and road communications. These communications run south from Sinuiju at the mouth of the Yalu river on the Manchurian border along the coastal region through the major industrial cities of Namsi-dong, Chongju, Anju and Sinanju at the mouth of the Chong-chong river, and on to the North Korean capital of Pyongyang, and Chinnampo at the mouth of the Taedong river.

The flat west coastal area of North Korea contained most of the principal military airfields, many built by the Japanese during the Second World War, and it was to this area that the US 5th Air Force directed the bulk of its offensive operations, leaving the narrow coastal strip of the east side of the country to the attention of the US Navy and Marine Corps operating from the Sea of Japan. The 5th Air Force conducted a continuous programme of air strikes on the North Korean airfields, areas of heavy industry together with attacks on the hydro-electric plants on which the industry depended, supply areas and storage facilities and the interdiction of all road and rail communications. The result of this constant pressure on the resources of North Korea was severe denial of the military infra-structure to the communists, and the attacks on the hydro-electric power sources severely inhibited the industrial potential of the North Koreans making them dependent upon Chinese and Soviet sources for their war material and supplies. The relentless day and night interdiction of supply, storage and communication centres, rail centres, bridges and roads restricted communist build ups for their land offensives forcing them to devise counter methods of supply, deployment, dispersal and concealment. With unlimited manpower resources the communists were very adept at repairing their infra-structure quickly and in the process provided many dummy road, rail and airfield targets to distract the attacking fighter-bombers, and it became almost a routine procedure to see these targets appearing regularly on the camera gun combat films.

Although the damage to the North Korean airfields was quickly and effectively repaired, the regular use of the airfields was denied to the North Korean, Chinese and Soviet fighter units. The communists conducted a continuous redeployment of their fighters so that although there were times when aircraft were seen on the airfields around the Sinuiju complex on the Yalu River, more generally they operated from the sanctuary of the air bases in Manchuria. To this end the communists operated their fighter force from advanced bases around Antung near the mouth of the Yalu River, or from rear bases situated around Mukden, 100 nm north of the border. With advance warning of approaching US fighters, the Mig-15 fighters could deploy forward of the Yalu river for an interception above the approaching US fighters and then return to the security of their bases around Antung or for added security return to the bases around Mukden. As a result of the USAF air strikes the communist land forces were denied any close air support during any of the communist land offensives as the communist air force had to fly 200–300 nm to reach the front line and then return to their safe bases in Manchuria. By the later part of 1952 and throughout 1953, the air operations of 5th Air Force resulted in the United Nations land forces being relieved of any threat of air attacks and the communist armies were forced to conduct any major offensive without any air support. Furthermore, the constant interdiction against communist supplies and communications throughout North Korea hindered the land support of the communist armies limiting any sustained penetration of their offensives.

Most accounts of the air war over Korea tend to concentrate on the more glamorous aspect of the fighter interceptor groups in combat with the Mig-15 and to the glorification of the 'aces'. Not enough consideration is given to the more important air battle carried out by the bomber and fighter-bomber groups and the main contributions by the US air forces in bringing the communists to a ceasefire. The area covering the top northwest corner of North Korea was the area of greatest air activity and became known as 'Mig Alley'. The air arena of combat covered the area between the Yalu and Chong-chong rivers, extending eastwards to the Suiho lakes formed by the Suiho Dam, some 60 miles up the Yalu River from the Antung-Sinuiju complex near the mouth of the Yalu. The two areas of intense AA defence were over the Sinuiju-Antung complex and around the Suiho Dam, where heavy concentrations of Soviet radar tracked 88 mm AA guns were sited. The Mig-15 officially had sanctuary north of the Yalu River in Manchuria and for the F-86s to seek out the Mig-15s and draw them into combat it was necessary to meet them on their terms. To reach 'Mig Alley' entailed a flight of 200 nm over enemy territory, about 20–30 minutes flying time, with about 15–20 minutes combat time before flying back over 200 nm to the nearest friendly base. For this reason those eager to become an 'ace' with five confirmed Mig kills would often break the rules of the game and fly across the border in the hope of catching the Migs heading for their bases. The penalty for crossing the border was a possible court martial and a return to the US with the loss of all claims and awards. The advantages lay with the Migs because they received warning of an F-86 sweep as the aircraft crossed the Han River heading north. The Mig, with its superior rate of climb, could climb and be at altitude well above the F-86s as they flew into 'Mig Alley'. The Mig with its superior altitude capability could always be above the F-86s and thereafter dictate the terms of combat. During the early days of the 'Mig Alley' F-86 sweeps the intense competition between the two USAF fighter interceptor groups would have them flying into Mig Alley in two big groups of aircraft with the result that they left the area at the same time and the Migs could bounce them while they were low on fuel. Later tactics were more sensible as the flights of F-86s were fed into the combat area in a stream so that aircraft were arriving as the first flights withdrew from the area leaving friendly fighters to protect them from attacking Migs.

In a comparison of performance and combat capability of the F-86 and the Mig-15 it can be said that the advantages and disadvantages of both aircraft were in some instances marginal. The Mig-15 could out-accelerate the F-86 with the advantage of less weight and a centrifugal turbine against the greater weight and axial flow turbine of the F-86. The Mig-15 had a higher rate of climb and a higher service ceiling than the F-86, and theoretically with a much lower wing loading by virtue of less weight, the Mig-15 could out turn an F-86 at all altitudes. However, in practice the Mig-15 with a much slower rate of roll, inferior longitudinal control and stall characteristics at high G and low speed, created by the high set tailplane and the aircraft's conventional Second World War design of its flying controls, was unstable at high Mach numbers and high G forces, thereby reducing its theoretical advantages. At high Mach speeds approaching the sonic barrier, the Mig-15 experienced heavy stick forces and a sluggish rate of roll. Flight instability resulted as the aircraft exceeded Mach 0.9 with severe buffeting and snaking, a flight progression known as 'Dutch Roll', and as the aircraft approached Mach 0.95 wing drop and pitch-up occurred. The Mig-15 could not be persuaded to exceed Mach 0.98 without loss of control, whereas, the F-86 was genuinely transonic and fully controllable in a dive above 35,000 feet to a maximum speed of Mach 1.01. We frequently operated within the transonic envelope and, although the Mig-15 held an advantage over the F-86 in climb and altitude performance, the F-86 was faster than the Mig-15 in level flight and in a dive, with superior handling and high speed stability at high Mach speeds. At high altitude the difference in speed between the F-86 and Mig-15 being small resulted in slow closure over long distance, and frequently we had to break off the chase owing to fuel requirements to return to base and to avoid infringement of the Manchurian border. At the lower altitudes the F-86, with its higher speed, faster rate of roll, greater high G stability and no vicious stalling characteristics, could out turn the Mig-15. The F-86 pilot also had the added advantage of a G-suit in low altitude manoeuvring to exceed the G threshold of the Mig-15 pilot flying without the assistance of a G-suit. The Mig-15 was susceptible to a high speed stall or a snap roll at low altitude in a high G turn, the stalling occurring without warning when an accelerated stall resulted in a spin.

The superior handling of the F-86 over the Mig-15 at lower altitudes allowed the inferior armament of the F-86 against the Mig-15 to be used most effectively. The Mig-15 was designed as a bomber destroyer and with its heavier armament of one 37 mm cannon and two 23 mm cannon the battle damage capability of the Mig-15 was far superior to the F-86 which was armed with six 0.5 inch machine-guns. The Soviets estimated that two hits from the 37 mm cannon or eight hits from the two 23 mm cannon were sufficient to shoot down a B-29 bomber which had a defensive armament of one 20 mm cannon and twelve 0.5 inch machine-guns remotely controlled by radar to provide automatic sighting, tracking and ranging. This may have been an optimistic assessment for the average Mig-15 pilot, but the Mig-15 was successful in its attacks against the B-29s to the extent that the USAF switched the heavy bombers from day to night operations. Certainly one hit with a 37 mm cannon shell on the F-86 would result in massive and probably fatal damage: this was all it took to shoot down Flight Lieutenant Graham Hulse. The Browning machine-guns on the F-86, although they had a far greater density of fire than the Mig-15's cannon, lacked the weight of fire to cause major structural damage to a Mig-15 at high altitude, or to slow it down for a kill. However, combat at lower altitudes presented a very different picture. Despite a high probability that a hit by a single 37 mm cannon shell could prove fatal, the F-86 proved to be superior to the Mig-15 when combat occurred at the lower altitudes. The superior manoeuvrability of the F-86 over the Mig-15 at low altitudes enabled the six 0.5 inch Browning guns with their reliability, superior range, accuracy and high rate of fire of around twenty rounds per second; combined with the tight bullet pattern assisted by superior sighting, ranging and tracking with either the A-1 or A-4 radar gun sight; to be very effective against the Mig-15. This was especially so when manoeuvring at high 'G' when the Mig-15's comparatively slow rate of fire of around seven rounds per second for the single 37mm cannon and twelve rounds per second for the two 23 mm cannon, decreased the probability of a strike during a sustained high 'G' turn; and I can attest to this from personal experience. Finally, the aiming, tracking and ranging of the Mig-15's armament was manually controlled using a gyro gun sight and this was far less accurate than the automatic radar gun sight on the F-86. In aircraft equipment generally the advantage was with the F-86 as the Mig-15 had equipment and systems inherited from the Second World War, nevertheless, the Mig-15 was a very formidable fighter when flown by experienced pilots.

The 4th ('Fourth but First') Fighter Interceptor Group (FIG) was the most famous fighter group of 8th Air Force in Europe during the Second World War. Then they were flying the P-51 Mustang. It became the first fighter group to fly the F-86 Sabre during the Korean War, finishing as the top scoring group against the Soviet Mig-15. The 4th FIG consisted of three squadrons, the 334th, 335th and 336th, and I joined the 335th FIS commanded by Lieutenant Colonel McElroy. Max Higson, Tom Sawyer, John Chick, Andy Devine and John King were the other RAF members of the 4th FIG. The group commander, Colonel James Johnson, had a flamboyant and extrovert personality much in the mould of General Curtis Lemay when commanding the US Strategic Air Command. Colonel Johnson did his operational flying with the 335th and at the time of my arrival was halfway to his goal of becoming a double ace. His initial words of greeting to me were succinct and to the point, 'Welcome to Korea, Captain. This is a God damned awful place and it is a God damned awful war, but it is the only one we've got, and we love it!'

The USAF had two major aims regarding their pilots. First, to update the experienced regular and reservist pilots in jet combat operations, and second, to create a pool of 10,000 jet pilots experienced in combat operations. The three squadrons consisted of a confident and diverse meld of experienced regular and reserve officers with very young newly graduating pilots straight from flight schools in the US. I was the only foreign representative on the squadron until Flight Lieutenant Bob Carew from the RCAF joined the squadron. Although the experienced air force reserve pilots from the Second World War and the newly graduated pilots from flying schools in the US made up the bulk of the fighter pilots on the USAF squadrons in Korea, there were a few regular career officers from the USAF reassigned from squadrons elsewhere. In addition to the small number of RAF and RCAF pilots were a few pilots on exchange from the US Marine Corps. As a consequence, the six squadrons of the two fighter interceptor groups consisted of a few relatively older but experienced senior pilots and a majority of young inexperienced junior pilots.

In the air glory lay with the fighter interceptor squadrons as these were the units in combat with the Mig-15s of the communist air forces. There was little or no opportunity to shoot down a Mig while flying fighter-bombers or tactical reconnaissance aircraft. It was the numbers game all over again. This resulted in intense competition between the two fighter interceptor groups, and for the 'firing slots' on the fighter sweeps in the 'Mig Alley' area along the border of North Korea and Manchuria, 200 nm from the front line. To this end K-14, home of the 4th Fighter Group, and K-13, home of the 51st Fighter Group, were the nearest USAF fighter bases to the front line. Each fighter group could put up sixteen F-86s from each of the three squadrons in the group. A maximum effort from both fighter groups on a sweep of the Yalu would average between seventy-two and ninety-six fighters over a period of two hours. To the RAF the designations Wing and Group were confusing because in the RAF a wing consisted of two or more squadrons and a group several wings. In the USAF at the time of the Korean War the 4th Fighter Interceptor Group was part of the 4th Fighter Interceptor Wing that consisted of a flying group, a maintenance and supply group, and an administrative base group. The basic element of a fighter squadron was a pair, and two pairs made up the operational unit of a flight. The tactics employed on the fighter sweeps during 1953 were to feed flights into the combat area at altitude under some radar control of limited capability. In the combat zone the flights operated virtually independently. There was no 'Big Wing' concept along the Yalu. The flight and pairs' leaders on a group sweep were the senior and experienced pilots, with the junior pilots as their wingmen and 'eyes'. The opportunities for the wingmen to fire at a Mig lay in the break-up of a flight during combat. The wing commander, the group commander, the squadron COs, the squadron executive officers and the flight commanders all jockeyed for the 'shooting slots' on the offensive sweeps, and added to this mix were the supernumeraries from Wing and Group Operations, and 5th Air Force Headquarters. *There be many Caesars.*

The commander of 5th Air Force during 1953 was Lieutenant General Barcus, a gung-ho air commander who liked to keep in current flying practice on the aircraft under his command. One anecdote concerning our flamboyant commander, that may be apocryphal, had him flying in an F-86 over the Yalu and calling over the R/T, 'This is General Barcus, commanding 5th Air Force; come up and fight you yellow bastards'! When the word got out at 5th Air Force Headquarters that – *Barkis is willin'* – many senior air staff officers tried to justify their flying pay and attempted to join the 'Mig Maulers' to share the glory. I was not alone in resenting these selective flyers imposing themselves on the 4th FIG, the nearest and more successful of the two fighter interceptor groups. Unfortunately, the 335th as the most successful squadron attracted more than their fair share of staff desk jockeys. Fortunately, the majority of the sweeps were conducted when fine weather offered the best prospects for engaging the Migs, as flying in adverse weather conditions with leaders that were not operationally competent was indeed more daunting than engaging the Mig-15s. Their presence and intrusion in the squadron could be hazardous to one's health and I experienced two examples showing how the air staff interlopers were not up to scratch in leading any fighter unit. The first was with a colonel from 5th Air Force in Seoul who led my flight on a Yalu sweep and while flying into Mig Alley and climbing through a high overcast of cirrus cloud managed to stall out the flight at 35,000 feet. Fortunately, we were not in tight formation in dense cloud and we did not lose contact with one another and were able to form up again quickly, but it might have been interesting if some Migs had been waiting above us. When queried as to why, the colonel said he thought we had reached the top of the cloud layer and tried to zoom into the clear. Even the most junior second lieutenant on the squadron knew how deceptive high cloud can be: fortunately, we did not experience that aspiring 'ace' again.

The next impressive bit of air leadership involved another gung-ho air staff colonel who tried to impress us with an affected burning desire for air combat with, 'Those damn Migs'! The weather was overcast with a high cloud base but we flew into 'Mig Alley' at 40,000 feet in the clear. Despite hearing calls from other flights that Migs were up, our gallant leader did an about turn and headed back south. I asked his intention to be told he wanted to have sufficient fuel for a bad weather let-down at base. About halfway back to the front line our leader started a let-down and I called that we were letting down over Pyongyang, the capital of North Korea. Our leader replied that his ADF indicated that we were over the base approach beacon and I suggested he look outside his cockpit as we were being bracketed by black puffs of flak from the radar tracked 88 mm AA guns around Pyongyang. After landing at base the colonel in a rather more subdued fashion regretted having to leave the fray and was surprised to learn of the two ADF beacons on the K-14 frequencies used by the communists as decoys to lure aircraft into a flak trap of AA guns. In all the other less glamorous missions of the group the 'one-day wonders' were conspicuous by their absence. For this I was grateful because their presence would certainly have been hazardous to one's health. With so many colonels, lieutenant colonels and majors leading the flights on the

'Charlie' Flight on alert at K-14, Korea 1953. Note the 'Witch's Tit' in the background.

Standby pilot for 'Charlie' Flight during squadron 'readiness'.

HMS *Ocean* on patrol in the Yellow Sea, Korea, 1953.

HMS *Ocean*'s crowded flight deck.

CWD flying as navigator in a Royal Navy Fairey Firefly mission from HMS *Ocean* in the Yellow Sea, Korea, 1953.

CWD standing next to a Sea Fury aboard HMS *Ocean* in the Inland Sea, Japan, 1953.

HMS *Ocean* arriving in Yokohama, Japan in 1953.

CWD with a Grumman F-9F Panther of the US Marine Corps at K-3, Korea, 1953.

The North Korean Mig-15 that defected to South Korea following the cease-fire in 1953.

A de Havilland T-11 Vampire seen at No. 4 FTS in 1955.

Hawker Hunter Mk VI of the Day Fighter Leader's Squadron, Central Fighter Establishment, West Raynham in 1956.

Fighter Combat Wing, Central Fighter Establishment, West Raynham, showing a Hunter Mk VI and a Javelin Mk IV in 1959. I am seated in the middle with the dog.

Hawker Hunter
cockpit.

Below: Flying the English
Electric Canberra on
overseas tours while with
the Central Fighter
Establishment.

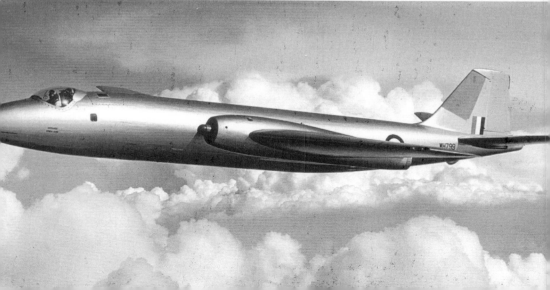

'The 1000 mph club'. The English Electric Lightning.

Handing over the fifth Handley Page Herald to ARKIA in 1967.

Mig sweeps it is not surprising that a large number of senior officers made up the ranks of the 'aces'. Captains and first lieutenants usually led the other missions undertaken by the 4th and 51st Fighter Groups: such missions included fighter-bomber escorts, photo recce escorts, the dawn and dusk airfield recce and weather flights, 'rescap' sorties and the tedious readiness alert. I certainly did my fair share of all such missions.

A young second lieutenant having completed his tour of 100 missions on the F-86 made the following comments at his farewell party in the K-14 Officers' Club, 'Well; I made my hundred missions and I suppose I should be grateful for that. One hundred missions and I never fired my guns at a Mig or anything else for that matter. I've been fired at from the ground; I've been fired at from the air, and I lost one F-86 in the process. So; a score of zero to one in their favour is not exactly an achievement I am proud of, but it is said one gets something out of a fighter tour in Korea and I'm sure glad to be able to say It's going to be my ass!' This is a fairly accurate assessment of the experience of the majority of the junior pilots joining either the 4th or the 51st Fighter Interceptor Groups of 5th Air Force during the later part of the Korean War.

The majority of ground attack operations of 5th Air Force during the later part of the war involved F-84 fighter-bombers; and by the spring of 1953 included F-86 fighter-bombers. The task of the fighter interceptor groups being to keep the Mig-15s off the backs of the fighter-bombers by drawing them up into air combat. In our operations from K-14 the favoured option of the 4th FIG was a full Group sweep of the Yalu area. To this end every day at dawn and at dusk a reconnaissance flight of F-86s would cover the Yalu area to establish the disposition and dispersal of the Mig-15s on the airfields, and the state of the weather. These circumstances dictated the decision whether to launch a full-scale sweep of Mig Alley. Often there were Migs in revetments on the airfields and often the airfields were deserted with the Migs deployed to their rear bases. We flew at high altitude and at a high Mach number if the weather was clear and I used binoculars to count the aircraft on the airfields. In the process of covering all the known Mig bases around the Sinuiju/Antung complex it was necessary to fly across the border into Manchuria, with the rationale that if one had engine failure one could glide back across the border to North Korea before ejecting from the aircraft to become a legitimate POW. If the weather was bad or there was cloud cover over the airfields, we would let down to a safety height of 6,000 feet to establish the cloud base. The safety height was necessary because, although the area was not as mountainous as it was further eastwards, there was still plenty of high inhospitable territory to be avoided. There were no navigational aids to assist us other than some initial positioning by the tactical radar sited on Chodo

Island. It was mostly a question of D/R navigation and failing all else the only other option was to let down over the Yellow Sea and fly in from the Yalu estuary. The only heavy and accurate AA fire encountered came from around the Antung–Sinuiju complex and around the Suiho Dam, about 60 nm up the Yalu River. These were both very sensitive areas for the communists and were heavily defended by batteries of Soviet radar tracking 88 mm anti-aircraft guns.

Not too late tomorrow to be brave. The competition to fly on the Yalu sweeps made it difficult for me as a foreigner to be scheduled other than as a wingman and my background and disposition rejected the 'lone wolf' approach to secure Mig scalps. I was given the opportunity to lead pairs and later flights on the other less popular missions, especially the airfield and weather recce flights where the squadron recognized that the RAF had more bad weather flying experience than could be gained flying at the flight schools in the United States. Interestingly, even when not leading a flight or a pair and there was a question of weather penetration, the lead was often handed over to me to lead the flight home, when the flight stuck to me as on the proverbial blanket. The average pilot from the US may have lacked experience in actual instrument flying but in holding formation they were tops.

I got an early introduction to 'Mig Alley' as wingman to Captain Clyde Curtin, who was initially my flight commander and later the squadron executive officer. I also flew as wingman to Captain Ralph Parr, with whom I shared a hut, but more often I flew with Captain Lonnie Moore, who gave me my most extensive tour of the Yalu and the Manchurian border. I also flew with Major Vermont Garrison, the squadron executive officer, before he took over command of the 335th. All four were experienced and aggressive fighter pilots, and as ambitious Mig killers all four were to join the list of the thirty-nine 'aces' of the Korean War. Curtin was a reserve officer hoping to become a career officer in the USAF, Parr joined the squadron from the staff of a tactical weapons school in the US, Moore came to the squadron as a test pilot from Edwards AFB in California and Garrison was a reservist with ten claims in Europe during the Second World War. Garrison was the oldest and most experienced pilot on the 4th Fighter Group; his snow white hair and his ability to see the Migs before anyone else earned him the respected sobriquet of 'Bald Eagle'.

The ability to see aircraft while flying at altitude requires not only excellent eyesight but also an aptitude to focus the eyes to scan at long range. The RAF aviation medicine establishment discovered while conducting trials that the average fighter pilot scanning the sky from within the aircraft cockpit focused his eyes thirty inches outside the canopy. A vitally important factor in scanning for enemy aircraft is the need to stay alert and it was common practice to take an amphetamine stimulant dispensed by the squadron sick bay as 'Mig Pills'. These did not prove detrimental when taken in moderation and the mission followed by a good night's sleep. Of the six enemy aircraft I saw shot down while flying my 100 missions with the 335th one fell to Garrison, two to Parr and three to Moore. There were two factors common to these kills: a non-deflection shot fired from the six o'clock position at close range. My experience of flying with these 'aces' showed me that their dedication to glory and possible Valhalla tended to cloud their judgment at times with a propensity towards tunnel vision.

Another frequent mission from K-14 was escorting the RF-80 reconnaissance flights from the 67th TRW on the south side of the airfield. The F-86 flew much faster and higher than the RF-80s, who generally covered their targets from around 30,000 feet at a speed of between 0.78 and 0.80 Mach. At this height and speed when over the Antung–Sinuiju complex, or the Suiho Dam area, the radar directed 88 mm AA guns would bracket the reconnaissance F-80, as the shell bursts were fairly accurate up to this height at this speed. However, in our F-86s we would set up a weave above the RF-80 at a speed of not less than 0.9 Mach, and at this speed the flak bursts were always behind us. Later in 1953 the 67th TRW received RF-86s and we would make up the recce flight with three of our F-86s as escort. The rationale for the odd number from the squadron was to make the communists think we were a regular flight of F-86s and thereby not attract so much attention from the AA guns, as the communists were very sensitive to reconnaissance aircraft in the 'Mig Alley' area. The change of aircraft equipment was very welcomed by the recce pilots who, now being able to fly higher and faster, were not troubled by flak, and we were seldom troubled by Migs while escorting the RF-86s on their reconnaissance missions. When flying cover for the fighter-bomber strikes we could rely on some protection from the flak by our high speed and this tended to keep us out of trouble while protecting the F-84s from the Migs.

Although the winter months provided the best flying weather for the fighter sweeps with periods of clear skies, the advent of the monsoon period saw a lot of activity in Mig Alley. It was our understanding that spotters in the hills to the north of the Han River overlooking K-14 would count the fighters heading north and telephone calls to the Mig bases enabled the Migs to scramble and to be at altitude above the incoming F-86s as they flew into the Yalu area. This would give the Migs three big advantages: first, they had the advantage of height and could make their attack out of the sun. Second, they could time their attacks as the F-86s flew out of the area on their 200 nm return to base, and third, after combat the F-86s had a long journey home over enemy territory whereas the Migs had only a short distance to fly to their secure bases on the other side of the Yalu. Therefore the Migs could break off combat at their convenience with a lower fuel state to return to their bases in Manchuria. A 'bingo' fuel call was an indication of the minimum fuel remaining for a safe return to base with a reserve. There were many factors that governed this call based on the distance, altitude and weather involved. If an F-86 was hit over 'Mig Alley' or had an engine failure some distance north of the front line, the main hope of survival was to head for the Yellow Sea, where the surveillance radar sited on the islands of Cho-do and Paengnyong-do could cover an aircraft in distress. A 'rescap' flight scrambled from K-14 with sufficient warning covered aircraft heading for the islands, where helicopters and amphibian aircraft were on patrol to retrieve pilots ejecting over the sea.

The two islands off the west coast of North Korea occupied by UN forces were bases for guerrilla raids on the mainland and both had rescue helicopters on readiness. The prospect for a pilot ejecting over the Yellow Sea in fair weather was good and many pilots were saved. However, the temperature of the water during winter and spring was such that without an immersion suit the pilot's expectancy of life was a matter of a few minutes. The rubber immersion suits gave the ejecting pilot a good chance of survival but were very uncomfortable to fly and to fight in, as the watertight seals around the neck and wrists chaffed the skin. Also, while wearing the suit on the ground one would sweat profusely and the boots filled with condensation, which resulted in the suit being very cold while in the aircraft at altitude. It was fortunate that the F-86 had a magnificent pressurization, air conditioning and heating system by which one could blow snowflakes in the cockpit while on the ground in summer and remove any frosting or icing from the cockpit canopy and windscreen while flying at fifty below zero at altitude. Some pilots preferred not to wear their immersion survival suits preferring to take a fatalistic attitude. Similarly, some did not bother to prepare or carry a land survival kit with them. The 'Catch-22' was to decide whether to be uncomfortable while flying and then possibly survive after an ejection over the sea, or be more comfortable while in the air and then probably die while in the sea.

On one sweep of the Yalu area in early June 1953 while flying at 40,000 feet as Captain Lonnie Moore's wingman, six Migs jumped us from above and we broke into them. I counted four Migs as they came towards us firing their cannon way out of range with no chance of a hit. In the ensuing mêlée our pairs separated with Moore chasing two of the Migs heading north. The second Mig or wingman was trailing his number one by at least 2,000 yards. Diving slightly to pick up speed and keeping below the Migs we were able to close on them and then ease up behind the trailing Mig. I called Moore clear and he opened fire at around 300 yards range to slow the Mig down or get him to turn. I saw some strikes on the Mig but did not see anything come off the aircraft as it went into a slight dive at maximum speed. Moore continued to fire as he closed on the Mig and I saw smoke coming from the jet-pipe. At this moment the Mig canopy came away and the pilot ejected. Moore then called that he had an explosion in the engine. I checked him over and called there was no fire visible but for him to head for the coast. Moore turned south-west and I asked if he could make Chodo Island and he replied affirmatively. As I could not see any Migs I told Moore I would cover him to the coast. I turned the IFF to the distress mode and put out a distress call on the R/T. Chodo replied they had a good 'paint' on my 'squawk' from the IFF and that a helicopter was on station over the island awaiting his arrival. Moore arrived over Chodo at 2,000 feet and I saw him eject and after seeing his chute open, I spotted the helicopter waiting for him. I was then anxious about my fuel state and wondered about going to Paengyong-do to the south as my fuel was well below my 'bingo' call of 1,500 lb of fuel. I cruise climbed to 30,000 feet before shutting down the engine for a quiet flight south as I decided to make for home. When the Han River came in sight I lit up the engine calling for a priority landing and taxied in with about 200 lb, around 30 gallons, showing on the gauges.

Moore told me later that the helicopter was overhead as he hit the water and although the sea was fairly calm the water was very cold. Although he was wearing an immersion survival suit, when the helicopter lowered the strop to him after a few minutes in the water his hands were so cold he could not grasp the strop and put it around him. The winch man went down to hook him up and the 'chopper' took him to Paengyong-do. A light communication aircraft flew him back to base and after a check up at the base hospital he joined me for debriefing and the confirmation of his first Mig. With the camera gun evidence and me as a witness this was routine and we celebrated his first Mig and safe return that evening at the Officers' Club. It was very reassuring that if one could make it to the coast the search and rescue facilities gave one a very good chance of survival. The Americans went to great lengths to retrieve downed pilots and we carried a homing beacon and an emergency UHF radio handset to contact searching aircraft. There was even a snatch pick-up retrieval system by which a C-47 would drop two poles with a line and harness. After attaching the harness to the line stretched between the poles, the pilot crouched down facing the rescue aircraft and the C-47 plucked him up with an arrester type hook. From 0 to 120 knots in about two seconds flat must have been quite some acceleration to experience, and better than a bungee jump. I witnessed a demonstration with no apparent ill effects to a brave volunteer when he landed, other than perhaps a higher pitch speaking tone. The territory over which we operated was mostly mountainous and I do not recall any of our pilots being rescued in this manner from the coastal strip, although I believe it was tried with some success with the fighter-bombers.

When Flight Lieutenant Graham Hulse was shot down the two fighter interceptor groups virtually stopped normal operations for two days to look for him. Hulse was an old friend who went to the US on an exchange posting before joining the 336th FIS on the 4th FIG at K-14. It appeared that Hulse was firing at a Mig and obtained visible strikes on the aircraft. As luck would have it he overran the Mig and in pulling up crossed in front of the aircraft that was in a climbing turn as it fired its guns. A 37 mm shell hit the F-86 by the right wing root and the wing folded back as the aircraft rolled over in a dive. Hulse's wingman was firing at the Mig as Hulse passed in front of it and his camera gun film recorded the cannon strike on the F-86 as he continued to fire at the Mig before destroying it. In his preoccupation with the Mig he did not see if the F-86 crashed or whether Hulse was able to eject. The 4th FIG felt the loss keenly and after making a great effort to find Hulse, awarded him a posthumous half share of the destroyed Mig-15. My own view is that he was in the aircraft when it crashed, but we never established his fate and his name did not appear on any POW lists.

How now! A rat? An interesting speculation of Moore's engine failure was whether his engine had failed because of the ingestion of some debris from the disintegrating Mig engine or whether his engine had exceeded its limitations through the use of a 'rat' or a 'mouse' attached to the jet-pipe. A 'rat' was a small steel plate about six inches long by two inches wide and curved to fit the contour of the inside of the end of the jet-pipe. A 'mouse' was half the size of a 'rat' with half the effect. These plates reduced the effective diameter of the jet-pipe efflux increasing the jet-pipe temperature and thereby increasing the thrust. We flew the F-86 at maximum power often exceeding the laid down maximum jet-pipe temperatures for a short period. Some aircraft due for engine overhaul would be down on percentage power and hence the use of this device to make up the shortfall. This was especially so if flying an earlier F-86E with an F-86F. After I complained to Lonnie Moore that I had difficulty staying with him when assigned an old aircraft, he introduced me to the practice of the rodents. Although officially frowned upon and needing the cooperation of an understanding crew chief, a lot of these rodents went flying on sweeps. They were very useful if applied judiciously to get that extra bit of thrust. Chasing a Mig at high altitude with only a fractional overtaking Mach number took time involving a considerable distance covered towards the out of bounds areas that was very frustrating, and we needed all the help we could get. No doubt at times they caused excessive jet-pipe temperatures and I only used one occasionally on an aircraft down on percentage power. I had no desire to risk a prolonged stay in the Antung 'Hilton' just to get a Mig-15, but others felt differently. On this occasion I did not see anything enter Moore's intake but it would only need a small piece of metal to throw a turbine blade and chew its way down the compressor. However, I did wonder if it was a question of the biter bit; with Moore being his own victim when in trying to catch the Mig to score his first claim, his turbine threw a blade as a result of exceeding the maximum jet-pipe temperature. If Moore knew he did not say, and although it may have been only a wee mouse that *gang aft a-gley*, in this instance *I smell a rat!*

The squadron had both the F-86E and the F-86F, with a GE-J47-13 engine in the 'E' model producing 5,200 lb of static thrust and a GE-J47-27 engine in the 'F' model producing 5,910 lb of static thrust. This gave the 'F' model a slightly better performance in speed, climb and altitude. When the first F-86Fs arrived on the squadron the 'shooters' took the 'F' models and with their wingmen still flying the older 'E' models they had problems in supporting their leaders. It did not occur to some 'leaders' to consider the advantages of keeping their wingmen with them the whole time even to the extent of reversing the assignment. If they did, then the consideration of the advantage of the 'F' model over the 'E' model in shooting down a Mig-15 put paid to the idea. It certainly did not appeal to those in the habit of breaking away from the flight during sweeps in a 'lone wolf' pursuit of the Mig-15s. The obvious answer was to fly the same models in the flight as the differences between the two types of F-86 were significant under combat conditions with the Mig-15. The most important difference of the two models for any would-be 'ace' was the installation of the A-4 radar gun sight in the 'F' model. The A-1 radar gun sight in the 'E' model was not only very unpredictable but also very unreliable.

On every mission the standard procedure was to level off at 15,000 feet during the climb to test fire the guns, this also allowed the engine oil that was scavenged during flight to drain forward. With the aircraft trimmed to fly straight and level we fired the guns, and frequently when flying an F-86E with the A-1 sight it went out never to reappear. The harmonization of the six Browning machine-guns bore sighted them for the bullets to converge at 1,000 feet. The first ten rounds in each gun were tracer rounds and a sighting dot made on the windscreen with a grease pencil where the rounds were seen to converge provided a reference mark for aiming when the sight failed. This allowed for a non-deflection shot from astern or for a fly through deflection shot, often referred to as

'Kentucky Windage'. The F-86F had an A-4 sight that was a great improvement, both in tracking and ranging the target, over the A-1 sight when it worked, and it was also very much more reliable. Sometimes the radar ranging did not work or it hunted in and out, but if the sight's two mil pipper was visible a useful rule of thumb was that it filled the Mig-15 jet-pipe at 1,000 feet.

A major modification to the F-86F provided a 6 inch by 3 inch leading edge extension to the wing. This removed the automatic leading edge slat with a fixed leading edge giving six more inches at the wing root and three inches at the wing tip. A later modification added a boundary layer fence at mid-wing five inches high. All of which gave additional speed with improved handling and increased the stalling speed by around ten knots, with the F-86E technically stalling at 111 knots and the F-86F at 125 knots. We therefore had three types of F-86s Sabres on the squadron in 1953 and we were very glad when our F-86Es went to No. 2 Squadron, South African Air Force, on the 18th FBW. These F-86s replaced their P-51 Mustangs, so they must have been very happy to receive the jets for their ground attack missions.

Air combat between the F-86 and the Mig-15 at high altitudes demonstrated that the F-86 armament of six Browning 0.5 inch machine-guns was inadequate for a high probability kill factor against the Mig-15, and indicated the need for a heavier cannon armament with a high rate of fire. All our F-86Fs had the modified hard wing and in June 1953 we received six F-86Fs equipped with four M-39 20 mm cannon installed in place of the six Browning guns at the nose intake. The M-39 cannon based on the design of the German Mauser MG-213 30 mm cannon had a revolver type ammunition feed for a high rate of fire, with the ammunition fired electronically. We were the only squadron on the 4th FIG to be so equipped as part of the GUNVAL operational armament trials. The four cannon had a rate of fire similar to that of the Browning machine-gun of around 1,100 to 1,200 rounds per minute. The Browning was a very reliable gun and the 0.5 inch calibre bullet was more accurate at a longer range than the 20 mm M-39 cannon shell; but even with armour piercing, incendiary and high explosive rounds the weight of fire from the Browning guns could not inflict sufficient damage to shoot down a Mig-15, or even slow it down for a kill, at altitudes above 30,000 feet. At altitudes over 40,000 feet, despite gun camera film clearly showing strikes hitting the Mig-15, the rarefied air would not provide sufficient oxygen to support combustion. Post-war studies by the USAF showed that about two-thirds of the Mig-15s attacked at high altitudes escaped destruction. During these attacks around two-thirds of the armament load of 1,600 rounds carried by the F-86 was expended over a firing time of ten seconds, even with the six 0.5 inch machine-guns point harmonized at 1,000 feet and the guns sighted, ranged and tracked with a radar gun sight. On the other hand hits from the Mig-15's two 23 mm cannon with a rate of fire of around 800 rounds per minute; or a single hit from the 37 mm cannon, with an even slower rate of fire of around 300–400 rounds per minute, could cause massive, and probably fatal, damage to the F-86.

'GUNVAL', the code name for the four 20 mm cannon gun evaluation trials on the F-86F, were not a success. When the four cannon were fired at altitudes above 30,000 feet the muzzle blast from the four cannon blanked the air intake creating an engine compressor stall, resulting in an engine flame-out. To overcome this it was necessary to fire the cannon in pairs, selecting the top pair followed by the lower pair; and to fire in short bursts. This not only halved the anticipated impact of the weight of fire of the 20 mm shells, but increased the kill probability firing time. In addition, the accuracy and range of the 20 mm shell was inferior to that of the 50 calibre bullet of the Browning machine-gun. Consequently, although the GUNVAL F-86s claimed six Mig-15 kills and in the process lost two aircraft, as the majority of Mig-15 kills resulted from an astern attack at close range many of the 'Old Hands' preferred to use the standard armament of six Browning machine-guns. I never did fly one of the 20 mm cannon aircraft but I did fly on one of the first combat trial missions. I flew as wingman to our squadron executive officer, Major Vermont Garrison, who later became the squadron commander. I had a standard F-86F and at 45,000 feet on a sweep south of the Yalu we spotted four Migs high above us. Garrison climbed in pursuit at full power after the Migs heading north. We crept up to nearly 50,000 feet but the Migs, although still strung out, remained above us and out of range. Although at maximum power I fell behind and below Garrison, and this was my first experience of the extent of the advantage the Mig-15 had over the F-86 in terms of climb and altitude capability, even against the improved 'F' model. We could never operate above 48,000 feet flying the 'E' model. We continued to follow the Migs as they crossed the Yalu into Manchuria. Our second pair had fallen well behind in the chase and as we continued after the Migs the number four called 'bingo'. Garrison told them to return to base and we continued after the Migs. It was obvious that at 50,000 feet with our marginal closing speed any combat was unlikely unless the Migs turned to fight. My fuel was down to a 'bingo' call of 1,500 lb and I suggested to Garrison that we fire towards the Migs in the hope that the tracer rounds loaded in his 20 mm cannon and in my 0.5 machine-guns would persuade them to turn. Garrison agreed and with the Migs still well above us and out of range, I eased the nose of my aircraft up slightly to get an upward line towards the Migs and fired my guns. The aircraft stalled but the engine kept running and as my nose dropped down I saw Garrison above me go into a spin. The Migs kept on their way, which was probably fortunate as I followed Garrison down, calling to him but getting no response. He continued in a spin and I kept calling him to recover. At around 25,000 feet he made an incoherent response and at around 20,000 feet the aircraft came out of the spin. The F-86 continued in a steep dive and eventually came out of the dive at around 10,000 feet. As the mountain tops were over 6,000 feet this was rather close for comfort. I continued to call to Garrison but he remained incoherent and dis-orientated due to severe anoxia. I continuously called attitude, heading and altitude to him all the way back to K-14, where I called for an emergency landing and talked him down to the runway before over-shooting for my landing. Garrison stopped at the end of the runway and an ambulance took him to the hospital.

Garrison told me later that before firing his cannon in the direction of the Migs he saw 50,000 feet on the altimeter. When he fired the four 20 mm cannon the aircraft stalled and there was a bang as the engine stalled with an explosive decompression of the pressurization system that filled the cockpit with white cloud. The effect of the decompression produced intense hypoxia. He became unconsciousness as his 11,000 feet cockpit altitude rose instantly to his aircraft altitude of 50,000 feet. The very efficient pressure demand oxygen system in the F-86 saved his life. He did not recollect the aircraft spinning or the recovery from the spin, and it is likely that the F-86 recovered from the spin by itself when it reached denser air. When he partially recovered his senses he realized the aircraft was diving steeply and while pulling the F-86 out of its dive he realized that he had no engine power. He must have done the right things for the engine started up when he resumed level flight. My instructions filtered through to him despite a blinding headache, dizziness and difficulty in focusing his eyes. By an intense concentration of survival he managed to handle the very difficult situation until at the end of the runway after stopping the aircraft he collapsed. It was a good thing there were no Migs around and the weather was clear otherwise the flight would have had a different ending. Although physiologically Garrison's age may have made him more vulnerable to the effects of hypoxia than a younger and fitter man, his great experience pulled him through. It was a couple of days before he returned to normal flight duties still suffering from headaches. To my recollection, despite the limitations imposed on firing the cannon in pairs, the squadron claimed several Mig-15s shot down, but one way and another none of the six aircraft survived to the cease-fire. I reported the result of the cannon trials to the Air Ministry in July 1953, but when I returned to Fighter Command early in 1954 I found that the Hunter, due to enter service in that year, suffered the same problem of an engine compressor stall when firing the four 30 mm Aden cannon at altitude. It appeared to me that a valuable year was lost in solving one of the many armament problems associated with the early Hunters. Interestingly, the Mig-15 did not appear to suffer from the same problem of intake blanking when firing the 37 mm and two 23 mm cannon. This was because the Mig-15 engine had a centrifugal compressor based on the Rolls Royce Nene engine given to the Soviet Union, as against the axial flow compressors in the General Electric J47-27 engine in the F-86 Sabre and the Rolls Royce Avon engine in the Hawker Hunter.

One mission for which there would be no pilots over the rank of captain and very few of those, was the alert readiness detail. Every day from dawn to dusk two squadrons positioned a flight with back-up aircraft on the alert strip at the east end of the runway. One flight would be on readiness with the pilots in their cockpits, and the other flight would be on standby with the ground crews near the aircraft and the pilots in the dispersal hut. The flights rotated hourly and were ready to scramble to intercept hostile aircraft that never came – at least by day. If a flight scrambled it would be to provide a 'rescap' for aircraft with an emergency over North Korea. The major concern was scrambling in bad weather conditions with little confidence in the local radar. The navigation aids were an ADF beacon on the airfield and one on the approach from the west. The use of a radio compass while flying in or near thunderstorms was unreliable as the needle would often turn towards the thunderheads. K-14 had its GCA radar positioned for the flat approach from the west and, as with the surveillance radar, it was often operated by grounded pilots with little controlling experience. The communists complicated the bad weather letdowns by citing a decoy ADF beacon on the approach frequency in the Haeju peninsula to confuse fighters returning to base.

'Flying in on a wing and a prayer' was a Second World War song that I recalled while leading a flight on readiness during the monsoon season. Bad weather had closed the airfield for normal operations with low cloud and heavy rain. I sat in the cockpit watching the rain thinking that with our inadequate navigational facilities we would not return to K-14 if scrambled. My reverie was shattered as Operations scrambled us on an unidentified target at an undetermined altitude to the north. We climbed through the overcast breaking into clear sky at around 30,000 feet. This was the good part as during the monsoon the cumulonimbus tops could exceed 45,000 feet. The bad part was four-day fighters not equipped with airborne interception radar, scrambled to intercept an unknown target in cloud, with the weather at base below minimums and no suitable diversions. Instructions came to orbit north of the front line and the operations radar could only maintain contact with us by use of our IFF. After twenty minutes spent enjoying the sunshine with no interception control forthcoming, instructions came to return to base. The weather conditions were the same as on take-off with no improvements at diversion airfields. On the premise, better the devil you know, I informed the tower we would position for a straight letdown into the GCA radar, and should the weather force us to overshoot we would try any available diversion and if this failed our letdown would be via our ejection seats. Assistance from radar and cross fixes on our ADFs positioned us for a straight descent from the west. The second pair elected to remain in tight close formation for the letdown and approach. Although the junior squadron pilots had little experience of weather flying before arriving in Korea, they were not lacking in their ability to hold tight formation. The approach from the west was over flat paddy fields, whereas from the east the approach was over hills, and close to the airfield in line with the runway was a small hill, 300 feet high, named 'Bust-your-Ass' mountain. The line-up on the runway from the west had to be precise because a few miles south-west of the airfield was a sharply pointed hill 1,500 feet high that we graphically referred to as 'The Witch's Tit'! The descent was through thick cloud with heavy rain and on reaching 2,000 feet we dropped landing gear and flap, and fed into the GCA. We passed our safety height without contact and at 200 feet we started to break out of cloud in heavy rain. I got a glimpse of the runway lead-in lights as we broke cloud and at 100 feet I could make out the runway and called contact, telling the second pair to ease back for the landing. Owing to the downwind touchdown in the wet we nearly aquaplaned off the end of the runway, but all four F-86s landed on the runway undamaged. It was the best GCA I was to experience in Korea under the worst flying conditions. We never did find out the reason for the scramble. Quite likely someone misread their CRTs radar paint or picked up a met balloon and hit the panic button. The result could certainly have been worse with a score of 0–4 in favour of the communists.

We never did get a daylight raid on K-14 while I was there but we did get some night raids carried out by single Russian built PO-2 biplane trainers dropping mortar bombs and hand grenades. Despite the searchlights and the heavy concentration of 40 mm AA guns and the quad mounted 50 calibre machine-guns, these gutsy North Koreans managed to cause considerable confusion and inconvenience to the base facilities. They succeeded in damaging several huts and F-86s in the revetments and I recall one F-86 destroyed when hit by a dropped mortar bomb. The flak barrage was something to be seen and would have done credit to any fireworks display on the 4 or 14 of July. One could hardly imagine anything flying across the airfield without being hit, yet these slow cumbersome night raiders named 'Bed Check Charlies' evaded all efforts by the AA guns on the base, and the Marine Corps Skyraider assigned to K-14, to intercept them. The PO-2 flew too low and slow for the F-94 Starfighter and the Marine Corps F-3D Skynight jets to intercept, and the only success I recall against them was a single kill by a Marine Corps F-7 Tigercat.

The only other memory of significance I carry from the irksome alert strip duties occurred after the cease fire at the end of July 1953, when in September a North Korean Mig-15 piloted by Lieutenant Kum Sok No defected to claim the US $100,000 reward offered by the United States during the war for a Mig-15. It was a fine day as I sat in my aircraft while leading a readiness flight watching a flight of F-86s overhead breaking and spreading for their landing from the east. Suddenly, a Mig-15 touched down from the west causing the four F-86s to overshoot. The Mig turned into the alert strip and stopped in front of me. I was able to take a photograph of it before hiding my camera, which was circumspect on my part because when the base police arrived at the alert strip they confiscated all the cameras they could find. We had a good look at the aircraft before it was towed to a hanger under a tarpaulin. The following day a military transport flew the Mig-15 to Okinawa for evaluation. The thing that impressed me the most while inspecting the Mig-15 was the superb high gloss finish on the aircraft. Although Russian aircraft construction looks somewhat agricultural in build quality when compared with US aircraft, the finish on the Mig was immaculate and highly polished.

We were able to talk to the North Korean pilot via an interpreter and he told us that after every flight a squad of mechanics would clean and polish the aircraft before it flew again to keep aerodynamic airframe drag to a minimum. This suggested to me that the communists accepted the fact that the F-86 was faster than the Mig-15. We learned a few things from Lieutenant Kum before he left K-14 for Okinawa to assist in the evaluation of the Mig-15, which had previously puzzled us. For example: why did the Migs appear to fire their guns even without a target in their sights? The reason given for this was that they had no official mission tour and in any event they had to fire their guns before being credited with a mission. There were airborne commissars flying the missions to monitor tactics and to confirm when and where the F-86s operated, and if air combat had taken place. Another query: the Mig cockpit canopy was a clear bubble hood yet why was it possible to close on a Mig at altitude from the astern position without the Mig taking any action? The reason given for this was the cockpit pressurization and heating system of the Mig was very inferior to that of the F-86 and the armoured glass plate behind the pilot's head would ice over cutting off rear vision. Several of the Mig-15's systems were inferior to that of the F-86 because they were

Second World War design; this applied in particular to the oxygen equipment, the radio equipment and the gyro gun sight.

The Mig pilots were also at a disadvantage compared to the F-86 pilots under high G conditions because they had no G-suits but wore a tight wide leather belt to lessen the G effects. An interesting aspect on which we were unable to get confirmation from the North Korean pilot was the colour schemes of the Migs and the pilots flying them. We saw some Migs with a beautiful camouflage on the upper wing and fuselage, and underneath a duck-egg blue. This was an effective combination when viewed from either above or below. We thought by the way they were flown these were North Korean Migs with Chinese and Soviet pilots flying with them as instructors and airborne commissars. There were also silver Migs that appeared to be flown more aggressively and handled more competently than the camouflaged Migs, and we assumed these to be flown by Chinese and Soviet pilots; although it was a silver Mig-15 flown by a North Korean pilot from the North Korean Air Force that defected and landed at Kimpo. Very occasionally, some grey Mig-15s appeared in the sky over the North Korean–Manchuria border that were believed to be Soviet Marine aircraft from Soviet bases around Vladivostok. I only saw the grey Mig-15s on one occasion and if they were Soviet Marine aircraft they were probably on detachment to one of the main Mig bases around Mukden. The North Korean Mig-15 was test flown in Okinawa by test pilots from the US, and by pilots detached from the 4th and 51st Fighter Groups for combat trials. Lieutenant Kum Sok No received his US$100,000 a little belatedly and reluctantly from the US authorities because they intended to withdraw the offer after the cease-fire. However, the US obtained its first and only Mig for technical and combat evaluation at a reasonable price. As for Lieutenant Kum, in addition to the money, he also received a visa for the US and enrolled in the University of Delaware, and eventually became a US citizen.

There were many variations of flying songs from the First and Second World Wars sung in the 4th FIW Officers' Club at Kimpo. One sung to the tune of 'On top of Old Smoky', included the following verse:

> *When up at the Yalu,*
> *Just turn up the grill.*
> *If the Migs don't get you,*
> *Then the '88s' will.*
> *It was over Antung,*
> *When covered in flak;*
> *I lost my poor wingman:*
> *He's not coming back!*

This was appropriate during a sweep of the Yalu on 18 June 1953, flying F-86E No. FU-852. The mission nearly resulted in disaster and its only achievement, as far as I was concerned, was in staying alive. The mission was certainly unusual in its duration, and also unique in being the only occasion when an F-86 landed on the beach of an offshore island of North Korea and flew back to base. The day started like so many others, rising at 5.00 am for a briefing at Group Operations at 6.00 am, followed by take-off at 8.00 am on a full Group sweep of the Yalu area. The briefing covered the usual weather and emergency procedures that included the facilities on the islands of Chodo and Paengnyong-do off the west coast of North Korea. Chodo was a small rocky island with no suitable landing beaches, 5 nm off the coast and 90 nm from the mouth of the Yalu. Paengnyong-do, 15 nm from the coast of the Haeju peninsula and 100 nm from K-14, was a slightly larger island 40 nm south of Chodo with a good beach on the east side. This beach was suitable for aircraft crash landing with battle damage, and at low tide the sand was firm enough for a normal landing. The radar on both islands provided surveillance cover for the west coast of North Korea with tactical information and guidance for parts of the 'Mig Alley' area. Helicopters on stand-by at both islands were ready to pick-up any downed pilots in the Yellow Sea and along the coast. These helicopters, together with patrolling SA-16 amphibian aircraft, saved many pilots unable to make it back to friendly territory. The briefing ended with the standard warning about the dire consequences of intruding into Manchuria.

The weather forecast was good with clear skies over the Yalu area established by the dawn Mig airfield reconnaissance flight along the Yalu. I took-off as wingman to Captain Lonnie Moore, the flight leader of four F-86Es, as we headed for the Yalu 200 nm away. As customary at 15,000 feet we test fired our guns and my radar gun sight appeared satisfactory. We dropped the external wing tanks as we flew into 'Mig Alley' at 45,000 feet and Mach 0.9. The 4th FIG flights were sweeping the south side of the Yalu from Sinuiju at the estuary, 100 nm up river to the Suiho lakes. The tactical radio frequencies were designated by a colour code and in line with Moore's briefing we used one of the colours, 'Silver', to change to the tower frequency at K-14. This was to avoid being monitored by the tactical controllers, and at 200 nm range our transmissions could not be heard at Kimpo.

Moore then swung north from the Suiho area where the GCI radar from Chodo had indefinite coverage and we crossed into Manchuria, heading towards Kuan-Tien airbase about 20 nm north-west of the Suiho Dam. Shortly after crossing the Yalu I looked down and saw four pairs of silver Migs flying in line-astern formation heading west towards Feng

Cheng, a large military airbase 25 nm north of Antung. The Migs had probably been above us at 48,000 feet waiting for the right moment to attack and now low on fuel were heading for one of their forward bases around Antung. The Feng Cheng airbase lay between the walled city of Feng Cheng, on the main road and rail communications between Mukden and Antung, and close to the Ai-Ho River flowing into the Yalu. Moore called the 'bounce' on the last pair of Migs and we rolled over in a sonic dive and found we were alone as the other pair called 'bingo' and headed back to the Yalu. As we continued down in our dive I reminded Moore of a previous occasion in making a similar attack on some Migs, when on pulling out of the dive at high G behind the Migs we both went into a violent longitudinal oscillation banging our helmets on the canopy as we bounced past the Migs trying to correct the oscillations. This was an aerodynamic phenomenon referred to as pilot induced oscillation, and in the confusion we lost sight of the Migs who were probably too low on fuel to react. This particular handling problem on the F-86Es was a function of the hydraulic controls, for in trying to correct the oscillation we got out of phase and over-corrected thereby increasing the oscillation. The solution was simple; either let go of the stick and the oscillation corrected itself, or apply steady back pressure to dampen the oscillation. On this occasion we pulled out of our dive at 3,000 feet without problems with two Migs ahead of us.

We closed rapidly on the Migs in front of us and I could see two more ahead of them, as they approached the Ai-Ho River with the runway of Feng Cheng visible ahead. I was to the right and behind Moore and I called him 'clear' as he closed on the trailing Mig. I asked if he was sure the pair in front of us were the last pair of Migs and received an 'Affirmative' answer from him that was incorrect! The Migs were flying at 2,000 feet and Moore opened fire on the Mig in front of him at 300 yards range. I saw some strikes around the aircraft as Moore closed rapidly to 100 yards still firing. The stream of bullets must have gone straight up the tail-pipe of the Mig for several pieces came away, followed quickly by the cockpit canopy as the pilot ejected at 1,500 feet. I did not see what happened to him as Moore, anticipating he would over-shoot the leading Mig, must have closed his throttle with his air-brake selected. I closed rapidly on him and in order to avoid over-running him I pulled up in a barrel roll around him. While inverted on the top of the roll, I saw two Migs closing in fast from our six o'clock position. I called Moore and told him that he had one Mig at six o'clock and one farther back at eight o'clock. I called for him to break left and take the wingman while I dropped down behind the leading Mig. Moore did not respond and I saw he was firing at the first Mig now approaching the runway. I repeated the call to break left and as he did so I dropped down behind the Mig chasing him. Moore's call of 'Roger, breaking left' was the last I was to hear or see of him for a while.

We passed over the airfield boundary and I saw Migs in the revetments: then the whole airfield seemed to light up as if it was a flashing Christmas tree as the AA guns opened up on us. I headed for the deck as the black puffs appeared everywhere and had a bumpy ride as I flashed through them at full throttle hugging the ground. I had a quick glimpse of a Mig on the over-run of the runway as I turned south away from the airfield thinking that the AA fire was just as likely to hit some of the Migs as my F-86, and there were more of them. I called Moore to say I had lost contact and asked if he was on the second Mig but I got no reply. I thought I had lost the Mig in front of me but then saw it above me, silhouetted against the sky and heading towards a 3,000 feet high sharply pointed hill to the south of the airfield. The black puffs were following me and I imagined the intense AA fire was as disconcerting for the Migs as they were for me, forgetting that the F-86, in common with all US jet aircraft, had the bad operational characteristic of trailing black smoke from its exhaust at low level. If I stayed down low level I was a marked man, but the alternative did not appeal either.

I started to track the Mig in front of me when clear of the airfield, easing up behind him to around 1,000 feet. In the turbulence with my flying helmet bobbing against the canopy while trying to rubber-neck looking for Migs, it was difficult to keep the gun sight pipper on the unsteady target ahead. In my anxiety to open fire and get out of the area before more reinforcements arrived, I opened fire too soon at 400 yards range. I saw strikes around the fuselage as the Mig broke to his left towards Feng Cheng. I followed and managed to put the pipper back on the Mig and opened fire again. A red 'cricket-ball' passed close to the top of my canopy and looking back I saw the underside of a Mig with flashes around the nose intake. I pulled left as hard as I could in a maximum G turn lowering the nose to increase speed, and as I did so another red 'cricket-ball' passed slowly ahead of me with a second passing behind the aircraft. I was probably lucky in two respects in that the Mig in front of me broke when he did, and the slow rate of fire of the 37 mm cannon placed a convenient distance between the shells in a high G turn.

I was now sandwiched between two Migs with no support, low on fuel and with other Migs in the vicinity; a veritable Catch-22 situation. In a game of chess the term 'zugzwang' would be appropriate: being a position where any move would be disadvantageous. Air combat is no game although chance can be a major factor in success. Turning towards the Mig behind me, I lost sight of the Mig in front of me but I was confident

I had inflicted sufficient damage to the aircraft, if not to the pilot, for it not to present an immediate problem. Anticipating other Migs arriving, and with the Mig having a superior acceleration and rate of climb performance over the F-86, I continued to turn at full power and maximum G. With a thumping G-suit and my flying helmet weighing like a sandbag on my head as it pushed my goggles down over my eyes, I strained to look back at the Mig following me. At around 7–8 G a few hundred feet above the ground and 'rat-racing' around the hill towering above us, the Mig pilot, following me without the benefit of a G-suit, should have been feeling an even greater strain. I was close to greying out as I kicked the top rudder bar hard to skid the aircraft before pulling harder into my turn. The desired effect was to upset the deflection sighting of the gyro gun sight of the Mig following me. It apparently succeeded for I saw the Mig take off some bank and I was no longer looking at its underside. The Mig pilot no longer had a deflection shot on me, but whether this was due to him anticipating a reversal on my part or a correction on his part to avoid a high speed stall, I had no way of knowing. Checking ahead and above, I looked back to catch a brief glimpse of the Mig as it slammed into the ground in an explosive ball of fire. I assumed the Mig had over controlled while trying to regain deflection; resulting in a high-speed stall that snap rolled the aircraft into the hillside.

I could no longer see any Migs following me and going down to the deck at full power I straightened out on a southerly course heading for the coast. When confident that any Migs following me would be unable to catch me and on seeing some cumulus cloud building up ahead, after a short buffeting ride at very low level, I eased up into cloud holding my altitude as I turned south-west to avoid the Antung area. After a short while I continued my climb breaking into the clear at 10,000 feet, and the only signs of aircraft were some contrails to the east. On crossing the coast I felt fairly secure although, with 800 lb of fuel remaining rather than a 'bingo' of 1,500 lb, I knew I had no chance of making it back to K-14. My only prospect was either to eject over Chodo with no means of communicating to the island, or a landing of sorts at Paengnyong-do.

I continued a cruise climb setting course south-east for Chodo. The weather and visibility were good with only some scattered cloud along the coast. I could see the many islands between the Yalu and Chong-Chong rivers quite clearly, but the mouth of the Taedong River was obscured by cloud and I was concerned that the cumulus cloud starting to build up might prevent a view of Chodo island. I tried all the R/T channels again without success and remained on the distress channel. The IFF was switched off for the excursion into Manchuria so I switched it back on and selected the emergency mode. Checking that I was below contrail height I levelled off at 30,000 feet and cruised until the fuel gauges registered 400 lb. I shut down the engine and switched off all non-essential services. The windmilling engine provided enough hydraulic power for the gentle operation of the flying controls, and the emergency battery supply took care of electrical requirements. I set up a glide angle at 160 knots that gave a still air distance covered of 14 nm per 5,000 feet of descent. I hoped the IFF was giving the Chodo and Paengnyong-do radars a good 'paint'; and it was with some relief I saw Chodo through breaks in the cloud as I passed overhead at 15,000 feet. This was sufficient altitude to make Paengnyong-do 40 nm to the south. I was thankful that Moore's ejection over Chodo with engine failure earlier in the month enabled me to recognize the island, for now I knew that with my remaining fuel I could land on the beach at Paengnyong-do.

The island of Paengnyong-do had a distinctive banana shaped beach running north-south on the east side of the island. The north end of the beach had a cliff rising to a low hill with the radar unit on top. The south approach to the beach was clear over sand dunes. Our briefing told us that at low tide the sand was firm enough for fighter aircraft to land. Many fighter types with battle damage were able to crash land on the beach, but no F-86s had landed on the beach from K-14. The briefing that morning stated that the sea would be halfway to full tide by the time I arrived. At 3,000 feet I saw Paengnyong-do ahead in the clear and fired up the engine. The 400 lb of fuel remaining would enable me to fly over the beach for a circuit, approach and an overshoot if necessary. I could see the tide was about halfway in and approaching from the north saw the northern half of the beach covered with people and the odd bullock cart. I pushed the nose down and buzzed the radar hut and continued down the beach at 50 feet as I buzzed the whole length of the beach. I pulled up at the sand dunes in a steep climbing turn and flew back along the beach dropping landing gear and flap as I touched down as close to the water as possible. I came up the beach and the congregation parted before me like Moses and the Red Sea. I reached the north end of the beach near the cliff and parked above the high water mark near a Meteor VIII of 77 Squadron and an F-84 fighter-bomber. I shut down the engine with, as the saying goes, nothing showing on the fuel gauges but the maker's name. There was probably about 20 gallons left in the tanks as I switched off everything, put the safety pin in the ejection seat, locked the flying controls and closed the hood.

I went over to the Australian ground crew working on the Meteor that crash landed on the beach with battle damage, and asked if it was possible to refuel my aircraft. The sergeant in charge answered that there was Avgas available but it would need hand pumping from fuel drums. I told him I could refuel through the fuel filler in the wing. I then asked if he had a suitable engine starter because the Australians used a trolley accumulator for the Meteor that was unsuitable for the US aircraft. He directed me to where the Americans working on the F-84 had a standard US generator for engine starting. Borrowing a screw driver from the American crew I removed the film magazine from the gun camera in the nose intake of the F-86, for no matter the fate of my aircraft I wanted camera confirmation for the claim of a damaged Mig-15. I asked for a guard to be placed on my aircraft as it was attracting a lot of attention from the large crowd of Korean peasants on the beach. The South Korean army was in the process of evacuating some North Korean refugees from the mainland and were using Paengnyong-do as a staging post while waiting for a boat to take them to South Korea.

It was then about 10.00 am and with the tide coming in it would be some hours before I could attempt a take-off. A Jeep drove me up the hill to the radar unit where they confirmed the fact that my radio and IFF were not transmitting, and they had wondered if I was a hostile aircraft. Presumably they identified me correctly as I had no AA reception overhead when I arrived. I asked if they could contact the 4th FIG at K-14 and 5th Air Force operations in Seoul to say that I was OK and attempting to refuel my aircraft and return to base. What transpired was that neither was informed and I was already listed as Missing in Action. Returning to the beach I prepared to refuel my aircraft: the Sabre carried 435 US gallons internal fuel and it was 100 nm back to K-14. I intended to fly back low level and I calculated that 150 gallons was sufficient for my return. Fortunately the weather was good because without a radio and radio compass I needed a visual approach. With the help of the American ground crew servicing the F-84, it took two hours to hand pump the fuel into the wing tanks. It was then 1.00 pm and I calculated it would be at least another three hours before the tide would allow me a firm beach on which to take-off. I went back up the hill to inform the radar unit of my intentions and they provided me with lunch.

Around 4.00 pm I prepared the aircraft for a start-up and we manhandled the F-86 facing down the beach. I attempted to start the engine but only got a wet start, and I shut down the engine. I now had a problem, for if the starter generator was supplying insufficient power the same result could occur on the second start-up attempt. To remove the excess fuel from the engine it was necessary to carry out a dry run, and to wait for the fuel to drain from the engine would take too long, so after a few minutes wait I carried out a dry run. After another short wait I prepared for the second attempt at start-up. It was now getting late in the afternoon and with some apprehension I tried again. As the engine lit-up a loud bang came from the jet pipe and ramming the throttle fully open I stood up ready to abandon ship. The excess fuel ignited sending a jet of flame torching 20 feet out of the jet pipe. The engine continued to run up to power and waving my starter crew away I headed for the beach while buckling up my harness. One good effect of the dramatic Roman candle firework display was to scatter the Korean bystanders who had been crowding in on the aircraft. People were still wandering about the beach despite the Jeep sent to clear them away. Running close to the water I opened up the throttle and started the take-off run. In similar fashion to my arrival, the people parted almost magically before me and the southern half of the beach was clear as I unstuck and cleared the sand dunes.

I throttled back at 200 feet and headed for K-14. This height was a compromise in keeping above the seabirds and below the radar: with my radio and IFF not functioning I wanted to avoid scrambling the alert on a 'hostile' aircraft approaching K-14. The sun had started to drop in the west with the prospect of a beautiful sunset, although this did not concern me as I headed south-east to avoid the Haeju peninsula before turning east for the Han estuary. There was no danger from enemy aircraft that far south but there was from North Korean AA fire along the Haeju peninsula. I assumed K-14 would not be expecting me, unless Paengnyong-do had managed to inform 5th Air Force, therefore, the radar would pick me up when close in and scramble the alert. I was a little uncertain of my landfall with the myriad small islands along the coast and I eased up as I crossed in to identify the Han River and saw the distinctive hill we called 'The Witch's Tit' in the distance to my right. I flew in low over the paddy fields and lined up for a straight in approach to the runway from the west. On seeing the runway and approach clear, I pulled up with air brake out, selected landing gear, flap and landed. I reached the end of the runway just in time to beat the scrambled alert flight taxiing for a take-off to the west.

With dusk approaching I taxied into my dispersal to be confronted by my crew chief with the words, 'Gee, Captain, you're reported shot down and Captain Moore said you were dead!' I replied that I was fine but the aircraft had a failure in the electrical system and that he should also check for turbine damage. As I wrote up the Form One there was a question whether the flight was one or two missions with the two landings. A chock-to-chock time of nearly ten hours was a very long mission for an F-86; and it had certainly been a long day for me. Moving to Group Operations I proceeded to give an edited debriefing to the intelligence officer omitting our excursion into Manchuria. Lonnie Moore arrived and his first comment was 'Did you confirm my two Migs?' I replied I confirmed the Mig where the pilot ejected. Unfortunately, our two reports did not tally with other combat reports of the group on the Mig activity.

The Group Commander, Colonel James Johnson, then ordered Moore's camera gun film shown after clearing the room of the others present, excepting the squadron commander. The film clearly showed Moore's attacks on two Migs but unfortunately, while attacking the second Mig, it also clearly showed the runway with Migs in revetments on the Manchurian airbase of Feng Cheng, 25 nm north of the Yalu. The group commander took possession of the film saying to Moore, 'You know this means a court-martial'! This dampened my confirmation of Moore's fifth Mig-15 to claim 'ace' status. In a sombre mood I returned to my hut to end the discussions regarding the disposal of my personal effects and to retrieve my record player.

Moore told me in the Officers' Club later that evening that the last call he heard from me was to break left and he did not see either of the two Migs I was involved with, although he saw my progress across Feng Cheng from the flak bursts. As he could not contribute to the situation and being low on fuel he headed south. None of the Migs milling around Feng Cheng caused him any trouble but he had to do a 'dead stick' landing on the runway when his fuel ran out while overhead K-14. In his combat report he claimed two Migs shot down and reported my probable demise. Regarding Moore's first claim there was no problem about confirmation as I saw the pilot eject and this was supported by his gun camera film. However, on the second claim, although I saw Moore firing at the Mig on the approach to the Feng Cheng runway, I observed no hits or visible damage. On seeing a Mig on the over-run of the runway as I passed overhead I assumed it was the same Mig. At best, this could only be considered a damaged claim. With the amount of light flak over Feng Cheng airfield it would not be surprising if the Chinese had managed to hit one of the Migs milling around the airfield. Ironically, I was thankful that when attacked by the Mig-15 following me it was not armed like the F-86. The more accurate and greater density of fire of the six 0.5-inch Browning machine-guns of an F-86 flown by an experienced pilot using a radar gun sight would probably have been successful in shooting me down. As it was, the slow rate of fire and the inferior ballistics of the Russian 37 mm cannon aimed by a gyro gun sight placed one 37 mm shell in front of me, with the following shell passing behind me in a maximum 'G' turn at low level.

My own claim for a damaged Mig came to naught as the camera film I nurtured so carefully on Paengnyong-do had not turned over showing a blank film. I only had myself to blame for this as I had changed from the standard black and white combat film to a new Kodak colour film that had teething problems. In speculating on Moore's two claims and the two Migs I was involved with, that I personally considered being a 'damaged' and a 'probable' claim; only those present at Feng Cheng at the time would be able to confirm this with the records office in Peking. Moore had certainly damaged the second Mig and probably would have shot it down if he had not been shot down himself in the process. I knew I had damaged the Mig I attacked but that was all. Similarly, I was convinced the Mig that attacked me crashed during our dog fight. It is therefore, just a possibility that the Chinese lost more than the one Mig-15 that day at Feng Cheng. I have known less plausible claims: on one such occasion during a debriefing of a Yalu sweep, a colonel placed his hand on the North-West corner of the map of North Korea and asked the assembled pilots, 'Did anyone see my Mig go down here?' A young second lieutenant answered, 'I thought I saw an explosion on the ground, Colonel.' The colonel turned to the debriefing intelligence officer and said 'This boy confirms my Mig, Captain!'

My analysis of our decision to cross the Yalu and of the mission as a whole, quite apart from any aspects of legality, discipline and plain folly, was the fundamental error in not determining the disposition of the Mig formation. This was a crucial blunder aggravated by an eagerness to engage any of the Migs before they reached the Feng Cheng circuit, with odds of four to one against us. Crossing the Yalu was like Caesar crossing the Rubicon – *Let the dice fly high!* Initially there was the prospect of picking off the last pair of the formation and withdrawing back to the Yalu with ample fuel to return to K-14. In becoming mixed up with the formation over Feng Cheng the die was cast for a very different scenario. My post mission impression was that we attacked the middle of the formation, as I saw two pairs of Migs ahead of us out of the original eight in pairs line-astern. Moore very effectively shot down the wingman of the second pair and while opening up on the lead Mig, the third or fourth pair bounced us. On giving the break I expected him to engage the wingman while I tackled the lead Mig. When I dropped down behind the Mig following Moore his wingman probably called my position and this dissuaded him from his attack, by which time we were over Feng Cheng. Moore heard no radio calls following the break or saw other Migs, and the reception over the airfield preoccupied his attention as he withdrew south. When south of the airfield I opened fire on the Mig and clearly saw some strikes on the aircraft before he broke north. Despite my continuous scanning for other Migs milling around Feng Cheng I saw nothing until attacked and I assume the second Mig was following me trying to get within range. During our low level dogfight this second Mig appeared to over control while pulling too much G, resulting in the high speed stall that snap rolled the aircraft into the hillside. Although I did not see the start of this manoeuvre, I had a momentary sighting of the impact followed by a big fireball on the ground. This impression was confirmed by the fact that I did not see the Mig again, or any other, as I withdrew south from the area. Although unconfirmed claims do not count I at least felt confident in my own mind with a 'damaged' and a 'probable' Mig claim.

There were precedents to our Feng Cheng affair: in February 1952, Major George Davis of the 4th FIG and the leading Korean War ace at the time with twelve kills was shot down and killed pursuing Migs across the Yalu River. He was awarded a posthumous Medal of Honour, the only Sabre pilot to receive this distinction. Again, in April 1953 Captain Harold Fischer, another double ace of the 51st FIG, was shot down pursuing Migs into Manchuria. He was to survive the war for the following two years as a guest of the Antung Hilton. I cannot view our Feng Cheng affair as the smartest operational sortie of my Korean tour: in retrospect it may have been the most foolish, but it was certainly the most exciting and interesting mission I was to fly with the 335th FIS. Fortunately, there was no court martial and with no proceedings against Moore he retained his four previous Mig claims; and so with the granting of a fifth Mig destroyed over Feng Cheng Moore became the 34th 'ace' of the Korean War. No further action occurred, nor was I questioned again on the incident. I believe the 'brass' viewed any proceedings against Moore, who received considerable publicity as a result of his 'ace' status, would create too many problems and backfire to the detriment of the 4th FIW. Also, I do not think they cared to have a foreign pilot involved. They decided to let the dogs lie.

I should like to think I learned something from the experience and although I did not venture to Feng Cheng again, I continued to fly with Moore to and over the Yalu. Despite his considerable experience of the 'Mig Alley' area, Moore always seemed to have a problem in navigation when approaching the Yalu. There was no question that infringement of Manchurian airspace was a frequent occurrence by aggressive pilots to find the Mig-15, in direct contravention of standing orders. I had no problem with this as I viewed Migs over Manchuria as fair game. The one-sided rule of engagement that restricted flight into Manchurian airspace during air combat over the Yalu was, in my opinion, an absurdity. The Migs could come out of China to attack us in North Korea but we could not respond by intruding into Manchuria. My sole reservations were with the possible consequences of such action and a natural concern for discretion therefore, apart from the Feng Cheng affair, I drew a line when it came to joining the Migs over their bases in their sanctuary of Manchuria. I flew with four successful 'aces' in Korea and, except for Vermont Garrison, they did not rate too highly in leadership in my opinion. Their flying ability was beyond question, and it was a great experience to fly with Lonnie Moore for although he had an individualist approach to flying, he was an aggressive fighter pilot with exceptional flying ability. He was certainly a genuine 'ace' and he would certainly figure in a short list of unforgettable characters I knew during my flying career. After the Cease Fire he returned to the flight test centre at Edwards AFB; sadly to lose his life while test flying the new McDonnell F-101 Voodoo fighter.

It was some years after the Korean War that I read Joseph Heller's satirical novel 'Catch-22', about an American bomber squadron operating in Italy during the Second World War. There have been plenty of incidents in my life when I could readily empathize with the definition contained within Heller's maxim that describes a 'Catch-22' situation as one characterized by obstacles that defeat any attempt of the victim to escape it. Possibly my most lasting memory of a 'Catch-22' situation in war is encapsulated within a very brief contribution to the ground war in Korea. The 4th FIG operational roles did not include ground attack, but for a brief period in early July 1953 all our normal operations ceased as we joined the fighter-bombers in supporting the UN land forces. The Chinese army, in a massive assault against the South Korean army in the centre of the front, broke through for a distance of several miles and threatened Seoul. The offensive made without air support was the first major offensive by the communist forces since 1951, and it proved to be the last major offensive of the Korean War. The breakthrough stalled when the Chinese army, unable to sustain the momentum, halted their advance for reinforcements and supplies. The continuous interdiction, both day and night, on all types of communications into the salient caused the Chinese to resort to lesser means of transportation such as horse and ox drawn wagons, together with thousands of men carrying supplies on A-frames.

The 4th FIG order of battle concentrated on the ground attack role to deny these supplies reaching the front line positions. The briefings were clear and adamant: to seek and destroy anything that moved as a potential weapon supply carrier. Although not equipped for bombing or rocket attacks our F-86s could carry out napalm and strafing attacks. In the four days the 4th FIG converted to a ground attack role I carried out two ground attack missions. Napalm can be a very effective weapon on suitable targets such as supply dumps and entrenched troops. The problem with napalm delivery is that it requires different sighting parameters to that of a gun or rocket attack. To achieve the optimum spread across the target requires a relatively low, slow, straight and level approach before release. Napalm released too high, or too low, or too fast, reduces the effective spread pattern and under these circumstances the napalm may not ignite. Such a delivery makes the pilot vulnerable to ground fire while providing any defending gunners with an optimum tracking time. Although the use of napalm has a psychological effect against ground troops, the same can be said for the attacking pilot.

On the first mission I was leading the second section of a flight and we each carried two 120 gallon drop tanks converted for napalm with phosphorus cap detonators. We flew to an initial point north of the line over rugged, bleak mountains laced with valleys of paddy fields. A forward air controller (FAC) operating from an L-19 light spotting aircraft called us on to a target of supplies and troop concentrations in some entrenchment. I could not see the target as I followed the flight leader in close formation down a valley at 150 feet and 300 knots, and we dropped our tanks on his call. Looking round as we climbed up I could see a good spread of fire from the eight tanks apparently across the target area, but I could see nothing else. The FAC called a good strike and for us to strafe targets of opportunity. Nothing appeared opportune and we returned to base without noticing any ground AA fire. The interesting aspect of flying over the battle front lines by day was the absence of any visible troops, guns, tanks or trucks. I noticed this fact during a tour of the front line with the British Commonwealth Division the previous April. In visiting the various units during my stay I was prevailed upon to fire a howitzer, a tank gun and a phosphorous bomb from a heavy mortar into the communist lines. I never did see any activity, apart from some return fire, across no-man's-land despite the thousands of Chinese and North Korean troops entrenched below ground.

The second and last ground attack mission I flew proved quite different from the first. Again I was flying as number three in the flight and again we carried napalm. After orbiting an initial point north of the line the FAC called the first pair in for an attack on some unspecified stores and troops. I could not make out the target clearly at the end of a narrow valley but it appeared to be a farm. The approach to the target was very tight and I was glad we were not attacking together. The four napalm tanks of the leading pair spread across the farm and the flight leader called there was some ground fire. My section then commenced an attack on an emplacement on the side of the hill, and as we dropped the tanks and pulled up sharply to avoid the hill I could see the four tanks had ignited in a wide spread of flame. There was no return fire during the attack and the FAC called two good strikes and instructed our two sections to seek targets of opportunity on an independent return to base. While flying low over the hills alongside a valley of paddy I saw a single ox-cart proceeding south down a dirt road in the valley. This was not an unusual sight in Korea and I was fairly sure what it was, but I was not alone and faced with implicit orders of engagement I told my wingman to give me top cover as I turned across the valley to the road. I flew low across the road and could see that the cart pulled by a single ox appeared loaded. The driver stayed where he was as I buzzed him at 50 feet and continued on his way. I cranked the aircraft hard round close to the hillside and made a run back down the road. I decided to give the driver one more chance to jump ship and fired a burst at long range to one side. The first ten rounds in each gun being tracer there could be no mistaking my intentions, but still the driver remained on the cart. I lined up on the road and started firing short of the cart and while still firing allowed the sight pipper to move up the road until stopping it on the cart. The six 50-calibre Browning guns delivered 120 rounds of armour-piercing explosive and incendiary bullets per second for 2–3 seconds. No explosion occurred as the driver, cart and ox, disappeared in a puff of brownish cloud, and I said the one and only appropriate word as we headed back to base.

On the debriefing the intelligence officer did not want to record one honey bucket wagon destroyed preferring to claim a military supply transport, together with the arms dumps destroyed. I could not bring myself to argue. The result of this mission did not bring any satisfaction for a job well done. For some time after I had visions of an old Korean *papa-san* in wind-blown white robes, with a black conical hat on his head as he acted out a rendition of Ben-Hur against an F-86 winged chariot. My attack and destruction of the honey bucket express exquisitely projects the absolute simplicity of 'Catch-22'. My orders were explicit and unequivocal: attack anything moving that could be conveying munitions and supplies to the front line. Not to do so was a dereliction of those orders, and despite a gut feeling to the contrary there would always be nagging doubts that failure to attack a farmer about to fertilize his paddy may have resulted in injury, mutilation or death to UN troops. In giving the driver a chance to escape I placed myself at some risk from any AA guns sited on the surrounding hills, and sentimentality has no place on ground attack missions. Quirks and absurdities are commonplace in war and it was no consolation to me that my instinct on this occasion was correct. As Heller says in his novel, 'That's some catch, that Catch-22!'

The time spent flying was a small percentage of the time spent on the ground in the mundane process of living in an unusual environment, for to quote out of context we were *Strangers in a strange land – Seeking the bubble reputation even in the cannon's mouth.* In common with most wars it was a time of brief moments of anticipation, apprehension, exhilaration and relief interspersed with long moments of boredom, inconvenience, discomfort and frustration. Consequently, certain minor factors and incidents tended to be exaggerated. The Americans were very good at providing all manner of things necessary and unnecessary to live and operate successfully, but it was up to the individual to make the best use of these facilities. At K-14 we lived in old Second World War huts once used by Japanese fighter pilots. The huts were allocated by squadrons and each hut was usually occupied by four to six pilots. This was preferable to the other bases where they lived in tents, as did our ground crew. Apart from the provision of a camp bed the rest was up to the occupants of the hut. In my hut we achieved some basic furnishing although not as elaborate as others, but I made sure I slept under a mosquito net in summer as there was a particularly virulent form of malaria in Korea in 1953. As a prophylactic we had to take one large chloro-quinine tablet a week instead of a previous daily dose of quinine. The weekly medical procedure to protect us against the effects of a very unpleasant, and possibly lifelong, disease was easy and convenient. Yet a few pilots appeared unable to carry out this simple regime, or bothered enough to draw a mosquito net from the base stores.

It was the same with the escape and evasion kits, where the variety of items available for survival was considerable. In addition to a silk-screen map of North Korea, marching compass, signalling mirror, torch and flares, I used to carry quite an assembly of camping, hunting and fishing gear attached to my Mae West. With my Colt 0.45 automatic I carried spare clips of ammunition with one clip loaded with tracer rounds and one loaded with bird shot. All this equipment was extra ballast to the Mae West, first aid kit, emergency radio, and the rescue items contained in the dinghy pack. In the event of a bale out I should probably have found it all quite superfluous. I was to discover later that a '45' tracer round was considered a dumdum bullet and therefore illegal under the terms of the Geneva Convention; not that the North Koreans would have needed that as an excuse! The tracer and bird shot rounds were in short supply and I did not test the tracer effect until after the Cease Fire, when I found it did not work anyway!! A five inch switch blade knife, together with some items for barter, completed my 'Escape, Evasion and Survival Pack', but there was one last very important item to be included – a small bottle of Dimple Haig Scotch for the 'last hurrah'. Many pilots did not bother about evasion and survival on land, and traded comfort for survival at sea by not wearing the immersion suits that were essential to survive in the sea during the winter and spring months. They held a fatalistic attitude towards possible capture or death.

On my arrival at Kimpo I was informed that the local village women could provide a laundry service. I tried it once and received back some unrecognisable remnants of grey and tattered rags infested with lice. When I witnessed their method of washing by thrashing the clothes against stones in the paddy water and saw the condition of the houses, I realized I had a fortunate escape from what might or could have been.

Clearly we could not rely on any outside laundry facilities and we engaged the services of a Korean room boy to take care of the hut cleaning, with a stove to provide a constant supply of hot water for washing and our laundry. The base Post Exchange (PX) together with a larger PX at our main supply and servicing base at Tsuiki in Japan provided most things we required, and as far as I was concerned it was the means by which I maintained a constant replenishment of shirts, socks and underwear. The PX also provided such luxuries as cameras, binoculars, watches, radios and record players at discounted prices and would order from the US any special items requested. A small portable record player and a small collection of long playing records was a particular pleasure for me, and I even carried it with me on R&R trips to Japan. In Korea when *England, home and beauty* was so very far away, lying on my iron cot listening to Mozart, Beethoven or Brahms was not only a pleasure but a comfort. In more sentimental mood a Puccini extract from '*La Boheme*', '*Tosca*' or more appropriately '*Madama Butterfly*', would fill the bill. There was, however, one peculiarity that would not have appealed to the musical purist in that the voltage and hertz in Korea was less than in Japan or the US, consequently a long playing 33 rpm record had to be played on the 45 rpm setting to achieve a nearer rendition of the original sound track.

Some of my more lasting memories of living at Kimpo are regretfully olfactory and lavatorial. One was continuously aware of living among the surrounding paddy fields, except perhaps in winter when the paddy was covered with ice. There was a daily ordeal in performing the normal bodily functions carried out in an impressive outhouse for twenty; reserved for the exclusive use of the officers of the 4th FIG. Between breakfast and the morning briefing it was fully occupied and after waiting in line for a vacant seat, one developed quite differing impressions while seated face to face, knee to knee and shoulder to shoulder with one's comrades at arms. Identification was often uncertain with the outhouse filled with dense clouds of defensive cigar smoke. During the summer months it was a particularly trying olfactory ordeal; and during the winter months the ritual while dressed as Eskimo in arctic clothing presented additional difficulties requiring the talents of Houdini. One particularly nasty experience to avoid was being present when the Korean 'honey bucket wagon' arrived and the long side flaps of the outhouse opened with a clang. The ensuing icy blast of arctic air may have been refreshing; but it also presented a distinct danger of mutilation or frost bite in the nether regions. There was, therefore, a definite advantage in knowing the time-table for the 'honey wagon express'.

More lasting and irritating problems were due to the constant sweating when dressed in survival suits in winter or in normal flying gear during the heat and humidity of summer. This resulted in constant skin problems that became aggravated during the summer months when torrential monsoon rains washed out our water supply, depriving us of washing water and showering facilities. There were occasions when the supply of one personal canteen of heavily chlorinated drinking water a day had to suffice during the day for drinking, cleaning teeth and other bodily ablutions. On two occasions this lasted for more than a week and we were lucky when a water wagon arrived enabling us to bathe under a water hose. For the rest of the time we waited for a convenient thunderstorm to take a shower in the rain. I had one particularly unpleasant experience while taking a shower from a visiting water bowser when, after I had completely soaped up, the bowser ran dry. Trying to remove the caked soap from my body with my meagre ration of drinking water was an ordeal not accomplished until I traded several cans of beer for a canteen of water. It was on these occasions that the beer sales increased considerably in the officers' club. The skin rashes that resulted from flying under these conditions were difficult to clear up and lasted for some time after I left Korea.

I rarely flew more than once a day and for the remainder of the time, unless released for the day, my time was spent at the squadron dispersal or on the alert strip. Occasionally if the weather was fine I would draw a shotgun from the armoury and spend some time on the skeet and trap shooting range. About once a month I would take an aircraft, preferably my own, down to the firing butts to harmonize the guns and the gun sight. The six 0.50-calibre Browning guns were bore sighted on a target to converge at 1,000 feet. On one occasion while waiting to put my aircraft on the firing base I watched the testing of another aircraft. A short burst of fire came from a machine-gun after which an airman marking the target stepped out of a bunker to check the target. As the airman marked the target a hot round in the gun fired and the 0.5 inch solid round hit the airman high in the thigh near the groin, sending him spinning like a top for several feet. The bullet passed through the upper leg causing a massive wound and severed the femoral artery. Despite efforts to staunch the spurting blood while unable to apply a tourniquet, the man died before reaching the base hospital.

As if to illustrate that death was often at hand without flying, I witnessed another accident shortly afterwards that was equally avoidable if more dramatic. The crew chiefs on the flight line often called on us to check out some servicing on an aircraft by ground running an engine and clear a fault written up in the Form One. It was a fine day as I sat outside the squadron dispersal talking with one of the pilots while another carried out a ground run on his aircraft. Suddenly, I saw one of the ground crew walk across the front of the F-86 and disappear. The engine running near full power at the time then exploded with a loud bang and the pilot shut it down and jumped out expecting an engine fire from the disintegrating turbine. I ran over to the aircraft and asked after the airman, but it appeared I was the only one who witnessed the incident and neither the pilot nor the crew chief was aware of what had taken place, until they realized the man was missing and that the engine intake guard was not in place for the engine run. This was contrary to standing orders and it was the responsibility of the person doing the engine run to see it was in place before starting the engine. Nothing could be found of the unfortunate airman and after towing the aircraft to the squadron hanger they removed the engine. Following a complete dismantling of the engine, two of the wing doctors spent several hours scraping every compressor blade in the axial flow turbine to accumulate enough human material to fill a small box for burial. The accident was quite unnecessary and due entirely to carelessness on the part of the pilot and the crew chief for not seeing that the safety guard was in place, and by the airman in walking in front of the aircraft during an engine run. However, the suction at the engine intake is so great at high rpm that even with the engine intake guard in place severe injury can occur and even death from asphyxiation if drawn against the intake. This was the second time I had seen a jet engine ingest a man and fortunately, it proved to be the last.

I was always careful while eating and drinking in Korea, but sometime during April I developed a particularly severe case of the 'runs' that made flying difficult and stressful. Overseas it was not unusual to suffer from loose bowels due to changes in diet and the water supply. The only ones immune to the problem and the local god's revenge were those who stuck rigidly to an intake of gin or whisky. Although I was susceptible to the problem I limited my alcoholic intake, as I hated flying hung-over. Beer consumption could be a problem overseas as beer produced for warmer climes contained a percentage of glycerine as an inhibitor, and this acted as an intestinal lubricant. However, on this occasion I started losing weight rapidly, with a looseness of the skin that indicated severe dehydration. The squadron flight surgeon after some tests diagnosed typhoid fever and shipped me off to the USAF hospital on the other side of the airfield. This was a considerable shock to me as no one else on the squadron seemed to be affected. I attributed it to a ferry trip to Japan where I may not have been so circumspect in my eating and drinking. My doctors asked to which hospital in Japan I wished to be evacuated to and I elected to go to the British hospital at the main Commonwealth forces base near Kure in Japan: the British military hospitals were less egalitarian than the US military hospitals. My evacuation process was delayed due to an influx

of casualties from the front and in the meantime the doctors started me on
a course of auromycin; a new antibiotic of the tetracycline group that
proved to be very effective against typhoid. The result was dramatic and
after a week, although I felt very weak, I elected to return to the squadron
where the squadron doctor grounded me for two weeks. In discussing my
ailment with an RAF colleague flying with No. 77 RAAF Squadron on
Meteors, he confessed that he suffered constantly with the same problem.
On one occasion during an interdiction sortie in North Korea he felt
unable to control himself before landing back at Kimpo. Trimming the
aircraft he released the seat and parachute harnesses, and while attempting to undress, partially standing up he continued to fly the aircraft.
Spreading his map on his seat he attempted to relieve himself. I expressed
incredulity at his attempt to achieve a feat not even the great Houdini
himself had attempted. I said he was fortunate the Migs were not flying
that far south. My friend replied his most satisfactory accomplishment
was to leave his map behind for the North Koreans to read. I mention this
vignette to illustrate the fact that not all our flying operations and their
associated problems were routine.

I returned to my hut to find my room mate, Ralph Parr, had opened his
account with two Migs confirmed, and in some frustration I drew a
shotgun from the armoury and borrowing a jeep did some pheasant and
partridge shooting in the hills to the south-east of the base. The weather
was by then spring and walking the hills was very enjoyable after my
depressing stay in hospital. My decision not to go back to Japan to
recuperate from the effects of typhoid fever was in retrospect perhaps a
mistake. In the frustration of my illness and my desire to complete my 100
missions I elected to stay with the squadron, and during my temporary
grounding a state of despondency set in with the Migs active while my
colleagues on the squadron achieved some success. Fortunately, I had
some diversions to my depression by walking the hills in search of game
birds, accompanying our squadron doctor on some of his visits to Korean
hospitals, and a visit to the British Commonwealth Division in the front
line.

Our squadron doctor was a very unusual service doctor who was a well-
known eye surgeon in Boston before he was called up from the reserve to
go to Korea. Eye complaints and injuries were rare events on the base and
in order to keep his hand in for his return to Boston he started to visit
surrounding hospitals offering his services during his off duty time. Most
of the demand on his time came from a request for cataract operations,
which were common among the Koreans due to deficiencies of diet. He
used no equipment or medications from the base during his visits to the
hospitals. He was able to persuade his wife to send the antibiotics and

whatever else he needed from the US. To pass the time I accompanied him on some of his visits, in particular to a bombed out hospital in Seoul run by an order of Italian nuns for the Italian Red Cross. The facilities in the civil hospitals around Seoul were very limited and the sanitation appalling or non-existent, yet the nuns went serenely about their work as true administrating angels. There were no wards as such and the patients just lay in rows on the floors of the hospital ruins, with their families camped about them. Our squadron flight surgeon carried out many eye operations under the most primitive conditions, leaving what valuable antibiotics he had with the nuns to administer to the patients. The Korean hospitals he visited regarded him with awe and great respect, and had he died while performing these good deeds I am sure the nuns would have called for his benediction by the Pope.

The extraneous medical services carried out by our flight surgeon certainly kept him in good practice for his return to the States, but there was one eye operation in particular he carried out that was very special. During my time in the hospital on the south side of K-14, the train bringing in supplies from the port of Inchon stopped to examine a body strapped to the line just outside the base. The Korean driver and the US guards on the train suspected a booby trap and were surprised to find a ten year old boy tied to the line. The boy was taken to the hospital and apart from a grotesque tumour in one eye the size of a golf ball appeared unhurt although very under-nourished. While the doctors were deciding what to do with the boy, I got our flight surgeon to see him. The doctor diagnosed a tumour but could not say to what extent it was malignant other than express his view that it should be removed as soon as possible. The boy's parents or relatives could not be traced and it appeared that they had decided to return the boy to God but being good Buddhists elected the Americans to be their executors. There being no hope for the boy if turned over to the Korean hospitals it was decided that our flight surgeon would operate and the eye was successfully removed without further complications. Our doctor ordered a matching false eye from the US that was fitted some months later. In the meantime the boy continued to live at the hospital and became a resident mascot. He proved to be of exceptional intelligence, learning English and playing chess and draughts with the patients. Eventually, an American serviceman formally adopted him and took him home to the US. This was typical of the generosity of the Americans in Korea and many of them adopted Korean children from orphanages and took them back home. In our squadron pilots' crew room we had a large box into which the pilots put money, food, candy, toys and clothing for an orphanage a few miles from the base. It became the 335th squadron's orphanage with the squadron's insignia of a North American

Indian chief's head at the entrance to the orphanage. The pilots set up a roster to visit the children with the gifts and donations, and judging by the excitement the children displayed they obviously looked forward to these visits from the foreign 'big noses'.

One of the outcomes of my convalescence from the effects of typhoid was to spend five days with the British Commonwealth Division in the front line. The US 1st Marine Division, the British Commonwealth Division and the US Army 2nd Division formed part of 1 Corps of the US 8th Army holding the left flank of the UN forces in the front line, with the South Korean ROK Army 2nd Corps on their right. The UN forces in the front line lived in hundreds of reinforced bunkers dug into the rugged hills, connected by a series of communication trenches resembling the Western Front in the First World War. Neither the UN nor the Communists showed any willingness to go beyond the demarcation line that had been agreed upon in November 1951. The purpose of the visit was entirely army-air force liaison and although the 4th FIG was not involved in air support for the front line, I accompanied an American captain from a fighter-bomber wing. At the time of my visit the British divisional commander was Major General Mike West, and he and his staff went out of their way to make our visit as interesting and entertaining as possible. The front line ran along the north side of a ridge of rocky hills overlooking a no-man's-land of paddy to the communist lines a few hundred yards away. The dominant positions on the hills were given names, such as 'Gibraltar' and 'The Hook' and many became famous during the war. The renowned stand and defence of the 'The Hook' by the Gloucestershire Regiment in 1952 became the best known British action of the war. It was the defence of this crucial position on the British left flank from 1951 until the cease fire in July 1953 that resulted in more British casualties than any other single battlefield during the Korean War.

The British forces defending the front line positions consisted of five battalions, and at the time of my visit a battalion from the Durham Light Infantry occupied 'Gibraltar' and a battalion from The Duke of Wellington's Regiment defended 'The Hook'. Accommodation although basic was remarkable under the circumstances as each battalion I visited had a mess dug into the rocks lined with wood panelling taken from packing cases and complete with the inevitable bar furnished with home-made furniture. In marked contrast to the British flair for creating a home-from-home atmosphere, the Americans lived in less decorative surroundings, although facilities such as iced drinks, ice cream and popcorn were available. During my stay at the front I visited the US 1st Marine Division on the British left and the US 2nd ('Second to None') Army Division on their right. The contrast between the two American divisions was very marked, and I was very impressed by what I saw with the Marines. Contained within the 2nd US Army division were other elements of the UN forces and of these we spent an afternoon and evening with the French Foreign Legion battalion, followed by a morning with the Turkish brigade. The Legion lived up to its reputation and most of the officers and men had previously fought in Indochina. All the officers were French with other ranks coming from various parts of Europe. The colonel commanding the battalion was a very professional soldier and ran a tight ship. Whether coincidental or planned, we were invited to stay for the formal monthly dining-in night. We sat either side of a long table with the colonel at the head, the American captain on his left and myself on his right. During the course of a lengthy dinner consisting of many courses and accompanied by copious servings of very palatable French wine, I noticed the conversation about me was entirely in English. It became obvious as the conversations diminished to silence at the far end of the table that the seating plan was not based on seniority but on the officers' proficiency in an English only conversation. This touch was typical of our host and I was very impressed by the French hospitality and their thoughtful arrangements for our visit. The meal was by far the best I ever had in Korea and the following day, after a very convivial evening when we were hard pressed to hold our own in after-dinner songs and games, two bleary-eyed and hung-over fighter pilots headed for the Turkish Brigade.

The contrast could not have been more marked, as there were certainly no frills with the Turks who fought and lived under the most basic conditions I ever saw with the UN forces. My companion expressed surprise and concern at the pay and conditions of the Turkish troops, who out of their very small entitlement of pay were only allowed to retain a pittance in Korea, while the remainder was retained in Turkey. Our escorting officer, a tough looking major, expressed the opinion that the honour of fighting for Turkey was sufficient recompense. Before we returned to the British lines we witnessed a bizarre event that made the visit memorable when the major asked us if we had killed any Chinese. We replied it was often difficult to be precise on those matters while flying. The major then produced a sniper's rifle that he gave to my companion, saying that now was our chance for some sport and to get ourselves a trophy each. The American looked somewhat nonplussed saying there was nothing to shoot at or even see. The major led us to a forward observation post and barked out some orders to a corporal who led out half a dozen soldiers into no-man's-land. The Turks moved through the wire and out into the combat area by leaps and bounds until they were some distance away. They then started to shout at one another while jumping up and down out in the dried up paddy. The major said, 'Get ready; you'll soon have a target.'

After watching this performance for a few minutes I saw through my binoculars a few heads starting to appear above ground in the Chinese lines as some of the communist troops could not contain their curiosity. The major started to become excited and kept saying, 'There that one, over there, shoot, shoot!' My companion continued to dither about with the rifle, muttering something about not shooting at a sitting bird. At last the major could contain himself no longer and in his impatience grabbed the rifle and fired at one of the heads. The heads disappeared and the major in visible disgust blew his whistle sharply and the Turks started to return in the same manner as before, while a mortar in the Chinese lines opened fire on them. The whole performance was quite extraordinary, and apparently was a common occurrence to relieve the boredom while occupying the front line positions when the only fighting action occurred during night reconnaissance raids. Our Turkish host appeared disappointed at our lack of enthusiasm for his efforts to entertain us and to provide some sport. It was a clear indication of the value placed on the lives of the Turkish troops.

Although the ROK and US forces bore the brunt of the casualties in Korea, it came as no surprise to learn after the war that the Turkish brigade suffered nearly as many battle casualties as the two British brigades combined, and double that of the total combat troops of the remaining nine participating nations. It was with some relief we thanked the Turks for an entertaining visit and returned to the British lines to spend the remainder of our time with the Hussars and their Centurion tanks, before bidding farewell to, and thanking General West and his staff for a very enlightening visit. The last two months of June and July before the armistice on 27 July 1953 was to see some of the heaviest action on the ground and in the air as the Chinese strove to improve their bargaining position prior to a cease-fire, and to humiliate and inflict as much harm as possible on the ROK army. General Mark Clark, the US and UN forces commander, later commented, 'There is no doubt in my mind that the principal reasons, if not the one reason, for the Communist offensive was to give the ROKs a bloody nose; to show them and the world that *Puk Chin* – Go North – was easier said than done.'

I returned to operational duty in May to find the Migs had been active during my absence from the squadron. The month of May saw the squadron add to its total of jet aces with Major Vermont Garrison, our executive officer or second-in-command, becoming the 32nd ace; to be followed in June by Captain Ralph Parr and Captain Lonnie Moore as the 33rd and 34th aces of the Korean war. As well as the increased Mig activity, with the warmer weather the US army engineers were busy extending and improving our runway. During the summer months the runway temperatures soared to well over 100°F and the F-86 with full combat load and two 120 US gallon metal drop tanks used most of the available 6,000 feet of the macadam strip to get airborne while using 15 degrees of take-off flap. The problem with the single east-west runway was two-fold. First, close to the east boundary of the airfield was a small hill 300 feet high, requiring a tight curved left approach turn to the runway on landing, and an equally tight right turn after take-off. For this reason it was given the name – 'Bust-your-ass-mountain.' Second, at the west end of the runway a sharp drop-off of 50 feet into a small hamlet gave us no over-run area in the event of engine failure on take-off or brake failure on landing. In helping to improve matters the US army engineers tackled the problem in typical American fashion. They carved about 100 feet off the top of the hill at the east end and deposited it in the drop-off at the west end of the runway. In doing this they provided an additional 300 feet of over-run with an aircraft carrier arrestor fence attached to heavy chains to stop aircraft over-running the runway overshoot area. Before this improvement to the runway I witnessed one shocking accident while on the alert strip. No. 77 Squadron, RAAF, took-off on an interdiction strike in the Haeju area with their Meteors carrying full over-load fuel tanks and armed with eight napalm rockets under the wings. One aircraft flown by an RAF pilot experienced an engine failure too soon to become airborne and too late to abort the take-off. The aircraft over-shot the runway and crashed into the hamlet below the drop-off erupting in a massive ball of fire and exploding ordnance.

All our missions were flown with drop-tanks and until the last three months of the war we used the US made 120 US gallon metal tanks. These were excellent tanks and the F-86 could land while carrying these tanks, although we always dropped them in the combat area. The technique used in dropping the tanks was to apply a positive upward G-force to ensure a clean separation of both tanks with the wings level so that a tank did not curl around the wing tip and damage an aileron. The US made tanks were expensive and a popular, plaintive call as they left the aircraft was, 'There goes another Chevrolet!' To help mitigate the cost of the tanks, some Japanese fibreglass tanks were tried but they were not a success as they were unreliable in fuel flow, they often leaked and they did not release cleanly. Consequently, regardless of the type of sortie flown they were always jettisoned before landing. During the last months of the war we received the large US made 200 gallon metal drop-tanks for long distance reconnaissance missions. During the hot months of the monsoon season my heart was often in my mouth on take-off when using these tanks as we used every foot of the runway before getting airborne. As with the Japanese tanks the 200 gallon tanks were always dropped before landing because the maximum amount of flap that could be lowered for landing was thirty degrees before the flap hit the tank; and landing under these conditions required a much longer runway than was available at K-14. The tanks were very much more expensive than the smaller 120 US gallon tanks, and when dropping these one often heard a heartfelt cry of, 'There goes another Cadillac!'

There was one other flight duty that was very popular but difficult to achieve by the junior pilots. This was ferrying our aircraft back to Japan for second line servicing and major overhauls. The squadrons were responsible for first line servicing and the maintenance group at K-14 carried out battle and accident repair to enable the aircraft to fly to Japan. Our main maintenance base was Tsuiki, a small airfield with a PSP runway 400 nm away on the north-east side of Kyushu and not far from the famous hot springs resort of Beppu. If the weather was bad we diverted to Itazuke near Fukuoka on the north side of the island; a large US base serving many types of aircraft for Korea. The procedure was to fly the F-86 to Tsuiki, night stop and then air test the replacement aircraft the following morning before ferrying it back to K-14. The pilots tended to be very fussy about these air tests in order to delay their departure by one more day. The temptation to indulge in the luxury of Japanese baths, fresh milk, fresh fruit, steaks, purchases from the PX and the other diversions not available in Korea were hard to resist. Those not fortunate in flying a ferry flight had to wait three or four months for a Rest and Recreational entitlement and a seat on a flight to Japan. As most headed for Tokyo this meant a flight to the main USAF transport base at Tachikowa near Tokyo. The squadron medics usually included a handful of 'No Sweat' antibiotic pills together with anti-malarial pills for pilots departing on their Rest and Recreational leave. One Kimpo bar song sung to the tune of 'On the Wabash' put R&R in Japan in perspective with a sentiment for getting away from it all in Korea.

> When the ice is on the rice in old Kyoto,
> And the sake in the cellar starts to freeze:
> If you turn to her and say – 'Ojo-san dozo';
> Well: you're getting just a little Nipponese!

The only way I could get my pay was to collect it from the British Embassy in Tokyo, and I made this the reason to have more than my fair share of the ferry flights. In hitching an airlift to Tokyo and back I saw quite a lot of 'Nippon – Land of the Rising Sun' as opposed to 'The Chosen – Land of the Morning Calm'. I considered myself fortunate to take advantage of this concession, and I was also fortunate in my contacts with the US Marines Corps. Shortly after my arrival in Korea I renewed my friendship with Major Willie Newendorp who was in my flight on 41 Squadron while he was on exchange with the RAF. He was the squadron executive officer of a fighter-bomber squadron flying F-9F Panthers at K-3 on the east coast. I visited him a couple of times at K-3, meeting some interesting reservists serving with the Marines, including the great baseball player, Ted Williams, and Woody Woodbury, a popular pianist and entertainer. One amusing reserve pilot on the squadron from Brooklyn had a fund of stories about New York and New Yorkers that he recounted with a broad Brooklyn accent. It appeared that a true native of Brooklyn had the same type of humour and sense of the ridiculous as a genuine London Cockney. One amusing tale that he swore was factual occurred while he was on an F-9F Panther Jet squadron at Cherry Point in North Carolina when he volunteered to demonstrate a Panther Jet at an air show at La Guardia Airport in New York. He had done so in the hope of spending some time at home in nearby Brooklyn. Owing to an air movement restriction the aircraft was not allowed to fly into La Guardia and so the Panther Jet with its wings folded upright on an aircraft transporter travelled with its pilot to New York by road. The transporter, while negotiating a bend in the Holland Tunnel, caused the aircraft's wing tips to strike the tunnel roof, creating a monumental traffic jam. Amid the chaos and the blaring of horns from irate motorists a tough looking New York traffic cop on a Harley Davidson motor cycle reached the scene of the accident and the following conversation took place:

Traffic cop, 'OK, Flyboy, is this your plane?'
Marine pilot, 'Yeah, I'm trying to get it to La Guardia.'
Traffic cop, 'Ok, Leatherneck, let's move it out of here!'
Marine pilot, 'How the hell am I to do that with the wings stuck on the roof?'
Traffic cop [jabbing with his index finger], 'Look, Buster, don't give me any goddamn static. You flew the goddamned plane in here, now you fly the goddamn thing out of here or I'll book you for obstruction!'

As a result of my contacts with the US Marine Corps I had an interesting liaison visit to HMS *Ocean* at the end of its west coast patrol in the Yellow Sea. My Marine friend arranged to fly me out to the carrier and while I was in the ward room, the pilot received instructions to return to base and did so without telling me, thinking I was remaining on board. It was all rather embarrassing being marooned aboard the carrier without being able to return to K-14. I therefore had no alternative other than to relax and enjoy the hospitality of the Royal Navy. The following day the Firefly squadron carried out their last mission to the Haeju escorted by the

Sea Fury squadron, and I went along for the ride as a navigator. Our assisted take-off from HMS *Ocean* was interesting; it being my first and only experience of being catapulted into the air. My pilot briefed me to brace myself firmly between the instrument combing and the seat, but in my haste I ignored one of Newton's laws of motion. The Firefly and I jerked forward violently on the release of the catapult and my face struck my camera now suspended in air from where I placed it before our launch. My goggles and oxygen mask probably saved me from a bloody nose or a broken tooth. Fortunately, the camera's carrying strap became caught up in the process saving it from finishing up in the rear of the fuselage. Whatever reservations I may have had flying from K-14 I modified after that comparatively slow, uncomfortable, noisy and bumpy ride in the Firefly. The flight was uneventful but it gave me an entirely different perspective operating from a carrier and flying low level interdiction over the Haeju, than from my F-86 high above the ground combat. We landed back on the carrier in time for cocktails and an enjoyable lunch in the wardroom as HMS *Ocean* set course for Sasebo in western Kyushu.

My hosts apologized for the poor fare, explaining that towards the end of their tour of duty the provisions supplied under contract by the Chinese victualler in Hong Kong ran a bit thin. I replied that they would have suited us very well at K-14. The US Navy visitors to Royal Navy ships always commented on the frequencies of meals aboard with breakfast, followed by a morning coffee break, lunch, afternoon tea, cocktails and dinner. After duty on a 'dry' US Navy ship the Americans appreciated the difference of the sociable wardroom with the added conviviality of the Royal Navy warships, especially with the Fleet Air Arm aircrew relaxing after their tour of operations. Only the skipper, Captain Evans, abstained as he maintained his lonely vigil in his quarters with an occasional invitation to visit the wardroom. After a short call at Sasebo, the port the Royal Navy used as a base when supporting the UN forces in the Yellow Sea, we paid a brief visit to Nagasaki. This port was the secondary and alternative target to Kokura for the second atomic bomb dropped on Japan. On 9 August 1945 the more powerful 10,000 lb plutonium 'Fat Man' bomb exploded over the city at 1,500 feet ending the war with Japan. The effects of the bomb were contained within the surrounding hills but still resulted in around 70,000 immediate casualties, with many others to follow as a result of radiation sickness. Emperor Hirohito sued for peace the following day. We cruised through the Inland Sea of Japan, under perfect weather conditions, to Yokohama. It had been a thoroughly enjoyable liaison visit and confirmed my view that although I had great respect for the Fleet Air Arm I had no desire to 'Fly Navy'; but I certainly appreciated 'Living Navy' when compared to our conditions ashore. HMS *Ocean* docked in

Yokohama to a ceremonial welcome before returning to Hong Kong for a full replenishment of supplies and aircraft before redeployment. Despite an invitation to stay and enjoy the festivities before their departure, I decided I should move on to Tokyo to organize my return to Korea before my prolonged absence was viewed as AWOL.

My first concern was to collect some pay from the British Embassy and following this I went to Tachikowa AFB near Tokyo, for a flight back to Korea. A big double-decker Douglas C-124 Globemaster aircraft was about to leave for Korea and as this was the USAF's latest and largest transport I thought it would be interesting to fly back on it. However, the dispatcher in charge had other ideas as I did not have the appropriate travel orders and would not allow me to board the aircraft. I returned to Tokyo to make alternative arrangements and heard that the aircraft had crashed into a rice paddy after take-off with a double engine failure. This was the worst transport aircraft accident during the Korean War with the largest loss of life. Investigations showed the cause was probably due to the second pilot feathering the inboard propeller by mistake when the outboard engine failed. It was a close call and I had reason to be grateful to the dispatcher who I viewed as officious and unsympathetic in following the inflexible travel order system of the USAF. When I did eventually arrive back at K-14 I found the 'brass' were a bit cool with my explanation for my prolonged absence and unimpressed with my narrow escape from terminating my USAF tour in a paddy field in Japan aboard the 'Globemaster'. I did have the advantage of being merely on exchange with the USAF, and so consequently any misunderstanding passed without repercussions.

I was to spend two R&Rs with Newendorp in Japan during which I experienced the differences in the US Armed Services. I was particularly impressed by the US Marine Corps facilities at and around their main air base at Itami near Kyoto, the ancient capital of Japan. It always appeared to me that although the US Air Force had better aircraft to fly; as was the case between the RAF and the Fleet Air Arm; when it came to organization both navies had it over their respective air forces. I always felt an affinity when with the Marine Corps, and after the cease-fire during a visit to K-3 to see Newendorp, I was fortunate enough to be allowed to fly the F-9F. Just one flight was enough for me to assess it as a good fighter-bomber, and it was as nice to fly as the F-80, however, it could not compare with the F-86 as a pilot's aircraft. Bill Newendorp was a good and generous friend. We spent some very enjoyable times together, both in the UK and while on my secondment to the USAF in Korea. Consequently it was distressing for me to hear when I returned to the UK that he was killed in a flying accident shortly after returning to the United States.

The peace talks at Panmunjon, a small village at the west end of the front just below the 38th parallel, dragged on through the spring and early summer of 1953. I can never see or hear the name Panmunjon without associating it with the word panjandrum. The catalyst being Syngnam Rhee, President of the Republic of Korea, who behaved just like *the Grand Panjandrum himself*. President Rhee was against the peace talks and wanted the UN, which meant the US, to continue the war. As the talks appeared close to reality during the summer, the South Korean President carried out acts devised to create as much inconvenience to the US forces as possible. The main stumbling block in the discussions centred on the repatriation of the North Korean POWs and after the communists walked out of the talks, Syngman Rhee started to disrupt the negotiations with organized protest marches. The rent-a-crowd demonstrations soon escalated to full scale riots in Seoul with girl students placed in the front ranks to hinder the reaction of the US troops, while the South Korean troops and police were conspicuous by their absence. The disturbances spread outside Seoul to the US bases and at K-14 crowds of screaming girls blockaded the entrance to the base. All UN personnel were confined to their bases, and it was disconcerting to those of us at K-14 to have random shots fired at us from outside the perimeter fences.

In June 1953 in response to the stalled armistice negotiations regarding the repatriation of the North Korean POWs the Chinese struck at the South Korean front. Syngman Rhee's response to the Chinese onslaught was to try to torpedo further negotiation by ordering the release of the North Korean POWs. At Inchon and Pusan the South Korean guards opened the gates of the prison camps and the North Koreans walked away. Out of the 27,000 POWs released only a few were recaptured and the rest being Korean faded into the countryside. Following the release of the North Korean POWs saboteurs cut the railway line from K-14 to Inchon, the main port for Seoul a few miles to the south-west, necessitating much tighter security. The double barbed wire fences around the base had South Korean guards patrolling the outer fence and USAF guards patrolling the inner fence. My hut was close to the inner perimeter fence and next to the hut occupied by the wing commander and the three group commanders. One night I was awakened by gunfire and ran outside with my '45' automatic and found that an American guard had shot dead an armed Korean attempting to cut through the inner fence. There were no South Korean guards in sight along the outer fence and there was nothing to distinguish the colonels' hut from any of the others. The intention of the intruder is speculative, but if his mission was to assassinate the colonels he knew where to cut the wire to reach their hut. President Eisenhower visited Seoul and made a very generous offer of aid to the

ROK that Syngman Rhee could not refuse. The USA agreed to a mutual security pact with the ROK, long term economic aid and a $200,000,000 down payment for the expansion of the ROK army to twenty divisions. The disturbances calmed down and the armistice negotiations continued until the cease-fire on 27 July 1953.

June produced the highest Mig count of the war and the last week of July saw a slackening of activity in the air war as the Migs pulled back to their bases around Mukden. Most of my missions involved reconnaissance flights with little or no opposition. By 27 July the 4th FIG claimed the most Mig kills, with my squadron, the 335th FIS, being the top scoring squadron of the Korean War. The new commanding officer of the 335th, Lieutenant Colonel Vermont Garrison, had reached a score of ten Mig-15s destroyed; the only pilot to claim ten kills in the Second World War and ten kills in the Korean War. Captain Lonnie Moore and the group commander, Colonel James Johnson who flew his missions with the 335th, also claimed ten Mig-15s destroyed. Major James Jabara and Captain Pete Fernandez of the 334th FIS each claimed fifteen Mig-15s destroyed, and only Captain Joseph McConnell of the 51st FIG beat these scores with sixteen Mig-15s claimed destroyed.

Captain Ralph Parr had claimed nine Mig-15s destroyed by the 27 July when he led a flight of four F-86s from the 335th on a reconnaissance sweep of all airfields in the Yalu area to check the disposition of Mig aircraft. I was flying as the second section leader and we flew with the big 200 gallon drop-tanks in order to cover all the airfields from the Chong-Chong River and the Sinanju/Anju airfields along the west coast to the mouth of the Yalu River. Around the Antung/Sinuiju complex were five airfields on both sides of the Yalu, and further north was the big Mig base of Feng-Cheng in Manchuria. Flying at 45,000 feet with no sightings of Migs on the airfields or reports of any Mig activity, we turned east towards the Suiho Dam and Tuan-Tien, an airfield in Manchuria north of the Suiho Dam. We had by now dropped our tanks and when turning over the Tuan-Tien airbase back towards the Yalu river I spotted an aircraft low down heading north-east from the Suiho lakes. I called the 'bogey' but Parr did not pick it up and fearful I should miss it against the rugged mountains I called 'lock-on' to keep it in sight and rolled over with my wingman into a dive to identify the aircraft, calling on Parr's section to provide top cover. On reaching 10,000 feet I identified the 'bogey' as an IL-12 flying at about 6,000 feet. The mountain tops were around 3,000–4,000 feet and as I closed on the aircraft at a reduced speed, to my surprise Parr passed me and closing to short range opened fire. The aircraft started smoking from both engines and went into a shallow dive until it crashed into the mountainside and exploded. On the debriefing Parr claimed his tenth aircraft destroyed, duly confirmed by his gun camera film and the rest of the flight, making it *the last hurrah* in the air battle and Parr the eleventh double ace of the Korean War.

The signing of the armistice occurred at 10.00 am on the 27 July with the cease-fire to take effect twelve hours later on 28 July. On the evening of the 27 July the whole of the 4th Fighter Group diverted to K-3 (Pohang), a Marine Corps base 150 nm to the south on the east coast. The deployment was to forestall any last minute attack on K-14 by the Communists before the cease-fire. We returned the following day to find that not even a 'Bed-Check Charlie' had paid us a visit. The shooting war was over and we were virtually back where it had all started four years before.

Two days later 5th Air Force conducted an inquiry at K-14 in response to a protest lodged at the United Nations by the Soviets into the shooting down of an unarmed civil IL-12 transport aircraft over Manchuria while on a flight from Port Arthur to Vladivostok. The US admitted shooting down a military IL-12 over North Korea and denied any infringement of Manchurian airspace. It was very obvious from the Soviet protest in the UN that the IL-12 aircraft was carrying important and high ranking passengers onboard who were in all probability Russian, or Chinese. The routeing of the flight so close to the war zone border was strange especially without a fighter escort, instead of flying to Vladivostok via Mukden, 100 miles north of the border. It seemed likely to me that the important passengers were viewing the big hydro-electric plants along the Yalu, of which the Suiho Dam was the biggest, supplying power to China and North Korea. The constant attacks by the USAF on the hydro-electric power sources severely damaged the industrial capability of North Korea, making the country dependent upon military supplies from either China or the Soviet Union. I often wondered about the consequences had I attacked the IL-12 instead of Parr, but under the circumstances I do not think I should have attacked a transport aircraft that far into Manchuria. As it was there was no international investigation and Parr was granted double ace status with ten confirmed kills.

In viewing the F-86 v Mig-15 combat during the Korean War and assessing the 'numbers game', there is the inevitable query regarding the kill-to-loss ratio and the 'aces'. Air combat started in the First World War and the politicians quickly saw a way of boosting a sagging national morale by firing the public imagination with the propagation of the image of knights of the air engaged in mortal combat. The media has continued the myth of a *mano-a-mano* concept of aerial combat by the fighter pilots ever since. Such propaganda was largely fantasy and is not supported by statistics, either in the First World War or in the succeeding air wars. The relevant national authorities claim not to recognize the established status of 'ace' and the respective unofficial definition of an ace varied. The generally accepted definition of a 'kill' required confirmation of an enemy aircraft destroyed. To some that meant an enemy fighter aircraft shot down in aerial combat. To others it meant any aircraft destroyed in the air or on the ground. The establishment of a kill requires confirmation of aircraft wreckage examined on the ground, the enemy pilot baling out, or later, ejecting from the aircraft; and the disintegration of the aircraft in flight by an independent witness and the gun camera film. Following these requirements a pilot credited with the personal destruction of five enemy aircraft in flight became an 'ace'.

Following the First and Second World Wars the claims for aircraft destroyed by both sides were found to be exaggerated by a factor of at least two and in some cases as much as three. There was a distinct grey area in relation to the claims in the First World War where the term 'victory' was applied to such claims as 'driven out of control', 'driven down' and the 'shared' claims. Such claims were added to the total of 'kills'. Although it is proved beyond doubt that the claims for aircraft destroyed in both World Wars was well in excess of the actual number of aircraft destroyed, the 'kills' credited to the aces remain as claimed. It is, therefore, left to personal assessment to establish the discrepancies of the claims and very obviously some 'kills' claimed can be reassessed as 'probable', 'damaged' or bogus claims.

The uncertainties of the First World War carried over to the Second World War in the need of public heroes for propaganda purposes, supported by commanders eager to promote morale, the offensive spirit and unit prowess with the reflected glory. The political dilemma arises between what is urgent or immediate recognition for propaganda purposes and what is accurate. For the politician and the propagandist, what constitutes the truth does not concern either and in the presentation of heroes once ace status is achieved, the unsubstantiated and uncon-firmed claims of the 'lone wolves' become acceptable and recognized. The result is that those writing of the 'aces' to perpetuate the myths actively support the claims, some of which must obviously fall within an area of speculation and suspicion. Further confusion arises following claims of aces in the Second World War and succeeding wars when the number of flying bombs and unarmed transport aircraft shot down, and the number of aircraft destroyed on the ground are added to the totals. Shooting down a V-1 or flying bomb was a very hazardous business but the fundamental fact as it applies to the 'ace' status is that it could not fight back and therefore no combat takes place. Similarly, ground attack in the face of defensive AA fire was also a very hazardous business, but again the aircraft attacked could not fire back. The shooting down of unarmed transport aircraft does not fall within any accepted definition of air combat. Therefore, such claims should not be accepted when establishing 'ace' status, or else the accepted definition of what constitutes the 'unofficial' recognition of an ace should be redefined.

Although the designation of 'ace' was not officially recognized by the RAF, during the Second World War the Air Ministry issued the following stipulations for approving combat claims:

'Destroyed'. The aircraft must be seen destroyed on the ground or in the air. Failing that, the aircraft must be seen to break up in the air or to be descending in flames: the claim was invalid if only smoke was seen. In all these circumstances there had to be independent confirmation either in the air or on the ground.

'Probable'. The pilot of the enemy aircraft must be seen to bale out of the aircraft. Failing that the aircraft must be seen to break off combat in circumstances that prove the aircraft is a loss.

'Damaged'. The aircraft must be seen to be considerably damaged as a result of the attack; for example, engine stopped, smoke issuing or parts shot away.

Therefore, all claims had to undergo scrutiny before officially approved. However, post-war research revealed that claims were exaggerated even though they were made in good faith and apparently verified at the time.

In the Korean War the USAF claimed nearly 800 Mig-15s destroyed for a loss of around 60 USAF F-86s, a kill-to-loss ratio of more than 10:1. Thirty-nine pilots claimed ace status with five kills or more, and of these eleven claimed double ace with ten or more kills, and three pilots claimed triple ace. Proponents for the glamorization and promotion of the fighter aces in general, such as Johnnie Johnson in 'The Story of Air Fighting'; Edward Simms in 'The Greatest Aces'; and Don McCaffery in 'Air Aces', readily and even wholeheartedly accepted and promoted the USAF claims. There were others who would stretch the kill-to-loss ratio to as much as 14:1 by suggesting that the aces had additional 'unofficial' claims to add to their totals. The Mig-15 claims were all destroyed over North Korea or Manchuria and therefore there were no wreckages available for inspection. The confirmation process was, therefore, entirely dependent upon gun camera film showing the disintegration of the aircraft or the ejection of the pilot. In support of the gun camera film was the confirmation by a witness, usually the wingman of the pilot making the claim. In the confirmation process rank had its privileges and in the Korean War, of the thirty-nine 'official' aces eight were of colonel rank, ten of major rank, sixteen of captain rank and five of first lieutenant rank. Only one second lieutenant F-86 pilot claimed a Mig-15 and it is uncertain if this was by ramming or an air collision. This shows, as would be expected, that the 'wingman' flying the F-86 missions did not share in the glory and rewards of Mig-15 combat to the same extent as the 'leaders'.

Only the communists can confirm the actual number of aircraft shot down and no actual loss figures for the Korean War were released by the North Korean, Chinese or Soviet Air Forces. The only so-called 'confirmation' to date stems from a North Korean pilot, Lieutenant Kum Sok No, who defected in a Mig-15 after the cease-fire. AVM Johnnie Johnson in his book 'The Story of Air Fighting' states: 'According to him (*Kum*) the communists lost more than 800 Migs, including two Russian units entirely wiped out; and the Chinese could not train pilots fast enough to replace those shot down.' It is hard to believe that a junior North Korean squadron pilot was in possession of this information at the time of the cease-fire. Under a communist regime it is inconceivable, and not even a senior ranking communist officer would have been aware of the total Mig losses sustained in the Korean War by the communist air forces. Such information could only be accessible in the top echelons of Peking and Moscow, and for obvious reasons this information would not be passed to the squadrons. An American fighter pilot would be unaware of the actual losses of USAF fighters operating in Korea beyond his own squadron or group. Obviously, under the circumstances of his defection, Lieutenant Kum, while under interrogation, would willingly confirm any figures suggested to him, and it is unlikely that he coincidentally conjured up by himself the same figures as claimed by the USAF. Regarding the comment about the Russian losses, if indeed he made this claim, one can only view it as spurious. It is also unlikely that a junior North Korean pilot flying with a North Korean Mig-15 squadron would be completely conversant with the Chinese Air Force flying training programme.

The post-war revisions and reassessments by the USAF reduced the claims of Mig-15s destroyed in air combat with the F-86 by as much as 50 per cent, to less than 400 Mig-15s destroyed. At the same time the USAF nearly doubled the admitted losses in combat to around 100 F-86s lost. This produced a modified kill-to-loss ratio of around 4:1. The process of reassessment is not known but the result indicates that confirmed 'destroyed' claims were revised down to lesser claims of 'probable' and 'damaged', or even 'not known'. The problem with the USAF's revised Mig-15 claims is that the details are not released and therefore, the individual claims remain unaltered. The USAF reduction by 50 per cent of the original claim of Mig-15 aircraft destroyed if factored to the claims of the thirty-nine 'official' aces would reduce the number of aces to around fifteen with no double aces. To account for where the discrepancies arise becomes a question of speculation. The official aces represented approximately

10 per cent of the F-86 pilots and accounted for 40 per cent of the total of Mig-15s claimed. It could be argued, with some logic, that by their success the aces demonstrated greater aggressiveness with superior flying skills and marksmanship. This argument implies that the discrepancies in claims lie mainly with the 90 per cent of the lesser claimants accounting for 60 per cent of the total of Mig-15s destroyed. A complete assessment of the kill–loss ratio of the F-86 versus Mig-15 combat is not feasible as it is virtually impossible to reassess the various claims against photographic evidence and the absence of the official communist losses. What the revised USAF figures indicate is a failure of the official USAF confirmation processes, as quite obviously some claims for confirmed kills were allowed that should not have been. To complicate the revision process there is the question of some unknown Mig-15 losses occurring in combat that have not been claimed for various reasons.

There is an interesting area of speculation resulting from the revised USAF claims regarding the claims of my own squadron, the 335th, as the top-scoring F-86 squadron of the six interceptor squadrons in continuous combat with the Mig-15. The squadron claimed 220 Mig-15 'destroyed', almost 30 per cent of the original total of nearly 800 Mig-15 claimed destroyed, and in making these claims the squadron provided 30 per cent of the recognized aces. If the individual claims pertain, this figure rises to more than 60 per cent of the revised total, which seems unlikely. In support of the number of 'destroyed' claims, the other claims were more modest with 80 'probable' and 185 'damaged' Mig-15 claims. The claims of the squadron during July 1953, the last month of the war, produced 12 Mig-15 'destroyed', mostly by the aces, against 2 Mig-15 'damaged'.

Russian figures from sources flying with the Soviet Mig-15 squadrons present a very different picture to that offered by the USAF. This is to be expected and in any event cannot be viewed as official and as such only cloud the question of the true kill-to-loss ratios of the combatants. The figures presented apply to the Russian pilots involved as neither the Chinese or North Koreans have offered any figures concerning their losses, official or otherwise. The Russian pilots were the most experienced in flying the Mig-15 and a higher kill-to-loss ratio can be expected than from the Chinese or North Korean squadrons. It is also probable that the Russian claims cover all types of USAF aircraft. The only certain con-clusion that emerges from a study of air-air combat is that the 'official' enemy aircraft 'destroyed' claims seldom correspond to the 'official' quartermaster 'loss' figures of the opposing air forces. The mathematics seldom match up. Therefore, despite the revised USAF kill-to-loss ratio figures, without the total communist loss rate any contention regarding the US 'aces' will remain unresolved, thereby maintaining the status quo and so avoid an embarrassing 'Catch-22' question – Who were the real aces? However, even if the total of Mig-15 aircraft destroyed is half of that originally claimed and the kill-to-loss ratio is reduced from 10:1 to 4:1, it is still an outstanding achievement. The Mig-15 was a formidable aircraft and had the advantage of forewarning with superior climb and altitude capability, with the advantage of operating over friendly territory from inviolate bases in Manchuria. The F-86 had to fly 400 nm over enemy territory to engage combat and return to the front line. This was an impressive display of the aggressive spirit, combative drive, superior training and flying skills shown by the USAF pilots, and a testament to their superior equipment.

In studying the few books available on the Korean War most confine their observations to the land battle and the air battle is covered cursorily, if at all. The war started on 25 June 1950 as North Korean troops crossed the 38th parallel and invaded South Korea. The land battle moved south to invest Pusan and then back north again as far as the Yalu River on the Manchurian boarder. The entry of China into the war caused a retreat back to the 38th parallel, where after one year of fighting, a stalemate developed resulting in a demarcation line just north of the 38th parallel in July 1951. The air battle continued with increasing intensity over North Korea until the cease-fire two years later on 27 July 1953. This cease-fire was the result of the USAF air battle over North Korea, together with the threat of escalation against the airfields in Manchuria. That this cease-fire was an armistice and not a surrender by the Communists is the result of the Communists being made aware early on in the war that it would be a limited war and no nuclear weapons would be used by the US. Also, no retaliation would be taken against communist forces outside the limits of North Korea, together with immunity for non-military targets within North Korea. This later aspect became a mute point when it was decided towards the end of the war to attack the Toksan and Chasan irrigation dams and the resulting floods destroyed rice crops and the rail communication to Pyongyang.

Whenever the air battle is mentioned emphasis is given to the more glamorous aspects of the Mig-15 versus F-86 aerial combat. Not enough consideration is given to the more important air battle of the bomber and fighter-bomber wings and the main contribution by the USAF in bringing the Communists to a cease-fire. The continuous pressure in attacking the airfields of North Korea forced the communist air forces to operate from rear bases in Manchuria. The fighter interceptor wings contribution was in protecting the day bomber, fighter-bomber and photo-reconnaissance aircraft from the Mig-15. This enabled massive and continuous damage to be inflicted on the North Korean airfields denying their use to the communists. In addition, attacks on the hydro-electric power sources reduced power down to 10 per cent of previous output. This had a great effect on the industrial potential of North Korea resulting in their war material and supplies being dependent upon Chinese and Soviet sources. The relentless day and night interdiction of supply and communication centres, rail centres, bridges and roads restricted communist build-ups for their land offensives forcing the communists to devise counter methods of supply, deployment, dispersal and concealment. With the UN land forces stabilized along a defensive front and the US politically denied the means to end the war, it was the USAF that brought about an armistice.

It is interesting to speculate on the outcome of the Mig versus Sabre combat had the Soviets supplied the Chinese with the Mig-17 by 1953 and the war had continued into 1954. The Mig-17 entered service with the Soviet Air Force in 1952 and its deployment to satellite air forces was restricted until its manufacture under licence in China in 1954. The Mig-17 had updated systems and equipment with improved stability control at high speed over the Mig-15. It was faster with a higher ceiling, although inferior in rate of climb. The Mig-17 still lacked a radar gun sight and an anti-G suit. The increased performance of the Mig-17 with a superior climb and altitude performance over the F-86, would undoubtedly have changed the parameters of air combat to some extent, and maybe the outcome with a different kill-to-loss ratio to that claimed against the Mig-15. However, I am sure the result would still have favoured the F-86 for other considerations, such as pilot ability and tactics. Had the Korean War continued into 1954 with the Mig-17 flying over North Korea, the United States had a counter with the North American F-100 that entered operational service in 1954. The F-100 was less manoeuvrable than the Mig-17, but faster with a genuine supersonic capability in level flight, and it also had a superior rate of climb. For combat the F-100 had a more lethal armament than the F-86 with four 20 mm cannon.

By 1952 the USAF B-29 raids changed from daylight to night attacks after suffering losses from the Mig-15. A friend of mine, Captain Chuck Edwards, whom I met in San Francisco while waiting to fly to Japan, flew A-26s from the island airfield of K-16 in the Han River outside Seoul. In addition to day and night interdiction missions his squadron carried out special missions such as dropping agents into North Korea. Apparently, on occasions these brave Koreans lost heart when they came to the drop zone and had to be persuaded to leave by means of a '45' automatic! The A-26s operated with two pilots and a navigator and the aircraft had tail warning radar. The B-29s and the B-26s were often intercepted at night by Soviet piston-engine all-weather fighters, but by 1953 there were reports of interceptions by jet fighters at night. While on a special mission over North Korea, Edwards told me his navigator reported a fighter closing at speed that indicated a jet fighter. After some evasive action he managed to shake off his pursuer, but shortly afterwards the fighter started closing in again and it required more violent evasive manoeuvring to lose the attacking fighter.

The USAF reports of night interceptions by jet aircraft over North Korea during 1953 showed that despite evasion tactics the Soviet fighters were still able to maintain contact, indicating a definite possibility that they had an airborne interception radar capability. The assumption was a development of the Mig-15, and I reported this to Air Ministry Intelligence. The reaction from London was to dismiss the reports, claiming it was not possible for the Soviets to be that advanced. It appeared that Air Ministry were unaware that the Mig-17 had been in squadron service in the Soviet Air Force since 1952, and it is now known the Soviets carried out a redesign of the nose section of the Mig-15 in 1950 to incorporate Izamrud airborne interception radar. The appearance was similar to the F-86D all-weather interceptor that became operational in 1950, with the difference that the Mig radar system had two scanners: one in the intake for tracking and the other in a lip above the intake for search. This necessitated the removal of the 37 mm cannon, leaving an armament of two 23 mm cannon. The aircraft became the Mig-15 SP1 and after a limited production run and successful trials during 1951, the Izumrud radar system was used in an all-weather variant of the Mig-17 in 1952. It is entirely feasible and quite probable that during 1953, either Mig-15 SP1 or Mig-17 PF all-weather fighters carried out operational trials against the USAF operating at night over North Korea and the Manchurian border. If so, it is likely that they operated clear of the North Korea border from one of the Chinese air bases around Mukden.

Following the cease-fire the flying was still good if a bit more routine and with less adrenaline flowing. The irksome readiness duties continued as 5th Air Force maintained a full alert status. I was by then a flight commander in charge of 'Charlie' flight, although this did not give me priority to lead my flight on sweeps. However, it did on any other missions and it entitled me to a personal aircraft with my name on the side of the cockpit canopy. My crew chief asked me what personal symbol I wanted painted on my aircraft and I was tempted to display a winged lime, but I decided instead to name it after my yacht in England, *Wild Goose*, showing a goose in flight with its neck outstretched like an index digit.

Our flying reverted to combat training and I gave my flight, including the wingmen, experience of briefing the sortie, leading a section or the flight, and debriefing the sortie. This was similar to a small fighter leader's school within the squadron. The change both surprised and pleased the junior pilots after flying permanently on someone's wing, and it gave them a chance to prove themselves. We carried out live gunnery training and camera gun dogfights, and we also tried to improve on the bad weather let-down procedures. The long range patrols along the west and east coasts of North Korea became the nearest to an operational mission, involving the use of the 200 gallon drop tanks in place of the standard 120 gallon tanks. With these tanks we flew long flights along the entire coastline of North Korea. On the west coast we flew up to Sinuiju at the mouth of the Yalu, and once I flew 100 nm west of Sinuiju almost to Port Arthur. The east coast patrols were much longer and of far greater concern in the event of engine failure. Although the US Navy had ships in the Sea of Japan and provided radar cover, one did not feel the prospect of rescue from the sea was as good as over the west coast. My longest flight took us past Chongjin to within sight of the USSR border where contrails were visible, presumably of Migs based in the Vladivostok area. Occasionally, three of our F-86s would join up with an RF-86 from the 67th TRW for a photo recce escort. Not once did we get any reaction from the Mig-15s and none came up to investigate. The patrols did not appear to achieve very much other than to present an alert and aggressive posture to the communists. There was no discernible naval activity and as officially we could not infringe on North Korean or Manchurian airspace we could not evaluate the state of Mig activity on the airfields, other than those within sight of the coast. In respect of the long-range coast patrols, I do not recall any of the senior pilots who were so eager to grab the 'shooting slots' on the sweeps flying on these missions.

After the cease-fire I had one puzzling experience for which I can find no satisfactory explanation. The tedious alert duties continued unabated during a nervous armistice, with an expectation of a renewal of hostilities. One day in August it was our turn for alert and I led my flight to the readiness dispersal at the end of the runway. The weather was hot and fine, although rain usually fell by late afternoon. I used to enjoy watching the cotton wool cumulus clouds form over the mountains and by afternoon they were transformed into cumulonimbus clouds with anvil tops towering over 30,000 feet, to be followed by the thunderheads turning into a tropical storm with heavy rain. We were on standby and I lay looking up at a blue sky with the cumulus clouds visibly boiling upwards, to be occasionally distracted as a flight of F-86s passed overhead. My attention was caught by a formation high overhead flying due south and I estimated by their speed they were F-86s at around 30,000 feet. I could see the silver forms reflected by the sunlight but I could neither distinguish their shape nor could I hear the jet engines. There were no condensation trails and the line astern formation indicated a camera-gun tail-chase exercise. As I lay looking at the four silvered specks against the blue sky, waiting for the leader to start manoeuvring, the formation suddenly reversed direction and headed back north. I then realized this was accomplished without any radius of turn or discernible change in speed.

In a flying career of many years and thousands of flying hours around the world up to altitudes in excess of 50,000 feet, I have never witnessed a phenomenon that I can only attribute to the extraterrestrial or to the presence of UFOs from outer space. As I know of no propulsion system capable of traversing a galaxy measured in light years, I remain a sceptic regarding any such visitations to this planet. I therefore looked for a practical explanation for an ability to turn in flight without a radius of turn. Nature has found a way to achieve this phenomenon in such creatures as dragon-flies and humming-birds, but only helicopters and vectored thrust jets can imitate them to some extent. The only conventional explanation was that the objects in formation were meteorological balloons. The height was feasible as even at high altitude it is possible to see weather balloons in bright sunlight. The speed was a problem for although a balloon at this altitude travelling in a jet stream can have a ground speed as much as 200 mph, I estimated the speed of the formation to be at least that of the F-86, or more than double the speed of the strongest jet wind. The main assumption that the objects were weather balloons, which in free flight have no radius of turn, lay in the feasibility of them travelling in a jet stream. The only explanation for the change in direction of their flight was that they were close to the edge of the shear line of a jet stream that shifted taking the balloons into an opposing jet stream. If this was the cause it did not follow the usual pattern of jet streams that are relatively narrow and shallow air flows circulating around the earth in the upper troposphere in one direction. The formation I watched appeared to change direction instantly through 180 degrees with no apparent change in formation or speed. I have no doubts that what I witnessed that hot summer afternoon in Korea in 1953 was not a hallucination or a figment of my imagination: it remains an enigma.

Social activities after the cease-fire were few and limited to visits to the officers' club at Kimpo or downtown in Seoul at the 5th Air Force club or the 8th Army club. The drive into Seoul was depressing but occasionally I made it for a change of scene. There was considerable battle damage to be seen on the way and all the bridges across the wide expanse of the Han River were destroyed during the early stages of the war and replaced with Bailey bridges. The central railway station in Seoul was virtually destroyed but the ancient south gate to the city remained intact, as were most of the Japanese built government buildings. The principal hotel, The Chosen, also escaped war damage and was used as the 8th Army officers' club. The 5th Air Force club was much less impressive being within a military compound. Our money was in military script and could only be used for purchases in military establishments, but despite this an active black market flourished covering a remarkable range of products and amenities. It was unwise to walk the streets but if one did the evident poverty and numerous beggars made it an unpleasant experience. It was not until I returned to Seoul some twenty years later that I did some sightseeing in the city. I visited the ancient palaces and gardens where in spring the Korean women in their very colourful national dress presented a pretty picture among the spring blossoms, in marked contrast to my memories of 1953. Seoul in the seventies looked very different in every way with western style buildings, clothes, cars and traffic jams. By the 1980s it was even more so as Seoul became a metropolis in a rapidly expanding economic miracle of development.

One memory of the 4th FIW officers' club at K-14 occurred when the administration decided in the spring of 1953 to redecorate the club and make it more presentable. Following its redecoration two C-47s flew in some furniture from Japan and the result was quite attractive, considering we were in a war zone. About a day or so after the official opening of the new club, Pyongyang Radio included in the daily hate session a reference to the club. Pyongyang Rose, named after Tokyo Rose from the Second World War, asked how the 4th was enjoying its nice new officers' club. She went on to tell us not to get too comfortable in it as the gallant aviators of the People's Republic would soon make a visit to blow it into oblivion. 'Bed Check Charlie' did pay a visit but all they could do with a hand grenade or mortar bomb they dropped was to put a hole in a Quonset hut and the club remained undamaged until the end. However, this incident did indicate the spread of the North Korean intelligence net, and they were probably aware of quite a lot that went on at Kimpo.

When not scheduled for flying I often borrowed a Jeep and drew a shotgun from the armoury. I explored the hills for pheasants, or the tidal flats along the Han River estuary for wildfowl, as before the Second World War Korea had an international reputation for its pheasant and duck shooting. The Korean War did not appear to have affected the number of pheasants and the amount and variety of wildfowl was phenomenal. At dusk with the paddy fields close to the shore, the huge flights of birds onto the fields from the mud flats were something to see and we were able to get some marvellous shooting. The bags of geese and ducks taken back to the mess hall to supplement our routine and monotonous menus were a welcomed change from fried chicken or pork chops, and were very much appreciated. I kept the pheasants for the squadron and friends. These were pleasant days and in the process I visited several Buddhist monasteries and ancient burial sites in the hills around Kimpo. On one occasion as I hunted pheasant, I climbed to the top of 'The Witch's Tit' for a fine view of the estuary and found out just how steep it was.

How it came about I do not know but the South Korean authorities became aware that the 4th FIW mess had occasional feasts on South Korean game birds. Anyway, someone in the Blue House, the ROK equivalent of the White House, resented us our sport. A presidential Decree filtered down to 5th Air Force HQ to the effect that any US personnel shooting Korean birds must first obtain a shooting and a game licence from the South Korean authorities. Under the circumstances, this appeared both unbelievable and ludicrous. The wing commander informed me of the edict, saying that it would be better under the circumstances to confine our shooting to the skeet and trap ranges. Not wishing to create another international incident I limited myself to bird watching on the Han estuary, although I did take the odd pheasant for myself. As a consequence of this farce I thought it appropriate to register my protest in song to the tune of a well-known Irish ballad and, with the help of RAF colleagues, formed a barber shop quartet that proved very popular in the K-14 officers' club.

The Kimpo Blues

A large lump of nightsoil fell from out the sky one day,
And it settled in a Chosen place; oh, so very far away,
That when the Top Brass saw it, sure it looked so grim and bare,
They said, 'That's what we're looking for, send the Air Force there.'
So they flew in Sabre Jets, Shooting Stars, and Meteors too;
And they sent 'The Fourth but First' – they'd nothing else to do.
Now you'll hear the pilots cry from that place so far remote –
'Where, oh where; Mother dear; where is that fucking boat?'
We've got the Kimpo Blues; and we've got the Kimchi Blues:
We're fowled-up; we're fed-up; and tired of this fucking ooze!
Oh, we tried to help old Syngman but that was just a fucking farce;
And now the Fourth has just one shout – 'Go shove it up your arse'!
We've got the Kimpo Blues; and we've got the Kimchi Blues:
And now we are fed up waiting for our fucking travel news!

At last the time came to say farewell to The Chosen – Land of the Morning Calm, and as the fighting was now over with no further prospects or aspirations of glory, there was *no sadness of farewell* on my part. My wartime recollection of Korea was that it was not a land that endeared itself and, apart from some brief moments, I found little to commend what was a brutally devastated and hard land with a trying climate, inhabited by rugged, tough, hard people suffering desperately from the impoverishment of war. This was in marked contrast to my first impressions of Japan during short visits to the Land of the Rising Sun recovering rapidly from the effects of the Second World War. However, to be fair, under the circumstances Korea was very much like the curate's egg – good in parts. Although I did not wish to repeat it, the experience of the Korean War was one I do not regret and from a flying point of view it was a wonderful experience flying the best fighter aircraft of its day under combat conditions. Flying the F-86 with the USAF in Korea was a privilege I shall always value, providing me with many exceptional memories.

Flying with the top scoring squadron of the top scoring fighter group was a most interesting experience, but it was to be detrimental to my chances of any Mig-15 claims. The only way I was able to participate on the fighter sweeps along the Yalu was as a wingman, when the chances of firing one's guns at a Mig-15 were rare. If given the choice I should have preferred flying with an RAF fighter squadron of F-86s as my seniority would have ensured that I had priority in leading flights and filling one of the shooting slots on the Yalu sweeps instead of flying the majority of my Mig sweeps as a wingman. In joining the top scoring squadron with the most Mig kills and the most aces in 5th Air Force, this not only attracted senior officers from headquarters 5th Air Force in search of glory, but severely limited my participation on the fighter sweeps to that of a wing-man. Although I led sections and flights on weather and airfield recon-naissance flights, photographic reconnaissance and fighter bomber escort missions, the opportunities for Mig claims on these missions were rare and limited. Unfortunately, although by 1953 the North American Aviation F-86E was in production in Canada, it did not arrive in the RAF until 1954 and under the Mutual Defence Aid Programme (MDAP), these air-craft were assigned to NATO and as such equipped squadrons of 2nd Tactical Air Force in West Germany or Fighter Command in the UK. In any event, had the RAF sent a fighter squadron to Korea it would have been with the Meteor VIII and involved in interdiction missions with No. 77 RAAF Squadron. As for the RAF losses on the USAF 4th Fighter Interceptor Group during 1953, they amounted to two missing in action and presumed killed, namely: Flight Lieutenant Graham Hulse and Flight Lieutenant John King.

The national flag of South Korea is unique in not denoting repre-sentation as in other national flags, but in displaying the Yin-Yang symbol it represents the principles of Chinese philosophy. The Yin-Yang school of Chinese philosophers teaches that history is the influence of the seasons and the five elements of earth, wood, metal, fire and water. Yin is representative of all that is negative and dark, while Yang depicts the positive and bright. The interaction of these influences decides the destinies of creatures and things. The symbol therefore graphically depicts the struggle between the North and South. It has been said that the Korean War was the wrong war, at the wrong place, at the wrong time and with the wrong enemy. Of course, this could be said of many wars and poses the question – Whenever is there a right war, at the right place, at the right time and with the right enemy? The Korean War was so very much smaller in scale than the major theatres of the Second World War that it has become little more than a footnote in history to most people, but for those who participated in that forgotten and unreserved war it remains imprinted in their memory. On Sunday, 25 June 1950, seven divisions of The People's Democratic Republic of Korea supported by tanks and aircraft invaded the Republic of Korea. With the Chinese made aware from the onset that the US would not fight an all-out war the die was cast. Three years and some five million casualties later, an armistice ended the fighting only miles from where it had begun. This armistice with no peace terms was to be no more than a cease-fire that has lasted until now. *The end crowns all and that old arbitrator, Time will one day end it.*

CHAPTER FOUR

Pleasant Hours Fly Fast

My departure from Korea to my arrival back in England was a leisurely affair taking about three months. The first stop-over was in Tokyo to settle affairs before moving south-west to the British Commonwealth base at Iwakuni by the Inland Sea and close by the infamous city of Hiroshima. The accommodation at Iwakuni, where the RAF operated a Sunderland flying-boat squadron in support of the UN forces, was very much more comfortable than had been the case at Kimpo. At Iwakuni I had a room to myself with a Japanese maid to make up my bed and clean the room. My used clothing was quickly removed for laundering and ironing; and fresh flowers were placed in the room each day. This sort of pampering, together with the pleasant mess, good food and a convivial atmosphere, made me wonder about my decision not to volunteer for occupational duties in Japan following VJ Day in 1945. During an enjoyable autumn stay I visited Hiroshima and, although eight years had passed since the first atomic bomb fell on a human target, there was evidence of the devastation it created. On 6 August 1945 the 9,000 lb uranium bomb, 'Little Boy', detonated over Hiroshima at 2,000 feet obliterating an area radiating out for 4 miles from the city centre. This resulted in around 80,000 immediate casualties, with many others to follow from the effects of radiation. At ground zero stands the skeletal domed remains of what was the city exhibition hall that now forms the memorial for the Peace Park and museum. Nearby was a more lasting memorial with the silhouette of one victim indelibly etched into the concrete of the bridge over the Ota River, illustrating the intensity of the searing thermal wave preceding the blast wave. A more enjoyable excursion took me through the many cultured pearl farms in the sheltered bay of the Inland Sea, past the distinctive torii of the famous Shinto Temple on the island of Etajima. After an interesting and relaxing stay at

Iwakuni I flew on to Hong Kong via Okinawa stopping off in the Philippines on the way. This was my first visit to both places and after a pleasant diversion in Hong Kong and Macao I flew on to Singapore via Borneo. Little did I imagine that this whole area of south-east Asia was to become very well known to me many years later after I retired from the RAF and during my time with Handley Page Aircraft and Hawker Siddeley Aviation. Following another pleasant few days in Singapore, I flew on westwards stopping in Ceylon, Pakistan, Iraq and Libya, before arriving back in the UK just in time for Christmas 1953. My round the world trip, courtesy of the RAF and USAF, had taken a few days short of one year.

Reporting to the Air Ministry in the New Year I requested a posting to my old squadron, No. 65 (East India) Squadron at Duxford near Cambridge, for I understood it was to be the first squadron to be re-equipped with the RAF's latest interceptor fighter, the Hawker Hunter. This was scheduled for the summer of 1954 but unfortunately for me it was not to be, and No. 43 Squadron, 'The Fighting Cocks', received the honour. In fact, No. 65 Squadron did not receive their Hunters until the arrival of the Mark 6 two years later in 1956, which was probably just as well in view of the many problems associated with the early marks of Hunters. Regrettably this was to be the last aircraft for this famous squadron before it disbanded to become a ground-to-air missile squadron, and thankfully I was not around then to witness this, or the ever diminishing fighter force in Fighter Command. Early in 1954 I arrived at Duxford to join No. 65 Squadron again and command 'A' Flight on my old war horse the Gloster Meteor Mk VIII. Duxford, a famous pre-war fighter base, was also occupied by No. 64 Squadron, an old squadron sparring partner from my Mustang days. Life followed very much the pattern of my time on No. 41 Squadron with me leading the squadron aerobatics team, only to be overshadowed by emerging Hunter aerobatics teams as squadrons became equipped with the Hunter Mk 1 and Hunter Mk 2. Apart from the disappointment of not being the first fighter wing to be equipped with the new interceptor, I was pleased with my posting to Duxford as it was a pleasant base conveniently situated for most of my interests, and because it enabled me to renew acquaintance with my old alma mater after a period of a dozen years. Much had happened to me in the intervening years but at Cambridge the apparent changes were more with 'town' than with 'gown'. In 1954 RAF Duxford was commanded by the highly respected fighter pilot Group Captain Jamie Rankin, DSO, DFC, who had replaced 'Sailor' Malan after the Battle of Britain in commanding the Biggin Hill wing. There were many experienced and knowledgeable wartime fighter pilots in the RAF who assessed both men as the two best RAF wing leaders of the war. Wing Commander Tommy Burn, DFC, who flew Meteors despite the handicap of two prosthetic legs, commanded the wing. Another aspect that pleased me was that the CO of No. 64 Squadron was an old friend, Squadron Leader Harry Bennett, AFC, who led the RAF aerobatics team when flying Vampires. I was his best man at his wedding and sadly in 1955 he was killed in a flying accident. In the space of little more than a year I lost three of my closest friends in the RAF through accidents.

Not much of significance occurred during the year apart from my promotion to squadron leader when I took over command of the squadron for a short while. As one of the principal RAF fighter bases Duxford had many VIP visitors and the most memorable and unique for me occurred with the visit of Emperor Haile Selassie of Abyssinia. He flew into Duxford for a visit to Cambridge University with a large and impressive entourage and accompanied by the British Minister of Defence and the Chief of the Air Staff. I was selected to escort him for a tour of the Duxford wing and to my surprise, and to the obvious discomfort of his towering Nubian bodyguards, when we arrived at my squadron he asked to see my personal Meteor and insisted on getting into the aircraft. Haile Selassie had a very imposing list of titles and although splendidly attired in full formal uniform and decorations, this could not disguise the fact that in stature he was a small man. After inserting him into the aircraft cockpit with some difficulty in as dignified manner as possible he disappeared from view. I leaned in to brief him on the controls while his two large and imposing bodyguards dressed in their flowing white robes and carrying gleaming scimitars, poised precariously on either side of me. I had the distinct and disconcerting impression that the slightest move on my part being wrongly interpreted by them would result in me being shish kebab. The Emperor was very friendly and appeared genuinely to enjoy his visit to the squadrons. The only sour note for me during his visit occurred when a pompous representative of the Ministry of Defence informed me that should the Emperor present me with an inscribed solid gold Rolex watch (that was his custom when favourably impressed) I must regard it as treasure-trove and hand it over to the Treasury Office. I wondered afterwards what the comptroller did with this imposing array of imperial largesse. As it turned out this caution was unnecessary for Haile Selassie was either keeping the watches for his visit to the University or else he had run out of them by the time he arrived at Duxford. Although I have owned a solid steel Rolex, this was the nearest I ever came to own a solid gold Rolex watch.

The New Year of 1955 brought a shock when my tenacious flying instructor's category popped-up again in the bowels of the Air Ministry and I found myself posted as the chief ground instructor to No. 4 Flying Training School at Middleton St. George in the north of England. I endeavoured to get this changed for the command of an F-86 squadron with 2nd ATAF in Germany without success. I spent the next year instructing and training *ab initio* fighter pilots while flying DH Chipmunks, Vampire Vs and the two-seat Vampire T-11, and in my spare time included some flying instruction at the local gliding club. During the year I did have one interesting break from a job I did not enjoy very much as my position presented an opportunity to attend a month's course on supersonic aeronautics at Bristol University that was both interesting and enjoyable. Then fortunately for me, although not for others, fate took a hand in February 1956 when two flights of Hunters from the Day Fighter Leader Squadron at the Central Fighter Establishment (CFE) were caught out low on fuel when a sudden sea fog closed the airfield at West Raynham and the aircraft diverted to the nearest airfield at Marham 10 miles away. As the eight Hunters flew overhead Marham the sea fog rolled in and only the first pair landed on the runway. The other six ran out of fuel with four pilots ejecting from their aircraft. One pilot attempted a forced landing and crashed on the airfield with injuries. The remaining pilot attempted a crash landing outside the airfield boundary and was killed. The loss of six Hunters with one pilot killed made headline news with a call for a parliamentary inquiry into the disaster and, as is the case when politics are involved, there had to be culprits and heads had to roll. The result of which was that in March 1956 I found myself at West Raynham as the senior instructor of the Day Fighter Leader School and CO of the Hunter squadron.

The Central Fighter Establishment moved from Tangmere on the south coast of Sussex to West Raynham on the north coast of Norfolk at the end of the Second World War in 1945. CFE was responsible for evaluating the tactical and operational abilities of new fighter aircraft and for the training of the leaders of the fighter squadrons. As such it comprised several flying departments or squadrons under the control of the Air Ministry: the Air Fighting Development Squadron (AFDS), the All Weather Development Squadron (AWFDS), the Instrument Rating and Examination Squadron (IRS), and the Day Fighter Leader School (DFLS) incorporating the Day Fighter Leader Squadron and the All Weather Fighter Leader Squadron, which became the Fighter Combat Wing (FCW). These squadrons were commanded by wing commanders who reported to a Group Captain Operations, who in turn reported to the air commodore Commandant. When I arrived on the DFLS the squadron operated Hunter aircraft and the Fighter Combat Wing had not formed. During war exercises the squadron reverted to its war designation of No. 122 'Bombay' Squadron of which I was the CO, and with its pick of the best of course graduates from the fighter squadrons on the staff, the squadron was the most experienced and elitist fighter squadron in the RAF. I was naturally very pleased and proud to be given this command although I was unhappy at the way it came about because the officer I replaced was an old friend. I knew No. 122 Squadron from my Mustang days and so things had turned out better than expected for me with my command of the Hunter squadron of all Hunter squadrons in the RAF. Many pundits scoffed that DFLS was a unit courting trouble and it was surprising such a disaster had not occurred before with the squadron operating to much lower limits than customary with the regular fighter squadrons. Unfortunately, the short duration of flight of the Hunter Mk 1 had been its undoing in that it did not allow for the vagaries of the weather along the north Norfolk coast, notorious for its sudden sea fogs sweeping in from The Wash and the North Sea. Such a moment of bad luck with no warning caught the Hunters too low on fuel for a diversion to where conditions were clear. The delay in the courses enabled me to get flying time on the Hunter and not for the first time was my conversion on type dictated by the study of the Pilot's Notes while sitting in the aircraft, starting up and then taking-off. By the time the courses resumed I had accomplished sufficient flying time to be both conversant and proficient with the aircraft; my only one mishap occurring when an engine failure on take-off resulted in me parking the Hunter in the runway over-shoot area, fortunately with no airframe damage to the aircraft or injury to myself. Had the turbine failed a little later in the take-off it would have been a different story and provided another field day for the press.

The history of the Hunter development into a satisfactory fighter is an interesting story and my years spent flying the aircraft through a progression of Marks 1, 2, 4, 5, 6, 7 and 9 provided some of the most satisfying flying of my RAF career, although initially fraught with frustration and disappointments. There is an old pilots' adage that if an aircraft looks right it flies right. If this is a truism then the Hunter should have performed like a dream, but such was not the case and my anticipation proved far greater than the realization until many modifications occurred culminating in the Hunter Mk 6 that did indeed fly right. There are some aircraft that defy this supposition and in this respect the McDonnell Douglas F-4 Phantom is a good example of an ugly aircraft proving to be very effective operationally. The F-4 Phantom proved to be one of the greatest multi-role combat aircraft ever designed.

The Hunter Mk 1 was arguably one of the best looking transonic jet fighters to enter service but was woefully deficient in some flying and operational characteristics. There were two main factors that affected the introduction of the Hunter into service. First, the advent of transonic fighters such as the Soviet Mig-15, the French Dassault Mystere and the US North American F-86 made the British Gloster Meteor obsolescent as an interceptor fighter, although it continued to provide a useful service in the ground attack and reconnaissance roles. Second, the national defence situation during the Korean War at the height of the Cold War, pushed for an early introduction of the Hunter into service and the initial order of only three prototypes was an incredible decision for a priority project. The result of this folly and pressure was that the Hunter entered RAF service in the summer of 1954 before the many shortcomings, difficulties and operational problems of the aircraft were sorted out in the development trials' programme.

The RAF philosophy for its new jet interceptor fighter remained the same as it was for the Spitfire and the Meteor in that the close proximity of the bomber threat from the European mainland required an interceptor with a high rate of climb. This was a fundamental operational requirement for the interception of high altitude bombers carrying nuclear bombs before reaching the UK. During the 1950s and 1960s the nuclear air threat to the UK was from the high altitude and high speed Soviet subsonic jet bombers, such as the TU-16 'Badger' protected by a defensive armament of 23 mm cannon in remote controlled turrets. The RAF counter to this threat was initially with the subsonic Meteor, to be replaced by the transonic Hunter day and Javelin all-weather fighters by the mid-1950s; with the supersonic Lightning all-weather fighter entering service in the early 1960s. The Hunter, Javelin and Lightning fighters were armed with 30 mm cannon until the Javelin became equipped with air-air guided weapons during the late 1950s, and the Lightning in the mid-1960s. During the era of the subsonic fighters the speed differential between the bombers and the interceptors was negligible, making accurate positioning for a successful interception essential in order to carry out a pursuit attack. In the Second World War the *Luftwaffe* was successful in head-on attacks to break up the packed formations of the USAF heavy bombers. However, with a single jet bomber the closing speed was such that the effective firing time available made the kill probability very low on a first-pass-only attack. Therefore, even with an accurate interception the prospect for the fighter invariably prescribed a lengthy pursuit attack that in the distance and time involved placed severe constraints on the fighter's performance, by which time a Soviet jet bomber would be within the UK airspace. While closing on the Soviet bomber the fighter pilot had time to consider and assess some ballistics factors and Newton's Laws of Motion in anticipating a reception from the bomber's defensive armament. The physics involved were to some extent in favour of the fighter as the effective range and accuracy of the bomber's return fire was resolved by the aircraft's speed because this had to be subtracted from the muzzle velocity of the guns to establish the adverse effect on the speed, accuracy and range of the bullets or shells. Conversely, the fighter's cannon fire was assisted by the speed of the fighter when added to the muzzle velocity of the cannon, thereby extending the effective range and accuracy of the cannon shells. The problem confronting a discretionary fighter pilot was to assess theoretically the effective range to open fire with some immunity from the bomber's multiple cannon. This was obviously a fine line to draw in order to silence the bomber's return fire before concentrating on the destruction of the aircraft. Fortunately for us such suppositions were academic in offering the encouragement that in addition to the greater firepower advantage of the fighter, there was an operational advantage while attacking a Soviet bomber. It was not until the advent of air–air guided weapons that this advantage over the bomber was complete, provided the interception profile was correct, in ensuring not only a higher interception probability but also a far greater kill probability.

In 1948 the Air Ministry issued two Operational Requirements (OR), OR.F-3 and OR.F-4. The Hawker Hunter was the chosen aircraft to meet the Day Fighter OR and the Gloster Javelin was selected for the All Weather Fighter OR. The Hawker Hunter Mk 1, the RAF's first British transonic fighter, was a single seat, single engine swept wing aircraft powered by a Rolls Royce Avon 107 axial-flow compressor turbine engine of 7,500 lb.s.t. This gave the Hunter an impressive initial rate of climb of approximately 10,000 feet per minute, with 45,000 feet reached in 13 minutes. The 40 degree swept wing at the inboard wing root increased to 44 degrees along the leading edge to the wing tip, and this gave the Hunter Mk 1 a maximum speed of Mach 0.93 with a service ceiling of 49,000 feet. An internal fuel capacity of 334 (Imp.) gallons limited the aircraft's duration of flight to around 30 minutes. Thus in order to achieve a high rate of climb over a short ground distance covered, the dilemma of all RAF interceptors of a short duration of flight continued until modified with additional external fuel tanks and increased engine power. The Hunter Mk 1 controlled by conventionally designed power-assisted ailerons and elevators resulted in poor handling characteristics at high altitude and high Mach numbers. Various modifications to the mainplane, tailplane and flying controls resulted before the pitch-up handling problems were cured. In parallel with the entry into service of the Hunter Mk 1 with the Rolls Royce Avon engine, the Hunter Mk 2 entered service with an Armstrong Siddeley Sapphire axial-flow compressor turbine engine giving 8,000 lb.s.t. The inclusion of the Sapphire engine as an alternative engine was an insurance in case of a shortage of Avon engines from Rolls

Royce. The Sapphire engine with its greater power gave the Hunter Mk 2 a better rate of climb and an increase in maximum speed to Mach 0.94 with an increased service ceiling of 50,000 feet. The Rolls Royce Avon's compressor design produced engine surges at high altitude at high angles of attack, with compressor stalling under slam throttle conditions that often resulted in an engine flame-out. Consequently, high altitude combat manoeuvring produced frequent practice of engine relighting in flight. The shortcoming of the Hunter Mk 1 operationally became apparent as the service trials progressed with the gun firing trials.

A study of the respective armament of the Hunter and the F-86 makes for an interesting comparison. In ordnance terms aircraft guns up to a calibre of 12.7 mm (0.5 in) are referred to as machine-guns and any calibre in excess of that is considered a cannon. The armament of the Hunter consisted of four 30 mm Aden cannon in a removable pack. The Aden cannon were a development of the revolver-fed design of the German Mauser MG-213 with electronically fired ammunition. The Hunter had a maximum load of 150 rounds per cannon with a rate of fire of 1,200 rounds per minute, giving a firing time of 8 seconds. The rounds were belt-fed to the five chamber revolver action by the recoil with a gas piston operation. This was a far more effective armament than that of the F-86 in meeting the anticipated threat of high flying and high speed Soviet bombers. The rates of fire of the 30 mm Aden cannon and the 12.7 mm Browning machine-gun was approximately the same. The Hunter carried 600 rounds for the four Aden cannon with a firing time of approximately 8 seconds, against the 1,600 rounds for the six Browning machine-guns carried by the F-86 with a firing time of approximately 13 seconds. This equates to around 80 of the 30 mm shells per second from the Hunter against 120 of the 12.7 mm bullets from the F-86. The average burst of fire with the sight steady on the target was around three seconds during a pursuit attack. In a head-on attack this would approximate to the maximum firing time available within firing range. During three seconds burst of fire the Hunter delivered 240 of the 30 mm shells against 360 of the 12.7 mm bullets from the F-86. However, the killing factor is not the density of fire but the weight of fire and here the Hunter held a big advantage, for although the 30 mm Aden cannon shell was more than twice the size of the 12.7 mm Browning machine-gun bullet, it was more than six times the weight. Consequently the Hunter would deliver more than four times the weight of fire of the armour piercing, incendiary and explosive 30 mm shells from its four cannon as against the same type of 12.7 mm ammunition from the six machine-guns of the F-86. Put in more practical terms, during three seconds burst of fire the Hunter could hit a target with close to 180 lb of lethal metal compared with a little less than

40 lb from the F-86. Obviously, 30 mm cannon fire had far greater destructiveness than the lighter 12.7 mm fire, and a single 30 mm shell had a far greater probability for a kill than a single 12.7 mm bullet.

During the Second World War the German Luftwaffe continually increased the weight of fire of their fighters in confronting the Allied bombers to increase the kill probability. The German fighter armament progressed from the early armament of 7 mm and 13 mm machine-guns to 20 mm and eventually 30 mm cannon. Luftwaffe studies showed that although twenty hits from a 20 mm cannon was sufficient to bring down a four-engine bomber, to achieve a 50 per cent kill probability required at least forty hits with the 30 mm shells fired from 500 yards range. With double this number of 30 mm strikes from the same range the probability kill factor rose against the defensive B-17 and B-24 USAF day bombers to 95 per cent. As experienced during the Korean War the 12.7 mm Browning although very accurate and effective at the lower level altitudes during air combat, was very ineffective at high altitudes as its weight of fire was insufficient to inflict the massive structural damage necessary to destroy a high flying and high speed bomber, or even a fighter. Unfortunately, in the early Hunter firing trials the muzzle blast from the four 30 mm cannon blanked the engine intakes at the wing root causing engine surges as the gun gases were drawn into the engine. This engine surging could occur at any altitude and speed, and it often resulted in an engine flame-out with the Avon engine. Rolls Royce modifications incorporated a fuel-dipping switch in the electrical firing circuit thereby reducing fuel flow to the engine. The recoil of the four cannon together with a loss of thrust from the engine resulted in a loss of speed and at the same time the aircraft experienced a marked nose-down pitch making gun sighting unsteady and erratic with a spray pattern from the cannon. Finally, the cannon shell links that were jettisoned in flight created the danger of the steel links being ingested by the engine. This state of affairs was hardly encouraging when considering that the firing range and the duration of fire was critical against the defensively armed Soviet bombers, or combat against the Mig-15 and the improved Mig-17. The nose-down pitch change of the Hunter while firing the cannon was countered by the installation of downward directed muzzle deflectors at the gun ports. The shell link hazard was corrected by the addition of two blisters on the nose of the aircraft to collect the expended links from the cannon. Both of these cannon firing modifications involved the penalty of a small increase in airframe drag.

The Hunter Mk 2 with the Armstrong Siddeley Sapphire engine did not suffer from the problem of compressibility stalling of the turbine as was the case with the Avon engine in the Hunter Mk 1. The superiority of the

Sapphire compressor over the Avon compressor was due to its heritage from the Metrovick Beryl engine used in the Saunders-Roe flying-boat fighter, the first aircraft to fly with an axial-flow designed compressor based on the design of industrial gas turbines by Metropolitan-Vickers (Metrovick). The advantage of the axial-flow compressor over the centri-fugal compressor as used in the earlier Rolls Royce Derwent and de Havilland Goblin and Ghost engines was a smaller overall diameter leading to more airframe design flexibility with the potential for greater power. As a result of the deficiencies in the design of the Avon compressor the Hunter production stalled. The Air Ministry with pressure from the government forced the cooperation of the two engine manufacturers in the national interest. Rolls Royce, with a little help from Armstrong Siddeley, was able to sort out their turbine design problems and produce the Avon Series 200 engine giving 10,150 lb.s.t. This engine entered service in the Hunter Mk 6 during 1956 and with this engine the Hunter came of age, becoming a rugged, reliable and much loved aircraft. With a newly designed engine giving a 30 per cent increase in thrust, the rate of climb improved dramatically over the Mk 1 and Mk 4 Avon engine Hunters reducing the time to 45,000 feet of 13 minutes down to 7 minutes, a comparative rate of climb to that of the Mk 2 and Mk 5 Sapphire engine Hunters. The maximum speed of the Hunter Mk 6 increased to Mach 0.95 and the service ceiling rose to 51,000 feet. An additional improved feature with the Series 200 Avon engine over the Series 100 engine was with the engine starting system. Initially, when starting the engine, the compressor was turned by an explosive gas charge supplied by one of three cartridges fired from the cockpit as the fuel cocks opened. This system had proved unreliable and was replaced by a quicker and more reliable liquid-fuel system of isopropyl nitrate called Avpin. The Hunter production pro-gramme continued with the Rolls Royce Avon, and an equivalent Armstrong Siddeley Sapphire engine producing 10,500 lb.s.t. was, unfor-tunately, never used in the Hunter. This engine became the production engine for the twin-engine Gloster Javelin All Weather interceptor fighter.

A further operational limitation of the initial Hunter design was the lack of an efficient air brake. Combat between the F-86 and the Mig-15 in Korea showed that this was an essential requirement during jet fighter combat. Sidney Camm in designing the Hunter was resistant to any excres-cence to detract from what he described as his 'most beautiful aeroplane.' Therefore, he assumed that the use of aircraft flap was sufficient to slow down the aircraft and this was true in so far as circuits and landings were concerned, but not while manoeuvring in aerial combat. Neville Duke, chief test pilot of Hawker Aircraft, was one of the RAF's premier fighter aces during the war and as Hawker's chief test pilot would become one of

Britain's premier test pilots. I knew him well from his time as CO of 615 RAuxAF Squadron at Biggin Hill, as well as the other test pilots at Hawker's test site at Dunsfold who were all ex-RAF pilots. I had the greatest respect for Duke not only as an exceptional test pilot but also as an individual, and I knew he had flown the F-86 and studied Korean combat reports. I asked him while on a visit to Dunsfold when flying the Hunter at the Central Fighter Establishment, how it was that Hawker Aircraft finished up with such an afterthought of an air brake attached beneath the rear fuselage instead of it being incorporated within the airframe. The air brake modification not only spoiled the clean lines of the aircraft but resulted in a less efficient air brake with more airframe drag. Duke shrugged, commenting that Sir Sidney Camm was a great aircraft designer but not the easiest man in the world to work with where his aircraft were concerned. The use of the flaps on the Hunter other than for take-off and landing had no operational function due to airspeed limitations and excessive nose-down trim. The air brake modification although visually unsightly and incorporating some airframe drag, nevertheless, was fairly effective in the air although not wholly satisfactory. Furthermore, it had to be retracted for landing otherwise in a tail down attitude at touch-down the 67 degree deflection of the air brake could strike the ground.

In producing the Hunter Mk 4 with the Avon 107 and the Hunter Mk 5 with the Sapphire 101, in addition to the modifications resulting from the firing trials, the aircraft's handling problems were partially improved but were not fully addressed until the arrival of the Hunter Mk 6. Although the Sapphire engine Hunter 5 was a better performing aircraft than the Hunter Mk 4, the Sapphire was not entirely without problems associated with the compressor, as there were instances of lost turbine blades during flight. Therefore, after the great expectations for the new RAF interceptor the realization for one who had flown the F-86 operationally and in combat was one of great disappointment, with some relief that we did not go to war with the aircraft. As it happened, it was the comparatively more effective Hunter Mk 5 that saw the only operational service of the early Hunters while escorting Canberra and Valiant bombers during the Suez fiasco in 1956, although without resorting to the use of their armament.

In reading Neville Duke's interesting biography 'Test Pilot', nowhere is there mention of the many problems associated with the early development of the Hunter. This is disappointing from the pilot best qualified to comment, and it may be a deliberate omission by the author and his collaborator. The impression given in the book is that the Hunter was a superb interceptor and combat fighter from its inception, but this was not so until the arrival in service of the Hunter Mk 6 in 1956. The Hunter Mk 6 had much improved flying controls and the ineffective longitudinal control at high altitude and high Mach number was corrected by fully powered elevators and ailerons with automatic reversion to manual control in the event of power failure. Most importantly, a variable incidence tailplane followed the movement of the elevator. Although not as effective as the full flying tail on the F-86, it was a great improvement both in feel and control. Modified gearing in the standby manual control greatly improved the feel and control on the ailerons and reduced the very heavy loads when flying in manual control. The automatic reversion to manual relieved the need to ensure that the aileron controls were neutral before selecting manual otherwise the locking jacks could jam on the control rods with disastrous results. The rudder control remained manual with an electric trim tab and auto stabilizer. The air brake operated hydraulically either in the fully extended or retracted position. The undercarriage, flaps and wheel brakes were hydraulically controlled with a pneumatic system for the emergency selection of wheels and flaps, while the anti-skid Dunlop Maxaret brakes were supplied by two oil accumulators. A leading edge 'saw tooth' extension at the wing tips improved the handling at altitude and corrected the pitch-up of the aircraft under G conditions. The aircraft's air-conditioning system was greatly improved with no more misting and icing up of the canopy that had restricted visibility at altitude. The short duration of flight of the Hunter was addressed in the Hunter Mk 6 by increasing the internal fuel capacity to 414 gallons by additional fuel tanks in the leading edge of the mainplane. In addition, two inboard 100 gallon drop tanks increased the total fuel capacity to 614 gallons giving flight duration of close to one hour. There was one interesting Hunter aircraft during the Hunter development that involved a racing version designated the Mk 3. This was a stripped down Mk 1 aircraft with a specially adapted windscreen and pointed nose, powered by an RR Avon 107 engine with reheat. During the summer of 1953 this aircraft, flown by Neville Duke, broke the airspeed record of 715 mph set by an F-86D with an average speed of 727 mph over the 3 km course, as well as the 100 km closed-circuit record. The sole version of the Hunter Mk 3, the only Hunter to be fitted with engine reheat, can be seen at the Tangmere Military Aviation Museum.

With the arrival of the Hunter Mk 6 during 1956 the aircraft finally came of age and realised its operational potential. It became a rugged, reliable, versatile and much liked interceptor fighter, and later a fine tactical reconnaissance fighter. It was a very pleasant and easy transonic aircraft to fly. The handling was now predictable with no particular vices at low speed manoeuvring where any mishandling resulting in a stalled condition was easily corrected. In traditional British fashion the cockpit could only be described as a close or intimate fit. Without the complications of an American designed fighter cockpit it unfortunately did not have their more logical layout. Although everything fell easily to hand when flying the aircraft there was still an impression of an absence of ergonomics in design. With a satisfying take-off and initial rate of climb of over 10,000 feet per minute aerobatics in the Hunter Mk 6 was a delight, as was exemplified by the many RAF formation aerobatics teams. To exceed Mach 1 required the Hunter to be dived at not less than a 40 degree dive above an altitude of 30,000 feet. Any dive of less than 30 degrees regardless of altitude and the Hunter Mk 6 could not be persuaded to exceed Mach 0.96. In going transonic there was little trim change as the aircraft attained a maximum speed of Mach 1.01. There were plans for further developments of the Hunter line by sweeping the 40 degree wing back to 50 degree with a thinner wing to further delay drag-rise generated by shock-waves while approaching Mach I, and by using a Rolls Royce Avon 200 engine with reheat. The 'thin wing' Hunter was designated the P.1083 project and we looked forward to its acceptance as it would have given the Hunter a true supersonic capability of Mach 1.2 in level flight, in line with the F-100 Super Sabre development from the F-86. Unfortunately, the project was cancelled after the end of the Korean War in favour of the English Electric supersonic Lightning to meet the Soviet bomber threat. With the advent of the Lightning, the RAF's first supersonic fighter, in the early 1960s the Hunter followed the progression of RAF interceptors into the ground attack and fighter reconnaissance roles. The Hunter Mk 6 became the Hunter FGA Mk 9 weighing some 600 lb more than the Hunter Mk 6, and the installation of a braking parachute in the tail resulted in improved braking distances on wet runways. The use of additional outboard 100 gallon drop tanks gave an increased fuel capacity of 814 gallons. For long range ferry flights 230 gallon tanks were fitted during which there were G limitations until the tanks emptied. The Hunter continued for many years into the supersonic fighter era to perform well in the ground attack and reconnaissance roles. The side-by-side two-seat trainer version of the Hunter, the Mk 7, followed the Hunter Mk 6 two years later in 1958. It can be said of the Hunter Mk 6 that it not only looked right, it flew right. It was certainly a pilot's aircraft and it became one of the most satisfying fighters to fly during my flying career, joining the Spitfire, the P-51 Mustang and the F-86 Sabre as my favourite aircraft. The Hunter finally equipped thirty-eight RAF squadrons and twenty other air forces around the world for a total production figure of 1,975 aircraft.

Flying with the Fighter Leader Squadron was the nearest thing to operational combat flying and while the previous zero limitations were raised slightly to avoid the danger of repeated bird strikes and a repetition of the Marham incident, it was still the most exhilarating flying and when the DFLS became the first squadron to receive the Hunter Mk 6, the flying was certainly the best available on RAF fighter squadrons.

The Day Fighter Leader course covered all types of fighter operations from high level fighter sweeps and interceptions to low level strikes. During all these exercises simulated combat resulted as directing staff pilots attacked the formations. The results of these missions were assessed by the directing staff flying in the formations and analysis of the camera gun films. Particularly stimulating were the strike missions carried out at low level and high speed. The navigation on such sorties required precise use of compass and watch, with accurate map reading while flying close to the ground to evade radar detection. At that time the sophisticated navigation systems currently available such as inertial navigation, moving map display and ground positioning from satellites to guide the aircraft and pinpoint its position were not in service. To assist the formation leader in his D/R navigation the sorties were flown at speeds in increments of 60 knots, so that a speed of 420 knots gave a still air ground distance covered of 7 nm per minute, and 480 knots a distance of 8 nm per minute. Low flying below 200 feet at over 400 knots while avoiding obstacles, scanning for hostile aircraft and map reading, can certainly concentrate the mind acutely. Course corrections required quick mental calculation to arrive accurately at the initial point for a timed run to the pull-up over the target. It was at this time that after a simulated attack on the target the lurking 'hostile' directing staff pilots attacked the formation. The course always terminated with a squadron sweep to Germany to be intercepted by the 2nd ATAF fighter squadrons, and on the following day the squadron returned to West Raynham to be intercepted by the squadrons of Fighter Command.

In addition to these visits to Germany the DFLS staff toured overseas to visit RAF air staff and fighter squadrons in the Middle East and Far East, when we flew on the several types of aircraft with the fighter squadrons and evaluated their operational proficiency. During these tours in the Middle East I flew with Meteor squadrons in Malta, Venom squadrons in Cyprus during the Suez campaign, and also with the Meteor FR squadron and the Venom fighter-bomber squadron operating from Aden and attacking the insurgents in the Radfan. By the time of the introduction of the Hunter to re-equip the Meteor squadrons in the UK, the Venom squadrons in Germany were re-equipped with the F-86. The Venom squadrons operated only in the Middle East and Far East Commands during their withdrawal from front-line service by 1962. Further developments of the Venom by de Havilland produced a two-seat night-fighter, and in 1959 the all-weather Sea Vixen for the Royal Navy. The Sea Vixen was powered by two RR Avon turbojets and carried four DH Fire-streak missiles. In the Far East I flew with Venom squadrons in Malaya and Singapore attacking communist encampments in Malaya. The Venom fighter-bomber was developed from the Vampire with modifications to the wing and tail, but the main difference was a change of engine from the DH Goblin of 3,350 lb.s.t. to the DH Ghost of 5,150 lb.s.t. Although these changes increased the weight of the aircraft, the considerable increase in power nearly doubled the initial rate of climb. This only resulted in a marginal increase in maximum speed to just over Mach 0.8. The big disappointment of the aircraft was that whereas the Vampire was one of the nicest handling of all jet aircraft to fly, the Venom could only be described as unpleasant in comparison. The main reason for this was the modifications that incorporated geared tabs to the ailerons and elevators. As an interceptor fighter the Venom was obsolescent when introduced into service and as a fighter-bomber the Venom had many failings in that, although it carried a useful armament of four 20 MM cannon, for rocket attacks it relied on Second World War 3-inch rockets on rails that had a considerable circular error of probability (CEP) factor. In bombing attacks the Venom became restricted to shallow dive attacks, and conse-quently the aiming errors were large and generally unacceptable.

In the Far East by 1956 the ground counter-insurgency operations in Malaya forced the communist insurgent cadres to withdraw to camps situated deep within the almost impenetrable jungle of the peninsula of Malaya. The result of this was to relieve many villages, hamlets, rubber and tea plantations of the attention of the revolutionary elements in obtaining information, provisions and equipment in order to terrorize the population and to attack the authorities. Consequently, in order to survive deep in their jungle encampments the insurgents cleared areas of jungle to provide for small farms and holdings to provide crops and vegetables. To protect the cultivation from the attention of marauding herds of wild boar it was necessary to build protective fences. The height and density of the jungle made detection of the encampments from the air difficult, and whenever they were identified the Venom fighter-bomber squadrons were tasked with their destruction by bomb, rocket and cannon attacks. Suitable targets were few and indistinct, with the rocket attacks being unique in attacking the farm fences to allow the wild animal population access to the cultivation. The best that could be claimed from the attacks was that they forced the communist insurgents to move to other locations, with the consequent problem of supply logistics and in feeding themselves.

The year was a busy one for apart from the Day Fighter Leader's courses and the All-weather Fighter Leader's courses, there were the visits to the RAF fighter squadrons overseas during the year. The Central Fighter Establishment also held its annual convention for fighter leaders from the RAF and Commonwealth air forces, with invitations to some foreign air forces to attend. Presentations were made on various specialist fighter subjects, followed by discussions on fighter tactics. In addition to these tours and the CFE conventions, the Central Fighter Establishment also toured overseas, visiting the RAF Middle East and the RAF Far East Commands as well as Commonwealth air forces in South-East Asia. The purpose was to lecture on the latest fighter developments and tactics. The personnel comprising the CFE visits usually consisted of a day fighter pilot, an all-weather fighter pilot and two specialist navigators flying in two Canberra jet bombers. As the day fighter representative I flew one of the Canberra on two of these tours, and it was my second tour of South-East Asia and the Far East that was the most interesting and eventful, during which we visited Pakistan, India, Burma, and the RAF in Malaya and Singapore.

I enjoyed flying the Canberra on these tours, although the large Perspex cockpit canopy acted like a greenhouse while in the tropics. Even with a shade over the cockpit canopy it was still like a hothouse while on the ground; and even in the air despite air conditioning it was often warm work. As we flew at altitudes above 45,000 feet for long periods, pressure oxygen masks and suits were a normal requirement for long high-altitude flights, but we found them too hot and uncomfortable and we discarded them, trusting in the pressurization system to function correctly. On one occasion, when flying from Rangoon to Kuala Lumpur while climbing close to 50,000 feet to try and clear the inter-tropical front that moves up and down Malaya during the seasons, the cumulonimbus thunderheads towered above us and we encountered a lightning strike that entered the aircraft at one wing tip and exited at the other. The lightning strike caused the gyrocompass repeater in the wing to malfunction and despite efforts to degauss the aircraft, the compass remained suspect for the rest of the tour. One of the benefits of taking a Canberra on these long distance flights was the luxury of a navigator, with his navigation aids, to guide me, and the absence of concern over weather and fuel, which was often the case when flying single-seat fighters in the tropics. I should have liked the opportunity to have flown the B-57 (the American version of the Canberra built by the Martin Aircraft Company and used by the USAF in Vietnam) in order to compare it with the RAF Canberra. This aircraft had a conventional fighter type tandem cockpit that must have been preferable for operating in the strike and reconnaissance roles, although the aircraft weighed more than the British built Canberra. I also regret not flying the last of the Canberra line, the PR9. This must have been a very pleasant Canberra to fly with a raised pilot's bubble canopy, although the navigator was still claustrophobically enclosed within the nose. The aircraft had an increased wingspan with hydraulically powered flight controls and although the maximum speed remained the same, the more powerful Avon 206 turbo-jets of 11,250 lb.st. greatly increased the Canberra's rate of climb and raised the aircraft's service ceiling to 60,000 feet.

One interesting adjunct for me prior to the visit to India, was a short detachment to the Aircraft and Armament Experimental Establishment (A&AEE) at Boscombe Down to fly the Folland Gnat. The Gnat was a development of the ultra lightweight Folland Midge fighter from the drawing-board of a brilliant designer, William Petter. When Folland merged with Hawker Siddeley Aviation, Petter joined English Electric where he was responsible for the design of the Canberra bomber and the Lightning all-weather supersonic interceptor. My subjects for lecturing during the tour mainly involved the Hunter VI that was coming into squadron service with the RAF; as it was hoped the aircraft would be purchased by India. The Folland Aircraft Company was in the process of promoting the Gnat to India, and to assist in this process it was considered useful for me to have some knowledge and an acquaintance of the aircraft. Despite a reluctance by A&AEE to entrust one of their two Gnats to my care, higher authority prevailed and I flew the aircraft. An interesting aspect of my endeavours on behalf of Folland in promoting the Gnat to India was meeting the Folland sales director, Air Vice-Marshal Richard 'Batchy' Atcherley. Although I never served under him in the RAF I was well aware of his reputation, and I knew his twin brother David when he was Air Vice-Marshall, Senior Air Staff Officer Fighter Command during my time as Personal Assistant to Air Officer Commanding No. 11 Group. The Atcherley twins were famous in the RAF and both became air marshals. Their exploits were legion and being legendry it was often confusing to identify which brother was connected with which anecdote, although 'Batchy' was the better known. I particularly recollect one anecdote attributed to AVM 'Batchy' Atcherley when he was AOC 12 Group. He was flying a Meteor jet from one of his bases in the Group when the weather closed in. Flying control had difficulty plotting his position accurately due to the brevity of his radio transmissions. After several requests for him to make a longer transmission, 'Batchy' finally started to slowly recite 'The Lord's Prayer' and on reaching the words, 'Thy will be done ...' 'Batchy' interjected his transmission saying, 'And you'll be bloody well done if you don't get me down quickly!' It was a tale typical of the twins and could have been attributed to either of them.

Sadly for the RAF, AVM David Atcherley disappeared without trace in 1952 while flying a Meteor from Egypt, where he was AOC No. 205 Group, to the armament practice base in Cyprus.

The Gnat was a single-seat lightweight interceptor fighter and first flew as a private venture in 1955. A total of six prototype aircraft were purchased by the Ministry of Supply (MOS) for evaluation trials. This was an improvement over the MOS order of only three prototypes of the Hunter. The Gnat and the Vampire were two of the most enjoyable jet fighters to fly from a pure handling point of view, but both fighters had limitations as multi-role fighters. The Gnat was a pocket rocket and a lot of fun to fly. Because the Gnat was much smaller and half the weight of the Hunter, one fitted into it like a glove. The aircraft was an absolute delight to handle with a very impressive rate of roll. The single Bristol Siddeley Orpheus turbojet of 4,700 lb.s.t. gave it a high rate of climb with 45,000 feet reached in less than six minutes and a service ceiling of 50,000 feet. It was also fast with a maximum speed of Mach 0.98 and it had a useful armament of two 30 mm Aden cannon. However, operational limitations in fuel and over-load stores made the aircraft unacceptable to the RAF as an operational fighter. The only export orders came from Finland and India, where it was manufactured under licence by the Hindustan Aircraft Company. In similar fashion to the original Hunter, the Gnat lacked the use of an airbrake, but whereas the designer of the Hunter, Sir Sidney Camm, decided on a partial use of the aircraft's flap to act as an airbrake, William Petter chose to use a partial lowering of the undercarriage when the 'D' doors would serve the same purpose as an airbrake in decelerating the Gnat. However, neither was an effective airbrake during aerial combat, although on the Gnat it may have provided a confusion factor for a following adversary. When the Folland Gnat became the Hawker Siddeley Gnat, the RAF recognized its potential as an operational trainer and ordered a redesigned two-seat trainer version. This aircraft served successfully as a trainer for the RAF until replaced by the British Aerospace Hawk multi-role strike-trainer. For many years the Gnat performed as the RAF's official aerobatics team when it replaced the supersonic Lightning due to the reduced airframe hours and the high cost of operating the Lightning. Flying the mini Gnat could be compared to an enthusiastic motorist driving a Mini Cooper motorcar. It would have been interesting to have operated the Gnat single-seat fighter against the Mig-15, and even the Mig-17. All three fighters had a similar operational ceiling, but the Gnat was not only superior in speed over the Soviet fighters, it had a better rate of climb with a faster rate of roll and it had an armament capable of inflicting massive structural damage on the Soviet fighters at altitude. India ordered the Hunter while Pakistan ordered the F-86 under favourable terms from the United States. During the short Indo-Pakistan war of 1965, the Pakistan F-86s acquitted themselves well in combat against the heavier armed Indian Air Force fighters, claiming the destruction of twelve Hunters, two Gnats and four Vampires against an admitted loss of seven Pakistani F-86s. While staying in both the Indian and Pakistan air force messes I saw the squadron photographs with Hindu, Sikh and Muslim pilots operating together during the British raj. It was sad for me to think that those pilots subsequently fought against one another during the Indo-Pakistan war. Before this conflict started and when lecturing to both air forces on fighter aircraft and tactics, a common question asked by the pilots of both air forces was how to operate the Hunter and F-86 against each other.

Another interesting and versatile fighter similar in concept to the Gnat which I should have liked to have flown was the Northrop F-5, a lightweight supersonic fighter that first flew in 1959. Although not adopted operationally for the USAF, it was exported as the Freedom Fighter to many air forces around the world that were friendly to the US. It was comparatively inexpensive, easy to operate, and with a good performance it had the attraction for developing air forces of being capable of supersonic flight. The USAF eventually used the two-seat trainer version of the aircraft and they also used a development of the F-5 as a realistic 'enemy' fighter for training in aerial combat. I recollect at a CFE fighter convention an American pilot describing and praising the F-5's flying qualities, while making the graphic analogy that flying the aircraft was like a blissful dream, until one woke up wondering what to do with it! Such a description could well be applied to both the Vampire and the Gnat operationally. However, the Gnat did have some success in aerial combat during the Indo-Pakistan wars.

One particularly interesting feature of this tour, after our presentations to the Pakistan Air Force in Karachi, was to visit the restricted area of the North-West frontier of Pakistan and Afghanistan, and the Pakistan AF base at Miramshah. This had been an important air base for the RAF in covering this hostile frontier area. The PAF at Miramshah entertained us with an amazing variety of the local tribal kebabs, and I felt it prudent to use my navigator as our official taster by claiming sovereign protection as pilot. Peshawar was another interesting port of call with its diverse arms industry, where identical replicas of every conceivable type of rifle was produced with rifled barrels made from mild steel rods used for reinforcing concrete. Although the appearance of these rifles was impressive, their range and accuracy was not because the first few rounds fired turned the rifles into smooth bore guns. A particularly interesting excursion from Peshawar was up the Khyber Pass to the Afghanistan border with the many memorials along the pass to the British Army regiments in their skirmishes along the frontier with the Afghan tribesmen. At the old Tochri fort in the Khyber Pass surrounded by barren brown hills, I tried to imagine how it was during those fractious years on the NW Frontier; and it seemed incongruous to be sitting on the green sward of the fort eating tiffin while listening to a Tochri Scout bagpipe band.

Flying on to India I recollect the magnificent views of the Himalayas as we passed Rawalpindi and Kashmir on our way to the Delhi. After our presentation to the Indian Air Force our hosts very thoughtfully arranged for us to visit Agra to see the Taj Mahal. My enjoyment of this, as we motored with the car windows open in the 100°F-plus heat, was marred by a blast furnace effect that seared the eyeballs. Flying south to Calcutta we 'night stopped' at Benares; and again the memory of this memorable place is of the intense heat as North-East India waited for the rains to come to relieve the drought and famine. The Indian Air Force entertained us to lunch in their mess; while a frail looking punka wallah endeavoured to get more movement in the slow moving punka fan overhead by attaching the cord to his big toe, and lying on his back while pedalling as if on the Tour de France. We stayed at a hotel overlooking the mighty River Ganges flowing from the snows of the Himalayas in Nepal, down to Calcutta and into the Bay of Bengal. That evening, while sipping a gin and tonic on the terrace, I watched as devoted Hindus carried out their ritual ablutions in the holy river. Occasionally, an unidentified body drifted by, until a swirl in the brown water indicated its disposal by a patrolling Ganges crocodile. It is unlikely that any of the bodies completed the journey to Calcutta, our last stop in India before flying on to Burma. Calcutta, the capital of Bengal, was a traumatic experience for the uninitiated, with its appalling poverty and teeming millions living, sleeping and dying in the streets, among the sacred and untouchable cows. A city of the quick and the dead; Calcutta is the only place I can recollect where children were deliberately mutilated in order to carry on the ancient profession of begging.

Our next port of call was Rangoon, capital of Burma, with its romantic Victorian image and its magnificent golden pagoda, where we walked in stocking feet through refuse and 'whatever'! The departure of the British was very evident as the golden city looked shabby, worn and run down while governed by an obscure and impecunious communist military regime. Although our presentations in Burma could be considered as entirely academic with the declining national economy and the Burmese Air Force flying obsolete aircraft, it was interesting to note that the audience contained women officers, who proved to be a distraction and a restraint on any risqué witticisms during the presentations. I wondered how much of the highly edited presentation would be of interest to recipients in Moscow. Our hosts very kindly decided to take us sightseeing and flew us up to the ancient capital of Mandalay, with its many pagodas on the Irrawaddy River. I must confess that having been brought up on a diet of Rudyard Kipling, and my experience at the Golden Pagoda, I found this rather disappointing. However, the flights to and from Mandalay were certainly interesting and attention grabing.

The last two legs of our journey in South-East Asia took us firstly to Butterworth to speak to the RAAF squadron operating the Australian built F-86 Sabre. While there we visited the island of Penang, before flying on to Kuala Lumpur to give a presentation to the RAF. After a quick sightseeing visit to the Cameron Highlands, we left for RAF Changi and the island city of Singapore, terminating our outward journey with a convivial stay in Singapore.

In 1956 some of us at CFE were involved in the Suez fiasco. I travelled out to Cyprus for a short stay to fly with and observe the Venom fighter-bomber squadrons. The Suez operation was a failure with incompetence on the grand scale and was an outstanding example of the breakdown that can occur between political and military thinking. The resultant fiasco owed much to the British Government's failure to define both the kind of war it wished to conduct with appropriate targets in pursuit of the political objectives. Clauswitz, in declaring that war is nothing more than the continuation of politics by other means, assessed the rights and wrongs on whether such action was successful or not. The political vacillations of the British Prime Minister, Anthony Eden, and his government, allied to the interminable period of preparation, guaranteed failure and gave the Americans and Soviets time to respond. Anthony Eden gave little thought to whether Britain had the military capacity to achieve his political aims against a totally hostile country, and his political objectives certainly exceeded the military capacity to achieve them. The British lacked not only a *casus belli* for a *coup de main*, but also the capacity for prompt action. The French, with the experience of recent operations in Indo-China and Algeria, were frustrated by the tedious complexity of British planning and the slow build-up of forces. Eden deliberately kept senior civil servants, military experts and his Foreign Service officials and ambassadors in the dark as to his intentions. Senior commanders were denied any knowledge of the political aims of the Cabinet. When asked by Field Marshal Viscount Montgomery for his political objectives and aims Eden is reported to have replied, 'To knock Nasser off his perch'! It was said at the time that of the twelve different plans prepared for the invasion of Suez, Eden chose the thirteenth.

Operation Musketeer for the retaking of the Suez Canal had three phases. The first was the obliteration of the Egyptian air force by attacks on the airfields. The second phase was the destruction of military installations. The third phase was an airborne and seaborne assault against Port Said and the occupation of the Canal Zone. The Egyptians were informed of targets beforehand to reduce civilian casualties and to this end the RAF bombers were restricted to a maximum bomb of 1,000 lb. To minimize interception of the RAF bombers by the Egyptian Air Force, the Valiant heavy bombers from Bomber Command operating out of Malta and the Canberra light bombers operating from Cyprus, flew at night and bombed from 40,000 feet. The result of all this was that few Egyptian aircraft were destroyed in the raids and Cairo International Airport was bombed in error. During the second phase of Musketeer, the Venom fighter-bombers with their Second World War 3-inch rocket attacks were very ineffective, and were not assisted by instructions to alert their targets before attacking them. During the third phase of Musketeer, the intended naval bombardment of Port Said in support of the landings was cancelled to minimize civilian casualties. The resultant humiliating withdrawal of the Anglo-French forces proved to be a political disaster for the irresolute British Prime Minister, who was a sick man at the time and who resigned from office the following year. Only the Israelis, and to a lesser extent the French, had a true appreciation of what was required for a rapid offensive to achieve their aims before the United Nations could react. It was for the Israelis a major victory against the Arab threat in clearing the blockaded port of Eilat, the capture of the Gaza Strip and the Sinai and the defeat of a much larger Egyptian army that was threatening Israel.

There was little I witnessed in Cyprus during 1956 that impressed me favourably. I found the RAF's performance hamstrung by staff edicts and its operational achievements negligible. Apart from the problems of the Venom fighter-bombers, who lost one aircraft to ground fire, the night-fighter Meteor squadrons patrolling between Cyprus and Egypt complained of orders that kept the loaded guns uncocked by the armourers. Although there was strong opposition in Britain to the Suez operation, especially from the opposition Labour Party, it was a considerable shock to the RAF when a young pacifist minded Canberra bomber pilot in a formation of Canberras about to take-off from Nicosia to bomb the airfields around Cairo, selected his wheels up on the runway thereby blocking the runway in protest against the British action. Lapses in security enabled a Greek EOKA terrorist to cycle onto the main RAF base at Akrotiri and place an explosive charge disguised as a milk container in a PR Canberra aircraft in a maintenance hanger causing considerable damage. The only organization and formations to impress me were the French Air Force and the two F-84 fighter-bomber squadrons with an FR-84 photo-reconnaissance squadron. The Egyptians flew their Soviet built IL-28 jet bombers 200 miles south of Cairo to Luxor to be out of range of RAF attacks, but the French F-84s flew via Israel to Luxor and destroyed all but two of the bombers parked on the airfield. The French photo-reconnaissance FR-84s following up the attack had their films developed and analysed that evening at Akrotiri and as a result the French F-84 fighter-bombers returned to Luxor the following morning to destroy the remaining IL-28 bombers. This was in marked contrast to the RAF photo reconnaissance Canberras who flew their films back to England for the photographic unit at RAF Benson to assess, before flying the results back to Cyprus. In addition to watching a British military fiasco I also witnessed the Greek EOKA terrorist attacks on the British forces in Cyprus that appeared to have support from some quarters of the British Labour Party. We all carried personal arms while in Cyprus and I rejected the general issue six-shot 0.38 inch service revolver in favour of a 9 mm fifteen-rounds Browning automatic. The main objective if caught in a cross-fire situation was to get off as many shots as possible in the direction of the assailant. To avoid an attack one made sure not to set-up a pattern of movement, and if in a public place to make sure to face the entrance and open area. If any servicemen became involved in a terrorist shoot-out it was unfortunate for them if there were any EOKA survivors because the survivors were brought before the courts, and the British servicemen involved had to be present to give evidence, and thus become a marked target by EOKA. Many service personnel involved in the court proceed-ings returned to the UK to find that they and their family were targets for letter or parcel bomb attacks. Under the circumstances, although I liked Cyprus very much I was relieved to return to some sanity in Norfolk.

About one year after my arrival at the Central Fighter Establishment it was decided to form an All-weather Fighter Leader Squadron (AWFLS) operating Meteor NF XII and NF XIV aircraft; and with the Day Fighter Leader Squadron (DFLS) flying Hunter VI aircraft, we became the Fighter Combat Wing (FCW). The two-seat radar-carrying Meteor night-fighters were the current RAF all-weather interceptors and owing to their considerable increase in weight were inferior in performance to the obsolescent Meteor VIII day-fighter. They were nice and comfortable aircraft to fly and if not up to the task of intercepting the current Soviet bomber threat were ideal personal transport at week-ends for flights to the south coast for sailing and crewing during the yachting season. The Meteors were replaced by the RAF's latest all-weather interceptor fighter, the Gloster Javelin, which although much bigger and heavier than the Hunter had a similar performance. The Javelin two-seat twin-engine all-weather interceptor was the result of Air Ministry Operational Requirement F-4 in 1948 for a transonic all-weather interceptor for the defence of the UK to meet the threat of a Soviet attack at the height of the Cold War.

Initially, and in a similar manner to the Hunter, the Javelin was plagued by development problems and the aircraft entered RAF service in 1956 to replace the obsolescent Vampire and Meteor all-weather night-fighters. The aircraft was a big leap forward in all-weather interception capability over the subsonic Vampire NF Mk 10, and the Meteor NF XII and NF XIV then flown by the FCW at CFE. The Javelin was a large and heavy aircraft powered initially by two Bristol Siddeley Sapphire turbojets of 8,500 lb.s.t. each; and was the first delta wing fighter in the RAF. The delta wing design was chosen to give stability and low drag at transonic speeds. It allowed the leading edge of the wing to be angled more sharply than a swept wing, thereby reducing drag and delaying the onset of compressibility without sacrificing control surfaces along the trailing edge. However, the modest sweep of 45 degrees and the moderate thickness cord ratio of the large delta wing and delta T-tail restricted the Javelin's maximum speed to Mach 0.95; comparable to the Hunter. Initially, the aircraft had handling problems at high speed and altitude when the elevator and rudder controls became very heavy. It also inherited the continuing initial problem of British interceptors carrying insufficient internal fuel for its role. The arrival of the Javelin Mk 4 in RAF service in 1957 with an all-moving tailplane, and the power from the Sapphire engines increased to 10,000 lb.s.t. resulted in a much more pleasant aircraft to fly. We now had a more serious contender to meet the Soviet strategic bomber force threat. The Javelin Mk 5 entered service with a modified wing and additional fuel, followed by the Mk 6 with American radar. The armament for these Javelins remained four standard 30 mm Aden cannon.

The Javelin Mk 7 was the definitive variant of the series with major modifications that included an improved and complicated flight control system incorporating a drooped leading edge wing, pitch autostabilization, a fully powered hydraulic rudder with yaw stabilization, control dampers, an autopilot for automatic approach and altitude control, in-flight refuelling capability and reheat to the two 11,000 lb.s.t. Sapphire engines. The use of reheat, or after-burning, was standard practice in US fighters from the mid-1950s and normally resulted in an augmentation of thrust by at least 25 per cent, giving the aircraft a considerable increase in performance. In the case of the Javelin Mk 7, Mk 8 and Mk 9 the simplified reheat system on the Sapphire engine increased the thrust by 12 per cent; from 11,000 lb.s.t. to 12,399 lb.s.t. Those of us flying the Javelin at CFE would refer to this augmentation as 'wee-heat'! Unfortunately, the use of the reheat was restricted in operation to heights above 20,000 feet, otherwise there was a paradoxical loss of thrust from the Sapphire engines. The use of the reheat above 20,000 feet did marginally improve the rate of climb of the Javelin Mk 7 and raised its service ceiling to around 60,000 feet. It also improved the Javelin's poor high speed and high altitude handling to some extent, but the increased thrust had no effect on the maximum level speed that remained at Mach 0.95. The armament of four 30 mm cannon installed in the wings in previous marks was reduced to two 30 mm cannon built into the fuselage, with the principal armament of four de Havilland Firestreak infra-red heat-seeking air-air missiles mounted under the wings. The Javelin Mk 7 was the first British built interceptor to be re-equipped with air-air homing missiles, and it could now be considered as an effective response to the Soviet bomber threat, allowing an interception out of range of the defensive fire from a Soviet bomber, such as the Tu-16 'Badger'. The Javelin Mk 7's range and endurance capability was further increased by the installation of an extended in-flight refuelling probe.

By 1959 Fighter Command operated Javelin Mk 8 and Mk 9 aircraft and these aircraft were virtually Mk 7s equipped with either the US built or the British built interception radar respectively. A comparison with the development of the contemporary US Convair F-102 interceptor fighter that also entered service in 1956 in contrast to that of the Javelin is of interest. The Convair F-102 had a 60 degree sweep delta wing with an exceptionally thin cord ratio. It was a single-seat interceptor powered by a single Pratt and Whitney J-57 turbojet of 11,700 lb.s.t. with after-burner, giving the aircraft a true supersonic level maximum speed of Mach 1.25. Three years later, with the later variants of the Javelin entering service, improved developments of the F-102 produced the F-106 powered by a P&W J-75 turbojet of 17,200 lb.s.t. and 24,000 lb.s.t. with after-burner; raising the maximum level speed to Mach 2.3. This aircraft became the principal air defence interceptor of the USAF Air Defence Command. The Javelin equipped fourteen RAF squadrons and remained in service with the RAF until withdrawn from service in 1967. The Gloster company obtained no export orders for the Javelin; and it was the last aircraft to be built by the Gloster Aircraft Company.

I liked to fly the Javelin in the same way I liked to fly the Canberra; although a big aircraft it was comfortable and easy to fly. From a pilot's viewpoint the aircraft was entirely what it was intended to be: a weapon carrier for bomber destruction and it would not have fared well in air combat against the current Soviet fighters. The Javelin handled well up to transonic speeds but with its thick delta wing and big delta tail it could not maintain speed through a high G-turn at altitude. During a tight G-turn the induced drag on a delta wing bleeds off energy quickly resulting in a loss of speed. The result of this was that the Javelin acquired the nickname of 'The Drag Master'. Allied to this was the significant effectiveness of the wing mounted air brakes: these were similar in design but larger than those on the Gloster Meteor, and the Javelin's air brakes were the most impressive of any aircraft I flew. The Javelin could be rolled on its back at high altitude and pulled through to a vertical dive, and with the air brakes out it stayed vertical under full control without any possibility of exceeding speed limitations. Selecting the air brake out at any speed had the apparent effect of running into a giant sponge, and in this respect the aircraft lived up to its nickname. Unfortunately, the wheel brakes were not as impressive because, for some incomprehensible reason in its development, the aircraft retained the former brake design of its predecessor, the Meteor, with differential wheel braking and no nose-wheel steering; requiring the use of brakes for turning while taxiing.

My main flying was with the Hunter squadron but in 1958 the wing commander in command of the Fighter Combat Wing left CFE and I took over command of the FCW while awaiting a replacement. As a result my flying on the wing became dependent upon approaching the two squadron commanders to be included in their operations. Despite this I still managed to get some flying on the Javelin Mk 7 before my departure from CFE. My three years spent at CFE were very enjoyable and produced the most variable and interesting flying of my RAF career. There were also ample opportunities for many recreational activities. I did a lot of sailing at week-ends with the RLondonYC at Cowes and the RAFYC at Hamble, and there was some good dinghy sailing to be had near West Raynham along the north Norfolk coast. My interest in shooting continued at CFE with some excellent wildfowl sport on the saltings of The Wash nearby, and some first class pheasant and partridge shooting with a syndicate that had extensive shooting rights in Norfolk.

There have always been dogs in my life both in my family and the RAF, and my Border Terrier died shortly after my posting to Biggin Hill in 1951. However, a friend stationed in Germany returned to England with a pregnant Long Hair Dachshund and he gave me one of her puppies with the grand Teutonic pedigree of Cassandra von Schleswig-Holstein, and I called her Cassie. This dog formed a closer bond with me than any other dog I have owned and I became aware of her incredible extra sensory perception (ESP). My father had a Border collie that always seemed to know when he was returning home and this dog had this same sense even when I was flying. At Biggin Hill the dog was my constant companion and when I left for Korea my best friend, Douglas Ford, flying with 615 RAuxAF Squadron prevailed upon me to let him keep the dog for me at Biggin Hill. During the year Douglas was promoted and took over command of a squadron in Suffolk. Just before my return to the UK he was killed in a flying accident and his fiancée living in Lancashire took the dog to her home. On my return to the UK I travelled to Lancashire to collect the dog and driving up a long driveway to the house I saw a small brown dog sitting in front of the house. I parked and got out of the car and while still some distance away the dog started to get agitated, then yelping, and as I neared the house it became frenetic. It is known that dogs have remarkable hearing and can differentiate the difference in car engine sounds, but in this particular case I had not seen this dog for a year and my car was unknown to her as it was new.

During my time at CFE no matter whether I was flying with the Hunter squadron or the Javelin squadron this dachshund demonstrated a degree of ESP that was uncanny. The procedure was always the same: this dog would accompany me from the squadron dispersal across some grass to the edge of the concrete aircraft parking area that she knew was out of bounds to her. Here she would sit and watch as I continued to the aircraft. She remained there until the aircraft taxied out and then she returned to the pilots' crew room where she occupied her favourite chair on which I had placed an old sheepskin flying jacket of mine, and here she stayed until my imminent return. The duration of the flight was generally about one hour when flying the Hunter and two hours when flying the Javelin. Occasionally, I landed away from base and returned later in the day, however, according to eyewitnesses the dog's response was the same. She indicated she wished to go out and she returned to where I had left her and waited. This occurred shortly before my aircraft arrived in the circuit. After I landed and parked the aircraft and walked back towards the squadron crew room the dog would recognize my approach from more than normal recognition distance, and start to jump and turn in circles with yelps of joy amounting to almost a dementia of delight as I reached her. This was a regular performance witnessed by the pilots and ground crew on the squadron. Looking for a human explanation, the possibility arises that the dog programmed its memory to the duration of flights based on the aircraft concerned. Such sorties were predictable but not all were routine. Ground crews by their activity could also convey some information to the dog regarding the return of the aircraft, although this would not be significant for a single aircraft flight. Also, there were the occasions when I visited another air base. Any significant engine noise from an individual aircraft although undetectable by human hearing could be distinguished by canine ears. However, I did not always fly the same aircraft which meant that she would have had to memorize the sound of that particular aircraft as I was taking off. On the other hand the dog always appeared to predict my return before it was possible to detect any sound from the aircraft. My only connection with the ground giving a precise indication of my arrival was by radio telephone to the control tower before landing. Whatever the stimulus for this phenomenon the dog's uncanny accuracy in predicting my return was truly amazing and can only be explained as ESP. Truly, *there are more things in heaven and earth, than are dreamt of in our philosophy.*

In 1959 I left Norfolk for France to join the headquarters of Allied Air Forces Central Europe (AAFCENT) under the command of Supreme Headquarters Allied Powers Europe (SHAPE). The headquarters of SHAPE at the time was based in Paris and the respective headquarters of the navy, army and air forces comprising Central Europe were at Fontainebleau 30 miles south of Paris. The commander of AIRCENT at Camp Guynemer was ACM Sir George Mills, ex-CinC RAF Bomber Command, and by an interesting turn of events the general commanding the Operations Division of AIRCENT to which I was attached was General Le Baron Michel Donnet, DFC, Belgian Air Force, who during the war made a famous escape from Belgium by sailing a small boat to England to join the RAF. He was my wing leader on No. 122 Mustang wing at Bentwaters in 1945 when I was with No. 65 Squadron, and he eventually retired as Chief of the Air Staff of the Belgian Air Force. My duties were mainly involved in the Tactical Strike Plan for the targeting and air delivery of tactical nuclear weapons. Fontainebleau was a pleasant small town at the edge of Fontainebleau Forest alongside the River Seine, and famous for its chateau from which Napoleon departed into exile on St. Helena following Waterloo. Living in the BOQ at Camp Guynemer did not appeal to me and I rented a small house by the river at Samois-sur-Seine, about 5 miles out of Fontainebleau. Samois was an interesting village perched above the river between Melun and Moret, a favoured location of the French Impressionists. With the surrounding forest and overlooking the Seine it was a pleasant place to live. The foundations of the house were very old and consisted of the remains of a Roman bridge crossing the Seine. Because this stretch of the river was shallow the bridge was replaced by locks which allowed large vessels to navigate up river to Dijon.

My duties involved considerable travel in France, my favourite country in Europe, for which I found the Guide Michelin invaluable in my quest of the coveted Michelin stars of culinary France. My other main area of travel involved Germany and this was usually undertaken by air with one of the headquarters communication aircraft based at an airfield a few miles north of Melun. These aircraft were light passenger transports of around twelve passenger capacity consisting of the Percival Pembroke powered by two Alvis Leonides engines and the de Havilland Dove or

Devon powered by two DH Gypsy Queen engines of 400 hp. In order to keep in current flying practice I qualified on type with a VIP endorsement so that I could fly very senior staff around Europe in the course of their visits to NATO forces. This gave me a legitimate reason to spend as much time out of the headquarters as possible. In order to keep current on jet flying and to maintain my jet instrument rating I had periodic visits to the RAF Flying College at Manby in Lincolnshire where I flew the Meteor. I also flew the French Fouga Magister jet trainer, a nice handling aircraft but not up to the performance of the RAF Gnat jet trainer.

As a result of my VIP endorsement I flew frequent flights to Northolt, the RAF air base for London and took advantage of the occasions to supplement those provisions unavailable in France and to take advantage of the very favourable currency rate of exchange in purchasing the French franc against the pound sterling. These trips also included flying 'The Brass' to such venues as the Farnborough Air Show and the Brussels World Fair. It was on the return from a weekend in Brussels that I experienced my only near flying incident while in France. On the approach to Melun airfield while flying the Pembroke with some senior staff aboard I started a gentle direct approach to the runway and in so doing reduced throttle and airspeed as I lowered the landing gear and some flap. With the wheels locked down and half flap selected I attempted to increase power but found the throttles jammed, and with this configuration the aircraft was scheduled for a crash landing in woods short of the airfield. I decided to retract the wheels and flaps but with the power still available this was insufficient to maintain height. Fortunately, I had made a high approach to give the passengers a smooth ride, for the prescribed pattern for VIP flying was to give the least impression of being airborne. I was able to continue a flapless approach selecting the wheels down as we crossed the airfield boundary. The passengers were surprised when cars came on the runway to collect them and a tractor towed the aircraft and crew back to the dispersal. The passengers were blissfully unaware that their weekend junket nearly ended in disaster, and the navigator and I decided to stop off for a thankful libation on our drive back home. That was the first and last time I ever experienced throttle linkage jamming, although the jamming of flying controls by a tool dropped carelessly during maintenance inspections was something I had experienced. It was indeed fortunate that the incident did not arise while on approach to Brussels airport.

It was while carrying out local flying from our airfield near Melun that I flew over the battlefields of the First World War. I had visited these with my father after the Second World War when he identified the areas where he had fought and the places where he was wounded. After a period of forty years of regrowth and cultivation it was often difficult from ground level to be sure of the battle areas of the Western Front with its network of entrenchment. However, the trench systems that stretched nearly 500 miles from the North Sea to the Alps could be seen quite clearly from the air as if revealed by X-ray. This was most evident when flying over the chalk-downs of the Somme where the armies of both sides burrowed like moles during the four years of fighting.

My father received his baptism of fire in his nineteenth year amid the coalfields around Loos in September 1915 during the Second Ypres Offensive. He was fortunate to survive the slaughter at Loos that resulted in 60,000 British Empire casualties, the majority occurring during the first day of the battle, for little or no strategic gain. The same result occurred the following year on the Somme where he was not so lucky, when on 14 July 1916 in an attempt by the 9th (Scottish) Division to capture the village of Longueville either machine-gun or rifle fire struck him in the chest and he fell with many others short of their objective. The bullet entered the upper right side and exited at the lower left, and he described the effect of first staggering back as if hit by a sledgehammer before pitching forward as if kicked in the back by a mule. A stretcher party found him late in the day and after sheltering in a shell-hole during an intense artillery barrage they left him to die. Some twenty-four hours later some Dragoons retiring to their lines after the loss of their horses found him while sheltering from machine-gun fire. They carried him back to a casualty station that was unable to treat his wound, and after being taken to a rear dressing station he was then transferred to a field hospital where he was put aside to give priority to the wounded considered more likely to survive. Apparently, it was not his time to go and he eventually recovered in England with the recollections during his conscious moments of jolting rides over bumpy roads that brought blood from his froth filled lungs gurgling into his throat, and pictures of the horrific overcrowded human charnel houses as if painted by Hieronymus Bosch.

The poets of the First World War of 1914–1918 produced many fine poems describing the appalling conditions that prevailed on the Western Front, and of those who passed through *the valley of the shadow of death*. None of them gave a more graphic description of trench warfare and the conditions under which the infantry lived and fought than Arthur Graeme West in his poem 'Night Patrol'.

> *... and everywhere the dead.*
> *Only the dead were always present – present*
> *As a vile sticky smell of rottenness;*
> *The rustling stubble and the earthy grass,*
> *The slimy pools – the dead men stank throughall,*

Pungent and sharp; as bodies loomed before,
And as we passed they stank: then dulled away
To that vague foetor, all encompassing,
Infecting earth and air.

As a result of a year spent in Flanders and on the Somme, my father decided it was time to leave the filthy, fetid and sodden trenches of the Western Front. He volunteered to transfer from the infantry to the emergent Tank Corps and he arrived back in Flanders as a tank commander in time for the Third Ypres Offensive in July 1917. The men who volunteered for the early tanks were similar to those who volunteered to crew the early submarines and they lived, worked and fought under similar conditions. Outside the tank the noise from the big diesel engine and the clacking, clanking caterpillar tracks was deafening. For the crew inside the confined space of the tank the noise was ear-splitting, the air was foul from the choking fumes and the heat intense from the engine. An eight men crew operated the tank and its guns while jammed between the engine and the guns in a dimly lit restricted space that allowed little movement or headroom. The tank crew consisted of the commander seated beside the driver with a Lewis machine-gun, he also operated the tank's brakes requiring the full use of his strength; the driver controlled the engine and steered the tank tracks; two gear-men manned the two independent gearboxes that controlled the independent tank tracks; two gunners in the sponsons manned the two six-pounder ex-naval guns in a male tank, or two Lewis machine-guns in a female tank and two additional gunners manned two other Lewis machine-guns.

Manoeuvring the tank required the coordinated actions of four men: the commander and the driver with the two gear-men to advance or stop and reverse the tank tracks alternately or in unison. As the noise inside the tank made speech impossible all communications and information were conveyed and orders given by hand signals, or tapped out on the engine for the two gear-men with their ears pressed against the sponsons of the tank. Hot steel splinters flew around the interior of the tank when it was hit by gunfire and shell fragments entered the tank through gapes in the armour plates. In addition, by 1917 the Germans had produced a long barrelled 12.75 mm Mauser anti-tank rifle that could penetrate the tank's armour with the bullet ricocheting around the interior of the tank. I consider myself indeed fortunate that the working conditions in my P-51 Mustang during the Second World War, and in my F-86 Sabre during the Korean War, were congenial by comparison and far removed from those prevailing in the tanks during the First World War.

The waterlogged conditions around Ypres not only made it almost impossible for the infantry to dig in but also to attack through the mud, water-filled shell-holes and a maze of barbed-wire in the face of intense machine-gun fire from the many small concrete pill-boxes just placed on top of the mud. Continuous artillery fire from the German guns sited on the higher ground overlooking the British positions harassed the attacking infantry and tanks. The continual rain and ensuing mud and flood water spelt disaster for men, horses and tanks alike, and under these conditions the manoeuvring of the tanks was limited to the few clearer areas with the Menin road from Ypres becoming a graveyard for the tanks. Despite this my father participated in three tank actions, losing his tank on each occasion. The first action during August resulted in his tank becoming immobilized soon after leaving the start line when the tank became bogged down in the morass around Ypres before being hit by artillery fire.

In his second action in September he was supporting some fellow Scots in the 51st (Highland) Division assaulting Passchendaele Ridge. The Highlanders were wallowing in the mud and water desperately trying to clear the barbed-wire while pinned down by machine-gun fire from one of the German pill-boxes. The tank's six-pounder guns had no effect on the concrete casemate that required a direct hit from heavy artillery or a grenade attack through the embrasures. My father directed his tank to climb on top of the pill-box and by alternately advancing and reversing the tracks the tank drove the pill-box down into the soft mud entombing the machine-gun crew inside. Shortly afterwards the tank's engine overheated and the two gearboxes controlling the tracks seized-up causing the tank to stall close by the pill-box when it became a stationary target for the German guns. The tank caught fire when hit in the rear and the crew abandoned the tank and made it back to the British lines with only minor injuries.

His third and last action involved an attack down the St Julian-Poelcappelle road to capture the village of Poelcappelle, only to lose it when the heavy rain made it impossible to consolidate their gains and forced the tanks to withdraw. My father's tank, while returning to the start line, became immobilized when it lost a track and the crew returned to their lines aboard another tank.

There is no better description of the conditions that prevailed during Third Ypres, when the rainfall was the heaviest for thirty years, than that written by Paul Nash with his painter's eye while serving as an official war artist in Flanders. His painting 'The Menin Road' brilliantly conveys the scene during the battles of Third Ypres – *No pen or drawing can convey this country – the normal setting of the battles taking place day and night, month after month. Evil and the incarnate fiend alone can be master of this war, and*

*no glimmer of God's hand is seen anywhere. Sunset and sunrise are blas-
phemous, they are mockeries to man, only the black rain out of the bruised
and swollen clouds all through the bitter black of night is fit atmosphere in
such land. The rain drives on, the stinking mud becomes evilly yellow, the
shell-holes fill with green-white water, the roads and tracks are covered in
inches of slime, the black dying trees ooze and sweat and the shells never
cease. They alone plunge overhead, tearing away the rotting tree stumps ...
annihilating maiming, maddening, they plunge into the grave which is this
land; one huge grave, and cast upon it the poor dead. It is unspeakable,
godless, hopeless.*

Before the capture of Passchendaele Ridge by the Canadian Corps in
November 1917 that effectively closed down the Third Ypres Offensive,
the perpetual quagmire forced the remnants of the demoralized, emasculated and immobile Tank Corps to move south for the first major tank
battle of the war at Cambrai in November 1917. Before doing so my
father celebrated his 21st birthday and his majority on 25 October,
St Chrispin's Day, becoming eligible to vote for his country, as well as to
bleed and die for it! Of all the statistics of the First World War none are
more inconceivable or horrific to contemplate than those of the three
months of fighting during the Third Ypres Offensive in 1917 that gained a
total advance of 4 miles at the cost of over 400,000 British Empire
casualties. This figure compares in its magnitude with those suffered
during the Somme Offensive the previous year over a slightly shorter
period, but with the horrific difference of 90,000 casualties listed as
'missing' and 40,000 never found who died in the waters of the battlefield
and were interred in the mud of Flanders.

The appalling conditions that prevailed in Flanders rendered the tanks
largely immobile, vulnerable and unproductive during the Third Ypres
Offensive. However, the tank offensive at Cambrai over good tank
country with rolling downland free from craters and standing water,
offered a chance for the Tank Corps to redeem itself. My father's contribution to the Battle of Cambrai was short-lived without him firing a shot
at the enemy. As the tanks advanced a thick mist covered the front line
around Havrincourt Wood hindering the manoeuvring of the tanks as
they moved towards the German trenches. My father walked ahead of his
tank guiding his section of three tanks by means of a red (Port) and green
(Starboard) torch through the gaps cut in the barbed-wire. A heavy
German artillery barrage opened up on the tanks as they approached the
first German trench and my father's lead tank received a direct hit by a
heavy calibre shell, killing the seven crew members inside the tank. My
father fell in front of his blazing tank with multiple injuries from shell
fragments to his back, arms and legs, while the remaining tanks and

supporting infantry passed and successfully crossed the first of the three German trenches. Later that morning some stretcher bearers found him and carried him back to a casualty station. Evacuated to a hospital in southern England, many shell fragments were removed from his body. His wounds kept him in hospital for several months. One wound in his back was large enough to place a fist, and another shell fragment had removed most of the calf muscle of his right leg. However, many small fragments remained and for the rest of his life they moved around his body, appearing at times on the surface of his skin. He commented that his recovery from the battlefield at Cambrai was far less traumatic than had been his experience at the Battle of the Somme; but this time there was the mental anguish at the loss of his entire crew. In losing his fourth tank in action, a quirk of fortune and the fog saved him from joining them at the moment of their destiny, on the Battle Roll of Honour. *Fortes Fortuna adjuvat!* – indeed!! In passing through his majority, three years of war had aged him, mentally and physically, at least a full decade.

He returned to the 1st Tank Brigade on the Somme in time for the great German spring offensive of 1918, and the British Fourth Army's counter attack at Hamel in July that checked the final German offensive. The Battle of Hamel prepared the Allies for the last great battle of the war at Amiens in August 1918 that decided the outcome of the fighting on the Western Front. Prior to the start of the Battle of Amiens my father flew on several reconnaissance flights with the RAF to coordinate operations between the tanks of 1st Tank Brigade, the Canadian Corps, the artillery and the RAF. On the second day of the offensive on 11 August 1918 his aircraft was shot down by ground fire and the aircraft crashed killing the pilot. My father received serious and extensive injuries for the third time and these injuries ended his war at the age of twenty-two, and he began his long and painful battle of rehabilitation. Post-war studies by the RAF reveal that by the end of the war 64 per cent of the pilots and observers flying on the Western Front became casualties. After many months in hospital by virtue of a combination of his youth, strength and luck he was able to return to civil life with a full disability pension that a grateful nation exempted from income tax. He was to survive this most horrible of all wars until his nineties. Comparing my father's war with my own experience of war at the same age always leaves me feeling humble, inadequate and very fortunate.

> *Died some,* pro patria,
> Non dulce non et décor . . . .
> *Walked eye-deep in Hell*
> *Believing in old men's lies,*

Then unbelieving
Came home, home to a lie,
Home to many deceits,
Home to old lies and new infamy.

Ezra Pound (1885–1972)

My duties at AAFCENT involved the targeting and delivery of tactical nuclear weapons under the NATO Atomic Strike Plan. For the safe delivery of the weapon by the fighter-bombers and a safe escape from the nuclear blast, the aircraft used a loft technique called Low Altitude Bombing System (LABS). The modus operandi called for a high speed, low-level approach to the target area to avoid radar detection. Then at a predetermined speed and distance from the target, the pilot pulled up into a loop at a constant high G and when near the vertical the weapon was released; the bomb being lobbed upwards towards the target. At a prescribed altitude it deployed a parachute; and descended towards the target. The bomb detonated at a preset height above the target. Meanwhile, the pilot, after releasing his weapon, completed his loop, rolling on his descent while diving steeply for a fast, low level return; hopefully, avoiding the consequences of the nuclear blast.

Headquarters considered it helpful that I should learn something of the consequences of my targeting with a short course at the US Army Atomic Weapons School in Germany, and I drove to a small town in Bavaria near Munich. Ironically, Oberammergau, the town chosen by the US Army for its Doomsday school, is more famous for the Passion play performed once every ten years. The play is performed entirely by the villagers, and initiated from a desire by the villagers in the seventeenth century to ward off the Black Plague sweeping across Europe. Fortunately, I attended the course in late winter and not only avoided the summer plague of tourists but was able to experience that unique and interesting German carnival of Fasching, or Shrovetide, that allows the dispensation of mortal sins prior to Lent. The inhabitants of Munich enjoy two such festivals where the consumption of strong beer is prodigious, with the second occurring after the harvest with the Oktoberfest. By all accounts both festivals were an inspiration for Martin Luther in his fight against the sale of indulgences to Rome. I stayed in a delightful small Bavarian style hotel and the close proximity of Garmische-Partenkirchen enabled me to enjoy some skiing on the Zugspitze. My return to France was via Mittenwald on the German-Austrian border for more skiing before crossing the border into Austria to initiate a survey of the ski resorts of Austria, Italy, Switzerland and France. So that one-way and another during my three years in France and afterwards I managed to ski at most of the major ski resorts of

Europe. After I retired from the RAF my skiing experience was extended to include Iran, Japan, New Zealand and North America.

Shortly after settling into my new appointment I suggested to General Donnet that we should sponsor an air firing competition for the air forces of AAFCENT. Donnet agreed and gave me the task of organizing the competition. The project became my main task and absolved me from some of the rather tedious tactical strike plan revisions and tests. I was conversant with both the RAF and USAF concepts in gunnery training and after considerable discussions with the respective air forces involved I devised the rules for the competition and acted as chairman of the organizing committee on behalf of General Donnet. The Americans and Canadians favoured a straight air-air firing competition whereas the RAF placed equal emphasis in the value of camera gun air combat. The committee resolved this by a combination of both exercises with emphasis on live firing, and the RAF were approached to provide a film assessing unit for the air combat part of the competition. The first competition took place at the French Air Force live firing air base at Cazeaux to the south of Bordeaux, with teams competing from 2nd ATAF and 4th ATAF. Judges were invited from AAFNORTH in Norway and AAFSOUTH in Italy, with the Chief Judge coming from AAFCENT. In absolving myself from the judging committee I became chairman of the Arbitration Committee. By the time of the third competition all the air forces of NATO were represented in the competition either as competitors or judges.

One interesting aspect in devising the competition was the acquisition of suitable trophies for the winning and runner-up teams because the head-quarters was reluctant to provide any expensive silverware. I asked to see Marcel Dassault of the Dassault Aircraft Company, the makers of the Mystere and Mirage fighters. Dassault, unlike the other major French aircraft company Aerospatiale, was an independent company and after I explained to Marcel Dassault the concept of the competition he expressed interest. I then asked if he would consider donating a trophy for the tournament. He agreed and asked my advice on a suitable trophy and I showed him a sketch I had done of a stylized delta wing Mirage fighter standing vertically with a detachable nose cone to reveal the cup inside. Dassault liked the idea and asked what we intended to call the trophy and I suggested the Dassault Trophy, but Marcel Dassault demurred saying that as the headquarters of AAFCENT was at Camp Guynemer named in honour of Georges Guynemer, France's second ranking fighter ace of the First World War, it would be more appropriate to name the trophy after him. My impression of Marcel Dassault was not only a brilliant designer of excellent fighter aircraft, but also a gentleman of class and distinction. A large silver Mirage cup duly arrived at the headquarters in time for the first competition and presentation to the winning RCAF team by General Donnet. The Canadians won again the following year with the RAF succeeding in the third and last competition at Cazeaux. For the runner-up trophy, Headquarters 4th ATAF presented a silver model of an F-86 Sabre jet. When France withdrew from NATO and the respective headquarters moved to Belgium the fourth competition was held at Leewarden in Holland. I had left France by then but was invited to continue for the last time as chairman of the Arbitration Committee and met Prince Bernhard of the Netherlands when he presented the Guynemer Trophy to the RAF team. By this time the advent of guided air-air missiles brought about a change to the competition. It was decided to incorporate an air-ground strike component to the competition, for which an additional trophy was required. The commander of AAFCENT was by then ACM Sir Harry Broadhurst, ex CinC RAF Bomber Command, who on retiring from the RAF to become CEO of the A.V.Roe Aircraft Company, agreed to present an appropriate trophy. The Broadhurst Trophy duly arrived from AVROs in time for the first strike competition. Each of the AAFCENT air firing competitions held at Cazeaux proved to be the highlight of my AIRCENT year and although my tour was nominally a staff appointment I still managed to achieve almost as much flying time as a full flying appointment.

When I arrived in France in 1959 the country was recovering from years of political instability as a succession of short-lived coalition governments ruled France following the retirement of General de Gaulle in 1947 until his return in 1958, firstly as Prime Minister and then as President of the Fifth Republic. De Gaulle's return came about because of the escalation of violence in Algeria as the nationalists struggled for independence. The French white settlers in Algeria, the Colons, backed by a French army still smarting from the loss of French Indo-China in 1954, took over control of Algeria against the FLN, the Algerian nationalists seeking independence. Algeria with its many French nationals was regarded constitutionally as an integral part of metropolitan France, and as the struggle between the Colons and the nationalists intensified and became more violent, the French army became deeply involved in Algerian politics as it decided against France granting independence to Algeria. Senior army generals threatened to seize power in France and the politicians in desperation persuaded General de Gaulle to come out of retirement as he was considered to be above party politics and also acceptable to the army. Given far greater powers at the expense of the National Assembly, President de Gaulle became ipso facto dictator of France as he set about solving the Algerian problem. The army generals and the Colons (anticipating a man of the extreme right in support of military government, who had proclaimed in 1940 '*Je suis la France*') expected de Gaulle to support them. However, he surprised them by being a realist in favouring colonial self-government with close ties with France in the French Union. This was regarded by the Colons and generals in Algeria as betrayal, with the result that during the following two years there were organized revolts against the French government. Extremist army officers attempted a military coup against the government and even assassination attempts on the president that nearly succeeded. At Fontainebleau we became aware of the purges in the French military, mostly the army, to uncover the conspirators and some officers were replaced. There was an air of possible civil war as rumours followed rumours. At AIRCENT I had friends and colleagues in the French Armed Forces, although they were mainly in the Armee de l'Air, and one speculated as we went about our duties on the loyalties involved as many officers had served in Algeria and were sympathetic to the Colons.

During 1960 the OAS, a secret army organization of extremist army officers supporting the *Algerie fancaise* movement, carried out random terrorist bomb attacks in the Paris area. Fanatic members of the OAS carried out nine assassination attempts on de Gaulle, and two nearly succeeded. The blast from a bomb planted in the road and detonated by remote control nearly blew up his car when en route to his home outside Paris at Colombey-Les-Deux-Eglises. Another attempt from a machine-gun ambush en route to a helicopter flight to his home riddled his limousine with bullet holes but both de Gaulle and his wife escaped injury. In Algeria the French CinC, General Raoul Salan, was replaced by General Maurice Challe and Salan became the military governor of Paris. Shortly afterwards, Challe returned to France to command the NATO Land Forces of Central Europe at Fontainebleau. Salan retired that year and took up residence in Spain to lead the OAS, and scarcely a day went by without some incident by the OAS. The military purges continued in the top echelons of the French high command in Algeria and France, and the atmosphere at Fontainebleau became electric when General Challe became implicated and he took French leave. His successor, General Hans Speidel, an ex-chief of staff to Field Marshal Irwin Rommel in France during 1944 who had escaped involvement in the unsuccessful bomb attempt in July 1944 to kill Hitler, became the first German commander of NATO land forces. General Challe joined General Salan in Spain and in 1961 both generals attempted to seize power in Algeria. They flew to Algiers in April and a French Foreign Legion parachute regiment seized the main government buildings in Algiers capturing the army CinC and the civilian head of government. In France all the airports were closed and an embargo placed on all supplies to Algeria as France hovered on the brink of civil war. President de Gaulle appeared on the TV dressed in his general's uniform and called upon the military to resist the revolt and to shoot the instigators. General Challe called off the revolt and gave himself up. He was flown back to France for trial and imprisonment. General Salan went into hiding but was eventually caught and imprisoned.

The war in Algeria between the French Colons and the nationalist FLN lasted eight years with great loss of life, until finally President de Gaulle's negotiations with the Algerian nationalists, following a national referendum, led to full Algerian independence in 1962. More than 200 officers and nearly 200 civilians were arrested or interned for supporting the revolt of the generals. General Salan and General Challe, the leaders of the coup attempt, were released from prison in 1968.

During the expectant days of 1960 we still carried out the NATO Air Firing Competition at Cazeaux in late summer and at the completion of the competition I decided that a change of scene was preferable to a return to Fontainebleau and took some leave to explore Spain and Portugal. Arriving in Lisbon I followed up on a hotel recommendation and booked into a small hotel in the old town. The hotel was sited below the walls of the Castelo Sao Jorge on top of a cliff with a perspective of the city below and was aptly named 'The Eagle's Nest'. I was sitting on the terrace of the hotel enjoying an early evening aperitif before dinner and admiring the view over Lisbon when I noticed some cars approaching rapidly below me and several men got out and hurried into the hotel. The group passed close by me and my attention was drawn towards two men being escorted by some very tough looking men. One man appeared familiar to me from photographs in the French press. The other man I had seen at the AFCENT headquarters at Fontainebleau. It was a considerable shock for me to realize that the two men were Raoul Salan and Maurice Challe, the two most important and sought after generals of the Algerian revolt; whose whereabouts were being actively pursued by the French security forces. My next thought was that my car was parked outside the hotel and it carried the SF plates denoting someone working at AFCENT. I did not fancy my chances if those tough looking bodyguards accompanying the missing generals, who did not flinch from an attempted assassination of the President of France, thought that I might be instrumental in putting the finger on their bosses. Assuming a nonchalance I did not feel, I sauntered out of the hotel to park my car some distance away, while I took my dinner at a café. When I returned on foot all was quiet and I retired to bed for an early departure south next morning on my first visit to the Algarve, and my return to Spain via Jerez. Some years later I returned to 'The Eagle's Nest' with Stuart Mackay, an RAF colleague at Fontaine-bleau, who had retired to live on the Estoril coast near Lisbon. The memory of my night with the generals returned vividly once more while enjoying a drink on the terrace overlooking the city.

During my time in France I had other flying interests that were unconnected with the RAF or AIRCENT when I flew sailplanes. Occasionally on a Sunday I joined a French gliding club either to fly the planes or act as a glider tug. The club operated from a grass airfield near Montargis, about 30 miles south of Fontainebleau. The raison d'être of the club was more social than functional as the morning flights were just a preliminary to a lengthy gastronomic endurance exercise at the local inn. Accompanying the many excellent courses le patron dispensed a remarkable selection of local wines, and the atmosphere soon became decidedly Rabelaisian until late in the afternoon and early evening when the members of the gliding club made their various and uncertain ways back to Paris.

Eventually the time came for me to leave France and when I did so it was with many regrets. One of my regrets was not taking back to the UK the magnificent eight litre 1927 French Hispano-Suiza limousine that I acquired from a British army friend who found it hidden in a chateau. I considered it superior to the Rolls in every way, but it was a ridiculous expense for me in operating costs with gasoline rationing; added to which was the question of availability and cost of spare parts and tyres. I had nowhere to store the car in England and so with great reluctance I parted with it for a song to an American friend in the headquarters who took it back to the USA. Over the succeeding years I have watched its value soar to seemingly infinite heights to remind me of an appropriate military axiom – *It's better not join if you can't take a joke!* That said I thoroughly enjoyed my time living in France and my work with the Allied Air Forces of Central Europe. I had the satisfaction of achieving something both personally and professionally. I managed to fly quite frequently while in France and although not much of it was of any significance, it was all interesting and enjoyable. I also saw a great deal of Europe and was able to enjoy many leisure activities such as skiing the Alps, competing in the Swiss skeleton and bobsleigh races, cruising the Baltic and participating in the Fastnet Race. I also survived a gruesome ship collision while aboard SS *Agamemnon* during a convalescent cruise of the Eastern Mediterranean recovering from a second bout of hepatitis. On reflection, although I may not have realized it at the time, the three and a half years living and working in France were certainly among the most enjoyable of my life.

Towards the end of 1961 I left France to return to England and moved to the Royal Radar Establishment (RRE) at Malvern and Pershore near the Welsh border. RRE was responsible for all types of radar detection, control and guidance of aircraft and weapon systems. My appointment involved programming the interception profiles for the Lightning Mk 3 all-weather interceptor equipped with Red Top infra-red guided missiles using the Ferranti Airpass radar system. This system allowed a collision course attack profile using semi-automatic attack and missile launch modes flown under autopilot control from the Ground Control Interception (GCI) station. The Lightning Mk 3 and Red Top were scheduled to enter RAF service in 1963 when the 30 mm Aden cannon armament would be deleted from service. The English Electric Lightning replaced the Hunter day and Javelin all-weather interceptors in 1960. The Lightning was the first and only British designed supersonic interceptor and although it gave the impression of a highly swept wing fighter it was basically of delta wing design with added separate tail control surfaces. The low drag delta-like wing swept back at 60 degrees had a triangular incision where the trailing edge of the wing met the fuselage. The fuselage of the Lightning was unique with vertically stacked Rolls Royce Avon 200 Series turbojets of 14,430 lb.s.t. with reheat or afterburner. This engine installation enabled the design to combine the thrust of the two turbojets without widening the fuselage and increasing fuselage drag. However, the single circular nose intake also housed a bullet shaped fairing for the installation of the air interception radar, and this design limited the diameter of the radar dish thereby limiting the airborne interception detection range. The Lightning Mk 1 had an impressive rate of climb of four minutes to 40,000 feet with a service ceiling of close to 60,000 feet, but it continued the tradition of RAF interceptors entering service with short range and endurance. This was remedied by the installation of an external ventral fuel tank attached to the rear of the fuselage, increasing the duration of flight from half an hour to over one hour. Although the Lightning Mk 1 was capable of supersonic level speed of Mach 1.2 in dry thrust or without reheat, it flew close to Mach 2 with reheat selected. Unfortunately, in the initial model there was no variable control of the reheat, giving a wide speed gap from controllable maximum dry thrust to the maximum reheat throttle position. The introduction of the Lightning Mk 2 in 1961 greatly improved the aircraft's performance with a fully variable reheat control; the provision for in-flight refuelling; and improved avionics with all-weather aids. The armament of these first two marks of Lightning was limited to a fuselage pack of two 30 mm Aden cannon with two DH Firestreak infra-red missiles mounted on the fuselage. This was in marked contrast to the McDonnell Douglas F-4 Phantom that followed the Lightning into service armed with four Sparrow radar guided missiles and four Sidewinder infra-red guided missiles, with one six-barrel high rate of fire 20 mm cannon. The definitive version of the Lightning in RAF service arrived after my retirement in 1963 as the Mk 3 with more powerful RR Avon 300 turbojets giving 13,200 lb dry thrust and 16,600 lb with reheat.

The performance of the Lightning Mk 3 improved to a maximum speed of Mach 2.25, an initial rate of climb of 30,000 feet per minute with 40,000 feet reached in three and half minutes and a service ceiling of 60,000 feet; very impressive figures. The aircraft also incorporated an integrated flight instrument system with autopilot and improved Ferranti radar for the launch of the Red Top infra-red missiles under autopilot control from the ground. Unfortunately, I never flew this Lightning although it was my task to evolve the tactics and interception profiles, and for this I had to attend an early computer programming course and study binary mathematics.

My only experience of flying the Lightning was limited to the early model and although it was a large fighter the cockpit was typically British in that it was cramped and confined. I was suitably impressed by the great thrust to weight ratio of the aircraft with its remarkable rate of climb, when in reheat, as it soared heavenwards like a homesick angel. In the early Lightning aircraft the absence of controllable reheat was unacceptable during an interception. Additionally, the short endurance of the aircraft and the small diameter radar scanner in the engine intake limited the range and effectiveness of pilot induced interceptions. However, the handling of the aircraft was very good and it was the first and last fighter I flew with the capability of thrust turns and climbs. Unfortunately, as experienced by the Lightning aerobatics teams, when the thrust turns and climbs were carried out at lower altitudes it resulted in airframe over-stressing with a consequent reduction in the airframe life of the aircraft. The RAF's Lightning aerobatics team made a great impression at various air shows in Europe such as the Farnborough Air Show and the Paris Air Show, until the team's aircraft were replaced by the smaller less spectacular and less expensive Gnat jet trainer in the interests of economy and national defence. When flying the Lightning for the first time, after an initial impression of being left behind by the aircraft, the sheer power of the aircraft made it completely different from any other fighter I had flown before. The general effect after flying the Lightning was that the flying had become less fun and more serious, as from being in supreme control of a flying machine one had become just another component in a complicated guided weapons projectile with the pilot as standby and back-up for the systems. The Lightning Mk 6 entered service in 1965 and it continued flying with the RAF as an interceptor well into the eighties; as did the Mk 7 although this version had an extended range with the fitting of over-wing fuel tanks in addition to the ventral tank. Although the Lightning failed generally to obtain export orders, Saudi Arabia and Kuwait operated export versions of the Mk 6 in the interceptor and ground-attack roles. By the mid-1960s the versatile multi-role McDonnell

Douglas F-4 Phantom supplemented the Lightning squadrons in the air defence role. The Phantom had set world records in speed, climb and ceiling, and subsequently a British version of the Phantom powered by Rolls Royce Spey turbojets was ordered for the RAF that proved inferior in performance to the US GE-J79 powered Phantoms. This aircraft continued the interceptor role until replaced by the multi-role Panavia Tornado in the mid-1980s.

My impressions of flying some of the RAF's jet aircraft of the late 1940s, 1950s and 1960s are based on flying four Marks of Vampire, eight Marks of Meteor, two Marks of Venom, seven Marks of Hunter, three Marks of Javelin, two Marks of Canberra, one Mark of Gnat and one Mark of Lightning, as well as the French Fouga Magister. My experience of flying US jet fighters over the same period is limited to one Mark of Lockheed P-80 Shooting Star, with one Mark of Lockheed T-33; one Mark of the US Marine Corps Grumman F-9F Panther; and three Marks of North American F-86 Sabre.

Which way shall I fly? A man is indeed fortunate when he can say on retirement that he enjoyed his working life. I enjoyed my flying career in the Royal Air Force and considered myself fortunate to have attained a degree of senior officer rank during my twenty years of continuous flying. After more than a year at the RRE and my involvement in the Lightning development programme I was faced with the likelihood of a progression of ground or staff appointments. I therefore made a request to the Air Ministry for a transfer from fixed wing to rotary wing aircraft. This was turned down on grounds of rank and age, and I elected to take an early retirement from the RAF and join the aircraft industry. These memoirs were intended to correlate to my military career and so *here is my journey's end.* I look back on my years in military aviation with a sense of satisfaction: the satisfaction of being part of the principal arm of the services that, despite political and inter-Service argument, was the deciding factor in winning the Second World War. It has been said that air power alone cannot win a war until a defeated country is occupied by land forces. This is the argument of semantics as one cannot view the unconditional surrender of Japan to any other cause than air power. It was air power that ensured that the survivors of the European conflict did not need the use of German as a second language. It was air power and nuclear missiles that kept Europe free during the years of the Cold War, and it was air power that brought about the armistice of the Korean War, with the US politically denied the means of victory. Victory by air power in the Vietnam War was also prevented by politicians. Air power could have ensured a definite conclusion to the first Gulf War and avoided a sequel.

On retiring from active service in the RAF I was not entirely divorced from military aviation while in the aircraft industry. I was involved with both military and civil aircraft: first, with the Herald and the Jetstream while with Handley Page, then the Hunter, Harrier, Hawk, HS-748 and HS-125 with Hawker Siddeley, and the Twin Otter, Caribou and Buffalo with de Havilland Canada. I also became responsible for the activities of British Aerospace in Asia. It was during my time with Handley Page that I came closest to a quasi-war experience, although as an interested observer rather than a participant, when I was caught up in the Arab-Israeli Six Day War of 1967. The national airline of Israel, El Al, operated on the international routes, while its subsidiary, Arkia, operated the domestic routes. The airline ordered six Handley Page Herald aircraft for the interior domestic services. The fifty-seat twin RR Dart turbo-prop Heralds operated from Sede Dov airport on the north side of Tel Aviv. Handley Page delivered four Heralds to Arkia and in May 1967 I delivered the fifth Herald to the airline. I landed at Tel Aviv to find the country in a state of high tension in anticipation of an attack by the surrounding Arab Alliance. Israel was in a process of mobilization and a call to full mobilization occurred just after I arrived. This resulted in the majority of the younger Arkia pilots leaving the airline to join their military units, with most of them flying on the French Dassault Mystere and Mirage fighter squadrons. The remainder of the more senior pilots formed a temporary cadre transport squadron of Heralds under the command of Colonel Hugo Agmon, chief pilot of Arkia. The new Herald had scarcely time for formal acceptance when it and the other four aircraft were stripped of their seats and usual furnishings, and fitted with racks containing litters or stretchers for medical evacuation. The full mobilization of the country was by now complete and within a twenty-four hour period the essential services and facilities of the country were taken over by non-combatants which freed able men and women and enabled them to report to their military units. I have never before or since witnessed such a rapid transformation, and the calm and efficient way Israel went about it was indeed most impressive to one who thought with other outsiders, that this time Israel was in for a likely defeat or at least a bloody nose with the massive superiority in numbers of the Arab Alliance.

My first indication that I was stuck in the middle of an Arab-Israeli war came when seeing elements of the Israeli Air Force (IAF) participating in 'Operation Focus' in the early hours of 5 June 1967. At 07.45 the IAF carried out a devastating pre-emptive strike against the Egyptian airfields in the Sinai and Egypt. Within a few hours the Egyptians lost the bulk of their Soviet built fighters and bombers, with around 300 aircraft destroyed in their parking areas. The timing of the strike was brilliant, but whether it will also be remembered as *a day that will live in infamy* is another matter! The Egyptian airfields were hit following a routine Egyptian Air Force (EAF) dawn patrol. With the bulk of the Egyptian fighter force on the ground for a turn-around the Israelis hit them and continued to do so throughout the morning until the EAF had virtually ceased to exist as a fighting force. With the destruction of the Egyptian Air Force, the Israeli Air Force switched their attention to the airfields in Jordan, Syria and Iraq. Only the Jordanian Hunters attempted a response but they were soon out of action and by late afternoon on 5 June the Arab air forces had ceased to be a factor in the conflict. This was the most important feature of the Six Day War as the Israelis were able to switch the IAF from attacking the Arab airfields and air forces to supporting the Israeli armoured thrust into the Sinai called 'Operation Red Sheet' that started at 08.15 hours. Although the Israeli ground forces met with stiff resistance in places from a superior number of Egyptian tanks and guns, the release of the IAF to support the armoured divisions, now relieved of attacks from the Egyptian Air Force, made the task easier. The intense daytime heat of the Sinai Desert was another factor against the Egyptian tanks supplied from the Soviet Union without air conditioning and still retaining the heaters necessary for Russian winters. The overall result was an overwhelming and devastating defeat of the Egyptian army.

A significant factor in the success of the IAF was not only the dedication and performance of their pilots but also the efficiency of their ground crews, who managed to reduce the normal turn-around times of the fighters by half to around ten minutes. As the Israeli armour advanced into the Sinai the IAF left the smoking remnants of the EAF fighters on the Sinai airfields, and bombed and strafed the Egyptian armour in front of the Israeli tanks. Meanwhile, Israeli paratroops dropped on the forward airfields in the Sinai supported by helicopter airborne troops. In Tel Aviv we did not know what was going on other than an extreme amount of aerial activity and the Heralds were held on constant readiness and loaded with medical staff and supplies together with drinking water and food. When Arkia received word that a Sinai airfield was captured by the Israeli troops and secure, the Heralds took-off for the airfield and un-loaded the medical staff and supplies, returning with the Israeli dead and the wounded for medical attention at the excellent hospitals in Tel Aviv.

The next two days were hectic for all concerned as the armoured units raced towards the Sinai escarpment to close the escape routes through the passes to Suez. The Israeli fighters ranged across the Sinai desert bombing and strafing the Egyptian army. Soon the Sinai became a shooting gallery for the Israeli fighters as the desert became strewn with burning, destroyed and abandoned Egyptian tanks, guns and transports that were rendered vulnerable by the destruction of the Egyptian Air Force. The Arkia Heralds flew into the Sinai airfields when they became occupied by the Israeli troops ferrying in vital supplies and carrying out the Israeli casualties. In front of the advancing Israeli armour the Egyptian tanks ran out of fuel and were attacked by Israeli fighters after their crews abandoned them and attempted to walk back to Suez. By 8 June advanced Israeli airborne troops secured road blocks in the Tassa and Gidi Passes, and the bigger and more important Mitla Pass through the Sinai Plateau to Suez. These Israeli units held the passes from both sides causing the few roads leading to the passes to become jammed with motorized columns attempting to retreat into Egypt. These columns stretched back many miles into the desert presenting the Israeli fighters with static targets as they systematically took a terrible toll with continuous strafing of the immobilized columns; and by the end of the day the Egyptian army as well as the air force had ceased to exist as a fighting force.

I did not fly on any of the medical evacuation (medevac) missions for the Israelis until after the cease-fire in the Sinai. For the first few days I was with the Heralds on the base at Tel Aviv acting in a technical support capacity. Obviously, my hosts did not want the embarrassment of a foreign casualty should the Heralds experience battle damage, but after the cease-fire things became more relaxed and I flew as supernumerary crew on supply missions. The following two days involved the taking of Jerusalem, the West Bank of the Jordan and the Golan Heights in Syria above Lake Tiberias, the Biblical Sea of Galilee. The Arkia Heralds continued to fly to the Sinai airfields as far as the southern tip of the Sinai at Sharm-el-Shiekh on the Red Sea. The scene in the desert of carnage and destruction of what had been an army of seven divisions amounting to 100,000 men was quite incredible. We flew over the Mitla Pass the day after the cease-fire and I could hardly believe my eyes as the stationary remnants of what had been the Egyptian army stretched back miles along the few roads leading to the pass. I took some photographs but kept to a safe height in case there were still Egyptian troops manning the vehicles eager to have a shot at us. As a result of maintaining a prudent height the photographs did not convey the impact of the total destruction of an army in the field, with the hundreds of tanks and trucks merely showing as black dots resembling lines of ants converging along the escarpment roads to the Mitla Pass.

Following the cease-fire I had a fascinating time with a grand aerial and ground tour of Biblical places that had not been possible before the 1967 War. The flight to Sharm-el-Sheikh on the southern tip of the Sinai Peninsula was particularly interesting as we flew low over the Sinai Massif, passing alongside the Monastery of St. Katherina perched like an eagle's nest at 8,000 feet near Mount Sinai. Another magic moment was flying over the Wilderness of Judah to land by the shore of the Dead Sea, 1,200 feet below sea level. The 1,000 feet climb up the escarpment to the ancient fortress site of Masada overlooking the Dead Sea, although exhausting, was spellbinding. This natural fortress was defended by the Zealots during the Jewish uprising against Roman rule in the first century AD. It resisted a siege for many months until the Romans had built a land bridge to position their assault towers. However, before the Romans could break into the fortress the 800 inhabitants committed mass suicide. The site is a required pilgrimage for the Israeli recruits into the armed forces.

Flying up the Jordan rift valley across Jericho and Samaria and the West Bank of the Jordan, we could at last fly over the Sea of Galilee and Nazareth without danger of being fired on from the Golan Heights in Syria. Then a visit to Jerusalem, without the restrictions that existed before the war, rounded off three of the most interesting weeks of my life, and changed many of the preconceived views I had of the Arab-Israeli disputes.

The nearest I came to any trouble was while standing on a hill on the Jordanian border overlooking Bethlehem, when someone took pot-shots at us causing us to beat a hasty retreat. With bad memories of the troubles after the Second World War in British Palestine and some sympathy for the Palestinian Arabs, I nevertheless formed a great respect for the proficiency and courage of the Israeli forces, and experienced the most friendly and generous hospitality before, during and after the war. I am sorry that after Israel's magnificent achievement during the Six Day War they could not find a process of magnanimity acceptable to the Arabs in avoiding what was to follow. I had the satisfaction that the Heralds performed immaculately with little or no unserviceability problems to ground them, and that they provided an invaluable service in the medical evacuation of Israeli casualties. Just before I left Israel to return to the UK I met the Israeli Air Force CinC General Ezer Weizman, a former Spitfire pilot and later to become President of Israel. During a conversation with the general I congratulated him on the performance of his air force and expressed my admiration for the Israeli forces in inflicting such a devastating defeat on an enemy that had out numbered them by at least 15:1. General Weizman with modesty and grace replied that although Israel was a small country with a population of around 3,000,000, it had the good fortune to have 11,000,000 taxpayers!

An interesting interlude followed later in the year when I was introduced to David Stirling, the creator of the SAS in 1941 during the North African campaign. Stirling expressed interest in securing the services of pilots for his security services company and he invited me to visit him in London. After a pleasant lunch a fairly intensive meeting followed with him and two of his lieutenants at his company headquarters. Although no specific enterprise was discussed, I came to the conclusion that such activity did not guarantee long term prospects and consequently was not for me. The feeling must have been mutual for although we parted with an assurance of further contact, I heard nothing more. On reflection this was probably just as well!

When I returned with the sixth Herald for Arkia the following year, the Egyptians sank the Israeli destroyer 'Eilat' with a surface-to-surface missile during my stay and I thought: here we go again! Fortunately, the Israeli reprisals that followed did not result in another Arab-Israeli war. During my second and last visit to Israel, I took the opportunity to take some leave to explore the southern Negeve and the Sinai coast along the Gulf of Aqaba. While staying at Eilat I enrolled in a scuba diving course with the Swedish Red Sea Diving School. The diving along the coral cliffs of the gulf was fascinating with more than 300 varieties of coral and 400 species of fish. I have dived on the Great Barrier Reef of Australia, the Bay of Islands in New Zealand, and in The Philippines, Indonesia and Thailand but the diving in the Red Sea was the finest of them all. Before leaving Israel I was able to dive at Caesarea, the submerged port and ancient capital of Roman Palestine, founded by Herod the Great. Although it could not compare with the Red Sea for the variety of coral and fish, and the water was a lot colder with poor visibility at times, it was fascinating to swim among the city ruins and see Roman and Greek amphorae scattered on the sea floor from ship wrecks.

While in Jerusalem, the holy city of three great religions, in order to gain some perspective I walked the Via Dolorosa through narrow streets cleared by the Israeli army to the Christian holy of holies, the Church of the Holy Sepulchre. It seemed incongruous that the official guide describing the crucifixion, burial and resurrection of Jesus was a Jordanian Arab. Throughout his presentation he punctuated his remarks with – 'so the story goes.' I could see some Americans were uncomfortable with this and it proved to be too much for one American woman, who had probably waited her whole life for this pilgrimage, as in evident exasperation she loudly interrupted him saying – 'It is not a story! It is true! It is in the Bible!' At which the guide shrugged commenting – 'Well; whatever pleases you to believe!' This was followed by a visit to the Jewish holy of holies, the site of the Jewish Temple where a group of Arab huts in the shadow of the Wailing Wall had been bulldozed away to leave the area clear. In an altercation between Israeli soldiers and some orthodox Jews who were complaining that the soldiers should show more respect for this holy place, I heard one soldier shout – 'What did you people do to preserve this? I shed my blood for this place! Many of my friends died for it!' Finally, after climbing up to the Mount of Olives I visited the Moslem holy of holies, the Dome of the Rock. Inside the vast mosque I descended some steps to a small cave in the rock beneath the mosque floor. A small blackened hole in the roof clearly indicated a chimney that suggested before the building of the mosque the cave was shelter for shepherds during the cold nights. The Jordanian Arab guide explained that through this hole while mounted on his horse, the Prophet Mahomet passed on his way to visit Allah. He was not interrupted.

The next major confrontation between Egypt and Israel occurred when President Sadat of Egypt launched an attack across the Suez Canal against the Israeli Bar-Lev Line on the east bank of the canal on 6 October 1973. This was Yom Kippur, the Day of Atonement, and the holiest day of the Jewish calendar during which neither public transport nor broadcasting operated. The Egyptians no doubt considered this a justified and overdue response to Israel's pre-emptive air strike that started the Six Day War of 1967. This time the Israelis had a much tougher time against a well-prepared Egyptian army. The Yom Kippur War lasted over two weeks with heavy casualties on both sides before the United Nations negotiated a cease-fire leading to peace terms that left the frontiers more or less unchanged, but returned the Sinai to Egypt with a recognized southern frontier.

It was with Handley Page that I experienced my second war situation as a civilian while in Vietnam. I was flying with Far Eastern Air Transport Corporation of Taiwan because Handley Page had sold the Dart Herald Turbo-prop to the airline which was an independent domestic carrier in competition with the Nationalist Government's China Airlines. I had taken the founder and president of the airline, T. C. Hwoo, to the Channel Islands to fly the Herald with Channel Airways before he bought the aircraft. Fortunately, I was able to establish a rapport with him when I realized that we had both flown P-51 Mustangs during the war and that we also shared an interest in Chinese porcelain. Following the war against Japan T. C. Hwoo left the Chinese air force and joined Civil Air Transport (CAT), then financed by the Americans with reportedly covert operations in support of the CIA. He moved with CAT from Chungking when the Nationalists under Chiang Kai-shek occupied Taiwan to create the Republic of China in 1949. The Communists on the mainland had created The People's Republic of China under the command of Mao Tse-tung. CAT was replaced by China Airlines as the national airline of Taiwan and T. C. Hwoo left CAT to form his own airline. He started by delivering the newspapers printed in Taipei to the three principal cities of Taichung,

Tainan and Kaohsiung in the south of the island with converted C-45 aircraft: the military version of the twelve-passenger Beech 18. He purchased twelve surplus aircraft and cannibalized them to produce six serviceable aircraft that formed the cadre that was to become the Far Eastern Air Transport Corporation in competition with China Airlines on the Taiwan domestic services. To start his passenger airline with Douglas C-47 aircraft, the military version of the Douglas DC-3 that formed the backbone and basis of civil aviation after the war, he flew to California and purchased one from surplus military aircraft sales and flew it back solo to Taiwan. Without a second pilot, navigator or flight engineer for a ferry flight lasting three days on an aircraft equipped only with a standard radio and radio compass as navigational aids was a remarkable feat of piloting and physical endurance. The normal range of a Douglas C-47 is 1,600 miles, and in order to extend this to 3,000 miles for the 7,500 miles ferry flight to Taipei, extra fuel tanks had to be installed in the cabin. Refuelling stops at Hawaii and Wake Island resulted in a total flight time of over 40 hours, and although the aircraft had an autopilot 'TC' said he was afraid to resort to it in case he fell asleep, and flying the aircraft forced him to stay awake.

This first acquisition for his nascent airline was typical of his courage and resolve. By this accomplishment he started his airline service around Taiwan. After increasing his fleet of refurbished and converted C-47 aircraft to civil use he progressed to turbo-prop aircraft. With a large fleet of turbo-prop aircraft operating in Taiwan, Vietnam and Indonesia, his airline eventually became an all jet fleet of Boeing 737s serving the domestic routes in Taiwan, and on international charter operations. In achieving this, although he had to give up flying, his hand controlled every aspect of the airline's organization from the flying and technical operations to the administration and finance. He recruited most of his operational and technical personnel from the air force, with most of his 'old hands' moving to Taiwan from the mainland in 1949. To encourage loyalty and incentive he gave ten percent of the airline equity to his employees thus giving them a sense of part ownership. 'TC' was a tough and entirely straight negotiator, being determined to achieve and maintain complete independence in the operation of his airline; consequently he did not permit any 'middle men' to figure in his airline interests. In following this policy he set up a complete engine overhaul and maintenance facility in Taipei, much to the consternation of the engine manufacturers.

I delivered the first RR Dart Turbo-prop Herald to Far Eastern Air Transport in Taipei in 1966 and my stay in Taiwan resulted in my first close call since retiring from the RAF. After delivering the first Herald to the airline, the first British aircraft sold in Taiwan, I stayed for the crew training and the aircraft's transition into the airline's domestic services. I flew as supernumerary crew with fifty passengers on the first service from Taipei to Kao-hsiung, Taiwan's second city in the south of the island. On our arrival the station manager asked if I would stand-down for the return flight owing to the heavy booking on the flight. As he offered lunch and some sightseeing as an incentive, I agreed. When I returned to the airport I learned that the Herald had crashed on its return to Taipei with the total loss of passengers and crew. We could only speculate on the cause of the accident because the wreckage revealed nothing to indicate a failure. This was the second occasion when giving up my place on an aircraft saved me from the grim reaper and I was left to reflect on the old saw – *Never two without three*! However, this did not occur for some time; not until I arranged to join an Airbus team visiting Malaysian Airlines. On the team's flight to Kuala Lumpur from Tokyo I arranged to join them at Hong Kong. There was no first class seat available on the aircraft and so I flew to Kuala Lumpur shortly afterwards on a Cathay Pacific flight. When I arrived I learned their aircraft had crashed in bad weather while on the approach to Kuala Lumpur with the loss of all onboard. I have since been spared a fourth close encounter with the grim reaper under similar circumstances, and can consider myself *a well-favoured man.*

During the Vietnam War T. C. Hwoo asked me if I would accompany him to Vietnam to help set up a subsidiary airline operation with Air Vietnam on their domestic routes, and it provided me with a chance not only to promote Handley Page, but also to see the country. When in Saigon I usually stayed at either the Continental or the Caravelle near the palace and parliament building in the city centre. Shortly after the European Gregorian New Year and before the Chinese Lunar New Year (Tet), late in January 1968, 'TC' said I should move into his airline compound near the airport and the main US air base at Tan Son Nhut on the north side of the city. The airline compound was next to a military compound occupied by a South Korean army division operating with the US ground forces. On the eve of the Lunar New Year, as the Vietnamese celebrated the festival, the communist led guerrilla forces and army of the National Liberation Front of South Vietnam, the Viet Cong, launched their Tet offensive against the US forces and the South Vietnam army and government. All hell broke lose as rockets and mortar shells rained in on the city with explosions occurring everywhere, and the parliament building and the US Embassy came under attack. Amid the chaos the South Korean compound remained an oasis of relative calm, with the adjacent FEAT (Far Eastern Air Transport) compound protected by the presence of the Koreans. I assumed that the well-deserved reputation of the Koreans as tough, well-disciplined and uncompromising fighting troops deterred the Viet Cong from getting them involved in the fighting. There is a Chinese equivalent to the proverb about letting sleeping dogs lie that says, '*He who rides the tiger can never dismount*'. In any event, we experienced no attacks and suffered no damage or casualties from the rockets and mortar shells while the rest of the city appeared to erupt in violence, and I was very glad not to be holed up in one of the hotels. It took some days for the South Vietnam forces to regain control of the city and even then isolated terrorist attacks made life in Saigon not only precarious but unpleasant. It also meant that the excellent restaurants that provided such a wonderful blend of French and Chinese cuisine remained closed, with the presence of the Viet Cong ensuring that Saigon was no longer a fun place to stay.

The Viet Cong Tet offensive conducted by well-equipped guerrilla forces, logistically supported by the Viet Minh army of North Vietnam, continued to escalate throughout the country. This came as a surprise to the US and a shock to the US army commander, General Westmoreland, with his failed policy of containment and attrition of the Viet Cong forces, and he was replaced shortly after the situation stabilized in mid year.

Before the Tet offensive of 1968 I had enjoyed my visits to Saigon, seeing much of the country on the east coast up to the second city of Da Nang and the ancient Annam capital of Hue near the border with North Vietnam (soon to be destroyed when the Viet Minh army invaded South Vietnam). I had also visited Cambodia to see the jungle-strangled temples of Angkor, part of the Buddhist Khmer Empire that flourished while Europe was in the Dark Ages. A visit to the lush mountains of Laos, 'Land of a Million Elephants', and the mighty Mekong River as it ran down the borders of Thailand and Cambodia to the Saigon delta was particularly memorable.

However, after the Tet offensive the war became a serious business for visitors as it was no longer safe to move around not knowing who were the Viet Cong and their supporters. My last and lasting memory of Saigon was of a clear night and seeing the fires from the explosions as rockets and mortar shells landed in the city, while from high above came a steady drone from the big USAF B-52 strategic bombers operating from Thailand, the Philippines and as far away as Guam, as they dropped hundreds of 1,000 lb high explosive bombs to the north of Saigon. We could see a glow in the sky as the stream of bombers laid a carpet of destruction along the Viet Cong supply routes, and we heard the thump and felt the tremor of the ground as the exploding bombs created a mild earthquake. The B-52 strategic bombers were used solely in a tactical role during the Vietnam War between 1965 and 1973. According to the official

USAF figures, these bombers dropped more than 2,600,000 tons of 'iron bombs' on targets in the former Indochina and lost thirty-one B-52s in the process.

Following his withdrawal from Vietnam, T. C. Hwoo transferred his operations to Indonesia before returning to Taiwan. In the process he made himself extremely wealthy with a vast collection of priceless Chinese antiques that he bequeathed to the national museum of Taiwan and to a museum in San Francisco. 'TC' was a convivial man who enjoyed life working hard and playing hard. To this extent it eventually caught up with him when he died suddenly and prematurely of a heart attack shortly after his sixtieth birthday. He was one of those rare individuals whose word was his bond and his handshake was a binding contract. In burning his candle at both ends he produced a bright light, not only in Taiwan but also among those who knew him. In my memory he was certainly one of the most remarkable personalities that it was my privilege to know in all my fifty years in the aviation business.

De Havilland Canada, then a member of the Hawker Siddeley Group of companies, delivered two DH Twin Otter aircraft to the Indonesian Government for support operations in West Irian, formally Dutch New Guinea. The aircraft were based on the island of Biak, on the northern coast of West Irian, and I recollect flying one of the Twin Otter aircraft out of Biak into the mountainous hinterland of West Irian at the time of the second Moon landing. Biak had been a large and important air base for the Japanese during the Second World War, and was the scene of much fighting, with resolute Japanese resistance, before falling to the Allies in 1944, with heavy Japanese casualties. It was fascinating to fly low level along the coastline looking for the many aircraft wrecks clearly visible as they lay on the seabed of the Philippine Sea. The Japanese and Allied fighter and bomber aircraft wrecks created artificial reefs attracting many species of fish, making this a very interesting fishing and diving area for scuba divers. While on the look out for the sunken wrecks, giant Manta rays were seen in the clear water and with wingspans approaching 20 feet they appeared to fly through the water, occasionally leaping clear to crash back with a huge splash. Occasionally an enormous spotted whale shark some 40 feet in length was seen cruising peacefully on the surface; and like the giant Manta rays they swam with their huge mouths open to vacuum up the vast amounts of plankton and krill present.

We were flying some emergency rice supplies for the Indonesian government into a small landing strip in the mountains of Irian Jaya when we experienced an engine failure, and, unable to take-off, we waited for a relief aircraft to arrive. The natives of the uncharted mountains of New Guinea are among the most primitive in the world and are virtually living fossils of a stone age, whose activities at the time involved the hunting of human heads to shrink as trophies, and cannibalism. There was a gruesome incident some time prior to my visit when an aircraft crashed in the mountains and examination of the wreckage concluded that some of the occupants survived the crash but the heads were missing with parts of the bodies. Retribution by the Indonesian army was swift and drastic for the village believed to be responsible for the atrocity. The adult males of the village were lined up in front of the assembled villagers and the more mature and influential executed. In a naked society status may not be readily apparent, however, with the natives of New Guinea there were two significant factors. Male adulthood commenced following the circumcision ritual, after which the men wore an elongated sheath covering the penis as their sole attire. For the immediate initiates this adornment usually hung from the waist but for the mature native status was often indicated by the degree of decoration and embellishment of the pellicle. The measure of wealth of the men was indicated by the strings of cowrie shells hanging around the neck. The cowrie shell was used as money to purchase the pigs that subsequently were exchanged for wives who cultivated the yams that fed the village. News of the dramatic reprisals by the Indonesian government spread rapidly throughout the territory as a graphic warning against further incidents of head taking and cannibalism. Shortly before our flight into Irian Jaya a missionary aircraft made a forced landing in the mountains with a family aboard and was quickly found by the natives who tended to the injured and carried the survivors back to civilization. Our mission was, therefore, not only an errand of mercy but a reward to indicate a paternal and benevolent government. The village consisted of a clearing for the airstrip and the cultivation of yams, with the villagers living in small beehive shaped straw huts. In a society that assessed wealth by the possession of cowrie shells, it is not surprising that the entire village crowded around us as if aliens from another planet.

We waited two days for the relief aircraft to arrive with a spare magneto to service our aircraft and spent the cold nights huddled around the village fire with the Dutch missionary who had spent the previous twenty years living with these people. During the day clouds built up over the mountains and by afternoon torrential rain fell, but at night the clouds left the mountains and at 5,000 feet it became very cold. The clear skies revealed a full moon with the galaxy and the solar system brilliantly clear in all its magnificence. As the naked village tribesmen gathered around us watching our every move, I turned to the Dutch missionary and said, 'These people regard us and our unsophisticated aircraft with awe more suited to gods. How can they start to appreciate that maybe right at this very moment there are two Americans walking on the surface of the moon?' The good Father replied that he would ask the village chief, and after doing so he turned to me and said, 'I'm sorry to disappoint you but the chief is not impressed. He tells me that his people have been visiting the moon for many generations'! This just goes to show that Einstein was indeed right and relativity applies to everything. Our Dutch host was a remarkable man who lived his life among the primitive aboriginal mountain tribes with only a small hut and an HF radio to serve his temporal needs, while a slightly larger corrugated iron shed served the spiritual needs of a parish that stretched in all directions through dense jungle for a distance of maybe a full walking week. Although the monthly missionary supply aircraft was two weeks overdue he insisted on exhausting his meagre stores during the two days we were stranded in the mountains. When I returned to civilization I arranged for an aircraft on a scheduled flight to Biak to carry a food hamper for delivery to our missionary friend by one of the two Twin Otters operated by the Indonesian government. The hamper included some of his precious Java coffee, some medicinal cognac and a box of his favourite Dutch cigars.

Marcel Proust in 'A la recherché du temps perdu' dipped into his memories to transport him back into his remembrances of things past. I have attempted to do the same with this memoir, rather as I did as a child in France with the ritual of the afternoon *gouter* when I would dip my *madeleine* into my *chocolat*. In similar fashion I have savoured the memories of flying some of the best combat aircraft the world had to offer at the time. It has been a good journey but in looking back on my good fortune there remains the memory of lost comrades in arms, including my best friends, who did not complete that journey with me. It took 400 years to progress from Leonardo da Vinci to the Wright Brothers for sustained human flight, and less than a lifetime from man's first flight to his walking on the moon. The achievements are mind boggling and yet in an age of TV media and computer video games they are regarded as commonplace. In the space of my lifetime aircraft had progressed from flimsy wood and fabric construction controlled by means of cables and pulleys, flying a short distance above the ground at a speed of a modern motor car to landing a man on the moon. In military aviation today pilots fly fighters and bombers of highly complex aircraft structures and designs. The fundamental airframes, controls and basic flight instruments of my generation replaced by complex fail-safe fly-by-wire computer generated and auto stabilized flight systems that control and guide the aircraft many miles into the stratosphere at speeds in excess of twice the speed of sound. The delivery of weapons progressing, if one can use the word, from a simple navigation-attack system consisting of pilot induced guidance in fair weather to deliver a hand grenade or a mortar bomb, to a fully automated navigation and weapon guidance system that launches a guided weapon under all-weather conditions at a target the pilot may only see on a radar scope.

A significant factor in the use of air power in any armed intervention, engagement or hostilities involves the Rules of Engagement. Certainly as far as the British Commonwealth and US armed forces are concerned, ever since the end of the Second World War the most efficient use of air power has been assessed and dictated to by politically inspired rules of engagement, and as a consequence of this the resulting amendments and the restrictions imposed have inhibited and frustrated the most effective use of air power. I witnessed and experienced such constraints in Korea and during the Suez Campaign. However, the most restrictive rules of engagement were experienced by the Americans during the Vietnam War and resulted in the loss of many aircraft and their crews in fighting not only the enemy but the rules of engagement.

My last memorable flight occurred after my second retirement to become a senior citizen. A fascinating drive across Australia from Perth to Sydney made me appreciate the immensity of the continent when I realised that this had been the equivalent to a drive from London to Moscow. This was further emphasised in a flight around Australia in a Cessna 180 owned by Tom Lucas; ex-RAAF fighter pilot on P-40s during the war, valued angling companion and a good and generous friend. It was one of my most enjoyable and unforgettable flying experiences.

In looking back over my flying career, I consider myself fortunate that my squadron flying included the two best and most versatile fighter aircraft in service at the time: the North American P-51 Mustang during the 1940s, and the North American F-86 Sabre Jet during the 1950s. Of course, there have been some regrets and wishes for a second chance, but more importantly, I am lucky to have an abundance of good memories. Any comparison and evaluation of flying and operating differing types of combat aircraft as their design and performance evolved during the twentieth century, becomes a relative process. My flying career involved thousands of flying hours on many different types of high performance aircraft flying at altitudes up to 50,000 feet. Although I flew some supersonic hours in the Concorde while with British Aerospace, the sum total of my supersonic flight time can be measured in minutes rather than hours. But then anyone willing to pay the high cost of a seat could cross the Atlantic in a few hours while seated comfortably at 60,000 feet nibbling on caviar canapés and sipping champagne as the Concorde flew at Mach 2 – twice the speed of sound. Flying a modern jet fighter aircraft, while monitoring highly complex aircraft, navigation and weapons delivery systems is no doubt just as exhilarating and satisfying to the pilots of today as it was to the pilots of years past who had to fly, navigate and fight entirely by means of their own flying skills without reference to modern avionics. However, I doubt if it is as much fun; and for me a service flying career lasting twenty years that included flying in two wars and five campaigns followed by the ensuing years of peace was, apart from a few anxious moments, a lot of fun even if I *left no foot prints on the sands of time!*

> *Old men forget: even when*
> *It was fun just to be alive;*
> *To be young was heaven.*
> *Now in trying to revive*
> *Recollections and things,*
> *To brighten up the day;*
> *'Laughter-silvered wings'*
> *Bring memories that stay.*

Colin Bernard Walker Downes

Epilogue

What has been, has been, and I have had my hour.

John Dryden

To-morrow, and to-morrow, and to-morrow,
Creeps in this petty pace from day to day,
To the last syllable of recorded time;
And all our yesterdays have lighted fools
The way to dusty death. Out, out, brief candle!
Life's but a walking shadow; a poor player,
That struts and frets his hour upon the stage,
And then is heard no more:
It is a tale told by an idiot, full of sound and fury,
Signifying nothing.

Macbeth

All is flux, nothing stands still.
The way up is the way down.

Heracleitus

Index